Masculinities, Gender Relations, and Sport

RESEARCH ON MEN AND MASCULINITIES SERIES

Series Editor:
MICHAEL S. KIMMEL, SUNY Stony Brook

Contemporary research on men and masculinity, informed by recent feminist thought and intellectual breakthroughs of women's studies and the women's movement, treats masculinity not as a normative referent but as a problematic gender construct. This series of interdisciplinary, edited volumes attempts to understand men and masculinity through this lens, providing a comprehensive understanding of gender and gender relationships in the contemporary world. Published in cooperation with the Men's Studies Association, a Task Group of the National Organization for Men Against Sexism.

EDITORIAL ADVISORY BOARD

Volumes in this Series

Masculinities, Gender Relations, and Sport

Edited by
JIM McKAY
MICHAEL A. MESSNER
DON SABO

RESEARCH ON MEN AND MASCULINITIES
Published in cooperation with the Men's Studies Association,
A Task Group of the National Organization for Men Against Sexism

Sage Publications, Inc.
International Educational and Professional Publisher
Thousand Oaks ■ London ■ New Delhi

For information:

Sage Publications, Inc.
2455 Teller Road
Thousand Oaks, California 91320
E-mail: order@sagepub.com

Sage Publications Ltd.
6 Bonhill Street
London EC2A 4PU
United Kingdom

Sage Publications India Pvt. Ltd.
M-32 Market
Greater Kailash I
New Delhi 110 048 India

Printed in the United States of America

Library of Congress Cataloging-in-Publication Data

Main entry under title:

Masculinities, Gender Relations, and Sport / edited by Jim McKay, Michael A. Messner, and Don Sabo.
     p. cm. — (Research on Men and Masculinities Series ; v. 13)
Includes bibliographical references and index.
   ISBN 0-7619-1271-1 (cloth: alk. paper)
   ISBN 0-7619-1272-X (pbk.: alk. paper)
  1. Sports—Social aspects. 2. Sports—Psychological aspects. 3. Masculinity. 4. Sex discrimination in sports. I. McKay, Jim. II. Messner, Michael A. III. Sabo, Donald F. IV. Research on men and masculinities series ; 13.
GV706.5 .M365 2000
796'.081—dc21
                                 00-008019

This book is printed on acid-free paper.

00 01 02 03 04 05 06 7 6 5 4 3 2 1

Acquisition Editor:	Peter Labella
Production Editor:	Sanford Robinson
Editorial Assistant:	Victoria Cheng
Typesetter:	Tina Hill
Indexer:	Molly Hall
Cover Designer:	Michelle Lee

Jim dedicates this book to John Carlos and Tommie Smith, whose extraordinary grace and courage under pressure—on and off the track—at the 1968 Olympic Games will always be an inspiration for activists both inside and outside sports. Mike dedicates this volume to Larry Wenzel—inspirational professor, passionate advocate of social justice, and fellow San Francisco Giants fan. Don dedicates this book to Eva Auchincloss, Linda Bunker, Deborah Slaner Larkin, and Carol Oglesby—each a beacon of energy and a visionary in the women's sports movement.

Contents

Acknowledgments

We are especially grateful for the scholarly support and friendships within the North American Society for the Sociology of Sport. Special thanks to Michael Kimmel, an indefatigable editor and guiding force behind the study of masculinities.

Series Editor's Foreword

The nation's recent love affair with the magnificent performance of the U.S. women's soccer team as it won the World Cup provided a revealing glimpse into the ways by which sport has become one of the primary sites of the reproduction of gender relations. A variety of promotional efforts transformed those gifted athletes from "soccer moms" to "soccer mamas" in David Letterman's felicitous phrasing, their femininity assured because of their wholesome sensuality and the persistent (and insistent) references to their heterosexuality. If excellence in sports is equated with masculinity, then the phrase "woman athlete" is almost an oxymoron—to the extent that one is a woman, one cannot excel at sports; to the extent that one excels at sports, one cannot be a real woman.

Such a historical moment of transformation, then, sets in stark relief the ways in which sports is a site for the demonstration and proof of manhood. Sports has become both metaphor and reality of American masculinity—its language dominates other discourses as metaphor, while sports have become increasingly important among young boys as the arena of demonstration and proof.

This volume, edited by three of the leading scholars at the intersection of masculinity studies and sports studies, offers a fascinating and important articulation of the state of the field. Each part of the volume examines a particularly significant arena, from the mechanisms by which masculinity is interwoven into sports, both as participant and observer, to the specific ways in which violence is encoded into athletic masculinity. The final section offers some interesting, if partial, approaches to uncoupling gender performance from athletic performance, or at least some of the more visible ways in which this entangled identity can begin to be disentangled. In the era of sports dominance of American culture, during the reign of the athlete as de facto role model, this process is even more urgent.

—MICHAEL S. KIMMEL
Series Editor

1

Studying Sport, Men, and Masculinities From Feminist Standpoints

JIM MCKAY
MICHAEL A. MESSNER
DON SABO

A decade ago, *Sport, Men and the Gender Order: Critical Feminist Perspectives* (Messner & Sabo, 1990) built on a framework developed by feminist analyses of women and sport to demonstrate the fundamental importance of gender in men's sports. Nearly two decades of feminist studies of women and sport had demonstrated the fundamental importance of gender as a category of analysis (e.g., Birrell, 1978; Duquin, 1978; Felshin, 1974; Greendorfer, 1978; Hall 1978, 1988; Hargreaves, 1994; Harris, 1972; Lenskyj, 1986; Oglesby, 1978; Theberge, 1987). Yet, with the exception of a few writings on masculinity and sport that had appeared earlier (Dunning & Sheard, 1979; Sabo & Runfola, 1980), gender was conspicuously absent from studies of men's sports.

Sport, Men and the Gender Order challenged this blind spot in sport studies by moving gender to the center of analyses of men's experiences in sport. The editors and contributors (both men and women) were writing from intellectual standpoints that were based in feminist theory, women's studies of sport, and the emerging area called "men's studies." They argued that one way men responded to various crises surrounding masculinity during the modern era was to construct sport—both materially and

1

symbolically—in ways that naturalized men's subordination of women. Fundamental to this analysis was Connell's (1987) theory of the gender order as a dynamic system of power relations, in which multiple masculinities and femininities were constantly being constructed, contested, and altered. Late 20th-century sport was portrayed as a conservative institution that tends mostly to reproduce existing unequal relations of power between women and men as well as existing unequal class, racial/ethnic, and sexual relations of power among men.

We still see sport as a predominantly conservative force in contemporary gender relations (Rowe & McKay, in press; Scraton, Fasting, Pfister, & Bunuel, 1999). However, some of the research during the past decade suggests that this perspective is too simplistic and deterministic. In this introduction, we outline some recent developments and discuss some of the ways that the study of gender, men, and sport is being pushed in newer and more nuanced directions.

The Centering of Gender in the
Study of Men and Sports

If gender was largely invisible in studies of men's sports in the 1980s, it moved to the center of analysis during the 1990s. Critical analyses of masculinities were fundamental to empirical studies of gay male athletes (Pronger, 1990); the lives of male athletes (Messner, 1992b); male body-builders (Klein, 1993); the sport media (Davis, 1997); the sporting cultures of Australia (McKay, 1991, 1997), Canada (Gruneau & Whitson, 1994), and the United States (Trujillo, 1991, 1995); and misogyny and violence against women (Brackenridge, 1997; Brackenridge & Kirby, 1997; Crosset, Benedict, & McDonald, 1995; Schact, 1996; Volkwein, Frauke, Schnell, Sherwood, & Livezey, 1997). Moreover, these scholarly analyses of masculinities moved into popular discourse on sport especially with respect to high-profile public debates about male athletes and sexual violence against women (Benedict, 1997; Nelson, 1994; Messner & Sabo, 1994; Robinson, 1998). The "success" of feminist analyses of masculinities in sport also was reflected in the tendency of some high-profile feminist scholars in the 1990s to draw insights from sport scholars to advance their understandings of gender and bodies (e.g., Connell, 1995; Lorber, 1994).

This volume, then, emerges in a different era (the end of the 1990s) than did *Sport, Men and the Gender Order* (the end of the 1980s). Rather than issuing a call to begin to pay serious scholarly attention to gender in sports, this book is published at a time when gender is already a visible and acceptable category of analysis in studies of sports. This "centering" of a gender analysis raises three new questions on which we hope to shed light: (a) How can the study of masculinities in sport be integrated with critical feminist studies? (b) How can scholars reckon with the tendency in critical sport sociology to overemphasize negative outcomes for men within dominant sport institutions? and (c) How can studies of masculinity and gender relations in sport be consolidated with analyses of race and ethnicity, social class, and sexual orientation?

Canonization, Dialogue, or Synergy?

As a "new men's studies" emerged in the early 1980s, feminist critics were concerned that instead of complementing and supporting feminist women's studies, this new focus would water down, oppose, or even displace women's radical scholarly interventions. Similarly, we ask how the study of masculinities in sport can be integrated into larger feminist frameworks for analyzing sport and gender.

When critical feminist analyses of men in sport were introduced in academic sport studies in the early 1990s, they were quickly and widely accepted and, some might even say, canonized. What factors were operating that might explain the rapid growth of interest in masculinities in sport studies? In retrospect, several explanations come to mind. It is true that the study of masculinities and sport was introduced and developed mostly by male scholars. Could it be, as Messner (1990c) wonders, that feminist ideas simply have more legitimacy when they are introduced by men and are aimed at studying men's lives? Can scholars of masculinities in sport now simply read a male feminist canon and ignore the work of feminist women scholars who laid the conceptual and theoretical groundwork for critical studies of men's sport with a turnover line?

In contrast to what might be labeled the "canonization thesis," we observe that both male and female scholars figured prominently in the development of the study of sport and masculinities during the 1990s. For example, 9 of the 22 editors and contributors to *Sport, Men and the Gender Order* were women, and much of the subsequent scholarly work done on men and masculinities in sport sociology was done by women. Likewise, a number of male scholars conducted research on women in athletics, calling attention to longstanding feminist concerns, such as gender inequity, homophobia, gender bias in media representations, and male athlete violence against women. There were cross-gender collaborations as well. In summary, under the banner of a "dialogue thesis," it could be argued that a good portion of the vitality of men's studies in sport is owed to the ongoing communication and collaboration between male and female scholars. Put another way, the study of men in sport has been informed and energized to a significant extent by dialogue between men and women scholars.

The study of men and sport was also partly fostered by synergy between feminist women's politics and profeminist men's politics. Many sport sociologists who studied gender, particularly those associated with the North American Society for the Sociology of Sport, attempted to yoke theory and analysis to political vision. Sport was not only studied, but recommendations often were made about how to transform and humanize gender, class, and race relations in and through sport. To the extent that sport sociology became a conduit through which some feminist women and profeminist men interacted and shared ideas, sport sociology in the 1990s may have differed somewhat from the larger pattern of gender segregation that existed in many scholarly and feminist circles. Many mainline male academics "didn't get" feminist theory and avoided or downplayed feminist scholars and women's movements. So, too, profeminist male scholars often were unsure about how to approach and work with women feminists. There were also walls between the genders that were constructed within feminism. As Sandra Bartky (1998) wrote, "The Second Wave feminism of the late sixties and seventies emerged and grew strong and confident in an environment where men were largely excluded" (p. xi). And so we wonder whether the political synergies between female and male critical scholars of gender and sport that emerged during the 1990s added wind to the sails of men's sports studies and extended and expanded the tradition of women's sport studies that emerged in the 1970s.

Staying the Critical Feminist Course

We suggest two ways for the critical studies of masculinities in sport to stay grounded in—rather than distracted from or antithetical to—feminist theory and women's policy goals. First, as many of the chapters in this book demonstrate, scholarly analyses of men's sports experiences should draw from, and dialogue with, studies of women's sports. We leave it to our readers to discern the extent to which the contributors to this volume tap feminist theories and writings (by women as well as men) in their work.

Second, there is a need to develop critical *relational* studies of gender and sport. Relational analyses take into account the reciprocal relationships between men's and women's lives, the fact that constructions of masculinity are interwoven with constructions of femininity. Perhaps because sport is such a gender-segregated institution, the tendency has been to conduct separate studies of "women's sports" and "men's sports." Indeed, these sorts of studies are important and should continue (for excellent examples, see Halbert, 1997; Hargreaves, 1997; Theberge, 1997). Yet, it is increasingly apparent that even when we are studying single-gender sport contexts, the analysis needs to take into account the larger contexts of unequal relations of power that exist between and among women and men. Studies that do this include Thompson's (1999) analysis of the ways that women's labor facilitates the sport participation of family members, Boyle and McKay's (1995) investigation of the exploitation of older women's labor and leisure in sport, and Kane's (1995) study of the ways that sport constructs categorical differences between women and men rather than reveals a continuum of bodily performances. Similarly, Messner, Duncan, and Wachs (1996) analyzed televised coverage of women's and men's sports, and Sabo (1997) compared inequities in intercollegiate women's and men's athletic programs. Miller, Sabo, Farrell, Barnes, and Melnick (1998) studied the associations among boys' and girls' athletic participation, sexual behavior, and risk for teen pregnancy, and Tomlinson and Yorganci (1997) analyzed male coach-female athlete relations.

Several of the chapters in this book develop a relational framework for understanding masculinities in sport. Cynthia A. Hasbrook and Othello Harris study interactions between first- and second-grade girls and boys, and Stephan R. Walk examines the experiences of women student trainers in men's college sports. Don Sabo, Philip M. Gray, and Linda A. Moore report on interviews with women who have experienced violence inflicted by male partners during and after televised sports programs. Readers also can find a relational context behind Todd Crosset's chapter on athletic affiliation and violence against women, Timothy Jon Curry's examination of relations of violence in sports bars, and Alan Bairner's look at the ties between soccer hooliganism and terrorist violence in Northern Ireland. Faye Linda Wachs and Shari Lee Dworkin deploy a relational approach to understanding the construction of gender in sport in their study of race, sexual orientation, and gender in media coverage of famous athletes who have announced that they were HIV-positive.

In one sense, relational approaches like these make it impossible to ignore women's experience while studying men and masculinities. A relational emphasis also makes it difficult to keep issues of power and inequality far from the center of analysis, thus carrying on the critical impulse in feminist analysis of sport. At the same time, relational approaches press feminist theories and political agendas to include analyses of men and masculinities, pointing the way toward the development of what Messner (1990c) called "inclusive feminisms." The emergence of more inclusive feminisms may mean that, just as profeminist male scholars seeking to understand the links between sport and masculinity need to take feminist theory and politics into account, so, too, do women feminists need to address somehow the "man question" in sport and the larger gender order. Although we recognize that such a vision of theoretical and political synergy is a formidable undertaking, we also think that the authors in this book are moving in this direction. Conceptually, we are addressing the larger issue of how to integrate the systematic study of men and masculinity into the theoretical and political purview of gender studies (Brod, 1987; Sabo, 1999). Conversely, our work also reflects and extends the profeminist political struggle to strengthen links with women and women's movements.

Overemphasis on Negative Outcomes

Most of the critical feminist writings on men's experiences in sport during the 1980s and 1990s focused on negative outcomes such as pain and injury, misogyny, homophobia, and violence against women by men. In some ways, sport was portrayed as a hostile cultural space for boys to grow up in and to develop relationships with one another and with women. When male athletes bonded with one another, for example, the resulting ties were viewed skeptically as forms of male solidarity that, in turn, reflected and reinforced men's collective domination over women. "Men's sports" were categorically compared with "women's sports," the former being characterized as hypercompetitive, aggressive, hierarchically organized, and detrimental to play and physical health. Drawing on historical themes that prevailed in the development of women's physical education and sport, the domination model of men's sports was readily contrasted with the more playful, less competitive, more health-inducing and body-affirmative culture of women's sports.

Ironically, during the same decades that the critical work on the male sports experience was gathering scholarly mass and momentum, girls and women were entering sport in ever-increasing numbers. The number of girls participating in high school sports in the United States, for example, increased from 1 in 27 girls in 1971 to more than 1 in 3 by 1994. Whereas

31,000 women participated in college athletics in 1972, more than 120,000 do so today. A team of 277 U.S. women competed in the 1996 Olympic Games, the largest number in history. In this context, scholars who critiqued men's sports were sometimes chided with the question, Why were so many girls and women flocking to enter an institutional setting that's so harmful to boys and men? This question is overly simplistic, but a more serious question deserves some attention.

Have sport studies scholars overstated the extent to which sport is a conservative institution that largely reproduces existing inequalities, while ignoring or downplaying the range and diversity of existing sport activities? What are the possibilities for disruption and resistance within dominant sport structures?

Throughout the 1980s and 1990s, most of the studies of masculinities in sport emphasized the extent to which men's actions in sport, as well as sport media's framing of sport, largely reproduce and ideologically naturalize existing gender, racial/ethnic, sexual, and class hierarchies. In contrast, scholars have viewed girls' and women's sports in more complex ways. Due to the history of sport being defined as a masculine (and masculinizing) practice, the very existence of athletic women challenges many assumptions underlying the gender order (Cahn, 1994a; Theberge, 1987). On the other hand, corporate interests and media framing of female athletes often serve to neutralize any challenge inherent in female athleticism and to facilitate and profit from the creation of new, but still subordinate, definitions of emphasized femininity. This feminist view of sport as a context in which the cultural meanings of female athletes are contested or "at play" suggests that scholars should study concrete contexts to determine under what conditions girls' and women's athleticism tends more toward a conservative "reproductive agency" or instead toward a more radical or disruptive "resistant agency" (Dworkin & Messner, 1999). The complexity of this perspective that refuses to see women's sport in either-or terms has been taken up in studies of female bodybuilders (Guthrie & Castelnuovo, 1992; Heywood, 1998) and women's professional golf (Crosset, 1995).

Adopting this perspective in the study of men's sports is more tricky. Clearly, sport continues to be an institutional practice through which men's collective power and privilege vis-à-vis women are reproduced and naturalized. Yet, the experiences of individual men or groups of men within sport settings are not uniform. Like racial or class differences, variations in gender identity and behavior also exist among male athletes, along with resistant inclinations and, sometimes, rebellion against forms of hegemonic masculinity. But when scholars go looking for "resistance" within men's sports, just what are men said to be resisting?

There are two directions that recent literature has suggested scholars might go with this question. First, the past decade's critical studies of masculinities in sport mainly examined men's experience in highly institutionalized team sports such as football, basketball, baseball, hockey, and rugby (e.g., Kidd, 1990; Messner, 1992b; Sabo & Panepinto, 1990; White & Vagi, 1990). Within these contexts, scholars found ritualized masculinization processes that rewarded and reproduced attitudes and practices that oppressed women and marginalized groups of men. However, research that focused on individual, less centralized sports such as swimming (Pronger, 1990) or bodybuilding (Klein, 1993) found a more paradoxical mix of practices that simultaneously reproduced and disrupted (or perhaps even overtly resisted) hegemonic masculinity. More recently, following this lead, Wheaton and Tomlinson (1998) found that the noninstitutionalized athletic context of windsurfing fosters a mix of masculine styles, identities, and practices, ranging from highly misogynistic to cooperative and egalitarian. This sort of research invites scholars to investigate the extent to which activities that are on the periphery (at least before they are commodified and incorporated by commercial interests) can create spaces for alternative relations of gender. Perhaps women and men who are already "turned off" by mainstream competitive sport are attracted to these alternative sports. It might also be that the less institutionalized, rationalized, and/or mediated contexts allow more room for the play of alternative gender display and relations.

A second direction for exploring more nuanced aspects of men's sports experiences concerns the extent to which, even within conventional and highly institutionalized athletic contexts, there is room for gender play, disruption, or even resistance to hegemonic masculinity. In this volume, Laurence de Garis's analysis of a certain kind of intimacy that develops in male boxers' relationships with each other suggests a need to reexamine our assumptions about the "shallowness" that often results from male athletes' competitiveness, violence, and homophobia among one another. Alan Klein's chapter on Mexican baseball players similarly challenges narrow and often racist assumptions about the "macho" behaviors of Mexican men. The issue of potential disruption and resistance in men's sports is also raised in this volume by Brian Pronger's discussion of gay athletes, and Suzanne Laberge and Mathieu Albert examine the gender transgressions among adolescent boys. Kevin Young and Philip White discuss the ways that sports injuries can disrupt the smooth reproduction of hegemonic masculinity. David Rowe, Jim McKay, and Toby Miller show how men's bodies are a "contested" site fraught with contradictions, and Michelle Dunbar analyzes gender contradictions in media portrayals of U.S. basketball player Dennis Rodman. To what extent do gay male athletes, the gender transgressions of adolescent boys, and men's various bodily experiences (including injuries) destabilize the gender order? Do the manipulations of gender images and sexual orientation of a famous athlete like Dennis Rodman really disrupt the reproduction of hegemonic masculinity in sport? Or does the highly mediated commercial context in which Rodman operates turn his "play" into just another commodity to be consumed?

Gender and Difference

Some might assert that in the critical studies of masculinity in sport during the last two decades, gender became too salient a category for analysis. Following the lead of women scholars in feminist research at large, scholars who study men in sport have begun to ask when an emphasis on gender analysis can obscure, rather than illuminate, a social or cultural context. More specifically, we ask whether the centering of gender analysis in men's sports risks the development of an oversimplified and falsely universalized conception of hegemonic masculinity that ignores or submerges analyses of race/ethnic inequalities, social class, or sexual orientation differences and inequalities.

Since the early 1980s, women of color have been in the forefront of those who express a need to move "beyond" gender, and, recently, some theorists have begun to point toward concrete ways to explore how gender intersects with multiple systems of inequality (Baca Zinn & Dill, 1996; Collins, 1999). The focus on "difference" among women (or among men) and on multiple systems of inequality does not mean ignoring gender. It means starting with the recognition that gender tends to vary in salience in different times and at different social locations. The variable salience of gender is operant simultaneously at the levels of individual identity, group interaction, institutional structures, and cultural symbols and discourse. Thus, a challenge facing sport and gender scholars today is how to retain one's critical feminist edge and to avoid the tendency to superimpose falsely a simple gender analysis on a social situation one is studying. Instead, researchers need to be sensitive to the varying salience of gender dynamics within the wider interplay of race/ethnicity, social class, sexual orientations, and other systems of difference and inequality.

Some of the more creative explorations of difference and the varying salience of gender in sport studies have come from scholars working within a cultural studies framework that is informed by recent post-structuralist thought. For example, critical analysis of advertisements by multinational sporting apparel companies like Nike, especially when they rely so heavily on exploited women workers in developing countries (Cole & Hribar, 1995; Dworkin & Messner, 1999; Goldman & Papson, 1998; Lafrance, 1998; McKay, 1995), and the analysis of portrayals of African American men in the popular media (Andrews, 1996a; Boyd, 1997b; Cole & King, 1998; Sabo, 1994; Wilson, 1997), connect with a critical analysis of institutionalized racism, black masculinity, and consumer culture in North America. Similarly, Wenner (1998b) examined the "postmodern sports bar" as a paradoxical, highly commercialized masculine space. Studies of sports media have been particularly productive sites for the study of difference and intersectionality (e.g., Sabo & Jansen, 1994, 1998).

Finally, some recent studies of masculinities have been heavily influenced by feminist contentions that human bodies play a pivotal role in both constituting and symbolizing the oppressive and emancipatory dimensions of social relations. As well as the aforementioned emphasis on the "costs" of masculinity to men, this strand of research also has shown how men obtain benefits from socially constructed definitions of their bodily superiority over women, even when the former are divided by race, sexuality, social class, and age. Indeed, most chapters in this volume at least allude to either the material or symbolic ways in which sport is implicated in complex processes surrounding the sexual politics of liberating sporting bodies with a turnover line to show the bottom line of this page.

Conclusion

This book is intended as a touchstone for scholars, researchers, and activists who seek to integrate feminist perspectives into their understandings of men, masculinities, gender relations, and sport. Sandra Harding (1998) asked, "Can men be not just the objects but also subjects of feminist thought? Can men create feminist insights for themselves and the rest of us too?" (p. 171). She answered affirmatively, arguing that men have much to gain from adopting feminist standpoints and, reciprocally, that feminist theory and practice can be enriched by men's insights and profeminist actions. We hope that the writings in this volume will further the dialogue and political synergy between women and men who seek to understand and transform gender relations in sport.

One of the most welcome developments in profeminist men's studies has been the increasingly sophisticated and pluralistic nature of research at both the theoretical and empirical levels. To reflect and support this healthy commitment to theoretical and empirical diversity, we have included chapters that analyze gender relations and identities at both the micro and macro levels and deploy many theoretical perspectives; blend feminist and profeminist perspectives with the disciplines of anthropology, history, and sociology; and draw on a variety of research techniques (e.g., semiotics, in-depth interviews, surveys, ethnographies). This standpoint aligns with feminist pleas for research on gender to be methodologically and theoretically inclusive and supportive of interdisciplinary research.

The book is organized into three sections. The authors in Part One discuss everyday constructions of masculinity in sport. The writings in Part Two focus on the triad of men's violence in sports. Finally, the authors in Part Three examine ways that dominant forms of gender relations in sport are being contested and transformed.

2

Wrestling With Gender

Physicality and Masculinities Among
Inner-City First and Second Graders

CYNTHIA A. HASBROOK
OTHELLO HARRIS

The achievement of a gendered identity and the invoking of gender as a means of making sense of the world are very important in the everyday lives of young children (Davies, 1989, 1993). Children engage in daily interactive practices that signify, reflect, and express gender. These gendering practices may be viewed as "disciplinary practices" that variously produce and privilege subordinate feminine and masculine bodies (Foucault, 1979). Children actively "do" gender (West & Zimmerman, 1991) by engaging in practices that create differences both between and among them. In the process, femininities (subordinate and emphasized) and masculinities (subordinate and hegemonic) are both reproduced and reinforced (Connell, 1987). This is not to imply that such practices simply replicate dominant, binary forms of gender relations. Indeed, our data demonstrate that children's practices often challenge and contradict a dichotomous understanding of gendered identities and relations.

AUTHORS' NOTE: The first author thanks the children for their friendships and their teachers and aides for their insights, support, and willingness to open their classrooms to her. Thanks are also extended to Jim McKay, Mike Messner, and Don Sabo for providing us with thoughtful comments and suggestions for revising the chapter.

13

Scholars acknowledge the particular importance of sport as a means of demonstrating physical prowess important to the display and achievement of hegemonic masculinity (Bryson, 1987; Connell, 1987; Messner, 1992b). Sport participation, allowing for the competitive display of physical skill and strength among older elementary school children and adolescents, long has been associated with masculinity and prestige (Adler, Kless, & Adler, 1992; Fine, 1987). Physical skill, strength, size, gesture, and posture provide us with gendered identities and communicate our gender to others. In this chapter, we focus on young children's displays of physical prowess and how it produces masculinities in particular.

Physicalities, femininities, and masculinities are also interleaved with divisions of social class, race, and ethnicity. For example, Majors and Billson (1992) suggested that many African American men, especially those from lower social class backgrounds, create and adopt particular physical gestures and postures in response to institutionalized racism. These gestures and postures, part of what Majors and Billson call "cool pose," connote toughness, control, and detachment. The focus of this chapter is at the micro, interactional level. However, class (as measured by income), race, and ethnicity are taken into account, not as variables by which to simply group, label, or compare the children but as important indicators of the institutional and cultural contexts in which masculinities are produced. Our attention is directed toward masculinities per se, as well as toward how the production of masculinities entails the subordination of girls' physicality and their resistance to such subjugation.

Method

In 1993, the first author[1] began a long-term participant observational study of a group of first-grade children in an inner-city school. The school, selected for its racially and ethnically diverse group of children and personnel supportive of the research, contained about 425 children, 70% of whom came from low-income families of African American (71%), Asian American (13%), Latin American (8%), and Anglo-American (8%) backgrounds.

While the children were in first grade, participant observation was conducted 3 to 4 days per week during a 4-month period. In the children's second year, observations were conducted 1 to 2 days a week for 4 months. There were 26 girls and 23 boys in the two first-grade classes and 28 girls and 24 boys in the second-grade classes. The racial/ethnic distributions of children at each grade level and within each classroom were consistent with the school's population. The children's interactions with each other and with adults were observed and recorded in the various social contexts of the school, including classroom instruction, lunch, restroom breaks, recess, special events such as assemblies and field trips, and transitional periods during which children moved from place to place within the school.

The first author gained extensive background information on most of the children from conversations with their first- and second-grade teachers. This information included the children's health status and physical and/or cognitive disabilities, their living arrangements (including with whom and where they lived; number of brothers and sisters, as well as their ages; and family income), whether the child's family received social welfare assistance, and occasional information about particular family members (e.g., a parent's occupation, an older sister's or brother's involvement in athletics or a neighborhood gang, or a family member's drug or alcohol addiction). The children were given pseudonyms consistent with their racial and ethnic backgrounds.

What Fine and Sandstrom (1988) term a "shallow cover" was established to offer the children a partial and brief explanation of the study. Although the intention was to enter the study and establish a friendly, "least-adult role" (Mandell, 1988), it was quickly discovered that this would be impossible. Instead, a fluid set of roles transpired, including being an adult friend of the children and privy to their thoughts, understandings, and secrets; an observer, in a position of authority necessitated by situations in which lack of intervention might have resulted in a child's health or safety being jeopardized; and an aide who helped the children complete projects, read stories, or learn new motor skills. Finally, the children were cognitively mature enough to categorize the first author as white and, as one child stated, "old enough to be my grandmother." Thus, it is likely that this author's gender, race, and age affected what she observed as well as what the children allowed her to see.

Five types of field notes were made: (a) abbreviated accounts of daily observations and impressions; (b) more developed accounts of daily observations; (c) daily descriptions of methodological concerns, problems, and ideas; (d) ongoing observational insights and questions; and (e) a provisional running record of data analysis and interpretation (Spradley, 1980). As observational data were gathered, notable and recurring interactions were identified that yielded categories of foci for further observation and informal interviewing. This procedure followed the constant comparison method of Glaser and Strauss (1967).

Results

Physicality and Masculinities

The data are intended to provide a series of "snapshots" of young elementary school children's productions of masculinities and femininities. These vignettes demonstrate the embodied nature of these productions and focus on three aspects of physicality: physical aggression, competitive displays of physical skill and strength, and gestures and postures. Care has been taken to select examples that reflect the much larger set of data and analysis that typify ethnographic work. We begin with observations and discussion of physical aggression.

Physical Aggression

Many of the children, particularly higher-status[2] boys, engaged in physical aggression, mostly toward other boys, but occasionally toward girls. Such physical aggression was usually unprovoked and took the form of shoving, pushing, hitting, and chasing. The intent of this aggression was most often intimidation, self-assertion, and demonstration and maintenance of one's status and dominance over others. However, in some instances, the intention was also to hurt another child out of dislike or disdain. We focus on situations in which higher-status boys directed physical aggression toward one another, toward boys with the least social status, and toward girls. First, we consider higher-status boys' physical aggression toward one another. To do so, we begin by describing the higher social status structures of the first- and second-grade classrooms.

Physical aggression among high-status boys. When the first author began observing the children in first grade, there was a dominant, most popular boy in each classroom. In one setting, Martin, an African American from a lower-income background, was authoritative. Martin was tough, cool, physically aggressive, wore baggy oversized clothes like those worn by older boys who were members of community gangs, and possessed a social sophistication that allowed him to negotiate and maintain his high social status and masculine domination. Harris (1992) argued that low-income African American men who are least likely to have access to conventional symbols of masculinity (e.g., educational success) often develop distinct mannerisms and behaviors, which include physical postures, speech, clothing, styles of walking and demeanor, as a strategy for coping with the pressures of being young, black, poor, and male.

Martin was joined by two less dominant and popular boys, Wallace and Nicholas, who were also African Americans from low-income backgrounds. Although these two boys had relatively high social status, they were not particularly aggressive, tough, or cool. Wallace, like Martin, was uninterested in school. Nicholas was fascinated with school and learning and most often dressed in jeans and a T-shirt. Within their classroom, the three often engaged in competitive displays of physical prowess and aggression. Their classroom teacher, Ms. W, was intentionally tolerant of such behavior. She believed that such behavior was "natural" for young boys and suggested that "the boys learn how to control their own behavior by engaging in it." Consequently, more than one-half hour seldom passed in which such displays of physicality were not noted.

In the other first-grade classroom, Zeek, an African American, was the most dominant and popular boy. Zeek's middle-class background was reflected in his style. He was not particularly physically aggressive, tough, or cool, was very much interested in school and learning, and usually dressed like a "preppy" in slacks and polo shirts. He was joined by Malcolm, a somewhat less dominant and popular African American boy also from a middle-income background. Malcolm was not physically aggressive, tough, or cool, liked school, and also dressed like a preppy. Close in status, but clearly less influential than Zeek and Malcolm, were Sedrick, J. J., Jamel, Ronald, and Naseem, African American boys from low-income backgrounds. These boys had styles more consistent with Martin's. They were cooler, tougher, and more aggressive than Zeek and Malcolm, and much less interested in school.

Zeek and Malcolm's classroom teacher, Ms. X, had a great deal to do with their high social status. Unlike most teachers in the school, she was African American, so perhaps the African American children identified more easily with her, because they accorded her great respect and power. She created an atmosphere that conferred status to Zeek and Malcolm and rewarded their "well-mannered" behavior and interest in learning. More important, this milieu, in sharp contrast to Ms. W's classroom, disallowed and constructed as inappropriate the competitive displays of physical strength and aggression that Sedrick, J. J., Jamel, Ronald, and Naseem liked to engage in. As a consequence, these boys were punished for such improper behavior and granted little classroom status by their teacher and classmates.

Ms. X's classroom environment appeared similar to that of an Australian kindergarten classroom described by Jordan and Cowan (1995), who suggested that this ambience is created when two definitions of masculinity are pitted against one another. The first denotation, one that is consistent with a "civil society" rooted in rationality, responsibility, and decorum, is reflective of education's (and the teacher's) expectations of "appropriate" student behavior. The other scenario of "warrior narratives" assumes that aggressive behavior depicting good against evil is justifiable and reflective of the kindergarten boys' preferred and initial classroom behavior. Jordan and Cowan argued that these warrior narratives are eventually "driven underground" within the classroom, emerge in the boys' play outside of the classroom, and later only exist in symbolic form as sport. Our data, although generally supportive of such an analysis and a gradual decrease in the frequency of classroom warrior narratives from first through second grade, indicate that not all teachers necessarily adopt or are able to discipline such behavior effectively. In addition, some boys actively resisted such reproaches and continued to act as classroom warriors in the second grade.

Martin and Zeek, the two boys possessing the most social status in first grade yet quite different masculine identities (attributable to some degree to their differing social class backgrounds), were placed together in one of the two second-grade classrooms.[3] They were joined by Wallace, Jamel, J. J., and Sedrick—boys with class backgrounds and values more similar to Martin's than to Zeek's. Their classroom teacher, Ms. Y, was white, and unlike Zeek's former teacher Ms. X, had great difficulty in maintaining order. This often resulted in a rather chaotic classroom situation that neither privileged nor encouraged Zeek to negotiate the serious student, middle-class, nonaggressive masculine identity he had been accustomed to in the first grade. Indeed, the situation fueled an embodied struggle for power and masculine identity among the high-status boys of the second grade. These encounters were often played out in competitive displays of physical strength and skill on the basketball court during recess and in aggression toward one another both during and after these games. The following field note entry exemplifies this struggle:

> At recess Martin, Wallace, Cheryl, Jamel, Sedrick, Zeek, and J. J. are playing basketball. Whoever gets the ball on a rebound or made-basket must clear it at

the circle before shooting. It's pretty much "every boy for himself" in that each boy drives to the basket and shoots. Only on occasion does a boy pass the ball. The play is careful, controlled, and slow—like you'd expect from players just learning the game. The kids are giving each other time and space to perform. J. J. is dribbling the ball and intentionally drives into Zeek. Zeek seems taken aback but doesn't do anything. J. J. shoots and Sedrick and Zeek try for the rebound. Sedrick gets the ball and shoves Zeek to one side. Zeek looks angry but doesn't do anything. Martin laughs and says something to Sedrick that I can't hear. They both laugh and look at Zeek. The bell rings to end recess. The kids stop playing and start walking to the building. Sedrick, Zeek, and Martin begin to fight. Martin is careful to stay on the borders of the fighting, but Sedrick and Zeek get into a knock-down, drag-out fight. A playground aide breaks up the fight.

Once back in the classroom, Sedrick, Zeek, and Martin are sent to the principal and each has a private talk with the teacher. They all come back and Sedrick has an ice bag held to the side of his face. J. J. and Wallace, who were not involved in the fighting, seem to wish they had been and are pretending they were and asking for ice bags for their heads. Sedrick, Zeek, and Martin seem very angry.

We are now going to the science classroom, but Sedrick, Zeek, Martin, and Jamel are kept behind so that the teacher can talk with them. Wallace and J. J. refuse to leave and stay behind. Zeek and Jamel arrive shortly. Sedrick has just arrived and goes to sit down in the back next to Zeek. Zeek makes a fist, and starts punching his upper leg and looking at Sedrick. Now J. J. has arrived and here come Wallace, Martin, and Ms. Y. Zeek still looks angry and Martin goes up to him with an ice bag (that J. J. had been using on his face) and challengingly puts it on the back of Zeek's neck and then on his face. Zeek does nothing and Martin walks away laughing. (Second grade, April 1994)

Five instances of physical aggression are described in this field note entry: J. J.'s intentional drive into Zeek; Sedrick's intentional shoving of Zeek; the fight between Sedrick, Zeek, and Martin; Zeek's punching his fist into his leg; and Martin's placement of an ice bag on Zeek's neck and face. The high status accorded Zeek by his first-grade classmates and teacher and his more middle-class masculine identity were clearly being challenged by other high-status boys possessing a different masculine identity, based, in part, on their low-class backgrounds. Whereas Zeek was an "only child" from a middle-income family in which both parents were present and employed, Martin, Sedrick, and J. J. all had older brothers and sisters, and they were from low-income backgrounds in which only one parent (the mother) was present and often unemployed outside of the home. In contrast to the other high-status boys, Zeek possessed different references of identity, for example, "appearance," "mind," "care" (Hearn & Collinson, 1994, p. 109). Zeek was usually quiet, well-mannered, non-aggressive, interested in school and learning, and he even dressed differently. His "difference," yet high status, threatened the others' status and masculine identities.

In the embodied struggle for status and identity that ensued, Zeek attempted to renegotiate his masculine identity to protect and maintain his status. Unlike his first-grade year, Zeek often found himself not only in trouble with school officials for fighting (in an effort to defend and assert himself) but also with his mother, who strongly disapproved both of his fighting and the second-grade classroom teacher whom she viewed as lacking control over the children. Interestingly, Zeek's attempts to renegotiate his masculine identity also involved the adoption of some of Martin's physical gestures and postures. For example, when Martin wanted to make an assertive point with someone, he would often place his feet wide apart with one foot slightly in front of the other and then, straightening and snapping his arm downward, point his index finger down and toward the person. Zeek began to display this same gesture and posture about halfway through his second-grade year.

One additional point is worthy of mention here. Martin often was able to negotiate his own dominant masculinity without having to demonstrate it explicitly. He avoided getting in the thick of the fight between Sedrick and Zeek and chose a means by which to show aggression toward Zeek that could be interpreted as a nonaggressive, caring, and nurturing act (putting the ice bag on Zeek's neck and face). This suggests that the correspondence between Martin's character and hegemonic masculinity is not simply achieved through demonstrations of physicality but through his careful avoidance of situations in which his physicality may have been challenged.

Physical aggression toward lower-status boys. Boys with the least social status tended to be nonaggressive, smaller, and/or have physical and cognitive disabilities. As a consequence, they were often physically threatened and accosted by boys with higher social status. The following field note entry serves as an example:

> During recess, Marcus decides to chase Eddie for no apparent reason. Dennis sees what's going on and joins Marcus in the chase. They wrestle Eddie to the wet blacktop and Marcus punches him hard again and again. Dennis punches him too, but more like he's "going along" (not very hard). Eddie is angry and

sticks up for himself, trying to fight back and run, but winds up soaking wet, very tired, and crying. When Marcus and Dennis stop chasing Eddie, they spot Trang and chase him. They wrestle him to the ground and Marcus hits him. Trang, like Eddie, fights back but can't hold off both boys. Trang winds up standing and soaking wet. He looks angry, confused, and hurt all at once. Marcus gets very close to him and yells (hatefully) in one ear: "Chinese boy." (First grade, February 1993)

In this example, Marcus and Dennis physically attacked two of the smallest and most nonaggressive, quiet boys in the first grade. Marcus, who initiated the attack, was almost as small as Eddie and Trang, but much more aggressive and of higher but not the highest social status. Marcus appeared to dislike both Eddie and Trang, as evidenced by how hard he hit Eddie and how hatefully he called Trang "Chinese boy." Dennis, who was bigger, aggressive, and possessed greater social status than Marcus, went along with the chasing and wrestling of the boys to the ground but was restrained in how hard he hit Eddie and chose not to hit Trang. Whereas all four boys are of similar lower-income backgrounds and three are African Americans, Trang is an Asian American. Physicality, in the form of unprovoked physical aggression, serves as a primary means by which subordinate masculinities may be produced and reinforced. Marcus's physical aggressiveness, in light of his own small size and social status, may be understood as a more extreme effort to enhance his own subordinate masculine identity and status. Hondagneu-Sotelo and Messner (1994) similarly summarized a set of power relationships among adult men: "Marginalized and subordinated men then, tend to overtly display exaggerated embodiments and verbalizations of masculinity that can be read as a desire to express power over others within contexts of relative powerlessness" (p. 214). In contrast, Dennis's greater size, social status, and less subordinate masculine identity may have permitted him to exhibit a less aggressive physicality.

Finally, Marcus's physical domination and abuse of Trang and his loud, hateful denunciation of Trang's race and ethnicity link three of Hearn and Collinson's (1994) proposed references of masculine identity (ethnicity, size, and violence) and produce a subordinated masculinity (p. 109). This example exposes the untenability of theorizing a single, unitary masculinity.

We turn finally to high-status boys' physical aggression toward girls. In each case, the aggression is unprovoked, directed at girls with high status, not physically resisted, and ignored by other students in the class.

Physical aggression toward girls. Chantel and Regina are two of the most popular and high-status girls in Ms. W's first-grade class. Rakella is one of the most popular and high-status girls in Ms. Y's second-grade classroom. The following three field note entries describe how each of these girls was physically threatened and/or accosted by a high-status boy in her class:

Entry 1

The kids have "free time" and are engaged in a number of different activities around the classroom. Martin asks Chantel why she is at a different table. She tells him that she wants to be, and he goes over to her, pushes her and loudly asks: "Why?!" He continues to push her and ask "why" three more times. She tries to ignore him. The teacher intercedes. (First grade, March 1993)

Entry 2

Now the class is going to fine arts. The fine arts specialist has taken a leave, so there is a new teacher who is much stricter. Martin comes into the classroom late and approaches Regina at her seat and says: "Get out of my seat!" He makes a half gesture with his forearm and hand as though he's going to hit her. Regina immediately and calmly obliged, showing no resentment or anger. The seat was not Martin's. (First grade, March 1993)

Entry 3

The kids are back at their tables. Jamel gets up from his seat and walks over to Chantel's table, picks up a box of felt markers, and takes one out. Chantel protests, Jamel puts down the marker, hits Chantel in the back of the head with his hand, and walks back to his table. He starts punching Rakella in the arm. Rakella does not react to the punching. Jamel continues to hit her harder and harder trying to get a reaction out of her—she absolutely does not react. She finally slides her chair away from his, but he slides his over and continues to punch her about as hard as he can. The teacher becomes aware of the situation and stops it. (Second grade, May 1994)

We argue, similar to Ghaill (1994), that to maintain and enhance their own classroom status and masculine identities, these two high-status boys physically threatened and assaulted some of the most popular and high-status girls in their classrooms. It is interesting to note that the boys' behavior went unchallenged and seemed almost acceptable to both the girls involved and the other girls and boys in the class. Thus, some degree of social permission was accorded these high-status boys to exert physical power and control over these particular girls. Given the racial and class oppression that the majority of these children grow up with, the exertion of physical power and control over girls (and social license for it) is not difficult to understand. Many of these children come from families in which there are marginalized and subordinated men and older boys, who have likely adopted masculinities that express resistance to their marginal and subordinate status and assert power and control over women.

Martin's and Jamel's social savvy and ability to negotiate their masculine identities were quite evident in whom they chose (and did not choose) to assert themselves. More important, there were a number of girls in the class who would not have tolerated such aggression and acts of subordination. These girls would have resisted such subordination and would have immediately responded physically and verbally to Martin's or Jamel's physical aggression.

However, these girls were seldom physically challenged by any of the boys and were never observed to be physically confronted by the most dominant, high-status boys. In this case, high-status boys carefully avoided boy-girl interactions in which their high status could be physically challenged by girls. Furthermore, girls were never observed to instigate unprovoked physical aggression toward the high-status boys. The high-status boys' recognition of some of the girls' potential abilities to challenge and overcome them physically offers a partial and potential contradiction of traditional gender relationships. Yet, the boys' avoidance of situations in which girls might physically dominate them and the girls' noninitiation of physical aggression toward the high-status boys also keeps such contradictions in check and helps to maintain traditional gender (and power) relationships.

Competitive Displays of Physical Strength and Skill

Many of the boys tended to engage in competitive physical displays, ranging from spontaneous contests between two or more boys—in which, for example, they would try to determine who could jump highest, lift a heavy object, make a basket, or perform Michael Jackson's moonwalk the best—to more routinized, daily contests of wrestling and running and chasing games in first grade, and basketball and wrestling competitions in second grade. Due to space limitations, we limit our discussion here to wrestling competitions. We have chosen to discuss these particular competitions because of the abundance of data we have about them.

The wrestling contests occurred daily, were short-lived, and always took place on a carpeted area at the back of each classroom. Unlike the playground activities (e.g., running and chasing games, basketball), the first author was able to position herself in very close proximity to these competitions at a desk just off the carpeted area where she could clearly see, hear, and record the children's physical and verbal interactions. The object of the competition was to win by physically subduing one's opponent by sitting or lying on him. To the children, the meaning of this competition was the acquisition and maintenance of status and power through the display of physical force and skill. We argue that these displays are also important in the production of dominant and subordinate masculinities and femininities.

The encounters were usually friendly and few words between competitors were exchanged. The high-status boys, who were accorded rank partly because of their display of physical skill, strength, and superiority in the competitions of first and second grade, were without exception African Americans from lower-income backgrounds. The lower-status boys, who tended to be nonaggressive, smaller, and/or boys with physical and/or cognitive disabilities, very seldom participated in these wrestling matches. Most of these boys were Asian American, Hispanic American, or Anglo-American from lower-income or middle-income backgrounds, or African American boys from middle-income backgrounds who told the first author that they did not like the activity or think it was fun. Such differences in physical activity levels and interests across children of varying class, racial, and ethnic backgrounds have been reported consistently by school ethnographers. As noted, lower-class African American children especially value physicality as a means of expressing and promoting group and self-identity within a dominant white culture in which racial discrimination and oppression have been commonplace (Hanna, 1988). Yates (1987) noted that in the culture of Asian immigrants, sporting activity is not particularly valued.

Most of the girls did not wrestle or display any interest in watching others wrestle. However, Madeline, who was the tallest, heaviest, and strongest student in the first and second grades, especially liked to wrestle and often did so with the boys. The high-status group of boys who wrestled consistently avoided wrestling with Madeline. They seemed to know they did not stand a chance and did not want to risk being beaten, especially by a girl. These boys possessed a savoir-faire beyond their years that helped them to negotiate their social dominance, popularity, and a dominant masculinity adroitly.[4] Their decisions to avoid Madeline were never questioned or challenged.

In contrast, other boys who customarily wrestled were usually willing to wrestle with Madeline. These boys, who tended to have less status and lacked the social sophistication of the higher-status boys, did not seem to view wrestling with Madeline as risky, even though Madeline usually wound up sitting on them. Although these boys were publicly and consistently "beaten" by Madeline, none of the boys was ever teased about it. Indeed, it was often after Madeline had physically subdued one of them that the higher-status boys would loudly ridicule her, calling her names such as "tomboy," "whale," and "fat ass." Madeline's frank and obvious physicality, and especially her ability to subdue some of the boys in her class, contradicted and challenged traditional gendered relations of power. At the same time, the very public verbal ridicule leveled against her also served to contain and render less problematic such incongruities.

The carpet wrestling episodes, although providing powerful contexts for the production and display of dominant and subordinate masculinities, the repudiation of feminine physicality, and the challenging and contradiction of traditional gender relations, are reflective of only one form of physicality that was important in the children's constructions of masculinities. Physical gestures and postures are a third and final aspect of physicality that is critical in the production of masculinities.

Physical Gestures and Postures

Throughout the first and second grades, many of the boys displayed a number of physical gestures and postures connoting toughness, tenderness, aloofness, dominance, caring, and vulnerability that were linked to the production of gender. Those boys who possessed savoir-faire were well aware of what these displays of masculinity conveyed and when they could (or should) be invoked. Others remained apparently unaware of the meanings of such performances and of the contexts in which exhibiting them would be socially acceptable. We discuss one physical gesture here—touch—and begin with field note entries made on three different days of observation.

Entry 1

A physical education class is just ending and the children are walking to the perimeters of the gym to pick up their shirts and sweaters. Tobias has been sitting out against the wall after being accidentally hit in the head by a classmate. Nicholas walks up to Tobias, looks at him with concern for a moment and then puts his arms under Tobias's arms, helps lift Tobias up from the floor, and pats him on the back. (Second grade, March 1994)

Entry 2

We are in gym. Five teams and leaders are being selected for relay races. The first race involves the first kid in line running to the end of the gym, touching the floor, racing back to his/her line, and taking the next person in line by the hand and together running to touch the floor and return. The race continues until the entire line of children has run, hand-in-hand, touched the floor, and returned. Martin is next to last in line, and when his turn comes up, he refuses to hold hands with his fellow team-mates (Wallace, Nicholas, Shardae, and Brad) and so they all run side-by-side. (First grade, February 1993)

Entry 3

The kids are coming over to the carpet and sitting down for a story. Michael sits down next to Bareep and tries to hug him. Bareep is taken aback and loudly exclaims: "Quit hugging me gay boy!" Michael seems embarrassed and says nothing. Bareep moves away from Michael. (First grade, January 1994)

What is to be made of these seemingly contradictory accounts of boys' willingness or unwillingness to offer and accept expressions of care and/or affection via gestures of physical touch? In the first example, Tobias and Nicholas shared positions of relatively high and similar status. Nicholas helped Tobias up after he incurred an injury during physical activity, like scenes they might see in a televised football or basketball game. Nicholas's physical expression of concern and care was accepted, even welcomed by Tobias, because they shared equal statuses and such physical gestures in the context of gym class are consistent with images of celebrated athletic forms of masculinity. It is "cool" and totally acceptable to offer a hand up and a pat on the back to a fellow participant in the context of athletic endeavor.

In the second example, Martin refused to hold hands during a relay race. He was the most dominant, highest-status boy in first grade and it was to his character, more than anyone else's, that the emerging hegemonic mode of masculinity corresponded.[5] His cunning ability to negotiate and maintain his social status and masculinity were impressive. Other boys fell over themselves trying to be friends with Martin. They mimicked his speech, gestures, and postures; they covered for him so that he would not get in trouble; sought him out as a partner; and wrote stories portraying him as their friend. Martin constantly negotiated a masculine identity that was physically aggressive, tough, distant, and cool, and his refusal to join hands both consolidated his ascendant position and constricted other expressions of masculinity.

In the third and final example, Michael, one of the lowest-status boys, tried to hug Bareep. Michael suffered from brain damage and a heart disorder. Brain surgery as an infant had left him with a very visible 10- to 12-inch-long scar just above the hairline on his forehead. He was thin and weak due to his heart condition, often finding it difficult to climb the stairs of the three-story school building or participate in physical education classes. Although cognitively disabled as well, Michael was well aware of who the popular and unpopular boys in the class were. He desperately wanted to be accepted by other boys. Bareep, although not a member of the highest-status group of boys, was liked by many and ranked well above Michael in the pecking order. Bareep's particularly strong rejection of Michael, calling him a gay boy, was not simply a reaction to Michael's gesture. It was a response to the boy and body that delivered the overture— a low-status boy whose body was viewed by his peers as looking and acting strange. Bareep's rejection served to set Bareep apart from, and make him superior to, Michael; it linked Michael's physicality (touching) to the term "gay." Although neither Bareep nor the other first-grade boys understood the meaning of this term, it is nonetheless interesting to note its negative usage in this context.[6]

A noticeable process in the production of hegemonic masculinity is the establishment of heterosexual rather than homosexual preferences and relationships (Lorber & Farrell, 1991), and scholars have noted the intensity with which "compulsory heterosexuality" is especially enforced within and surrounding physicality in the context of male sport (Connell, 1990; Curry, 1991; Kane & Disch, 1993; Messner, 1994; Pronger, 1990). Studies of prepubescent schoolchildren often report how, for example, boys use homophobic labels such as "fag" or "homo" to tease and insult other boys displaying behavior that does not measure up to a hegemonic masculinity (e.g., too much physical contact with other boys, feminine dress and posture, or low skill in physical activities; Adler et al., 1992; Thorne, 1993).

Finally, Michael's clearly visible physical disabilities often prompted children to laugh at and verbally ridicule him. Thus, physical disability should not be overlooked in relation to the production of dominant and subordinate masculinities. As Hearn and Collinson (1994) pointed out, disability is one of many possible "sources or references of identity that cuts across notions of unified masculinity" (p. 109).

Conclusion

We have examined how first- and second-grade boys from a predominantly black, lower-income, inner-city school relied on their moving bodies, or physicality, in the production of masculinities. Through corporeal displays of aggression, strength, and skill via wrestling, basketball, and physical gestures, the boys negotiated with greater or lesser degrees of social awareness and skill their masculine identities and relative positions of power and status. African American boys from low-income backgrounds possessed the highest social status and displayed the most authoritative masculinity of the classroom cultures. Their physically negotiated dominant masculine identities and positions of power often marginalized and subordinated the masculinities of boys with less physical prowess; smaller boys; a boy with disabilities; African American counterparts from middle-income backgrounds; Hispanic American, Asian American, and Anglo-American boys from low- and middle-income backgrounds; and girls. Such physical domination over other boys and girls can be understood as the expression of a masculinity shaped by racial and class oppression. These boys mature in social contexts in which older boys and men, marginalized and subordinated by their class and color, display masculinities that resist other men's power and exercise control over women.

A hegemonic masculinity was evident that incorporated a particular set of references of identity, including African American racial and ethnic background, low social class, superior physical skill and strength, physical aggression, able-bodiedness, an uninterest in school, and a disregard for femininities and especially feminine physicality. This dominant masculinity does not appear to differ extensively from that of boys from the predominantly white, upper-middle-income school studied by Adler et al. (1992), who found that the most popular boys were physically tough, competitive, dominating, and involved in sport. Furthermore, they found that those accorded the greatest status challenged authority and expressed a detachment from teachers, school, and academic efforts. Of course, not all African American male persons employ the ascendant masculinity described in this study—those from middle- and upper-income levels with access to conventional symbols of masculinity were less likely to exhibit it. Such was the case with Zeek, whose masculine identity reflected his middle-class background, interest in school, and nonaggressive demeanor.

Finally, Asian American, Hispanic American, and Anglo-American boys, regardless of class background, were absent from the ranks of the high-status boys. Perhaps sport may, in part, explain this finding. The highest-status boys tended to engage in, like, and demonstrate competence in sport. If sport interest and ability are associated with race (e.g., African Americans are frequently attributed as possessing some mysterious "natural" athletic talent), perhaps some of the non-African American boys did not value sport or perceived themselves to be less proficient at sport than African Americans. Certainly, significant others may intentionally or unwittingly reinforce interracial beliefs about sport competence, much as they do intergender beliefs.

Perhaps these boys could have compensated for their lack of proficiency at sport by being more aggressive toward others. But even this may have been difficult in a setting in which they were a numerical minority, and race, ethnicity, physical strength, and skill, among other attributes, greatly determined status. Marcus illustrated this with his assaults on two lower-status boys, Eddie and Trang. The assault of Eddie was only physical, but the assault of Trang was followed by a verbal assault intended to inferiorize him. Had Asian American students constituted the majority of students in the school, the interracial group dynamics and the effect of this name-calling would likely have been decidedly different.

Notes

1. The second author participated in the data analysis, interpretation, and writing phases of the study.

2. Status was defined as popularity or social prestige. Children with high status were those liked by the greatest number of their peers and who were most influential in setting class atmosphere, making group decisions, establishing group opinions, and initiating group activities.

3. The children were not "tracked" according to academic achievement. There was, however, a conscious attempt to create mixes of students within each classroom at each grade level that might help particular "problem" students. For example, Zeek, who was viewed as a well-mannered and diligent student, and Martin, who was considered to be a

"discipline problem," were placed in the same second-grade classroom in the hopes that Zeek would be a "positive influence" on Martin.

4. Adler, Kless, and Adler (1992) noted that among the older elementary school children they observed, those boys who were most popular possessed a higher degree of social sophistication and interpersonal skills than did their peers. We are not suggesting that among the boys we observed, only those boys displaying a more hegemonic form of masculinity possessed such finesse, nor are we implying that only boys possess savoir-faire. Several of the highest-status girls also possessed such social skill.

5. The thesis that hegemonic forms of masculinity only correspond to the characters of a few men (Carrigan, Connell, & Lee, 1985) was evident among the first- and second-grade boys.

6. On several occasions, when a boy would use the term "gay," the first author would ask the boy what he meant by the term. Boys responding to this inquiry appeared to do so honestly, but with great difficulty. They did not seem to really know, or at least could not articulate, what the word meant other than to understand that it had a negative connotation.

3

Moms, Sisters, and Ladies

Women Student Trainers in Men's Intercollegiate Sport

STEPHAN R. WALK

Few areas of contemporary society construct dualism of gender and sexuality and maintain heterosexual male dominance more vigorously than sport. Historically, sport has been characterized by bonding activities that are linked to antisocial and misogynistic behavior by male athletes, coaches, and other members of the male sporting fraternity (McKay, 1997; Messner, 1992b; Messner & Sabo, 1994; Schacht, 1996). As was demonstrated vividly in the 1990 sexual harassment of Boston Herald sportswriter Lisa Olsen by several members of the New England Patriots, the locker room has become a flash point for the conflicts that can arise when the misogynist milieus of some sporting subcultures encounter the small but increasing number of women who are entering this traditionally androcentric domain (Kane & Disch, 1993). Despite such incidents, the sexual harassment of women in sport is only beginning to be documented (Brackenridge, 1997; Katz, 1995c; Lenskyj, 1992b, 1992c; Volkwein, Frauke, Schnell, Sherwood, & Livezey, 1997).

Athletic trainers, who provide ongoing acute and chronic health care services to athletes, have started to enter sport in expanding numbers. Like sports journalism, the profession of athletic training is characterized by a gender hierarchy. The National Athletic Trainers Association does not publish figures for percentages of men and women trainers, but one of its representatives stated that women make up only 2% of the athletic training staffs for professional baseball, basketball, football, and ice hockey, and about 20% of head athletic trainers in intercollegiate sports programs (B. Unruh, telephone conversation with the author, March 6, 1997). Nevertheless, the number of women in intercollegiate athletic training positions represents a substantial increase in recent years, and it appears that these women have joined a number of others who are challenging hegemonic forms of masculinity in traditionally male sporting subcultures (Young, 1997).

This study extends the growing literature on sexualities in organizations (Hearn & Parkin, 1995; Hearn, Sheppard, Tancred-Sherrif, & Burrel, 1989) by investigating the experiences of women working as athletic trainers in an intercollegiate sports program at a large Midwestern university, hereafter referred to as Great State University (GSU). It involved interviews with 9 women student athletic trainers (SATs) in an internship program and was part of a larger study that also included men SATs (Walk, 1994). The central focus of the study was the process by which students become athletic trainers and the nature of student-trainer relationships among peer athletes and others within the social structures of intercollegiate athletics. Given the scant literature detailing the experiences of women within male athletic subcultures, the interactions of these women with men during assignments to traditionally male athletic teams were of particular interest.

Participants

All of the women were either college seniors or graduate students in a program that required both course work and internship experience. All of the participants had at least 2 years of experience as interns as well as a series of assignments to various collegiate athletic teams. They also had either previous or current assignments to the football team, along with placements with other sports in the GSU athletic department. Out of concern for revealing identities, the teams to which particular student trainers in the study were assigned cannot be reported.

Methodology

I began with the premise that the student-trainers belonged to multiple and overlapping subcultures (e.g., athletic training, intercollegiate athletics, college student life). Each participant took part in a group session and a subsequent individual interview. The questions discussed in both situations focused on a number of issues, including the students' personal expectations of their internships, the daily problems they confronted, and the role of gender in their work. All of the interviews were tape-recorded and subsequently transcribed and analyzed by using a qualitative software program called HyperQual (Padilla, 1991).

Limitations and Epistemological Issues

The interview method carries a number of important limitations, including a lack of generalizability and other controls stemming from interviewing volunteers at a single institution. I also must note the gendered nature of the interview settings (Morgan, 1981), including my status as a white male scholar conducting the interviews, and the fact that two of the four group interviews involved combinations of men and women (i.e., 3 women and 3 men, and 1 woman and 7 men). Finally, as Jardine and Smith (1987) and Messner (1990c) noted, there are epistemological problems that arise when a male scholar employs a profeminist approach to the study of masculinity. In this case, this point makes problematic my attempt to construct a narrative of the experiences of women. Moreover, as Ramazanoglu (1992) argued, a pervasive lack of agreement on conceptions of social power, in addition to theoretical cleavages between profeminist studies of masculinity and feminist work on women's oppression, have left unclear the links between research of this kind and larger issues of political transformation. These issues, which transcend strictly "methodological" concerns, remain substantially unresolved in the extant methodological and theoretical literature.

My intention was to allow the participants to determine, as much as possible, the context and content of their responses in the interviews and to adopt a profeminist perspective in my analysis of their accounts. As is standard in such research, the women were free to refuse to participate in the interviews, in part or in whole, and were assured of the confidentiality of their identities and statements. Of some reassurance was the fact that, at least for some of the women, the group session appeared almost therapeutic, in that it allowed a confidential atmosphere in which to express some of their frustrations about working as interns.

Results

The outcomes are presented in two major segments. The first section describes how the women were placed in traditionally feminine roles, and the second examines the ways in which their interactions with men were sexualized and occasionally characterized by sexual harassment. To provide some measure of context, it is essential to describe the larger circumstances in which these women worked. Most noteworthy in this respect are the exploitation and humiliation to which they were subjected, the restrictions placed on their social interactions, and the ways they were assigned to sports teams at GSU.

"Water Girls"

As I have reported elsewhere, SATs are generally underpaid or unpaid interns who function as allied health care workers for athletes involved in university-sponsored sports programs (Walk, 1997). Some SATs spent from 40 to 70 hours per week in their internships, in addition to being full-time students. Perhaps their most publicly visible activity is when they rush onto the field to deliver water to athletes. This basic duty leads some to label the student-trainers as "water boys" and "water girls." The SATs resented these labels, particularly when used by football players, who engaged in a number of actions that demeaned them. Humiliating behavior by both male athletes and coaches appeared to open the door to other forms of denigration and harassment.

A salient issue among the SATs and their professional supervisors concerned the fact that the former form close friendships with athletes and with each other. Most commonly reported were social friendships and cohabitation, in addition to intimate friendships and amorous relationships. These relationships existed even though the GSU program maintained a "no-socializing policy" forbidding close relationships between SATs and athletes, ostensibly implemented to maintain the professional respect and authority of the former. Nearly all the men and women SATs were insulted by the no-socializing policy and violated it routinely. Nevertheless, in the presence of coaches and supervising staff trainers, the SATs had to work to control the nature of their relationships with athletes, including the perceptions of those relationships. Although all SATs were restrained by the no-socializing policy, it is my firm conclusion that all of these problems were considerably more complicated for the women than for the men.

Finally, the distribution of internships among the GSU teams, which were made by the head staff trainers, was neither random nor without political implications, that is, the student-trainers almost universally considered their assignments as indications of their status in the program. The top assignments were considered to be ice hockey (men's), football, men's basketball, and gymnastics (men's and women's), whereas fencing, swimming and diving, and tennis were perceived to be at the bottom of the hierarchy. Within this ranking, women SATs were never assigned to ice hockey, were restricted to the training room (i.e., not allowed by the head coach to watch practice) during assignments to the men's basketball team, and were excluded from some activities and felt a considerable degree of hostility from both players and coaches on the football team. For example, women reported being prohibited by football coaches from a postpractice huddle due to the obscene language used, including the naming of football plays with terms related to women's sexual anatomy. Hence, one's gender not only directly affected one's placement within the hierarchy of sports but also one's experiences within the sport once assigned.

Moms, sisters, ladies. As the women explained how their experiences differed from those of men, it became clear that one of the ways male members of athletic teams were able to come to grips with the presence of women student-trainers was to fit them into stereotypical feminine roles, that is, it was evident that often the very presence of women seemed incongruous with the practices that take place in traditionally male sports. Some of the women explained how many athletes used stereotypes when referring to them, and to some degree the women accepted these labels. As my title indicates, these stereotypes and their associated roles included those of mother, sister, and lady.

The most frequently mentioned role that women SATs adopted was explained, both by themselves and by athletes, as "motherly." One woman SAT explained, "You become motherly, you start taking care of them. And that's when they get to thinking you're a mom to them." Another noted, "You get that knock on the door at 5 o'clock in the morning: 'I don't feel good. Can you give me something to make me go to sleep?' " [laughs]. Moreover, some women indicated that not only did athletes treat them this way, but they also became "protective" of athletes, particularly after spending entire seasons with them. Indeed, one woman went as far as calling her demeanor a "motherly instinct," stating that she had gotten to the point of empathizing with the difficulties of intercollegiate athletic participation:

> I feel it's kind of a compliment that they feel comfortable enough with me. I mean, being an athletic trainer is difficult enough. But being an athlete you can't overlook either. I mean these people work umpteen hours a day [at] school, they get yelled at if their grades aren't good enough. At practice, they get yelled at

because they . . . were studying late because they hadn't made the grades, and now they're tired during practice and they can get worn out just as fast as you can. Every now and then they do need a shoulder to cry on or someone to just give them a little back rub and be like: "It's okay. Next game what if you try this?" or "This will work better." I've even helped athletes with their classes. So, you do . . . become a mom-figure. . . . I've had that with both men's sports and women's sports. But I think that's nice that athletes feel that they have that kind of crutch when they're away from home, especially the freshmen. I was up one night for three hours with someone that was homesick. A lot of people would feel that that's not my job description. No, it's not, but if that girl's up all night, she's not going to perform well either and she runs the risk of getting hurt. It's kind of really piecing it together to wind up with the athletic participation part.

As in this quotation, a number of other women and a few men SATs shared the belief that, despite the fact that forming a close relationship with an athlete violated the no-socializing policy and might undermine their professional authority, sometimes the trust they established made it possible to obtain important medical information or to initiate actions that might prevent injury.

However, consistent with what Connell (1987) calls "emphasized femininity," women's acceptance of this mothering status was also consistent with their further subordination to men, because it reinforced traditionally feminine notions of "compliance, nurturance, and empathy" (p. 188). This point brings up two related questions. As Curry (1991) noted in his discussion of locker room talk, male athletes generally avoid intimacy and are particularly hesitant to engage in disclosure among their peers. Hence, the first question was whether the SATs felt that male athletes were more likely to see women trainers as motherly figures or whether this occurred with both men and women athletes. One SAT stated her impression:

Sometimes the men are more accepting of you because you're female and they feel you are more nurturing and can take care of them, which is what I found. The men like to come to me because I think they feel like the more maternal thing, taking care of them.

Another stated that she thought she was more motherly in the presence of male athletes, stating, "They just came to me with everything, everything." One woman, however, disagreed with the notion that she was more motherly to men than to women, saying, "It doesn't matter whether they're male or female, it works on both sides." However, another doubted that men SATs would act in a motherly way:

When you have a guy laying in bed with a 104 fever for three days, you're the one checking on him every ten or fifteen minutes, just what a mom would do. And so that's how you get that type of thing. And I think sometimes that a man [trainer] might not be quite as sensitive to those type[s] of things, but that's just my personal feeling. I don't know for sure because I have never seen a man handle it before.

Indeed, the other question I asked about the motherly role was whether men SATs also adopted it. The response was generally "No," although in some cases these responses were qualified, as seen in one man's comparison of men and women SATs:

They [women SATs] get things that we don't. . . . Women are more motherly figures. . . . You can get closer to them. . . . A guy's relationship with a guy is like, you know [long pause] sex, sports, etc. There's a fine line that you only talk about certain things with guys. And then a girl can talk to a guy, and they'll discuss relationships and stuff. Guys don't talk about that kind of thing. They get a different perspective than I'd say a male trainer does.

Hence, this trainer suggested, consistent with the findings of Curry (1991), that certain barriers exist for male trainers in pursuing personal matters with male athletes that are perhaps not there for women. One woman responded to a question about male trainers and mothering:

You can't make guys feminine just to be a mom kind of role. I mean in their own subtle, guy way, yeah, I think they do help each other out. I've seen it. I have seen men trainers really help out their male athletes emotionally. I mean it's the same thing. You see it. Do you not intervene or just help them out a little bit, just because you don't want to cross that professional barrier? But at the same time, if that kid's not going to be happy, and he's going to be miserable, there are going to be detrimental effects that come out of it. So, it's kind of like a Catch-22.

Indeed, crossing a professional barrier was the principal issue these trainers spoke of as complicating the mothering role. Although they emphasized the importance of having athletes trust them, they also noted that staff trainers believed they were becoming too close to athletes. One group recounted how they believed an SAT was removed from an assignment for this very reason. What might tip off the staff to the status of these relationships was not mentioned, although a few student-trainers described how athletes occasionally lobbied staff trainers to reassign their current SATs for the following season, as opposed to moving them to another team, as was the common practice. Such pressure seemed to suggest that these favored SATs had become too close to their athletes.

One of the apparent results of this closeness—interestingly associated with the replacement of the word "mother" with "sister"—was that not only did SATs "protect" athletes as mothers, male athletes were also said to protect women SATs as they would sisters. This notion came up exclusively in the case of women SATs who worked with male athletes. In some instances, the sister label was described as simply part of the nature of the relationship between women trainers and male athletes. In other contexts, the expression was used to describe how, in some kind of crisis, a male athlete would come to the defense of a woman trainer. In one case, a woman SAT stated that a rumor had circulated about her alleged sexual proclivities. The protective athletes, described as "leaders on the team," identified the source of the rumor, and, as she stated, "shut them down." She described several instances in which athletes would come to her with gossip about her personal life or her skills as a trainer. She concluded by saying, "You've got to make friends or you're dead meat."

A final kind of stereotype was that of "lady" (see Yount, 1991). Some women noted that football coaches would apologize for swearing in their presence by speaking of "offending the ladies." Again, as in the example of the postpractice football huddle, this kind of protection was presumably the basis for some of the exclusionary practices at GSU. One group of women laughed about how some male athletes would criticize their peers for discussing "crude topics" in the presence of women SATs, saying, "Hey, there's a lady in the room!" One woman added that such behavior was "nice to hear," given the apparently common pattern whereby male athletes, and football players in particular, did not seem to mind who heard such talk.

In summary, the main stereotypes assigned to, and enacted by, women in the program were those of mother, sister, and lady, with the latter also implying that these women were, to some degree, seen as potential romantic contact interests or sexual partners. I now explore how the women SATs were sexualized, that is, where sexual innuendo and imagery pervaded the work atmosphere, as well as incidents of male athletes engaging in overt sexual harassment.

Sexualization and Sexual Harassment

Several women believed that the most politically powerful male coaches looked for incidents in which women "screwed up" or "got in the way" to prove their gender-based incompetence. Recounting what was perhaps the most notorious example of this hostility, one woman reported the following remark made by the head football coach to a staff trainer about the SATs on the football practice field, a remark that combines sexualization and sexual hostility: "[The coach] calls us pussies. . . . And he's, 'Why the fuck do we have all of these pussies out here? Look, [gestures, as if counting] pussy, pussy, dick, pussy, pussy.' That is what he said."

Several of the women perceived that the real reason for their exclusion from and/or hostility within the prestigious sports of football, basketball, and ice hockey was that, regardless of their intentions, professional or otherwise, they were a "distraction" to the male athletes. In other words, they were a sexual diversion that was not permissible by high-profile and revenue-generating coaches who are under pressure to win. To understand this sexually based distraction, one must recall the no-socializing policy mentioned previously. As might be imagined, women felt differentially affected by this policy. Some reported that they had received unfair evaluations of their performance due to rumors or a reputation that they were overly friendly with, or even dating, an athlete with whom they worked as a trainer. For example, one woman, not in the study, was reported to have been "blackballed," receiving an assignment to a "less prestigious" sport, due to allegations that she had been dating an athlete.

Considerable portions of two group interviews were spent discussing the implications of the policy prohibiting socializing and other types of nonprofessional interaction between SATs and athletes. Several women spoke about needing to choose between orientations toward male athletes, which were characterized as either "bitch" (essentially synonymous with being professional and rude) or "friendly" (described in terms such as "nice" and "sociable"). The underlying assumption about these interactions with male athletes was that they presumably involved a "pickup situation." For instance, one of the complaints lodged against some women SATs by staff trainers and coaches was that their appearance was distracting to athletes. One male SAT spoke of "trouble with them wearing their shorts too short or putting on lipstick on the field," which he said had led to hostility from a coach. One group also spoke of how the issue of makeup was included in comments one woman SAT received on an annual evaluation of her skills. Another woman alleged that she was told to ignore compliments on her appearance from players and coaches. Nor were male SATs immune from scrutiny of their appearance. One described an incident in which a football coach told a male SAT to remove an earring, with the former saying, "Guys don't wear earrings out here."

I asked women what they were expected to do in response to the initiation of a social conversation with a male athlete. One woman responded that she assumed she was expected to be courteous but standoffish: "If they say, 'Hi,' you say, 'Hi,' but you go and scurry off and start reading or something." She added that she refused to engage in such behavior and instead liked to "be involved with what people were doing." Her understanding of these prohibitions and warnings were the following:

> Because I guess they think it's unprofessional. That's what they say. Because then we're being women, as far as we're being nice and giggly. Even if we were not being giggly. "You're being too nice. You're acting weak. You're acting pretty. You're acting like a girl." And we're not supposed to do that.

When asked whether there were equivalent restrictions on male SATs, one woman responded, "No. The guys can talk, they can joke, they can party, they can do whatever they really want." Indeed, what struck many of these women about the no-socializing policy was that not only did it seem to apply only to women, it was part of a larger system of double standards about social relationships. Several women were aware of male SATs who lived with athletes, which was presumably against the no-socializing policy. Women SATs had lived with women athletes and some women SATs had plans to live with women athletes. But although both men and women reported cohabitation in violation of the no-socializing policy, there seemed to be little evidence that male trainers had sexualized assumptions attached to their everyday interactions with athletes. As one woman SAT concluded, to which several men and women trainers concurred, "It's your standard thing, you know. Guys who are social and flirtatious are studs and women who are like that are sluts."

Sexualization of women SATs was also linked with the general talk that pervaded their everyday work activities. A number of women spoke of needing to "set the tone" in their training rooms, given the proclivity of college athletes to discuss sexual topics. One described such talk as "getting way out of hand," and in some cases involving coaches. As mentioned, such behavior was part of the rationale for excluding women from ice hockey and from certain portions of football practice. In the case of football, one SAT claimed that the coach's basis for prohibiting women was that "our daddies never talked to us that way, so he doesn't want us to hear those words from him." She added, however, that such protection from vulgarity did little good when so many others in the work context were engaged in such behavior.

Other examples of such talk included male and female athletes talking about sex on a bus during a road trip and football players discussing the past weekend's "sexual conquests" in the training room. Moreover, as more than one woman stated, these latter conversations were intentionally started when they were in the room:

> Just foul comments. Like . . . if certain athletes know you're in the room, and you may be cleaning something or minding your own business, they will start up conversations that degrade women just to get a rise out of you. . . . I don't know, maybe it's the stereotype that women are softer emotionally that the guys constantly try to break you or try to get to you.

All women reported experiencing either subtle or overt sexual harassment by male athletes, the most common being these general "atmospheric" conversations. Most agreed that the best strategy to use in confronting these activities was to ignore the behavior. Again, this tactic often was described as being professional, although some described how they had fought back with some success in various, although unspecified, ways.

It should not be surprising, then, that sexual conversations among male athletes in the presence of women SATs also were accompanied by more direct forms of sexual harassment. Again, the women stated that most often this came in small doses, as one woman put it, "a comment here, a remark there." On the other hand, some women related being harassed on a daily basis, as in the following case:

> There are certain guys on the team that won't leave you alone. Well, say like there was this one guy who is known as one of the really rude guys on the team. He was always, "Yeah I know about you. I know what you're like." And there was nothing to know. So he was harassing me in that way. Then he'd always say, basically to everybody, "So baby, when we going out? I know you want me," all this crap. So you just learned how to deal with it. There were just a couple other incidences of that. In that respect, you know, I can see why they don't want you to date the athletes because then that would probably be even worse.

A few women also reported incidents in which physical contact was made by male athletes. One reported being "kissed on the cheek" in a "friendly" manner. Another reported that she had been approached several times by a player who made suggestive comments, would ask for hugs, and "look for excuses to touch" her. The player eventually approached her and said, "Hey, I got a condom. Let's get busy." Although she claimed that she did not feel "threatened" by the player, she did report the latter comment to her supervisors, who informed the coach, and the player did not engage in the behavior again.

In another case, an athlete had engaged in a pattern of verbal harassment but was continually rebuffed by the SAT, who said, "I had to be a total bitch to him, or he would think he could get away with it." However, the woman said the harassment escalated and she found herself alone in a room with the perpetrator. After verbal harassment, the athlete had her "nearly backed into a corner." This incident was dealt with severely, with the player being prohibited from interacting with women trainers.

Recalling the exclusion of women from ice hockey, one male SAT noted that the "mentality of hockey" was such that sexual harassment "could turn into a bad situation." One example he recounted involved ice hockey players joking about how a woman reporter and a woman SAT had seen them naked. The incident occurred during a competition at which the two women entered the locker room to investigate an athlete who had sustained a fairly severe injury. The women were told that it was OK to enter the locker room and assumed that the male athletes would cover themselves knowing that women were present. Instead, the injured athlete and several other players deliberately failed to cover their genitalia. Although the offenders were said to have been reprimanded, the incident appeared to have assumed a legendary status and was regarded with some humor among the players on the ice hockey team.

Although all of the previously described incidents were reported to have been handled to the satisfaction of the women involved, they are indicative of the types of actual and potential experiences that are exclusive to women SATs. However, the harassment summarized so far, along with the rest of the incidences of the sexualization of women SATs, has been essentially outside of the context of actually performing the tasks that fall under athletic training duties. When it is recalled that a substantial amount of physical contact is required of athletic trainers with athletes, the potential for sexualized construals in the situation at GSU seems to be great. Indeed, physical contact between trainers and athletes turned out to be an issue about which both men and women SATs were equally concerned.

Ironically, the issue of the legal liability of trainers was a point of discussion in all the group interviews. In most cases, this related to the fear of being sued by athletes for sexual harassment, as one woman interviewee noted:

Even if you just put your hand on someone's back, that could be sexual. Whether I was to do it with a female or male, depending on how they view it, 99% of the people wouldn't mind, if there's that one percentage that would say, "That's harassment." Because . . . with any profession, you just have to cover yourself any more.

Although the issue of contact between trainers and athletes might be thought of as being similar to that between, for example, nurses and patients, the context of the SATs' work made certain kinds of contact taboo. In particular, contact in or around the genital area was described as basically prohibited, although this seemed to depend on the context and individual comfort levels of the particular SAT and athlete. Some SATs spoke of finding replacement trainers to perform tasks, such as groin wraps, with which they or the athletes were uncomfortable. Similarly, some brought in witnesses during certain potentially sensitive treatments. Others spoke of simply keeping the athlete informed about what they were doing while performing a procedure and reminding athletes to alert them should they become uneasy about the process. Accompanying this latter approach with a "professional demeanor," as one trainer phrased it, seemed to work well.

However, one woman disclosed an example of an athlete who attempted to turn a stretching exercise into a sexual encounter by "pressing into" her genital area. She asserted that the player "had some problems with this before" and had been reprimanded by coaches for harassing women trainers. The incident involved a football player for whom she was performing a hamstring stretch. Although the SAT reported being extremely upset by the incident, she reported it to staff trainers and had it resolved to her satisfaction.

Although handling potentially litigious situations appeared to have been systematically addressed in the GSU program, in most other cases, it appeared that the SATs were on their own with respect to sexualized assumptions about interactions, sexual talk among male athletes, and associated problems. In some cases, serious problems were referred to staff and adequately addressed in the views of the women SATs. Although it appeared that the women were satisfied with these responses, they also reported that the incidents were handled on a case-by-case basis, and not through a policy or announcement to teams. So even though the SATs operated under a no-socializing policy and took precautions in light of potential sexual harassment charges by athletes, there were apparently no equivalent policies and precautions about the behavior of athletes toward SATs.

Summary and Conclusion

Nearly all the women in this study were positioned in contradictory ways. The constant energy and attention required to "do" gender (West & Zimmerman, 1987) was a constant diversion from the women's professional development. Indeed, it appeared impossible for these women to be seen primarily in terms of their professional status, that is, as appropriately present for the prevention and care of athletic injuries. In general, the presence of women among the male sporting fraternity at GSU represented an intrusion not just into the physical spaces of male sport "but into certainties about gender relations and sex differences that sport serves to guarantee" (Disch & Kane, 1996, p. 282).

Kane and Disch (1993) argued that what made the assault of Lisa Olsen culturally significant was that a physical space, in which the display of the male body, masculine power, and male privilege are central, was broached by a woman with the professional credentials to question these androcentric entitlements. If the "superior" male body, and physicality in general, forms the foundation for the cultural dominance of male athletes and the systematic denial of power to women, it might have been suspected that the ailing or injured male body in the presence of women student-trainers would undermine such power. Instead, the role of women SATs is constructed in ways similar to that of women physicians who attend male patients—as "servicing" male bodies (Phillips & Schneider, 1993). So even though the women SATs possessed paramedical knowledge and athletic training skills, these were articulated as performing tasks that fitted easily into traditionally subordinate roles for women.

The working environment at GSU forced the women either to adopt conventional feminine orientations (i.e., moms, sisters, ladies) or to display a gender-neutral professional persona. The women risked being considered as outsiders, either by being bitches in the view of student peers or girls in the view of professional authority figures. Of course, these student peers and professional authorities were two male-dominated groups whose demands were essentially contradictory. Chase (1988) provided a useful framework for understanding how the women SATs attempted to avoid being both "deprofessionalized," by being seen primarily as conventionally defined women, and being "defeminized," by being seen as strong women who "refus[ed] to use or trade on [their] femininity to gain the security of a place" (p. 284).

For women working in male sports contexts, a "professional/bitch" attitude may mute concerns about socializing, earn some limited protection from harassment, and make one gender invisible to coaches worried about "sexual distractions" (Disch & Kane, 1996). Yet, both women and men SATs considered the bitch element inimical to the kind of relationships they desired with student-athletes. Indeed, the latter relationships were the very basis for their resistance to authority figures in the program. Again, using Chase's (1988) terms, the price of such a "professional" strategy was defeminization, wherein a woman's desire to "make the fact of being a woman unnoticeable or invisible or silent or neutral" (p. 285) comes at the expense of casting doubt on her status as a woman. For women SATs, such a professional orientation also signaled, at the very least, sexual unavailability, so excluded the label of lady and essentially rendered a professional woman unsociable, unfriendly, and an outsider.

On the other hand, the very sociality that might be desired, in this case, by fellow student-trainers, athletes, and others is often taken as a sexual invitation by men (Saal, Johnson, & Weber, 1989; Stockdale, 1993). Because such sexualized interpretations prevail, the adoption of friendliness as the most pleasant path for maintaining social relationships among peers may be met by hostility among superiors, because women may be seen as attempting to get dates with male athletes rather than acquiring professional experience. Moreover, the sister or lady stereotypes legitimize the sexualization of all manners of male-female interactions. Such sexualization was most clear in the incidents of harassment to which women were subjected, perhaps thematized in the case of the coach who identified student-trainers as "dicks" and "pussies." Even if such sociality is not seen as sexual invitation, but rather in the form of stereotypical mothering (which, it must be reiterated, men but especially women SATs believed helped them do their work more effectively), one's professional credibility is again undermined because it is premised not on a command of professional skills and knowledge but rather on the basis of a presumably "natural" proclivity to nurture. More generally, historically feminine behavior deprofessionalizes the woman because it implies that she is attempting to trade on her femininity in the pursuit of status in the organization (Chase, 1988). In this study, such behavior rendered the nurturing, friendly, or ladylike SAT an unprofessional outsider to her superiors.

Some researchers have found that women in a male-dominated sport have been able to carve out pockets of resistance to masculine hegemony (Theberge, 1995; Young, 1997). However, most women in this study mainly had to accommodate to an androcentric environment. Although it is precisely the command of professional skills and knowledge, presumably attainable regardless of gender, that is the ticket into these masculine circles, such credentials are far from a guarantee of survival, because they will please some and antagonize others. Of particular consequence for women SATs was their atomization and sense of relative powerlessness within the program, with the result being that instances of sexual harassment were seen as isolated problems requiring individualized solutions. Although it may be possible for women to enter professional careers that place them at the center of a sport subculture historically exclusive to men, such entry has not necessarily cracked the edifice of the hegemonic masculinity on which it has been built.

4

The Morality/Manhood Paradox

Masculinity, Sport, and the Media

SHARI LEE DWORKIN
FAYE LINDA WACHS

In a world where women do not say no, the man is never forced to settle down and make serious choices. His sex drive—the most powerful compulsion in his life—is never used to make him part of civilization as the supporter of a family. If a woman does not force him to make a long-term commitment—to marry—in general, he doesn't. It is maternity that requires commitment. His sex drive only demands conquest, driving him from body to body in an unsettling hunt for variety and excitement in which much of the thrill is in the chase itself. (Gilder, 1986, p. 47)

Journalists articulated the "body panic" surrounding HIV/AIDS and sport in ways that framed heterosexual women as the virulent agents and heterosexual men as the "innocent" victims. These accounts are readily acceptable because they simultaneously produce and reproduce a gender regime that privileges heterosexual male "promiscuity" and devalues, pathologizes, or criminalizes other forms of sexuality. (McKay, 1993, p. 77)

On November 7, 1991, Earvin "Magic" Johnson announced that he had tested positive for the HIV virus. The public registered immediate shock and dismay that arguably one of the greatest and most beloved players in NBA history contracted the highly stigmatized virus. After Johnson, a self-identified heterosexual, made his announcement, once-quiet HIV/

AUTHORS' NOTE: Both authors contributed equally to the research and writing of this project.

AIDS information hot lines were suddenly jam-packed with millions of concerned inquiries as to who gets HIV and how. Johnson became a national spokesman for safe sex and began to urge abstinence, citing his unsafe "accommodation" of thousands of women. More than 4 years later, on February 22, 1996, professional diver Greg Louganis announced that he had AIDS and that he had been HIV-positive during the 1988 Seoul Olympics. Mainstream news coverage focused on the now infamous "blood in the pool" incident after Louganis struck his head on a spring-board and still went on to win an Olympic gold. Although no shock or dis-may was expressed vis-à-vis Louganis, concern was expressed that Louganis, who identifies as gay, had not informed others of his HIV sta-tus—and what effect his virus may have had on the doctors who stitched his bleeding head and on others in the pool. During the same month, on February 11, 1996, white working-class professional boxer Tommy Morrison let the public hear his own HIV story. Morrison expressed shock, regretfully blamed his "fast lane lifestyle," and is described by friends as the "world's biggest bimbo magnet." This chapter examines paradoxes that juxtapose the public perception of athletes as role models against me-dia accounts rife with "moral" turpitude. These paradoxes are particularly timely in the wake of recent attention paid to AIDS in sport. Our explor-ation of the widespread print media coverage of these prominent sports figures reveals cultural and historical assumptions about masculinity, sex-uality, and HIV/AIDS.

In U.S. mainstream culture, athletes and sports have specific cultural meanings. Athletes in mediated sports are role models, heroes, and are often featured as successful individuals. Our analysis of dominant print media coverage of these athletes' HIV announcements highlights two im-portant and interrelated issues surrounding bodies, morality, sexuality, and masculinity (the Appendix contains citations to all articles examined in this study). First, a contradiction between dominant norms of morality and masculinity becomes apparent. Second, the complexity of current and historical dynamics of race/class/gender/sexuality are explicated.

Hegemonic Masculinity, Sport, and Bodies

Hegemonic masculinity provides cultural icons or mythic images of masculinity that privilege the most powerful half of multiple dichotomous social locations. Hegemonic masculinity, the most dominant form of mas-culinity (white, middle-class, heterosexual) in a given historical period, is defined in relation to femininity and subordinated masculinities (Connell, 1987). As Foucault (1979) demonstrated, individuals live at the intersection of multiple hierarchicalized dualities, some of which are privileged, others of which are stigmatized. An individual's social location is determined by his or her positioning within multiple and fragmented hierarchies and dualities. For example, African Americans historically have been framed by the media as being "closer to nature" (Collins, 1990). Within sport, African American male athletes are assumed to be "natural" athletes, whereas white men are praised for their intelligence and hard work (Edwards, 1973). Although at times both privileged and subordinated male bodies may be said to enjoy male privilege and are seen as physically superior to female athletes, marginalized masculinities are indubitably stigmatized through comparisons with white middle-class norms (Majors, 1990). The body, then, and its discursive interpretations, are sites at which the material effects of power can be explored (Foucault, 1979). It is a tangible enactment and representation of these intersections.

In Western thought, the athletic male body has been a mark of power and moral superiority for those who bear it (Dutton, 1995; Synnott, 1993). Those who have these characteristics, along with others such as the "correct" race and class status, are assumed to be inherently "morally" superior. Which bodies are marked as superior is not static, but is contested. At the turn of the 20th century, the definition of morality was being debated within and between many social institutions, especially religious, medical, legislative, psychiatric, and social welfare agencies. The definition of morality was influenced by religious norms of good versus evil, prohibitions on nonprocreative sex (Katz, 1995b), and the Protestant work ethic that stressed hard work, individualism, and self-abnegation (Turner, 1984). This definition privileged the white, heterosexual middle class as "moral" against assumptions made about subordinated "others."

When urbanization and industrialization created changes in economic opportunities at the turn of the 20th century, many of these changes presented challenges to ideologies of gender and the position defined as hegemonic masculinity. The creation of white-collar occupations, an expanding middle class, and greater acceptance of women in the workforce facilitated a crisis in the definition of masculinity. Women's increasing presence in the public sphere, coupled with changes in men's work, fed fears of social feminization. The rise of competitive team sports in the United States is said to be a backlash, a means for white middle-class men to reaffirm symbolically their physical and moral superiority over women and socially subordinated men (Crosset, 1990; Kimmel, 1990; Messner, 1988). The sports that were popularized in the United States did not promote any type of masculinity and femininity but rather reflected specifically middle-class ideals of masculinity and femininity (Gorn & Goldstein, 1993). Individuals who participated in hegemonic sports were deemed heroes by virtue of their participation. Their bodies became signifiers of power and masculinity. With this power came the assumption of not only physical but also moral superiority.

In recent decades, most of the American public have increasingly experienced sport through the mass media (Sage, 1990; Wenner, 1989). This is not surprising, as sport and the mass media have enjoyed a mutually beneficial or "symbiotic" relationship over the last century (Jhally, 1989; McChesney, 1989). Mediated sports function largely to naturalize values and points of view that are generally consistent with cultural hegemony and come to appear as "common sense" (Jhally, 1989). Ideologies about gender, race, class, and sexuality are reproduced explicitly in media texts, in the assumptions that underlie the text, and in which sports and athletes are valued as culturally significant (Duncan & Hasbrook, 1988; Duncan, Messner, & Jensen, 1994; Kane, 1988, 1996; Messner, Duncan, & Wachs, 1996). For example, numerous works demonstrate how women and femininity are constructed as inferior through mediated sports and how men and masculinity are implicitly defined and constructed as superior (Duncan & Hasbrook, 1988; Kane, 1995; Kane & Snyder, 1989; Messner et al., 1996; Nelson, 1994; Theberge, 1987; Whitson, 1990). Furthermore, other works demonstrate how mediated sports reinforce stigmatizations of marginalized masculinities (Cole & Andrews, 1996; Cole & Denny, 1994; Dworkin & Wachs, 1998; Lule, 1995; Messner & Solomon, 1993; Pronger, 1990; Wachs & Dworkin, 1997). Although some works have examined HIV in sport (Cole & Denny, 1994; King, 1993; McKay, 1993), the cultural paradox that simultaneously represents male athletes as "moral" leaders and protects male privileges that are inconsistent with dominant norms of morality has not yet been problematized.

Given that sport is one of the most powerful socializing institutions for masculinity (Messner, 1992b) that privileges male heterosexual bodies, it provides an interesting forum for exploring norms of sexual behavior. Some scholars have argued that hegemonic male sexuality contributes to sexually aggressive locker room talk (Curry, 1991; Kane & Disch, 1993), violence against women (Crosset, Benedict, & McDonald, 1995; Kane & Disch, 1993; Messner & Sabo, 1994; Nelson, 1994), violence against other men (Messner, 1988; Young, 1993), and as contributing to difficulty in having lasting intimate relationships with women (Connell, 1990; Klein, 1993; Messner, 1992b). To be a man in our culture (and in sport in particular) is to have an assumed naturally aggressive sexual virility that brings with it access to multiple women's bodies. The case of athletes with HIV/AIDS presents a compelling arena in which to explore the discourse on masculinity and sexuality, and specifically "promiscuity" or "virility." Without the stigma that comes with HIV/AIDS, sexually active (heterosexual) men, by definition, are adhering to masculinity successfully. Given that HIV/AIDS is associated with the gay community (Connell, 1987; Patton, 1990; Sontag, 1989; Watney, 1989; Weeks, 1985) and carries a heavy "moral" stigma, we ask: How does the dominant print media frame male athletes and their concomitant normative sexual privilege when they acquire the highly socially stigmatized virus HIV? How will the public discourse—in our example, print media coverage—frame these announcements in the mass cultural discourse given its dual tendency to support hegemonic masculinity and stigmatize and blame infected (and often othered) bodies as immoral? How does mainstream media coverage reconcile hero status, dominant norms of masculinity, and morality in the body of the HIV-positive athlete? For which men?

Methodology

We used textual analysis to explore how cultural discourses that define gendered norms of sexuality shape and constrain men's and women's behaviors. Foucault (1979) observed that power operates both constitutively and repressively. Power operates to constitute dominant discourses, whereby some assumptions shape the acceptable public discourse and appear as common sense; this leaves many potentialities outside the realm of the fathomable. This constitution of power then creates a basis for power to operate repressively, whereby it seems "natural" to accept certain behaviors as "normal" and "moral" while policing "deviant" and "immoral" behaviors (Foucault, 1979). We explored dominant print media framings as one of power's material effects. Our interest was to deconstruct dominant assumptions about male and female sexual agency that survey and police "public" bodies and acts. We also explore the tensions and contradictions within these assumptions.

To explore these assumptions, we performed a textual analysis on all available articles from the *Los Angeles Times, New York Times,* and *Washington Post* that followed the HIV-positive announcements of professional basketball player Earvin "Magic" Johnson, Olympic diver Greg Louganis, and professional boxer Tommy Morrison. Articles were coded for content, tone, and implications and were cross-coded for validity. Out of the initial read of the articles emerged two areas for analysis. First, articles were analyzed as to how the status of the HIV-positive athlete was framed: Was he framed as a hero or as a "carrier"? The selective usage of the word hero in titles and/or bodies of articles demonstrates the morality/manhood paradox and reveals how the social location of individuals predetermines their access to hero status. Second, articles were coded for how men's and women's sexual agency is framed. This theme demonstrates how mainstream media coverage maintains this paradox by reinforcing cultural discourses that protect norms of hegemonic masculinity and male (hetero) sexual privilege while blaming and stigmatizing women and subordinated men.

Due to the enormous number of articles on Magic Johnson, many of which focused exclusively on his career, we limited our collection to all articles for 3 months following his announcement and 10% of the articles that appeared thereafter. Three mainstream newspapers were chosen from three major cities in the United States to represent the dominant or mainstream print media's treatment of gender norms, sexuality, and HIV/AIDS. Indeed, other newspapers, such as USA Today, may have large circulations, and the gay and alternative press might offer different framings of these events. However, the selected newspapers garner prestige and respect as mainstream media sources and, as such, are valuable sites in which to analyze dominant discourses on these subjects.

One striking feature of the HIV-positive announcements of Johnson, Louganis, and Morrison is the vast difference in the number of articles written. There are more than 100 articles about Magic Johnson, 12 articles about Greg Louganis, and 8 articles about Tommy Morrison. Perhaps the difference in sheer number of articles highlights not only Magic Johnson's celebrity status within the basketball community but also the fact that basketball is part of the triad of sports that reinforces hegemonic masculinity and is one of the most watched sports in our culture. By contrast, the fewer number of articles about Louganis and Morrison may reflect their lesser popularity as individuals or the status of the sports in which they participate. Furthermore, one cannot ignore the effect of the symbiotic relation between sports and the mass media (Jhally, 1989; Sage, 1990). Sport is promoted by the mass media as a means for targeting the hard-to-reach male middle-class market aged 18 to 45 years. Hence, sports that are considered middle-class and "masculine appropriate" (Kane, 1988) garner the bulk of media coverage (Jhally, 1989; Messner, 1988).

Boxing is a blood sport that has been widely contested as violent and immoral. Participation in such a sport has been largely linked to working-class men, who have been disproportionately represented in the sport since its inception (Gorn & Goldstein, 1993). Although boxing is widely accepted, popularized, and aired in mainstream sports media, it still retains stigma through its historical association with the working class. Thus, although Morrison participates in a sport with heavy doses of physical contact that aids the status of boxing in terms of hegemonic masculinity, its popularity suffers because it is not a team sport with signifiers linked to the dominant class. Although it is true that Morrison is hardly the equivalent of Johnson in terms of the success of his career, it is interesting to note that he received almost as much coverage as did Louganis despite his being a mediocre professional compared to Louganis, who dominated his sport for most of his career.

The relative lack of coverage of Louganis likely reflects that diving, which involves no direct physical confrontation, is not linked to the construction of hegemonic masculinity. In general, team sports are considered male-appropriate, whereas sports that emphasize grace are associated with femininity (Kane, 1988). Male team sports often involve overcoming opponents' defenses and asserting mastery and control of the field of play. The "female-appropriate" sports, like gymnastics and figure skating, involve one receiving an individual score that (in theory) is in no way dependent on the other participants' actions. Men who participate in sports that are not "masculine-appropriate" do not acquire the status of hegemonic masculinity; indeed, their participation may even mark them as less than masculine. Greg Louganis participates in an individual, graceful sport. His athletic body does not have the same status as an exemplar of hegemonic masculinity. Furthermore, as a gay man, he is linked to a number of negative body stigmatizations, especially the (assumed to be) diseased body. Thus, all of these factors contributed to keeping the mainstream media from more in-depth coverage of his announcement.

The "Hero" and the "Whore": Privileging and Protecting Hegemonic Masculinity

In mainstream Western culture, AIDS is associated with the gay community (Connell, 1987; Eisenstein, 1994; Sontag, 1989; Watney, 1989; Weeks, 1985) and other marginalized subpopulations and is therefore highly stigmatized. Despite the widespread invisibility and marginalization of gay men with AIDS, Magic Johnson, a self-identified heterosexual man, was not stigmatized when he publically announced he had contracted the HIV virus. He was framed by the mainstream American print media unequivocally as a hero and was lauded for courageously battling a socially stigmatized illness (Wachs & Dworkin, 1997). Although coverage of Johnson's announcement may destabilize popular assumptions around AIDS and sexual identity through its statements that "straights can get it too," racist ideologies of black male sexuality most likely linger in the public imagination. As is demonstrated by the print media coverage, ideologies reveal a way in which power relations operate to reproduce the stigmatization of subordinated men and women while protecting the privileges of dominant social categories.

More than 100 articles covered Magic Johnson's announcement. Although the primary framing and content of 27 was that Magic Johnson is a hero, numerous other articles also framed him as a hero through reference to his exemplary career and described his profound influence in professional basketball. Articles titled "Magic Johnson's Legacy" (Berkow, *New York Times,* 11/8/91) and "A Career of Impact, a Player of Heart" (Brown, *New York Times,* 11/8/91) ran the day after his announcement. Off the court, Johnson was framed as a hero to at-risk subpopulations, sports fans, activists, the medical community, and the public at large. One article featured Los Angeles Mayor Bradley's comparison of this news to the assassination of former President Kennedy (Thomas, *New York Times,* 11/9/91). Other articles stated that Magic Johnson "became a hero to a new set of fans—the community of activists and medical professionals" (Harris, *Los Angeles Times,* 11/8/91) and "I think he's obviously a hero to many Americans . . . so I think he would have a tremendous impact" (Cimons, *Los Angeles Times,* 11/11/91). Johnson's hero status was even openly conferred by President George Bush: "President Bush on Friday described Los Angeles Lakers basketball star Earvin (Magic) Johnson as 'a hero to me' and 'to everyone (who) loves sports'" (Gerstenzang & Cimons, *Los Angeles Times,* 11/9/91). This status conferral was also reflected in the titles of several articles in which the words hero and icon became synonymous with Johnson: "Los Angeles Stunned as Hero Begins Future With HIV" (Mathews, *Washington Post,* 11/9/91), "An Icon Falls and His Public Suffers the Pain" (Murphy & Griego, *Los Angeles Times,* 11/8/91). Furthermore, Johnson was framed as a hero for gracefully and honestly dealing with a socially stigmatized illness. For example, he was described as handling his announcement as a "gentleman" (Gerstenzang & Cimons, *Los Angeles Times,* 11/9/91), "with grace and candor," and as a "challenge to fans to put aside shock and dismay" (Kindred, *Los Angeles Times,* 11/8/91). Despite the long negative history of HIV/AIDS, when Magic was found to have contracted the disease, the press reported, "You don't have to avoid Magic Johnson. He is not contaminated. He is not a leper. He is still Magic Johnson" (Downey, *Los Angeles Times,* 11/8/91). These articles demonstrate the media's willingness to remove the stigma of HIV/AIDS when it was contracted by a self-identified heterosexual sports star.

Other articles framed Johnson as a hero for his role as an educator about HIV/AIDS to the heterosexual community and the role he would play as a national spokesman for AIDS. For example, the *Los Angeles Times* and the *Washington Post* published articles titled "Announcement Hailed as a Way to Teach Public" (Harris, *Los Angeles Times,* 11/8/91) and "Hero's Shocker Leaves Teens Grasping for Answers" (Shen, *Washington Post,* 11/9/91). Johnson was credited with bringing AIDS to the general public's attention and for putting AIDS on the national agenda, for example, "An Epidemic the Public Might Finally Confront: Johnson Could Help End Stigma of AIDS" (Gladwell, *Washington Post,* 11/10/91), "Legend's Latest Challenge: Sports Hero's Message May Resonate" (Gladwell & Muscatine, *Washington Post,* 11/8/91), and "They say he can help shatter myths about HIV, AIDS" (Harris, *Los Angeles Times,* 11/8/91).

However, given the fact that the social discourse that has surrounded AIDS has been one of individual blame, it is interesting to note that Magic Johnson was not vilified for the risk at which he put himself, nor the risk at which he put the numerous people with whom he was physically intimate. The way in which the blame for AIDS transmission was framed shows how the discourse on sexuality serves to exonerate heterosexual men, blame women, and marginalize gay men. Magic Johnson's "promiscuity" was not problematized as his responsibility or his "risk" but rather was blamed on aggressive female groupies. As McKay (1993) argued, the media coverage of Johnson privileged and protected virile male heterosexuality in sport, while making consistent references to "wanton" women who wait for the athletes. What is implied is that any "normal man" would have done the same thing (e.g., "boys will be boys"). Magic Johnson's "promiscuity" is not only blamed on women, but he is painted as a kind man who is quoted as "accommodating" as many women as possible. In one article, Magic Johnson was quoted as saying, "There were just some bachelors that almost every woman in Los Angeles wanted to be with: Eddie Murphy, Arsenio Hall and Magic Johnson. I confess that after I arrived in L.A. in 1979 I did my best to accommodate as many women as I could" (Editor, "Sorry but Magic Isn't a Hero," *New York Times,* 11/14/91). A second article agreed: "The groupies, the 'Annies.' They are the ancient entitlements of the locker room, the customary fringe benefits of muscles" (Callahan, *Washington Post,* 11/10/91). It is assumed that sports stars, as icons of masculinity, have a right to abundant sexual access to women's bodies.

Four years later, when white, working-class, heterosexual, professional boxer Tommy Morrison announced his HIV-positive status, he was not similarly valorized. Rather than elevating Morrison to hero status for over-coming the stigma of the illness, mainstream print media coverage treated him as a tragic figure, who, through his own "ignorance" about HIV trans-mission, destroyed a promising career. However, heterosexual masculine privilege was protected, through a reassignment of blame to women's sex-ual aggressiveness. As in the coverage of Johnson, women were framed as pursuers in the Morrison coverage, and Morrison is framed as a man who is unable to resist temptation. For example, one article pointed to the women who "wait outside the door fighting over who was going to get Tommy that night" (Romano, *Washington Post,* 2/16/96) as the problem, not Morrison's pursuit of these women or his failure to practice safe sex. Although Morrison was blamed on an individual level for making "irratio-nal, immature decisions," in his fast-lane lifestyle, he clearly was not framed as the pursuer, threat, or sexual agent, but rather as the "world's biggest bimbo magnet." Although the articles held Morrison accountable for his ignorance of HIV/AIDS, he was not held responsible for the risk at which he may have put others. One article highlighted how Morrison's in-ner circle summed up the situation: "It wasn't uncommon for me to go to his hotel room and find three or four women outside the door fighting over who was going to get Tommy that night. We had groupies all the way up to career women" (Romano, *Washington Post,* 2/16/96). As in their treat-ment of Johnson, the media confirmed Morrison's heterosexuality and af-firmed his sexual desirability to women through his acquiescence to temp-tation—what any "normal" man also would have done.

"Normal" under Western ideals of masculinity can include sexual con-quest with multiple desirable women. Because sports define and repro-duce ideologies of masculinity, it is hardly surprising that athletes are ex-pected to demonstrate their masculinity off as well as on the field. Even when media framings call men into question for their actions, agency and responsibility are displaced onto the bodies of women, while masculine privilege is protected. As noted, women are framed as aggressive groupies who are responsible for tempting men, whereas men are framed as doing what "any normal" man would have done. Reminiscent of 19th century ideologies of gender and sexuality, these ideologies featured cultural nar-ratives that claimed that men's sexual appetites were naturally more powerful and aggressive than women's. Given this claim, it is women who were (and are still) held responsible for controlling men's sexuality (Gilder, 1973). Repopularized during the Reagan and Bush era by leading conservative thinkers such as George Gilder (1986), these ideologies are maintained, reinforced, and celebrated under the rubric of "family values." This conceptual framework refers to women as the "moral guardians of civilization" through the expectation that they will not elicit, provoke, or satisfy male desire outside of heterosexual monogamous marriage. Hence, when mainstream media coverage presents Magic Johnson and other athletes as having "accommodated" as many "bimbos" as they could, the implication is that these men were merely yielding to aggressive females who are depicted as "out of control." Thus, through the framing of female groupies as responsible for tempting male sports stars into "promiscuity," the norm of aggressive male (hetero)sexual conquest common under masculinity remains unproblematized. Furthermore, the idea that women are responsible for control of men's morality means that male athletes are still presumed to be inherently moral. As we show, when individual athletes' morality is called into question, media frames do not link the "moral" transgressions to the norms of hegemonic masculinity but to each man's subordinate status.

Blaming Marginalized Masculinities

The mainstream print media coverage of Greg Louganis reveals a compelling contrast to the coverage of Johnson and Morrison. Although "shock" and "surprise" were abundantly referenced with regard to Johnson's and Morrison's announcements, there were no references to shock or surprise in the print media when Greg Louganis made his HIV-positive announcement. Unlike the articles on Morrison and Johnson, which featured phrases like "he got it from heterosexual sex," there were no inquiries as to how Louganis could have contracted the virus. The assumed linkage between homosexuality and AIDS was so profound that none of the 11 articles on Louganis even posed the question as to how he contracted HIV/AIDS. We argue that the profound questioning as to how self-identified heterosexual men contracted the virus, coupled with the lack of inquiry into how Louganis could have contracted the disease, works to reinforce the idea that HIV/AIDS is a "natural" and expected part of the gay life course (Dworkin & Wachs, 1998; Wachs & Dworkin, 1997;

Watney, 1989; Weeks, 1985). This works to perpetuate the historic assumption that gay bodies are inherently diseased and immoral. The athletes also were framed differently vis-à-vis the risk of transmission they present to others. Although the "blame" or responsibility for the pollution of the bodies of Magic Johnson and Tommy Morrison was placed on the aggressive women who pursued successful male sports stars, there is no corollary absolution of blame or fault for Greg Louganis. There was no discussion surrounding male groupies who may have pursued Louganis. Furthermore, Magic Johnson and Tommy Morrison's threat to women was nearly always discussed in relation to their wife and fiancée, respectively; they generally were not presented as a threat to their numerous other sex partners. In contrast, the print media did not even begin to ponder the men Greg Louganis may have infected in sex, nor did they ever mention his long-term partner. Several stories, however, expressed concern for the presumably heterosexual divers and doctor who came into contact with Louganis and his blood during the 1988 Olympics. All articles that covered Louganis's announcement discussed this incident and the potential risk of transmission. In this way, gay men and "promiscuous" women are viewed as the virulent agents or problematic vehicle for transmission (Treichler, 1988) while hegemonic masculinity, and the norm of virile male (hetero)sexuality is protected and reaffirmed.

Although data show how heterosexual masculinity is protected at the expense of women and gay men, print media coverage simultaneously subtly reinvigorates the link between blame and working-class and minority status. Johnson was presented as being an African American man with "special" importance as an educator and role model for minority communities. Although he was lauded more generally for raising public awareness on heterosexual AIDS and its prevention, numerous articles focused specifically on this special importance. For example, one article highlighted that the National Minority AIDS Council wanted Johnson to lobby for much-needed increases in financing for health care and prevention (Gross, *New York Times,* 11/13/91), whereas Johnson himself "has indicated that his personal efforts will focus on AIDS education in the black community" (Harris, *Los Angeles Times,* 11/13/91). Articles claimed, "He speaks best for African Americans" (Gross, *New York Times,* 11/13/91) and focused explicitly on how "the message" would be loudest for those "who need to hear it most," as quoted in an article titled "Magic's Loud Message for Young Black Men" (Specter, *New York Times,* 11/8/91, p. B12). Although funding and education are of paramount importance in often-overlooked minority communities whose AIDS rates are disproportionately high, the suggestion that African Americans "need to hear

it most" can all too easily become a historical "reminder" that links minorities to stereotypes of excess and a lack of control (Adam, 1978;
Collins, 1990). Similarly, articles cited Morrison's poor rural upbringing
and broken home and concurrently noted his "irresponsible, irrational,
immature descisions," how he "lacked the discipline to say no" (Romano,
Washington Post, 2/16/96), and his "ignorance" (Vecsey, *New York Times,*
2/16/96).

We find it ironic that in the furor over cases involving sexual assaults
and athletes, particularly athletes in hegemonic sports, the norm of male
sexual conquest in sport goes largely unquestioned (Crossett et al., 1995;
Curry, 1991; Nelson, 1994). However, when an athlete acquires a highly
stigmatized, potentially deadly virus such as HIV/AIDS, which historically is associated with the gay community, "mistakes" and "ignorance"
regarding male (hetero)sexuality are abundantly recognized by the media.
Print media coverage of both Morrison and Johnson simultaneously displaced blame onto the bodies of women and framed the two men as having
made bad "choices" or "mistakes." For instance, articles on Morrison
noted his "ignorance" around proper HIV and AIDS transmission information, quoted him as saying that he thought he had a "better chance of
winning the lottery than contracting this disease," and featured how he
"lacked the discipline to say no" (Romano, *Washington Post,* 2/16/96). An
article on Johnson featured a young man who was cited in a *Los Angeles
Times* article as saying, "It is good [Magic Johnson] is not ashamed he
made a mistake" (Almond & Ford, 11/18/91, *Los Angeles Times*). What,
however, is the mistake, precisely—is it "promiscuity"? Or is it "getting
caught" conforming to the norm of male sexual conquest only when men
have acquired HIV? Instead of highlighting how hegemonic masculinity
in sport fuels the discourse on male sexual conquest as part of its cultural
norm, popular discourse embraces the idea that it is the individual athlete's bad decision making or ignorance that is to blame.

We also argue that the transgression does not just stand on its own as a
bad "individual" decision, but becomes available as a negative signifier of
subordinate social categories, that is, in the same way that male privilege
is protected while women are blamed, we argue that white middle-class
heterosexuality is protected, whereas working-class, black, and gay male
sexualities are blamed. The social location of white middle-class heterosexuals is left out of the picture, and working-class, black, and gay male
sporting bodies are featured in the spotlight as "guilty." Because the dominant position remains unscrutinized by the mainstream media press, it
becomes the "normal" or moral category against which the "other" categories are negatively compared. Indeed, this is the case because working-

class and minority men are the ones held up in the sports limelight due to a limited structure of opportunity that disproportionately funnels subordinated men into a sports career (Edwards, 1973; Messner, 1992b). By featuring Morrison's working-class background and "ignorance," along with Johnson's "mistakes" and his role in speaking to African Americans who "need to hear it most," the print media reinforces "others'" bad individual decision making. Those in the dominant race, class, and sexuality position remain the invisible good against which the "bad" sexually excessive and/or out of control "other" is juxtaposed.

Myths in Sport: Productive Bodies, Moral Men?

We have noted the historical significance of how the muscled male body has been associated with moral superiority (Dutton, 1995). Male athletes who display this body and are successful at culturally valued sports receive widespread public attention and are elevated to the status of hero. As "heroes" with cultural fame and popularity, these athletes enjoy numerous social and economic privileges, one of which is the assumption of morality. Yet, simultaneously, one of the social privileges that (heterosexual) men in hegemonic sports are said to enjoy is access to the bodies of numerous women. We are left with a paradox between "moral" standards of heterosexual monogamy and how to attain high status under dominant norms of masculinity. For "fallen heroes" in sport, print media coverage rarely if ever acknowledges norms in sport or in U.S. culture at large that equate masculinity with sexual prowess. Sexual access to women is a cultural privilege associated with being a man, yet, in turn, the powerful then use this privilege to stigmatize subordinated masculinities and women while dominant men remain invisible to the watchful media eye.

Our analysis of print media coverage of the HIV announcements of Magic Johnson, Tommy Morrison, and Greg Louganis is consistent with those who argue that our culture gradually will add to the list of "others" who have been tagged as "deserving AIDS," to distinguish them from "innocent" victims (Eisenstein, 1994). The lack of inquiry into how Louganis acquired HIV, coupled with concern for the threat of transmission only to the heterosexual public, reinforces a tendency to blame gay sexuality for HIV transmission. It is also notable that lesbians are often left out of the discourse on HIV/AIDS, and sexuality in general, because popular culture tends to render lesbians and the kinds of sex they have invisible (Butler, 1993; Kane & Lenskyj, 1998). For Morrison and Johnson, media frames that emphasize "better decision making" for individual "promiscuous" black and working-class bodies reinvigorate negative stigmatizations as to which bodies are inherently "bad" or immoral. Heterosexual male privilege is protected, and "immorality" is linked to "other" categories. Johnson and Morrison are simultaneously featured for behaving "as any normal" man would, while also highlighting their "ignorant" individual decisions and "mistakes" amid discussions of their class and race, respectively. Thus, it is masculinity that is privileged as "normal," whereas it is the social categories of otherness upon which the responsibility for "deviance" is subtly foisted. Thus, dominant coverage works to displace blame onto the bodies of gay, working-class, and black male bodies, and what becomes implied is that through the proper education and assimilation (to heterosexual middle-class values), "the problem" will be solved. This is consistent with Cole and Denny's (1994) argument that such rhetoric "obscures the responsibility of multinational capitalism and the Reagan-Bush administration for the erosion of social welfare programs and the neglect of AIDS" (p. 123). Furthermore, we argue that the articles reinvigorate a white, heterosexual, middle-class moral gaze on gay, black, and working-class manhood.

Afterward: "God Saved Me": Family Values, Masculinity, and Sexual Conquest

Rather than revealing the paradox between the dominant norms of morality and masculinity, the position of sports stars with AIDS demonstrates how the social location of individuals defines their moral status, not their behavior. Although gay male bodies with HIV are featured often in the media as decaying, diseased, and unproductive (Crimp, 1990), recently, Magic Johnson's body was featured as healing, healthy, and productive. Johnson even announced that the virus in his blood has dropped to "undetectable levels," proof that "God" has "saved him" (Editor, *New York Times*, 4/5/97). Whereas earlier articles featured Johnson as a spokesman for safe sex, later articles featured his pro-God, promonogamy, profamily rhetoric. Whereas gay men are not framed as having the option of "being saved" from HIV, Johnson, a self-identified newly monogamous heterosexual, is lauded for battling the virus to a level at which it is undetectable. Instead of seeing Johnson as having access to the finest medical care in the world due to his class status, his body is held up as morally deserving of beating the stigmatized illness. Once Johnson renounces his "fast-lane lifestyle" in favor of marriage, family, and monogamy, he is saved. The power of this rhetoric also underlies the critiques of Morrison as irresponsible and assumes that a fast-lane lifestyle is the culprit. The discourse on risk assumes that particular lifestyles and family statuses are safe, and others are dangerous. By conflating lifestyle with risk, erroneous information about HIV transmission is perpetuated (Dworkin & Wachs, 1998). Furthermore, these assumptions reproduce ideologies that privilege particular family forms and relationships and stigmatize others. By contrast, Louganis and other gay men, even if monogamous or family-oriented, are rarely if ever featured for courageously battling HIV or for educating the public; rather, media accounts seem to imply that they "deserve" their fate (Wachs & Dworkin, 1997). For instance, whereas Johnson has become an acclaimed national spokesman and educator for people with HIV/AIDS, a U.S. senator attempted to ban Greg Louganis from speaking on a college campus, citing his talk as "immoral" (Associated Press, *Los Angeles Times,* 1/26/97). Because mainstream print media have identified (assumed to be) immoral acts that require blame, and they have reassigned this blame to "others," coverage of HIV/AIDS announcements reveals the paradox between manhood in hegemonic sports and dominant notions of morality. This is accomplished without ever problematizing hegemonic masculinity in sport or long-held mythic ideals associated with gender, family, and sexuality.

Appendix

Print Media Coverage of HIV Announcements
by Prominent Athletes

Magic Johnson

11/8/91 Aldridge, David. Lakers Star Put Imprint on Finals, Records, Money. *The Washington Post,* p. C1.

11/8/91 Araton, Harvey. Riley Leads the Prayers. *The New York Times,* p. B11.

11/8/91 Berkow, Ira. Magic Johnson's Legacy. *The New York Times,* p. B11.

11/8/91 Bonk, Thomas. Even Hearing News Was Not Believing It. *The Los Angeles Times,* p. C1.

11/8/91 Brown, Clifton. A Career of Impact, A Player With Heart. *The New York Times,* p. B11.

11/8/91 Cannon, Lou. Basketball Star Magic Johnson Retires With AIDS Virus. *The Washington Post,* p. A1.

11/8/91 Castaneda, Ruben, & Rene Sanchez. Johnson's AIDS Virus Revelation Moves Teenagers, Fans. *The Washington Post,* p. D1.

11/8/91 Downey, Mike. Earvin Leaves NBA, But His Smile Remains. *The Los Angeles Times,* p. C1.

11/8/91 Gladwell, Malcolm, & Alison Muscatine. Legend's Latest Challenge. *The Washington Post,* p. A1.

11/8/91 Harris, Scott. Announcement Hailed as a Way to Teach Public. *The Los Angeles Times,* p. A32.

11/8/91 Heisler, Mark. Magic Johnson's Career Ended by HIV-Positive Test. *The Los Angeles Times,* p. A1.

11/8/91 Kindred, Dave. Magic's Gift for Inspiring Us Tests Reality. *The Los Angeles Times,* p. B7.

11/8/91 Murphy, Dean E., & Tina Griego. An Icon Falls and His Public Suffers the Pain. *The Los Angeles Times,* p. A1.

11/8/91 Specter, Michael. Magic's Loud Message for Young Black Men. *The New York Times,* p. B12.

11/8/91 Springer, Steve. Through the Years, He Stayed the Same. *The Los Angeles Times,* p. C1.

11/8/91 Stevenson, Richard W. Basketball Star Retires on Advice of His Doctors. *The New York Times,* p. A1.

11/8/91 Thomas, Robert McG., Jr. News Reverberates Through Basketball and Well Beyond It. *The New York Times,* p. B13.

11/9/91 Bonk, Thomas, & Janny Scott. "Don't Feel Sorry for Me," Magic Says. *The Los Angeles Times,* p. A1.

11/9/91 Cannon, Lou, & Anthony Cotton. Johnson's HIV Caused by Sex: "Heterosexual Transmission" Cited; Wife Is Pregnant. *The Washington Post,* p. A1.

11/9/91 Editor. A Magical Cure for Lethargy. *The Los Angeles Times,* p. B5.

11/9/91 Lacey, Marc, & Hugo Martin. Student's Cry a Bit, Learn Life Lessons. *The Los Angeles Times,* p. A26.

11/9/91 Gerstenzang, James, & Marlene Cimons. Bush Calls Johnson a Hero, Defends Administration's Policy on AIDS. *The Los Angeles Times,* p. A26.

11/9/91 Horovitz, Bruce. Sponsors May Use Magic in Ads to Encourage Safe Sex. *The Los Angeles Times,* p. D1.

11/9/91 Mathews, Jay. Los Angeles Stunned As Hero Begins Future With HIV. *The Washington Post,* p. A12.

11/9/91 McMillen, Tom. "Magic, Now and Forever. *The New York Times,* p. 23.

11/9/91 Shen, Fern. Hero's Shocker Leaves Teens Grasping for Answers. *The Washington Post,* p. A1.

11/9/91 Specter, Michael. When AIDS Taps Hero, His "Children" Feel Pain. *The New York Times,* p. A1.

11/9/91 Stevenson, Richard W. Johnson's Frankness Continues. *The New York Times,* p. 33.

11/9/91 Thomas, Robert McG., Jr. A Day Later, It Remains a Shock Felt Around the World. *The New York Times,* p. A33.

11/10/91 Aldridge, David. For Moments Like These. *The Washington Post,* p. D4.

11/10/91 Callahan, Tom. What It Boils Down to Is Playing With Fire. *The Washington Post,* p. D2.

11/10/91 Gladwell, Malcolm. An Epidemic the Public Might Finally Confront. *The Washington Post,* p. A1.

11/10/91 Jones, Robert A. A Shock That Shifted the World. *The Los Angeles Times,* p. A3.

11/10/91 Lipsyte, Robert. A Jarring Reveille for Sports. *The New York Times,* p. S1.

11/10/91 McNeil, Donald. On the Court or Off, Still Magic. *The New York Times,* p. E9.

11/10/91 Muscatine, Alison. Magic's Revelations Transcends Sports. *The Washington Post,* p. D1.

11/11/91 Chase, Marilyn. Johnson Disclosure Underscores Facts of AIDS in Heterosexual Population. *The Wall Street Journal,* p. B1.

11/11/91 Cimons, Marlene. White House May Name Johnson to AIDS Panel. *The Los Angeles Times,* p. A1.

11/11/91 Horovitz, Bruce. Advertisers Try to Handle This Magic Moment Carefully. *The Los Angeles Times,* p. D1.

11/13/91 Gross, Jane. For Anyone but Johnson, a Daunting Pile of Requests for Help. *The NewYork Times,* p. A14.

11/13/91 Harris, Scott. Johnson Brings New Stature to AIDS Funding. *The Los Angeles Times,* p. A1.

11/14/91 Editor. Converse's AIDS Efforts Features Magic Johnson. *The New York Times,* p. D10.

11/14/91 Editor. Sorry but Magic Isn't a Hero. *The New York Times,* p. B19.

11/18/91 Almond, Elliot, & Andrea Ford. Wild Ovation Greets Magic at Lakers Game. *The Los Angeles Times,* p. A1.

11/31/91 Editor. Keep Magic in the Mainstream. *The New York Times,* p. B7.

1/1/92 Araton, Harvey. Advertisers Shying From Magic's Touch. *The New York Times,* p. 44.

1/14/92 French, Mary Ann. Magic, Rewriting the Rules of Romance. *The Washington Post,* p. B1.

4/5/97 Editor. Johnson's HIV Level Drops (Aids Virus in Earvin "Magic" Johnson Is Significantly Reduced). *The New York Times,* p. 36.

Greg Louganis

2/23/95 Longman, Jere. Doctor at Games Supports Louganis. *The New York Times,* p. B15.

2/23/95 Sandomir, Richard. Louganis, Olympic Champion, Says He Has AIDS. *The New York Times,* p. B11.

2/23/95 Weyler, John. Olympic Diver Louganis Reveals That He Has AIDS. *The Los Angeles Times,* p. A1.

2/24/95 Boxall, Bettina, & Frank Williams. Louganis Disclosure Greeted With Sadness. *The Los Angeles Times,* p. B1.

2/24/95 Editor. Louganis: Breaks His Silence, Another World-Famous Athlete Disclosed He Has AIDS. *The Los Angeles Times,* p. B6.

2/24/95 Longman, Jere. Olympians Won't Have to Take H.I.V. Test. *The New York Times,* p. B7.

2/24/95 Vecsey, George. Tolerance, Not Blame, For Louganis. *The New York Times,* p. B7.

2/26/95 Longman, Jere. Olympian Blood: Debate About HIV Tests Sparked by Diver With AIDS. *The New York Times,* p. 2.

2/28/95 Quintanilla, Michael. The Truth Shall Set You Free. *The Los Angeles Times,* p. E11.

3/5/95 Alfano, Peter. The Louganis Disclosure: AIDS in the Age of Hype. *The New York Times Magazine,* p. E1.

5/5/95 Ammon, Richard. Gay Athletes. *The Los Angeles Times,* p. M5.

1/26/97 Associated Press. Senator Seeks to Ban Louganis. *The Los Angeles Times.*

Tommy Morrison

2/12/96 Eskenazi, Gerald. Morrison Suspension: An HIV Concern. *The New York Times,* p. B6.

2/13/96 Eskenazi, Gerald. Morrison Confirms Positive HIV Test. *The New York Times,* p. B13.

2/13/96 Springer, Steve. Magic Johnson Plans to Call Boxer. *The Los Angeles Times,* p. A9.

2/13/96 Springer, Steve, & Earl Gustkey. Boxer's HIV Test Heats Up Debate Over Risk to Others. *The Los Angeles Times,* p. A1.

2/14/96 HIV Test for Morrison Ref. *The New York Times,* p. B11.

2/16/96 Eskenazi, Gerald. Remorseful Morrison Has Words of Caution. *The New York Times,* p. B7.

2/16/96 Romano, Lois. Heavyweight Deals With Serious Blow. *The Washington Post,* p. A1.

2/16/96 Vecsey, George. Morrison Didn't Pay Enough Attention. *The New York Times,* p. B20.

9/20/96 Kawakami, Tim. HIV-Positive Morrison Says He'll Fight Again. *The Los Angeles Times,* p. C9.

5

Dueling Machos

Masculinity and Sport in Mexican Baseball

ALAN M. KLEIN

Through a professional Mexican baseball team, this chapter critiques the concept of machismo as it has been used to describe Latino masculinity. The way that Latino masculinity has been presented, both among scholars and the public, is so problematic that a brief discussion of its history must precede any more specific examination. Following this, I use data from my own work on Mexican baseball to highlight particular aspects of Latino masculinity (Klein 1995b, 1997). The dearth of case studies about Latino masculinity has done little to deter the overgeneralization that has characterized research on Latino men. Even within the more geographically limited context of Mexican studies, students of the topic of masculinity often have ventured into the area with too little data, so my brief foray into this area is offered as suggestive rather than definitive. Only when studies begin to accumulate to an appreciable depth will we be able to conclude anything that approaches certainty.

The data for this study were ethnographically and archivally collected between 1992 and 1994 when I studied the Tecolotes de los Dos Laredos (The Owls of the Two Laredos), a franchise in the storied Mexican League. I observed the Tecos for the 1993 and 1994 seasons, making certain to be present at every phase of their season (beginning in spring training through the final game). I traveled, ate, and socialized with them. During that time, I conducted dozens of formal and informal interviews with the players and team officials, in addition to my regular observations. I also sought to conduct life histories of the players to amplify and provide a context for the observations I gathered. When I was not doing work directly on the team, I was conducting archival research on the history of the team and baseball on the border. Although the core of my research had to do with how nationalism is constructed on the border through this unusual binational franchise, the subject of the traditional role of machismo seemed to enter my analysis regularly.

The Concept of Machismo

Why is it that when it really describes categories of male behavior and attitudes in a wide range of societies, the term "macho" has become synonymous with Latino men? That an entire segment of the world's population should be characterized by a single trait may have been acceptable in the 1940s when anthropologists characterized whole nations on the basis of toilet training (Japan) or swaddling (U.S.S.R), but it cannot be now. We pretty much expect explanations to be multivariate, yet there must be something appealing about the simplicity of the concept of machismo that enables it to continue to be in such wide use.

Machismo has been used by scholars and authors to describe male assertiveness and control over everything from nature to society. In its most succinct form, machismo is defined as a template for male behavior that reifies aggression and domination as uniquely male attributes and reprojects them to every area of culture. The behavioral traits most commonly associated with machismo include hypermasculine bravado and posturing, willingness to confront physically any perceived slight, domination of women and other men through act and language, drinking to excess, sexual conquest, and squiring children. It is more than a collection of traits, however. In his study of a working-class neighborhood in Managua, Nicaragua, Roger Lancaster (1992) reminded us that "machismo is resilient because it constitutes not simply a form of 'consciousness,' not 'ideology' in the classical understanding of the concept, but a field of productive relations" (p. 19). As such, machismo is not particularly Latino and can just as easily describe men in New Guinea (Strathern, 1971), those among the Lakota (Hassrick, 1962), or those in the United States (Gilmore, 1990).

Although studies on Latino machismo from a variety of countries have been carried out (e.g., Brandes, 1980; Lancaster, 1992; Parker, 1991), the vast majority of them have been carried out in Mexico (e.g., Lewis, 1961; Mendoza, 1962; Paredes, 1967; Paz, 1961; Ramos, 1962). There is an implicit acceptance of machismo as synonymous with Mexican masculinity, and the person most responsible for this fusion, although by no means the originator, is Mexican essayist and poet Octavio Paz. *The Labyrinth of Solitude* was originally published in Paz's native Spanish in 1950. A decade later (1961), it was translated into English, and its impact was almost immediate. The literary elegance and provocative nature of its thesis assured it a wide audience despite mounting critiques, one that continues to the present.[1] At the heart of this study of Mexican culture was a definition of masculinity that wed psychoanalytic elements with history. The original conquest of the Aztec forebears by conquistadors was seen, by Paz, as so traumatic as to imprint itself on all subsequent generations. Overall Spanish brutality toward Aztecs was converted into the sexual act of raping Aztec women, and with it came the implications that the Aztec men were unable to prevent it. For Paz (1961), this historic act is summed up in the vulgar use of the Spanish verb *"chingar"*—to fuck up, or to fuck:

> There are two possibilities in life for the Mexican male. He either inflicts actions implied by *chingar* or he suffers them himself. . . . The person who suffers this action is passive, inert, and open, in contrast to the active, aggressive and closed person who inflicts it. The *chingon* is the macho, the male; he rips open the *chingada,* the female, who is pure passivity. (p. 77)

Almost 30 years earlier, in a much less known work, Samuel Ramos (1962) already had viewed the violent actions of the Spanish, the rape of Indian women, and the mestizo culture that resulted as a conversion reaction. For him, Mexican masculinity was predicated on Alfred Adler's sense of "protest masculinity," in which Mexican men who feel inferior conceal those feelings behind a substantial display of power and virility. Ramos came to view the Mexican urban working-class male (the *pelado*) as the embodiment of this masculinity. With no economic or political clout, the *pelado* was content to present himself as someone with *muchos huevos* (i.e., a lot of balls), aggressive, suspicious, insecure, and prone to acting out (Ramos, 1962, pp. 61-62).

Ramos and Paz were remarkably successful in promoting the concept of Mexican machismo. Still, their theses were so provocative that other Mexican scholars quickly reacted to these views. Vincente Mendoza (1962) studied ballads and folk songs and concluded that the data revealed bipolar conceptions of machismo in Mexican culture. There is an "authentic machismo" in which courage, generosity, and stoicism defines masculinity; and there also exists a "false machismo" consisting of cowardice masquerading as bravado and posturing. These conceptions of Mexican masculinity allow for the existence of hypermasculine macho of the sort Paz describes to exist alongside a more positive construction of masculinity. Americo Paredes (1967), examining Mexican folklore, deepened this view by showing that the word "macho" is of quite recent 20th century origins, but it is almost entirely negatively viewed within Mexican culture. Of equal import was the existence of a masculine depiction in opposition to machismo. *Hombres de verdad* (real men) were seen as honest, valiant, and defending the country and family.

Sociologists Maxine Baca Zinn (1975, 1982), Alfredo Mirandé (1982, 1988), and, more recently, Pierrette Hondagneu-Sotelo (1992), among others, have carried out research on Mexican American men that has furthered the critique of a one-dimensional view of Latino masculinity. These scholars variously have shown that Latino men come to play more active roles in the family (e.g., child rearing, shopping), in direct relation to changes in the economy and other structural factors. There is a pronounced sense of egalitarianism that also begins to alter traditional notions of machismo. Cultural notions of machismo may exist alongside these structural arrangements, but they do not determine the content of the relations (Baca Zinn, 1975).

Most recently, we have been fortunate to have two book-length examinations of Latino masculinity. The work of Matthew Gutmann (1996) and Alfredo Mirandé (1997) comprises two substantial critiques of the old school of machismo. Gutmann's ethnography of a working-class neighborhood in Mexico City beams right in on the issue of manhood. *"Ni macho, ni mandilón"* (neither macho, nor tied to apron strings) succinctly captures the thesis of this study. Gutmann examined a wide range of traditional activities associated exclusively with men or women (e.g., sexuality, child care, abuse of women, housework) and showed them to be carried out by the other sex. The sharing of tasks in the Mexican division of labor is predicated on structural shifts within the economy of the household and neighborhood that have occurred over the past two decades, in particular, women moving into the workforce and becoming political leaders in the struggle for recognition of the neighborhood. In response to these changes came those of the men who had to accommodate shifts of gender relations. Yet, traditions of male macho continue to exist in thought and deed. Clearly, we must expand our thinking to include varying degrees of contradictory ideology and behavior as existing within the individuals we study.

Similarly, in Mirandé's study of Latino masculinity, we see a multilevel critique of the idea that Latino masculinity is brutish. Using autobiography and history and providing a culturally sensitized version of Bem's (1974, 1975) sex role inventory, Mirandé (1997) echoed Mendoza's argument for distinguishing between true macho (or *hombria*) and false macho. In using this revised sex role inventory, Mirandé showed that Latino men blur the bipolar characterization of gender that Bem constructed. Hence, Latino men can be caring and sensitive (Bem's scale lists these as traditional feminine qualities) and at the same time be strong and protectively male (traditional masculine qualities). However much we have seen these gender constructions offered in a North American context, these two studies provide valuable insights into Latino masculinity. The objections to viewing all Latino men by hypermasculine characteristics are valid once class, race, and ethnic dimensions are factored in, but cultural comparisons to North American men are also implicit in these studies.

Mirandé and Gutmann differ from each other in certain ways, as well. Gutmann's critique of "macho" seeks to do away with the concept altogether by showing how vague it becomes when looking at real behavior and explanations of behavior in the neighborhood he studied. Mirandé's critique, on the other hand, is not willing to part with the term. Instead, he follows Mendoza and Paredes in chronicling a two-tiered view of Latino masculinity.

Studying Masculinity in and Through Sport

In the presentation of my findings, I use the Gutmann and Mirandé studies as a guideline for looking at some of the material collected during my ethnographic fieldwork on the U.S.-Mexico border. The dichotomizing of masculinity between the hypermasculine machismo and softer masculinity is, despite the aforementioned critique of machismo, continued in my analysis of men in Mexican baseball. At bottom, hypermasculine male role modeling continues alongside softer forms. More important, I would like to view sport as a lens for studying the process of looking at cross-cultural masculinity. In this instance, if sports were simply a mirror for gender construction, there would be little purpose in writing this chapter. We have no shortage of studies of sport as a socializing agency or reflection of social norms (e.g., Coakley, 1993, 1994; Foley, 1991). Presenting one more example would not push us forward much. Rather, we ought to be looking at the subtle ways in which sport differs from other institutions, ways that exaggerate or obscure social realities.

In some ways, sport is different from other institutions, making it better suited to examine social process. Although institutions such as family, politics, or religion are, with occasional exceptions, conducted in restricted venues (i.e. within the home, the capital, and the church), sport is totally public. It is designed to be performed for an unlimited audience, and with the aid of the media the sport performance is no longer simply confined to the actual contest. Increased attention is paid to the "up close and personal" dimensions of the athletes and the spectacle. The athlete is now a subject that transcends the sporting event. Both on and off the field, athletes are watched, and as their behavior and lives become more and more accessed, they are less and less likely to censure themselves. Even formerly private areas of sport (e.g., the sideline and locker rooms) are now part of our viewing scrutiny. The public and private persona are confused just as is the difference between hero and celebrity (Lasch, 1979). As a result, sport can give us a view of ourselves that is possibly more candid than any other institution. On the other hand, sport, unlike other areas of the entertainment industry, is a phenomenon whose performance and outcome is not predetermined. Other components of popular culture, such as music, dance, film, or television, are much more choreographed, with more rigid boundaries. Compared to most other social institutions, sport is both more public and more authentic. Sport may be a highly enhanced form of social realism.

The following study also draws a bit from an emerging study of the sociology and culture of emotions. Hochschild's (1979, 1983) use of emotion management through "social constructionism" (i.e., through a social milieu) is used in the study. Similarly, Rosaldo (1993), in his *Culture and Truth,* outlined a cultural approach to emotions within both the investigator and the people he or she studies. These works seek to take the fogginess out of emotions and ground them to the degree that social analysts may use them. But there is something unique to sport that makes it ideally suited to the social study of emotions, because in sport private emotions can be more easily expressed in public. In the heat of competition, defenses are down and feelings that are normally repressed rise more easily to the surface. The result is a potentially significant social display of emotions.

The Tecos

Founded in 1939, the Mexican League is an official AAA minor league, the only foreign baseball league to hold official status in the National

Association of Professional Baseball Leagues. The Tecolotes, or Owls (known more by the abbreviated "Tecos"), were one of the league's charter franchises. Originally named *La Junta Federales de Mejoras Materiales* after the enterprise headed by a group of Army generals, they came to be known as the Owls (Tecolotes) for instituting the first night games in the Mexican League in 1943. The team was wholly affiliated with the Mexican border city of Nuevo Laredo, yet the game historically reveals a binational character. The players, fans, and contests all reflected the easy access that always has characterized the cities of Laredo, Texas, and Nuevo Laredo, Tamaulipas. No matter which side of the Rio Grande fielded teams, the players and fans were just as likely to come from the other side. When, during the 1920s and 1930s, teams from elsewhere in the United States or Mexico played on the border, the twin cities fielded a single team comprised of the best athletes to represent the region. This binationalism was finally formalized in 1985 when the Tecos finally became known as the Owls of the Two Laredos, becoming in the bargain the only binational sports franchise in the world. The Tecos, then, came to have two home fields in two countries, played two national anthems before each game, had the owner living in Nuevo Laredo and the general manager and vice president living in Laredo, had a constituency in both countries, and had a team made up of Anglos and Mexicans.

The Mexican League consists of 16 teams divided evenly into northern and southern zones. They play a 132-game schedule most years, sometimes a bit more abbreviated if franchises fail. Each team's roster comprises 29 players: 24 Mexicans and 4 to 5 *importados* (foreign imports, mostly North Americans). The larger study of the Tecos sought to examine the structural, behavioral, and emotional relations of these two very different groups operating within a single intimate setting.

The Mexican Tecos came from all parts of Mexico but particularly from the baseball-rich regions of Veracruz, Sinaloa, and the Yucatan. The racial makeup of the team, reflecting Mexican history, is primarily mestizo (a mixture of native American and Spanish), with a bit of Afro-Caribbean (Veracruz), and even one Native American (Yaqui Indian) thrown in for good measure. With only two exceptions, the players are from struggling lower- and marginally middle-class families.

Structurally, the Mexican and Import players are differently treated by team owners. Imports are better paid, receive better accommodations, are not subject to the same behavioral demands as Mexican players, and, in the case of the Tecos, do not even live in the same city as their Mexican teammates. Going back a decade, the Tecos Imports all (with one exception) lived in Laredo, Texas, rather than across the river in Mexico. Other situations unique to the Tecos exacerbate the Anglo-Mexican tensions. For the Tecos, the first few weeks of the season were unusual because their "working agreement" (see Klein, 1991) with the Atlanta Braves precluded the arrival of the Imports in time for the opening of the Mexican League season. Unlike the Imports on other Mexican League clubs, Tecos Imports were expected to attend Atlanta spring training. This placed the Tecos in a difficult position for several weeks at the start of the season, but the late arrival of the Imports also structurally impaired relations between Anglo and *Mexicano* players.[2]

The privileged treatment of Anglo Imports is most dramatic in the travel arrangements made for both groups. As with many minor league teams, there is a good deal of road travel, but in Mexico the distance can at times be frightening. Travel from the northern border to cities in southern Mexico can sometimes be 40 hours (Klein, 1997). Mexican Tecos players were, in 1994, forced to make many of these trips by bus, whereas their Import counterparts were flown in any trip of more than 400 miles as dictated by the terms of their contracts. Although cultural differences posed serious problems for Anglos and Latinos playing in any Latin countries (Klein, 1991), the Tecos case proved particularly vexing for the players.

Making Sense of Tecos Macho

Many of the manifestations of the antagonisms between groups of players were cultural and nationalistic, but they were played out along masculine lines. The most direct antagonism between Anglos and Mexicans was chronicled over the 2-year period of the study, but it was the more subtle areas of emotions and attitude that revealed significant differences in masculinity between the two groups. I observed three areas of behavior in which Mexican players seemed to pose a clear difference both from conventional views of machismo and from their Anglo counterparts: attitudes toward children, ability to express vulnerability, and touching between men. These three areas not only invite a critique of traditional views of machismo, but they also reveal cultural differences along lines of masculinity.

Like the previously cited studies, I dichotomize masculinity and set it on a continuum ranging from excessively macho or hypermasculine, through androgyny, to feminine. I do this because I want to show that machismo as gender identity continues to be struggled with by some, easily accommodated by others. By dichotomizing, I do not think of gender construction as existing along a linear track but rather as pieced together. Nevertheless, the elements used to fashion gender identity stem from attitudes and behavior that exist between poles of masculinity and femininity as conventionally defined in time and place. I use the terms "Tough Machos" and "Tender Machos" to show that men can retain elements of both ends of the continuum within themselves and, following Gutmann, such Mexican men are *ni machos, ni mandilóns*.

Tough Machos

With 10 straight playoff appearances and two League championships, the 1993 Tecos were a recognized force to be dealt with in Mexican baseball. Their signature, appropriately enough, was power. A trio, led by the number two career home run hitter of Mexican baseball, Andres Mora, live and die by hitting the long ball. Also included was Alejandro Ortiz and Marco Antonio Romero, who were regularly among the top five in home runs. Their look was studied "macho": multiple days' growth of beard, cut-off sleeves on their uniforms, home run swings and trots around the bases designed to showcase their power. They routinely pounded their plastic cups (for protection of their groin) and proclaimed to all within earshot *Tenemos huevos!*—We have balls (eggs). There was no sign of self-derision in these statements or presentation of self. Like their north-of-the-border counterparts, following a home run, there was a good deal of choreographed chest-bumping between team members and the hitter, but there were excellent examples of the purely Mexican nature of this macho as well. Paz (1961, p. 81) noted that the "macho" is characterized by, among other things, a "great sinister laugh," turning even humor into aggressiveness via the put-down. The following was taken from field notes regarding Tecos slugger Marco Antonio Romero. Romero is one of the most macho acting of the Tecos. He cultivates the look (thick mustache offset by 2 days' growth of beard, powerful, beer-swilling body that swaggers). But what one remembers most about him was his laugh: loud, explosive, and potentially a bludgeon. In my early fieldwork, before I had been taken in by these men, I was very much perceived as an outsider imposing on the Tecos community:

Reynosa, Mexico: This afternoon the veterans were giving a workshop on Teco-lore in the dugout. Seeking respite from the mid-day heat, they straggled in one by one until a small group had gathered. Then each of the veterans (Mora, Ortiz, Romero) would take turns holding the center stage regaling the others with stories of having bested or humiliated someone. Always sentences are punctuated with "*Chinga*" (fuck) or "*Pinche*" (damn). . . . Romero recounts a time when he took off after an opposing pitcher, mimicking the feeble, cowardly way the latter ran around the diamond trying to avoid Romero and his bat. Ballistically, Romero flew into the face of one of the players in imitation of his fury. . . . Then, that menacing laugh of his boomed from his mustachioed face, and was joined by a chorus of laughter. . . . Turning his attention to me [he noticed me listening], Romero's smile slid smoothly to a sneer, and he used what limited English he knew to refer to my purpose in being with the team, making it clear that he does not welcome my presence. He used the English word "book" in his otherwise Spanish diatribe: "Look at this one, el barbón [bearded one], writing a 'book.' . . . fuckin' book, fuckin' book." Each time he spit it out more loudly and more threateningly, and always the sneer-smile and gravelly laugh. He was sitting on the edge between a frontal and oblique attack on me, smiling as if just joking and sneering as if not. The others were keenly interested in seeing what I would do.

Although I would eventually develop a good relationship with Romero, hearing and seeing his menacing laughter and smile always stayed with me, for it was the hallmark of the tough-seeming character of Mexican lore.

Traditional gender inequality is another important aspect of machismo. Although Gutmann has claimed that such relations have been eroded in Mexico (certainly within the colonia or neighborhood he studied), the same is not really true among Tecos. Only one Tecos wife was employed in the labor force (and she was Mexican American), and only one had postsecondary education. The others all saw their roles as being dutiful mothers and wives. The wife of one of the players summed up her view of what a man needed to be:

What he says goes with his girlfriend or family. He has to be in control. My husband had to be tough. His no's were no's. His yes was yes. If he wanted to go out, he'd go out. It wasn't a matter of asking. They'd call each other *mandilón* if the wife said no and he listened.

Another characteristic of the macho has always been womanizing. Here the line between Mexican macho and the life of a high-visibility athlete is unclear. Tecos players fooled around with women. "Groupies" were referred to in Mexico as *cachuchas* (baseball caps) because, like a baseball cap, you can put it on, take it off, or exchange it at will. Tecos players (and their Anglo counterparts) commonly engaged in dalliances with these women: "We go back to our hotel and we're too pumped, so we shower and go down for a few drinks. The women seem to know who we are. They're pretty upfront. Hey, you gotta be crazy not to go for that." Even though the Tecos players wouldn't talk about it in formal interviews, informally they discussed the several teammates that had *las casas chicas* (mistresses, second houses or families). Again, by itself this really does not distinguish Mexican from Anglo, but taken together a strain of machismo characterizes many of the Tecos. Still, although it may be the case that machismo is alive and well among the Tecos, it would be wrong to claim that these Tecos are one-dimensional machos. One Tecos wife cautioned me, saying, "Sure maybe Cuevas and Romero or others are a little macho, but they also bend the rules. They wash dishes. They carry the baby. They change diapers. So, that's not a real macho."

Tender Machos

Mirandé (1997) argued that for Latinos the expression of masculinity is determined by one's response to the group, one's public demeanor (p. 131). Again, because it is such a public display, sport offers an important measure of this. In Gutmann's (1996) study, we saw the easy coexistence of discordant traits (*ni macho, ni mandilón*), some of which were publicly played out. The following example from my work is noteworthy in that although taking place in pubic, it was not sport-related.

When a call went out to the Tecos to take part in a fashion show in Laredo one of the most surprising volunteers was Luis Fernando Díaz. He was considered by many to be muy macho. The woman who staged the show, a Tecos wife, said of Díaz, "I invited him to take part in the show, and thought, 'They're never gonna buy this.' But he showed up with his family. He wanted to come and he took his wife to pick out his clothes. And I'm like, 'What? This is one of the last guys I expected to show. And here is his wife picking out his clothes. And he comes out of the dressing room and asks, 'Is this okay?' She's dressing him!"

We might add that Díaz was completely nonplussed by this incident. The perception of Díaz as having somehow violated the macho code is interesting because it reveals to us that Mexican women also internalize a sense of what macho is, considering it noteworthy when they see it transgressed. The subsequent discussion details three areas in which I was able to observe contrasts with both one-dimensional views of Mexican men as machos and cultural differences between Mexican and Anglo players.

Attitudes toward children. Only the briefest of descriptions for the three areas of tender macho can be provided, but they are fairly representative of the data collected. Both Gutmann (1996, pp. 74-76) and Mirandé (1997) commented on the sensitive and caring nature of Latino fatherhood. For Gutmann, it may be a function of recent structural changes in family life, but for Mirandé it has always been there. Gender differences in the domestic sphere (which includes child care) continue to exist in Mexico, but there is evidence to support the view that men are increasingly playing roles in these areas (Gutmann, 1996). Moreover, in the area of emotions, a related indicator of some of these larger changes, Gutmann's survey revealed that for a "sizable number" of interviewees, "fathers are more or much more tender with their children (than mothers)" (p. 76). The Tecos, too, seemed unable to resist attending to children, as the following typical observation reveals:

> April 4, 1994 (West Martin Field, Laredo): On the field following batting practice and 30 minutes to game time. Romero, with his three-day growth of beard looks like central-casting's choice for a Mexican bandito. He laughs like a three-pack-a-day convict, but when he holds his little baby girl and zooms her around like a little pink dirigible (she's wearing a pink headband), he's the warmest, most comforting man imaginable. Each time he stops she cries to be picked up and zoomed, and so he and the others continue to take turns suspending her as effortlessly as the big moon hanging overhead.

In a related instance also taken from field notes, Alejandro Ortiz, following his third straight strikeout, stormed over to the "Time Out" corner [my term for a place in the dugout where players vent emotions freely], cursed loudly, and slammed his bat against the bat rack. Without losing a step he moved to the other side of the dugout still glowering, cleats clicking angrily up the steps to the chain-link fence that separates the players from the fans. Out of a mixture of his need for privacy and our fear of his outbursts we all avoided making eye contact with him. Looking out at the field, he continued seething, and the heat visibly rose from his head in a menacing way. Suddenly, out of the corner of his eye, he spotted a baby sitting on its mother's lap, and without missing a beat he swept from fury to smile, losing 20 years in the bargain. In a voice piping up at least two full octaves, he puckered up his lips and cooed, "Give me a little kiss, Alexis." Ortiz's ability to switch emotional gears so dramatically and quickly underscores the powerful and disarming place of children in the lives of many men.

Expressing vulnerability. Gutmann (1996) presented us with the case of Gabriel, one of his key cultural resource people, who openly discussed his traumatic family history, at one point actually breaking down and crying. Gutmann noted that, after wiping his tears, Gabriel was not embarrassed: "I think he wanted me to know how badly he was feeling" (p. 82). A similar instance from the Tecos involved Alejandro Ortiz. During the championship series in 1993, the Tecos lost Game 2 due to a fielding error by Ortiz. Predictably, Ortiz took it hard. He stayed out all night drinking and driving around, keeping his wife and children up with worry. The following morning, it was a haggard Ortiz who appeared at, of all places, the office of Esther Firova, the manager's wife. Although the two families were close, seeking out the wife of a fellow Tecos to unload some of his feelings went way beyond the emotional rules (Hochschild, 1979). In both venting and asking for help from a woman who was known to the community, Ortiz violated the protocol of a traditional macho. Esther recalled the meeting:

> He comes to my office, practically gets on his knees and wants me to tell him that he's doing okay, that he didn't make a mistake, that he's gonna snap out of his slump. He went to *my* office. He'd been drinking all night, and like, "God, where have you been?" And he sits down, puts his head down, grabs his forehead and says, . . . "I let the team down. I let my friends down." He was real emotional. He said, "I tried! I lost the ball and couldn't make up for it with a hit. I let Dan [the manager] down, and you don't know how much that hurts me. I'm trying. What am I doing wrong?" he kept asking me, practically crying. He was in my office for two hours, and I'm thinking, "Man, this macho guy. And him coming to a woman."

Ortiz often went out drinking with teammates during which they would "unload" their concerns, but going to a woman was considered by Esther an emotional departure from the conventions of machismo.

Even more stoic players on occasion surprised me with the depth of their feelings. An aging Andres Mora, facing declining skills and injury problems, had begun to consider the inevitable retirement from the game. I had never really been able to crack his emotional surface. Having been in the Major Leagues, and following a lifetime in the Mexican baseball lime-light, he was not about to present a public persona of anything short of be-ing in control. This governed his dealings with fans, media, and team-mates, everyone except his drinking buddies. Suddenly, one night early in the 1994 season, he turned to me, placed his hand on my arm and made a statement:

> "You know, I'm thinking of quitting after this year." I asked why, and he replied, "You see my bat [speed] slowed down. I have aches and pains everywhere. I can't move my leg any further than this [he shows me]. It's just that I don't know what to do. Baseball has been my life. I'm lost without it. It's very sad."

I was taken aback by his sudden expression of vulnerability right in the middle of a game. Again, the public nature of the response in the dug-out with teammates milling about reflects a sense of masculine comport-ment and emotion management that is simultaneously open, secure, and sensitive.

Physical expression.   Perhaps no area of male behavior in U.S. society is as charged as that of men touching other men. The problem is that physical contact between men is generally perceived homophobically, yet giving and receiving hugs and touches is so integral a part of our so-cial and psychological makeup. Moreover, the nature of sport, with its male-to-male focus, fosters considerable physical expression between men. Completely ruling out physical expression between men is impos-sible, yet the need for male companionship that goes unmet because of homophobic censorship creates a dilemma (e.g., Connell, 1995, p. 133; Lehne, 1980; Sherrod, 1987). Sport is only one institution that regulates how men may touch each other. Displays of affection and/or hugging are limited to public hugging, slaps on the behind, even a macho kiss on the top of the head is permitted. That same hug in the parking lot could get someone punched, but in front of 50 million television viewers, it is fine. Former basketball greats Magic Johnson and Isiah Thomas routinely would kiss each other on the cheek before games, making it a part of their public performance. In this instance, the overly public display of physi-cal affection is not only permitted, but required. In the more informal and private confines of the locker room, physical expression between men is even more controlled, in this instance, through joking (Curry, 1991; White & Vagi, 1990).

Gutmann (1996) examined this same phenomenon in Mexico City, concluding, "There is a lot of touching that occurs between men in public in Colonia Santo Domingo" (p. 123). Much of this involves formal touching (e.g., handshakes) but includes forms that we would regard with suspicion. Leaning one's head on another's shoulder, for instance, or instances in which "a younger man, perhaps a teenager, will rest himself against an older man who in turn is engaged in a conversation with a third man. Or a teenager might walk down the street with his arm around another boy's shoulder" (p. 124); all are informal and normative examples of men touching each other. They do not require homosexual joking to occur, because the homophobia, although present, is differently configured.[3]

The Tecos also provided me with dramatic examples of this. One night during a game, two Mexican players had begun mock boxing with each other in the dugout. Each was throwing phantom punches at the other, eventually progressing to more physically aggressive and moderate slaps and then body slams. As is too often the case, I feared that this kind of play fighting might turn more serious. After about a minute of this sort of combat, the two moved aggressive posturing to gliding around the dugout in a waltzlike embrace, settling finally into watching the game with their arms around each other's waists.

Some time later, I saw an even more striking incident. During a home game, the Tecos players were sitting in a row of plastic seats that had been placed at field level rather than in the dugout. The nights were already quite warm, and players wanted to take advantage of whatever wind there might be. The players seated were soon joined by others who stood behind them. Several of the standing players (all Mexican) rested their hands on the shoulders of their seated compatriots, but one player was absentmindedly stroking the hair (in a grooming sort of motion, front to back) of his seated teammate while talking to the man on his right about how his pitching had fallen on hard times of late. All this in front of some 9,000 fans. No one seemed to take notice of this.

I thought I might try to more systematically determine how many men on the team engaged in some form of physical contact and how often it might occur. For two periods of 1 week each, I tried to keep tabs on the number of times I saw players showing physical affection (here defined as touching someone informally, other than handshakes). I wrote down the names of the players and the form of the physical contact. Not all of the Tecos were physically demonstrative. I counted 9 men whom I regularly saw touching others and another 7 who did so occasionally (at least once a day). Sixteen of 24 (two thirds) Mexican players engaged in touching behavior.

Differences between Anglo and Mexican players along all three dimensions were noted, but most dramatically in physical expression. Among the 4 Anglo players, there was not a single instance of such touching, leaning, or hugging. When I queried one of them about this absence, he was somewhat surprised that I would be considering such a thing:

> Yeah, now that you mention it, I sorta noticed that too. But I can't get behind that kinda thing. I mean, I can bear hug a guy or "five" him or "mosh" [mutual body slam] him, but these [Mexican] guys. I don't know. It's different, they put their arms around each other and leave 'em there.

In follow-up conversations with the Mexican players pointing out my observations, one suddenly lit up as if just realizing something for the first time:

> When I went to spring training in the States, I remember once putting my arm around one of the gringos who was a good guy. He looked at me like [face recoiling in horror]. I thought he just didn't like me and I was surprised because we got along good. But now maybe I understand this thing better.

Anglo players were also less likely to talk openly about their vulnerability. In private conversation, I managed to get 2 of them to discuss some of their issues, but never in the midst of their fellow players. Even in discussing sensitive topics, there was tendency to cloak it in toughness with swearing ("Hey shit man! I'm gonna be thirty, and I'm fuckin' wasting my time here") or dismissing some coaching advice on how to move up the ranks ("No way do I listen to that pissant. Man, you can't fuck with a man's swing like that"). Mexican players, by comparison, employ language more in keeping with their emotions when expressing vulnerability. The need to cloak vulnerability (i.e., emotional pain or confusion) with expletives is noticeably absent in the following typical response:

> I got an invitation to West Palm Beach with the Braves [for spring training]. They wanted to pay me $40 a week. Then . . . my Dad died last year and I have to send my money to my Mom. I told them I'll stay here if you send $200 a month to my Mom. Don't give me anything, just send it to her. They said they couldn't do that. . . . Call the Tecos front office and tell them to send the money. The Tecos never talked to me about this. I said "Okay, I'm gonna go back to Laredo." Then

a Braves pitching coach says, "We want you here. If you go back to Mexico you're not coming here no more." I said, "I'm sorry." I told him that I have a certificate of my father's death and I'd show it to him, but he didn't care. What kind of man is this that doesn't care about family?

Similarly, in demonstrating affection toward children, the Anglos were somewhat less demonstrative, spending overall less time cuddling and playing with all children (not only their own). For Anglo players, the purpose of the pregame period was to get ready, to put their "game faces" on. Rolling around on the ground with children or talking candidly was not in keeping with their seriousness. This was not lost on the Mexican players and their families, prompting one of the Tecos wives to comment, "In our culture a gringo, we know, is cold. They may be good guys—not mean— not machos, but they're also not gonna be emotional." This observation mirrors some of Mirandé's (1997) conclusions on Latino masculinity: "Many traits which are defined as 'feminine' in the dominant [North American] culture such as being affectionate, warm, sympathetic, tender, emotional, and sensitive are much more acceptable behaviors in Latino men than they are in Anglo men" (p.131). These observed differences, as indicated by the Tecos wife, also are articulated by the people involved.

In looking at national differences, we have been looking at only these three areas of behavior, but there exists a more direct contrast between Anglos and Mexicans that also gives expression to machismo. The antipathy felt between the two groups was often manifested in very traditional macho confrontational style (Klein, 1996, 1997). Emotionally, there were barriers between the players that ensured that they almost never interacted with each other off the field. Disparaging perceptions of each other were thickly layered. "Hey," boasted one Anglo in the locker room, "I do the work of any three Mexicans." A perception like this can be countered by a Mexican one claiming, "You *pinches* (damn) Gringos come here to be served. You think we're your damn slaves." But even in this realm, I noted that Mexican players differed from their Anglo counterparts. Anglos, for the most part, would express their feelings about Mexico and Mexicans more openly. When a Mexican hotel employee did not respond quickly enough to an American's request, the latter ranted publicly about the "shit conditions in this shitbox of a country." Mexican players bear tremendous resentment against these Americans, but they prefer to express it more privately among themselves. Thus, even so small a unit as a single team can reveal larger national and cultural differences.

Conclusions

Connell's (1987) notion of "hegemonic masculinity," in which dominant templates for gender identity are, to varying degrees, accepted uncritically, fretted over, fought with, and/or rejected by men provides us a useful framework for looking at how masculinity operates within this cross-cultural team.

It is also important to understand that despite the lack of agreement as to what machismo is, there remains a vague shared sense, among scholars and others, of its existence as an attitude and set of behaviors that is hypermasculine. Whether it has always been part of Mexican masculinity or a mutation of an older and more honorable form of masculinity, machismo is something that scholars (North American and Mexican) acknowledge as a standard of behavior that exists either at one end of a range of masculinity or as one of many forms of masculinity. More important, however, perceived machismo is capable of coexisting alongside other (even contradictory) dimensions of masculinity within an individual and/ or culture. Hence, there is an awareness that these Latino men continue to hold certain "macho" views and that periodic departures from them pose little in the way of problems. In this more contemporary sense of Mexican masculinity, men may cry, let their wives dress them in public, or show physical affection, while also brawling or refusing to do things that they consider only women's work.

The Tecos case study also reveals intercultural and intracultural differences among the men. Clearly, there exists a range of attitudes about masculinity, prompted in part by class, ethnicity, and regional differences in both the Anglo and Mexican male players. Still, this study suggests that, despite internal variation, there were larger cultural patterns that turned up as differences between national populations, that is, larger cultural patterns may be discerned. Three areas of behavior and feeling were examined showing differences between Anglo and Mexican players. These differences were expressed as a combination of what these men did and what they thought about what they did, that is, behavior and emotions. Hochschild (1983) discussed the relation between "display" and "feeling" in her work on airline employees, arguing that over time the discrepancy that may exist between display and feeling for people engaged in public domains is narrowed by employing various techniques. Within this context of the sociology of emotions, the Tecos material is interesting. Most of the observations I used in this examination were public displays, that is, in full view of the fans, but the gap between display and feeling seemed nonexistent. In the three areas of behavior that I observed, the Mexican Tecos seemed emotionally open and unguarded, a situation that may reflect the relatively less commercialized business of Mexican baseball (compared to Hochschild's airline industry). One area in which display and feeling were separated had to do with the acrimonious relations between Anglo and Mexican players. The national and cultural antipathy that existed outside the white lines was never evidenced on the field (Klein, 1996, 1997); moreover, the discrepancy between public display and private feeling was not ameliorated over time. For the purposes of saving the social experiment (i.e., the group), this is precisely where internal controls are most needed. It is not surprising that this is where Hochschild's sense of "emotion management" is most pervasive, but here the wide gap between display and feeling did not appear to narrow over time. The jaundiced views of the other held by each group were countered by the performance on the field that emphasized team play with its accompanying unstated sense of positive team emotions, a situation highly reminiscent of Goffman's (1959) "front stage" and "back stage" behaviors. What was interesting in this regard was how the area containing the most virulent feelings (and among the most outward displays of machismo) was masked by the performance.

However one decides to look at the Tecos material, whether through the lens of nationalism, male/female relations, body language, emotions, or social relations, the template of masculinity may be found. It matters little whether one looks at unmistakable signs or subtleties, forms of behavior and feeling show up as differences in masculinity. In any case, what surfaces is that sports studies, even microanalyses such as this, reveal elements of social realities that might be more concealed in other institutions.

Notes

1. Paz built an entire cultural description around a single act, a culture that continued unabated through history, and Ramos simply psychoanalyzed all Mexican men as if they came out of a single mold; their conclusions continue to hold wide currency.

2. Although other teams use the preseason to bond, the Tecos have a group of Anglo late arrivals with bad attitudes and, in many cases, an unrealistic sense of entitlement (Klein, 1997).

3. Latino men continue to hold disparaging views of homosexuality (Lancaster, 1992), but they are different from the views often held in North America. For Latino men, homosexual sex is not damaging to one's sense of masculinity if one is the aggressor, the male who penetrates the other (see Paz, 1961).

PART TWO

MEN'S VIOLENCE AND SPORT

6

"Be a Buddy to Your Buddy"

Male Identity, Aggression, and
Intimacy in a Boxing Gym

LAURENCE DE GARIS

Boxing has been represented as a powerful metaphor for (Early, 1994) or
symbol of (Oates, 1995) masculinity. However, the role of gender relations is conspicuously absent in most previous empirical research on
boxing culture (Hare, 1973; Sugden, 1987; Weinberg & Arond, 1969).
Where gender relations are mentioned, they are dismissed matter-of-
factly, as if no explanation is needed (Wacquant, 1992). To the contrary,
gender relations in boxing culture are not unitary and self-explanatory.
Rather, gender identities in boxing culture are historically diverse and actively negotiated and interpreted, with significant variations in subjective
experiences.

Therefore, this chapter questions the presumption of masculinity in
boxing. By examining masculinity both as a rhetorical construct and as
patterns of behavior, this chapter explores the complexities and variations of masculine identity and expression in boxing culture. Based on

AUTHOR'S NOTE: Data for this study were collected as part of my doctoral dissertation at
the University of Connecticut. An earlier version of this chapter was presented at the 1997
meeting of the North American Society for the Sociology of Sport in Toronto. I thank Todd
Crosset and Alan Klein for their comments on earlier versions of this chapter. I especially
thank Don Sabo and Michael Messner for their insightful editorial comments.

the results of a 10-month ethnography of a New York City boxing gym, I discuss the salience of gender in the construction of male boxers' identities; aspects of sparring and men's friendships that do not conform with an aggressive, emotionally repressed masculinity; and the influence of age in moderating dominant forms of masculinity.

Boxing and Masculinity

Wacquant (1992) asserted but failed to articulate his position that "Needless to say, all members are men: The gym is a *quintessentially masculine space*" (p. 234). In her textual reading of boxing, Oates (1995) explained in a bit more detail how boxing is a "purely masculine activity," discussing the representation of masculine bodies and raw aggression through boxing's vocabulary. Oates suggested that boxing appeals to an innate male misogyny in that boxing repudiates femininity. In a more complete and compassionate textual reading, Early (1994) discussed how elements of race, ethnicity, class, and industrial culture interact with masculine identity in boxing culture.

Most writing on boxing focuses almost exclusively on young, African American, male professional boxers. Consequently, the literature often provides monolithic notions of both the meaning of "boxing" and the identity of the "boxer." Monolithic notions of masculinity and the boxer are now being challenged by recent research that provides insight into variations within boxing culture. In his study of National Collegiate Athletic Associated boxing, Wallenfeldt (1994) lamented that professional boxing has dominated representations and writing about the entire sport. He discussed the experiences and meanings collegiate boxers—mostly white and middle class—associate with boxing, but did not specifically address questions of masculinity. Jones (1997) discussed the motivations and experiences of a participant in unlicensed boxing matches, focusing primarily on the issue of deviance and mentioning masculine identity only in passing. Interestingly, the only study on boxing to focus exclusively on the formation of gender identity was Halbert's (1997) study of women professional boxers, as if gender relations are salient for women but not for men. No research on boxing has systematically approached the question of gender relations as they relate to men. Masculinity has been a presumption, rather than a problem, in writing on boxing.

Masculinity, the Body, and Intimacy

Messner (1992b) argued that masculinity is a "problem" in sport because, among other reasons, the dominant form of masculinity in sporting cultures is destructive to the body and denies emotional intimacy. Aggression, or a will to dominate, has long been associated with masculinity (Klein, 1995b; Oates, 1995). An aggressive attempt to dominate "others" (opponents, teammates, women, racial and ethnic minorities, members of the working class, and gay men) both promotes destruction of bodies and prohibits intimate personal relationships.

Dominant masculinity in sport, Messner argued, promotes an attitude in which the body is used as a weapon, as a tool to achieve goals. Two former professional football players in Messner's study suggested that masculine prowess is enhanced by being "hard-hitters," by tackling so hard as to cause injuries in one's opponents. The goal is domination. The body is both the medium and the target. As Messner noted, these practices carry enormous health costs to athletes, especially those in American football.

Insults and jibes, or a kind of verbal jousting, often have been seen as characteristic of men's friendships in sporting cultures (Curry, 1991; Klein, 1995b). In his ethnography of a Mexican League baseball team, Klein (1995b) argued that many players use jokes as a "weapon." In his analysis of the locker room talk of collegiate football and wrestling teams, Curry (1991) suggested that competition extends into male athletes' personal relationships. Similarly, Messner (1992b) argued that relationships among teammates are characterized by an "antagonistic cooperation," in which friendship is balanced by competition. The goal is domination. The medium is language. Messner (1992a) argued that men's friendships are impoverished by competition and aggression. When male athletes do bond with each other, it often takes the form of sexist and homophobic talk and actions (Curry, 1991; Messner, 1992b). Again, the goal is domination. The targets are women, gay men, and racial and ethnic minorities.

Aggression in personal relationships prohibits intimacy. As Rubin (1983) argued, "Intimacy is some kind of reciprocal expression of feeling and thought, not out of fear or dependent need, but out of a wish to know another's inner life and to be able to share one's own" (p. 90). Positions of power in personal relationships must reach some kind of equilibrium to reciprocate and share. Therefore, relationships characterized by attempts to impose a will preclude intimate sharing and reciprocity.

However, Messner's research, like most research on masculine ideology in sport, has been limited to young males in mainstream organized
sports. The influence of age is largely absent from discussions of masculine ideology in sport, as are experiences from nonmainstream, or marginalized, sporting activities. Albert (1991) argued that cooperative elements in bicycle racing are marginalized because they run against the
hegemonic ideology of competition in sport. Whether or not competitive
practices have been selectively observed, the study of masculine ideology
in sport has been limited to competitive activities.

Resistance and Transformation

Messner (1992a) suggested that the men in his study developed a *"covert intimacy,* an intimacy that is characterized by *doing* together, rather
than by mutual talk about their inner lives" (p. 232). Rather than eval-
uate styles of intimacy in a gendered framework, Messner asked, "How
do male friendships fit into an overall system of power?" (1992a, p. 217).
As Crosset and Beal (1997) pointed out, caution must be exercised in analyzing the relation between sporting practices, on the one hand, and larger
social structures such as economics, politics, and notions of national
or ethnic cultures on the other. Efforts to "pigeonhole" specific practices as hegemonic or resistant to dominant ideologies overlook anoma-
lous practices (such as egalitarian practices in a hierarchical culture) and
may impose a moral order or psychological framework that is alien to the
population being studied (Albert, 1991; Crosset & Beal, 1997; Ortner,
1996).

During the 1970s, critics of Western culture and American sport, notably Leonard (1974), looked to the East for alternatives to dominant ideologies in sport. In his volume on revisioning sport, physical education,
and the body, Leonard outlined the problems of competitive sport, such as
violence and anxiety, and proposed "Oriental" sporting practices, such as
aikido, as alternatives. During the 1980s, feminist critics proposed alternatives to dominant sporting ideologies. Birrell and Richter (1994) suggested, "Through reflexive social action, women (and by extension other
traditionally disenfranchised groups) can overcome the hegemonic grasp
of alienating ideologies and institute social practices which have authentic
meaning in their own lives" (p. 221). During these periods, many people
sought and found personal freedom and deep meaning in "Eastern" or
"feminist" sporting practices. By no means do I suggest that these solu-

tions are based on a false consciousness or are somehow disingenuous. However, the potential problem with Eastern and feminist critiques of competitive sporting ideologies is that, by "Orientalizing" or "feminizing" alternative ideologies, we run the risk of reifying the very gender and ethnic differences that constitute the relations of domination we wish to disrupt.

Klein (1995b) described machismo as a "system" that operates along a bipolar continuum with extreme forms of masculinity and femininity at opposing ends. Klein discussed many behaviors exhibited by Mexican baseball players that, by American standards, would be considered less masculine and more feminine. As Flax (1987) argued, the meanings attributed to gender relations require socially critical and self-reflexive analysis. What is unclear in Klein's study is how the Mexican players themselves attribute meanings to their behaviors. Klein ascribed primacy to gender relations by conforming specific behaviors to a masculine continuum that he himself created.

Messner's notion of "the larger gender order" and Klein's "masculine continuum" are bipolar systems. For Klein, men's behaviors are either masculine, to a greater or lesser degree, or feminine, to a greater or lesser degree. For Messner, men's behaviors either disrupt or contribute to "the gender order." A problem arises when conforming fragmented field experiences to unified analytical wholes (Tyler, 1986). What is missing are the possibilities that men's and women's identities are not formed around an axis of gender, and that some discourses, logics, and practices are simply "there," "other," or "different" (Ortner, 1996).

What needs to be teased out is the salience of gender in sporting cultures. Because most sporting cultures historically have been predominantly male, there has been a tendency to attribute characteristics of sporting cultures, such as aggression, to masculine ideology and/or personality traits. In her study of Walpiri widows in Australia, Dussart (1992) proposed an approach that "avoids a normative and rule-bound perspective that would depict women categorically and dichotomously vis-à-vis men" (p. 337). This approach questions, rather than presumes, the salience of gender in women's lives.

The amount and quality of data being collected regarding men's experiences in sporting cultures now place us in a position to examine the salience of gender in the study of men's experiences in sport. In their study of masculinity, sport, and violence, Messner and Sabo (1994) searched for possible alternatives to "hegemonic" masculinity in sporting practices. In an 11-point strategy, Sabo and Messner (1994) suggested practices that they hope will change men by changing their sporting experiences, as seen in their first point, "Be a Buddy to Your Body":

> Resist definitions of masculinity that put bodies at risk, glorify pain, and promote or ignore injury. Develop athletic potential in ways that are challenging but not physically harmful. Renounce painful and risky training practices. Confront and report instances of verbal or physical abuse of players by coaches. Reject locker-room clichés that encourage athletes to disregard the limits and vulnerability of their bodies, such as "No pain, no gain," and "You gotta pay the price to win." (p. 214)

Sabo and Messner (1994) did not specify under what conditions we might "resist," "develop," "renounce," or "reject," that is, the point is more ideology than strategy. At any rate, Sabo and Messner associated physical risk with masculine ideology. In their second point, Sabo and Messner suggested, "Change the rules and challenge the underlying values of games that promote violence and excessive aggression" (p. 215). Here, the focus shifts from a hegemonic masculine ideology to a hegemonic sporting ideology.

New questions must now be addressed: Are aggressive sporting practices attributable to masculine ideology, a competitive ethos, or both? Under what conditions? What are the "axes of prestige" (Ortner, 1996) for men's identities in sporting cultures? What is the salience of gender in the construction of male athletes' identities? Are egalitarian practices possible in a competitive and hierarchical culture? If so, are they constructed so as to contribute to or disrupt hegemonic ideologies? Or both? Or neither?

The Study

Data Collection

The research design for this study followed MacAloon's (1992) outline for an ethnography of sport, an "intensive, long-term, and face-to-face participant observation in natural settings and the systematic recording of conceptions, discourses, relations, and behaviors of the sports actors, agencies, and communities selected for analysis" (p. 104). The site for this study was a commercial boxing gym, which I call the "Gym," located on the second floor of an industrial warehouse in downtown Brooklyn, New York. Participants for this study were all active members of the Gym. For the ethnographic portion of the study, participants consisted of a core of about 50 active boxers, trainers, and Gym employees. In addition, this study includes visitors to the Gym—journalists, camera crews, photographers, and other observers—who did not maintain a consistent presence at the Gym. Descriptive data were collected for the participants who participated in formal interviews ($N = 30$). Most of the participants who were formally interviewed were active boxers ($n = 19, 63\%$). Other interview participants included trainers ($n = 6, 20\%$), retired boxers ($n = 2, 7\%$), the Gym owner, and an agent who books boxers for personal appearances. Of the participants interviewed, 46% ($n = 14$) identified themselves as "white," 30% ($n = 9$) as "black," 17% as "Latino" or "Hispanic," and 7% ($n = 2$) as Asian or Pacific Islander. The mean age for boxers was 32.8 years and for trainers was 52 years. Four of the participants interviewed were women, all of whom were boxers. Twelve of the 30 interviews were recorded on tape and transcribed. Skill levels of Gym members ranged from novice to active world champion professional.[1] Almost all boxers, except for 2, had previous or active competitive careers in boxing.

Data were collected over a period of 10 months, from July 1996 through April 1997. During that period, I was an active member of the Gym, where I trained as a wrestler and trained aspiring wrestlers at a professional wrestling school. Data collection techniques included participation, observation, and interviews. The study was conducted under the principle and guidelines of informed consent. Participants' privacy was protected by the use of pseudonyms.

The Political Economy of the Gym

The political economy of the boxing industry has changed drastically during the last decade. According to the Gym owner, the number of boxing gyms in New York City has decreased from approximately 100 to 5 during the last 10 years. Unlike gyms studied in previous ethnographic research (Sugden, 1987; Wacquant, 1992), the Gym is a commercial gym, not a neighborhood club. Rather than rely on patronage or percentages of purses from professional matches, the main source of revenue for the Gym owner is monthly dues ($45 per month). Likewise, trainers, who in the past were paid only a percentage of professional purses, are wage laborers paid on an hourly, weekly, or monthly basis by their trainees. Therefore, there is a vested interest in maintaining the health and safety of Gym members.

Only 1 out of approximately 10 to 15 trainers relied solely on boxing for income. In fact, 3 trainers in this study charged nothing at all for their services. Other trainers commonly charge $5 to $10 per session.

In addition, opportunities for competition in boxing have become extremely limited during the past 10 years. There are currently two amateur tournaments in the New York area—the Metros and the Golden Gloves. Because the tournaments are single elimination, an amateur boxer may have a maximum of 8 to 10 matches in a year, coming within a span of 2 to 3 months. A professional boxer who boxes every 3 months would be considered prolific. Because of the paucity of competitive matches, sparring becomes less "practice" in the sense of preparation and more of a practice in that it is an action in and of itself. Furthermore, the Gym sponsors public sparring exhibitions called "White-Collar Sparring," in which participants spar in front of spectators but no winners are declared. All participants have their hands raised and receive a trophy at the end of the bout. However, the title of the event often precludes, without formally excluding, individuals on the basis of class, and to a large extent race (but not gender).[2] Gym membership swells during the months prior to the Golden Gloves, but there is a core membership that trains year-round.

Sparring and the Body

As Gorn (1986) argued, masculinity is most often proven in a homosocial world of other men. With respect to time, boxing is primarily a solitary practice. Many more hours are spent jumping rope, shadow boxing, and working the bags than are spent in actual matches or sparring. The interactions in "floor workouts," in which there is no contact, take place between an individual boxer and a trainer. Social interactions among boxers, therefore, are limited to sparring, showering, dressing, and perhaps hanging out in the Gym, though most Gym members are not sociable in that respect.

Wacquant (1992) argued that sparring warrants close examination because it illustrates the "codified and collectively managed nature of pugilistic violence" (p. 242). Perhaps more important, sparring is a social relation in which social identities are formed and expressed. Sparring is strongly associated with masculine identities because the practice involves a negotiation and representation of dominance and subordination.

Boxers in this study engaged in sparring practices that varied in intensity, violence, and contact. In many cases, boxers practiced noncontact sparring in which two boxers face each other and throw punches without ever touching. This practice hones skills of seeing punches, bobbing, weaving, and countering without even a remote chance of injury. The violence of sparring sessions ranged from gentle tapping punches to full-force. Intensity in sparring ranged from very active to lackadaisical. However, sparring intensity was described in a rhetoric that invoked masculinity and social class. Variations in sparring practices were observed along the lines of class, ethnicity,[3] and age, adding further evidence that these variables influence the expression of male identities.

Violence, aggression, and the body. Many novice boxers are motivated to join the Gym because they want to be competitive. Contrary to the mainstream sport motto, "practice the way you play," novices are quickly taught that competition is for amateur and professional matches but has little place in the Gym. The more experienced participants in this study stressed the importance of cooperating during sparring in an effort to learn. This is often accomplished through caring and trust. Nigel, a 43-year-old Guyanese trainer, described his philosophy on sparring:

Sparring aspect is that you do not want your fighters to spar like they're in a fight. In sparring you come to learn so you need that aspect of looking at your fight and learning, not hurting each other in training. Any kind of serious sparring is when you're fighting, that's a fight. In the Gym, you're supposed to just try to learn from each other. (December 18, 1997)

Trainers and boxers both accept responsibility for the well-being of sparring partners. A sparring partner accepts responsibility for preventing injuries while learning techniques and improving fitness.

Often, the rhetoric used to describe sparring intensity invokes masculinity. Particularly aggressive sparring partners are said to be "macho." Many boxers in this study were originally attracted to boxing because it seemed to be a macho quest to assert dominance through violent competitive victories. As Mickey, a 73-year-old Jewish trainer, put it, novice boxers "gotta have that macho feeling. Otherwise they're going to fall short." But then Mickey argued that with few exceptions, novice boxers quickly learn differently. Mack, a 63-year-old Irish American trainer, said, "You've got to be macho to come in here. But then, that's the first thing you lose."

Historically, the practice of sparring has been strongly associated with upper social classes, whereas competitive and professional fights have been strongly associated with the lower classes (Gorn, 1986; Isenberg, 1988). Referring to 19th-century England, Gorn (1986) argued that the contrast between the "professors of pugilism" and their prizefighting counterparts is a clear example of the manifestation of class divisions in popular culture, suggesting that sparring matches were not as "gory" as the prizefights preferred by members of the lower classes and therefore a "fine compromise" for members of the gentry. Perhaps as a historical artifact of the interpretation of class differences in boxing, cooperative sparring practices are described in a rhetoric of class as well as gender. Cooperative sparring is widely referred to as being "gentlemanly." Red, a "white-collar boxer," put it this way:

> Yeah, you know what? I've been here a couple of months. But I've noticed it. I never would have thought that before. You mean—watching these guys spar. If someone gets hurt, they back off. You know, if someone loses a mouthpiece or whatever it's a, it's more of a friendly thing when they're sparring, which surprised me. You know, I thought that that killer instinct would take over. A guy sees blood and it's over. But I've seen guys back off, and they're almost *gentlemanly* about it. (January 17, 1997)

"Gentlemanly" sparring was not limited to middle- or upper-class boxers. Many trainers, professional boxers, and other Gym members, paradoxically including women,[4] referred to cooperative sparring as gentlemanly. Unlike Klein's (1995b) "masculine continuum," Gym members' rejection of a macho ethos did not imply femininity. No Gym members suggested that cooperative sparring was in any way "feminine." Rather, Gym members invoked an alternate masculinity based on a vocabulary of historical class differences.

The costs and benefits of aggressive sparring are weighed by many boxers. Because modern boxing is a relatively new sport, developed in this century for the most part, little was known in the past about the long-term physiological effects of regular, repeated, aggressive sparring or competitive matches. Rocky described his training for a Police Athletic League boxing team in 1964:

> To be honest with you, I took my lumps. We had [two guys], two real good—a heavyweight and a light heavyweight. And, uh, you know, learning the rudiments of boxing and everything, I took my lumps. But anyway, I made the team and I went to the Golden Gloves. (January 15, 1997)

Historically, boxers trained more aggressively and did not hesitate to assert their physical superiority over lesser-skilled opponents. This view was supported by other "old-timers" in the Gym. However, all boxers are now acutely aware of the potential damage, and most moderate their sparring practices accordingly. The consequences of aggressive sparring and excessive fighting are illustrated daily by the slurred speech of some older retired professionals in the Gym and elsewhere.

Somatic intimacy. The decision to renounce aggressive sparring is not purely rational and reasoned. To suggest so would deny the exuberance of shared intimacy and reciprocity many boxers experience and enjoy during sparring. Sparring offers a space in which men may share a somatic intimacy that otherwise would not be socially sanctioned. As Theberge (1994) argued, sport is often "an exclusively male realm that allows for expressiveness and intimacy—qualities that are typically absent from what is generally viewed as appropriate behavior" (p. 190). One of the few times in which two scantily clad men may, in a socially acceptable manner, emotionally and intimately embrace each other is immediately after they beat each other up. The Gym is a "safe" place to express intimacy because the textual representations of boxing as masculine and violent deter allegations of weakness or femininity.

Wacquant (1992) argued that choosing a sparring partner requires looking for some kind of equilibrium with respect to weight, experience, or skill. Birrell and Richter (1994) argued that skill too often assumes a privileged position in sport and proposed that more opportunities should be made available for lesser-skilled individuals. For the boxers and trainers in this study, the most crucial element in choosing a partner was trust, not skill. Trust was culturally encoded by boxers and structurally supported by trainers.

Trust was assumed or negotiated in different ways. Red recounted an invitation to spar:

> Some guy—actually in the shower, in the locker room, an older fellow, I found out he was 45, he told me he was 45—asked me if I ever did the white-collar boxing. I said, "No, I just started. Maybe in six months." And he just started, "Would I like to come down this Friday to this white-collar thing and box with him?" We're about the same size and it looks like he'll take it easy on me. So he picked me out and said, "Why don't you come down and we'll spar together?" 'Cause he got the feeling I wouldn't kick his ass and that I wouldn't kick his ass. But I said no, forget about it. I said, in three months. (January 15, 1997)

Red was approached because of similar physical attributes, but perhaps also because of his "white-collar" looks and the assumptions that this identity entails. Red declined the invitation largely because his trainer had already told him that he would not be ready to spar for another 3 months.

Beginners who are unable to control the intensity of sparring sessions are often matched by their trainers with other beginners who are unable to hurt them. Jimmy discussed a beginner's sparring experiences:

> He's not, he's not beating guys—he's not boxing with good men in the Gym. He thinks he is, and thinks because he hurts them, he's good, you know. And I said . . . this is not a real, a real fight. This is a workout. That's all this is. This here, I tell you so many times that don't try and hurt a guy cause you're just sparring with him. He's learning just as much as you are. And he can continue—I don't throw him in with good guys. I just throw him in with guys who are equal with him. (December 18, 1996)

In this case, a bullying beginner was being protected by his trainer from the potential wrath of more experienced fighters. In response to this bullying tactic, I asked Jimmy if he thought it would be a good idea for the bullying beginner to be "taught a lesson" by a more experienced fighter. However, Jimmy held hope that the young boxer would learn how to cooperate in sparring without being humiliated or injured.

Giles, a 31-year-old Guyanese trainer, disagreed with holding a bullying beginner back from more experienced boxers. Instead of verbal reasoning, this trainer advocated sending a physical message:

> When you sparring with somebody who don't know how to control himself, you gotta hit him hard so they will know. Now, if you hit me hard, I will hit you hard. So then, they will go easy because they don't want to get hit hard. (January 24, 1997)

It is important to note, however, that increased intensity is a response to inappropriate aggression. Furthermore, the experienced boxer physically communicates the message without causing injury. The intention is to sting the transgressor without a knockout or severe injury. Few boxers undergo a "trial-by-fire"-type masculine rite of passage in which a beginner is hurt as a test of toughness or courage. However, if rough sparring is initiated by a novice, some trainers advocate a measured violent response as a method of teaching proper sparring etiquette.

However, similar experience, skill, and physical strength are not sufficient to establish trust. Many participants in this study preferred to spar with boxers of unequal skill. Contrary to Wacquant's (1992) requirement for an equilibrium of skill in sparring, many participants in this study actively sought a disequilibrium as an opportunity to learn different skills. Lou, a 63-year-old boxer aspiring to box professionally, sparred only with professionals:

> Well, we have a lot of guys in the Gym here and I like to box with somebody who's professional. I don't like to go in with just like amateur-type fighters and take a chance with getting hit with a wild, swinging punch. So I like to box with professionals, guys who've been around, that know how to work with you in the ring. And move. And, uh, try new different things, and experiment. And, you know, you're working out in a nice pace without trying to take somebody's head off. (January 20, 1997)

Ironically, amateur boxers are more dangerous than professional boxers to this older boxer. This sentiment was shared by many others. Experienced, highly skilled boxers have more control of their strength and rarely slip up and cause injury. Furthermore, Lou sought the increased educational benefits derived from sparring with someone who is more skilled. But Lou's comments suggested more than the routine acquisition of skill. Lou desired a partner who knows how to "work with you," who can safely share a learning experience. Lou also stressed creativity and experimentation.

Similarly, Nigel strongly advocated that professionals spar with amateurs as a learning experience. He suggested that when sparring with a lesser-skilled partner

> you don't try to kill him. You try to learn from him. As much, as much as you are better than him you can still learn from him. That is why it's good for a professional to spar with amateur because an amateur do things unorthodox, things that are not really expected to be done by a seasoned professional. So that is why it's good to spar with amateurs from time to time. You make them miss and slip and roll, so as to create an awareness that anything can come at you. Because when you're fighting, hey, anything goes.

Like Lou, Nigel stressed sparring as a shared learning experience in which each partner recognizes and values the other's skills and efforts. When sparring with a lesser-skilled partner, the focus is often on defense, but hardly ever is the partner's weakness exploited. Unlike the participants in Wacquant's study, the boxers in this Gym often were deliberately matched, or matched themselves, in a disequilibrium of skill. The disequilibrium is managed safely by establishing and maintaining an ethos of partnership.

Wacquant (1992) argued, "There must always be a measure of equilibrium between partners, even if that requires purposefully handicapping one of them" (p. 242). What is unclear is how, or by whom, boxers are handicapped in sparring. Wacquant's use of the passive voice suggests that boxers are handicapped by some outside force or because they receive orders from a trainer. Wacquant failed to consider the process of self-handicapping, as articulated by Boulton and Smith (1992). Because sparring partners are hardly ever perfectly matched, and because trainers are not capable of accurately monitoring and completely directing sparring intensity, equilibrium in sparring requires the establishment and internalization of trust and caring.

Sparring sessions are sometimes opportunities for touching experiences of warmth and sharing. Immediately after a sparring session with a long-time partner, Barry, a 47-year-old Jewish professional turned white-collar boxer, was exuberant: "It was great. We were waling on each other. But we've sparred so many times, and know each other so well that it didn't even hurt." Lou recounted a sparring session with a current professional world champion, after which the champion kissed him on the head and said, "You're like my grandfather. How do you do it? God bless you." For Lou, this sparring session was an intimate experience of sharing. He recalled the sparring session quite warmly. The 31-year-old African American middleweight champ's use of "grandfather" suggests that he, too, experienced the sparring session as intimate, shared, and familial.

Cooperative, nonaggressive sparring fits in with Rubin's (1983) definition of intimacy as sharing one's inner life. That sparring is a shared experience is expressed in a vocabulary of cooperation: sparring "partners" work "together with" each other. Such experiences of sharing do not constitute a "covert" intimacy, as Messner (1992a) argued. Sparring is not hidden or disavowed. Rather, I suggest that cooperative sparring is "somatic" intimacy. Like dance partners, sparring partners share their inner (and outer) selves via their bodies. What is being shared is knowledge, creativity, and the bodies themselves. In this sense, the sparring body is simultaneously medium and message.

Nonviolent aggression. The avoidance of violence and injury does not preclude aggressive attempts at domination. It is possible to assert masculine domination without transgressing sparring codes and causing injury. Higher-skilled boxers who spar with novices sometimes taunt the novices' inability to connect with solid punches, although the higher-skilled boxers hold back from inflicting physical punishment. Sometimes, experienced boxers "pull" punches but nonetheless assert their dominance.

Denzel, a recently retired 31-year-old African American professional, argued that an experienced boxer could frustrate another boxer by tapping the other boxer at will. He demonstrated on me by tapping me in the stomach, and in the head, and back to the stomach, all at will. He said, "You know, after a while he gets frustrated and starts swinging wildly." I could easily imagine because I was humiliated by my inability to deflect or block any of his blows and wanted to grab him myself. I witnessed similar sparring sessions several times. In one instance, for example, a seasoned professional sparred with three amateurs in succession. In an attempt to improve conditioning and work on defense, he did not throw any punches but did not allow himself to be hit. However, his demeanor was aggressive and taunting and a couple of the amateurs became visibly frustrated. The professional demonstrated what could easily be interpreted as masculine aggression, but not at the physical expense of the amateurs. In no way could the session be interpreted as intimate, because there was no ethos of partnership. The session was characterized by antagonism rather than warmth. Nonviolent aggressive sparring may serve as a way to maintain a masculine trait without transgressing the Gym's cultural code of physical safety. The practice is somewhat evocative of the Native American practice of "counting coup" during warfare. In this practice, warriors would come close enough to kill their enemies but tap them with a stick instead of inflicting a lethal blow. Both the tapping described by this participant and "counting coup" are attempts at domination. But the target of domination is the will or soul rather than the body.

It also should be emphasized that the partnership ethos exhibited by Gym members in this study does not extend to the "world of boxing." Josh traveled from his home in the Bronx to train at the Gym because the Police Athletic League gyms near his home are "too rough." Josh said that the Gym takes care of its members much more than do other gyms. On a continuum of aggression in sparring, the Gym, as a whole, is likely on the less aggressive end. This is likely because of the generally older membership relative to youth clubs and boxing teams.

Age and experience. Many boxers in their mid-20s or older expressed an aversion to sparring with younger men, whom they deemed likely to be more aggressive in asserting their masculinity. It is difficult, however, to judge the effects of age without considering experience. Many novices who are older are as aggressive as their younger counterparts; that is, exposure to and internalization of sparring etiquette moderates aggression more so than does chronological age.

One possible reason why older boxers are likely to be less aggressive is an appreciation for pain and injuries. Veteran boxers often have experienced injuries during their boxing careers and may subsequently develop sympathy for others. Lou conceived the process of becoming a "fighter" as a rite of passage:

> I think it kind of makes men out of boys, you know, being a fighter. It gives you a little more insight into who you are and how vulnerable you are. Good point. I like the way I just said that. Vulnerable. (January 20, 1997)

For Lou, learning not to be aggressive was a sign of "being a man." Ironically, Lou constructed a mature masculinity in which the recognition and acceptance of vulnerability is an asset.

Age, Locker Room Talk, and Verbal Intimacy

Age moderates masculinity most noticeably in the nature and content of locker room talk. In Curry's (1991) study, the participants were all undergraduate college students. Although Curry did not include the ages of his participants, no participant could have been more than 25 years old because of Division I regulations. The locker room talk in this Gym (restricted to the men's locker room) was very different from the locker room talk in Curry's study. The men in this study were much less concerned with asserting dominance through verbal taunts. In fact, I shared several moments of emotional intimacy with male Gym members, especially in discussing relationships with women.

There is a contingent of teenage male Gym members who sometimes engage in a kind of locker room talk similar to the talk in Curry's study (I witnessed two "outbursts" during the period of this study). However, this kind of behavior is closely monitored and discouraged by older Gym members, myself included. Older Gym members rarely issue verbal sanctions. But that is not necessary to moderate the scope and content of the teenage braggadocio. Furtive glances and looks of disapproval almost always do the trick. Furthermore, successful professionals who are more concerned with their wives, children, and making a living establish and monitor models of appropriate locker room talk and behavior. Sexist locker room talk was successfully resisted (see Sabo & Messner, 1994, p. 215) by integrating adolescent and adult male athletes. Perhaps the sharpest difference between the results of this study and Curry's study is in talk about women. First, the increasing number of women Gym members is widely, and often enthusiastically, accepted by male Gym members. Most of the male participants in this study talked about their relationships with women in an emotionally sensitive way. Of course, most of the participants in this study were in their mid-20s or older. Furthermore, unlike many other professional and collegiate athletes, professional boxers are not coddled and sheltered and must keep full-time jobs to support themselves, that is, male Gym members are, by and large, adult men, sharing the same concerns many men face: making a living, finding a life's partner, and raising a family.

As a 32-year-old recently married man, I was a likely candidate for discussions with men who were considering marriage. Stretch, a 26-year-old Guyanese American professional boxer and a 6-feet-tall welterweight, often discussed his live-in girlfriend and asked about my feelings on marriage. Stretch spoke openly, freely, and warmly of his relationship, and he was more interested in discussing romantic relationships than in boxing or wrestling (even though he was an avid wrestling fan). One day while getting dressed in the locker room, Paisan, a 33-year-old Italian American amateur and aspiring professional, lamented that he wanted to get married, but "I guess I haven't met the right girl." Our conversation was warm and open, albeit brief. He shared a sense of emptiness because he was not involved in an intimate relationship with a woman. I shared the emotional fulfillment I derive from being married and offered encouragement for him to actively pursue his desires. Far from treating women as objects, these men openly spoke of their desire to establish and maintain intimate emotional relationships with women.

As Rubin (1983) noted, desires for intimacy often are associated with fears of intimacy. After discussing at length how his wife was his best friend, Nigel noted that he also fathered several children with other women during his marriage. After discussing an emotional turmoil caused by ambivalent feelings toward his live-in girlfriend, Denzel emphasized that he was still always willing to engage in sexual intercourse because, as he said, "I'm a man, you know?" After discussing vulnerabilities he attributed to a recovery from drug addiction, Paisan discussed his prediction that "no one will hurt me" during the Golden Gloves tournament. Biker Dude, a 37-year-old Puerto Rican man, followed his discussion of the emotional pain he experienced in a failed marriage with the sexual objectification of a younger woman with whom he was currently involved. Male boxers were able to express vulnerability and emotion at times, but they often (though not always) balanced such moments with assertions of masculine dominance.

Like Klein's (1995b) Mexican baseball players, many boxers in this study exhibited a broad range of seemingly inconsistent behaviors. One teenage boxer who recently turned professional was particularly aggressive with his peers in locker room talk and competitive matches, yet he was one of the more delicate and gracious sparring partners. Conversely, Paisan was delicate and warm in locker room talk but aggressive in sparring sessions.

Conclusions

Boxing culture in the Gym promotes sparring practices that avoid injury, treats the "opponent" as a partner, and often is characterized by a shared intimacy. Here, I return to Sabo and Messner's (1994) strategy, "Be a Buddy to Your Body," and address some of the questions raised earlier in this chapter. According to the sparring practices in the Gym, this strategy might better be changed to "Be a Buddy to Your Buddy." To avoid violence and injury, boxers in this study adopted a view in which the "opponent" is a partner. This ethos of partnership facilitates the expression of a somatic intimacy in which sparring partners share their bodies, their knowledge, and their creativity. The presence of older men in the Gym facilitated expressions of verbal intimacy and vulnerability.

However, there is no evidence to suggest that the men in this study considered their practices and ideologies as either subversive or supportive of male dominance. With respect to expressions of emotion and vulnerability, masculinity and manhood were redefined in a way that perpetuates a somewhat ironic notion of masculine strength and virility: "Be man enough to be gentle (as in a *gentle*man)" or "Be man enough to cry," so to speak. One might argue that these redefinitions were attempts to shore up threats to hegemonic masculinity (though certainly none of the men in this study did). Yet, benevolent attitudes toward the body and intimate relations with other men (either somatic or verbal) are at many levels inconsistent with dominant forms of masculinity.

In his theorization of male dominance in sport practices, Dunning (1994) argued that social conditions profoundly influence the intensity of male aggression. Similarly, Messner (1992b, pp. 171-172) argued that changes in macrolevel social institutions—such as child rearing, family, politics, and education—are necessary to effect the "humanization" of sport. Although macrolevel influences are undoubtedly significant, these positions neglect the possibility of specific, fragmented egalitarian practices within hierarchical structures.

Ideologies and practices in the Gym that are inconsistent with dominant forms of masculinity can be only partly resolved by structural considerations of age and the political economy of the Gym. At this point, many people would agree that isolating groups of young males, notably in college fraternities, the military, and athletic teams, has a potential for deleterious outcomes. For many men in this study, intimacy, the rejection of women's objectification, and the expression of emotion and vulnerability were redefined as symbols of strength in a framework of an adult masculinity. Perhaps as adult men develop intimate relationships with female partners and children, they also develop empathy for girls' and women's issues (see Early, 1994). For the men in this study, the primary axis for verbal intimacy is age, not gender.

Although verbal intimacy may be attributed in large part to the influence of age, cooperative sparring cannot be so attributed. Structured cooperation and the economic benefits of participation for trainers and the Gym owner are enabling conditions for a benign approach to the body, but not sufficient explanations in and of themselves. Boxers are actively engaged in maintaining cultural codes that engender an ethos of partnership in sparring practices that often provide a space for somatic intimacy, creative expression, and exuberance. A rejection of physical aggression in sparring did not entail a rejection of masculinity. Rather, definitions of masculinity were redefined so as to be congruous with boxers' cultural codes, that is, deterring physical aggression in sparring had less to do with new definitions of masculinity than with an enculturation into boxing culture.

The broad range of men's behaviors and ideologies exhibited in this study presents problems for the theorization of gender. Psychoanalytic frameworks of dichotomously opposed masculine and feminine traits alone fail to address the situationally specific experiences and meanings and the range and inconsistencies of ideologies and practices exhibited by boxers in this study. Messner's (1992b) combination of personal agency, personality, and social structure is particularly useful in dealing with broadly diverse ideologies, discourse, and practices. But although Messner (1992a) enjoined us to locate these ideologies and practices within a "gender order," I suggest that the egalitarian discourses and practices in the Gym neither disrupt nor contribute to broad relations of male dominance. Although certain egalitarian practices in the Gym may be related to sexual egalitarianism (e.g., accepting women as Gym members of equal status), there is no evidence to suggest that men in this study reached an epiphany of egalitarian enlightenment that extended to other areas of their lives. In fact, some men who treated women as equals inside the Gym objectified and oppressed women outside the Gym. Finally, the salience of gender relative to age and sport's institutional structure is called into question.

Boxers in this study successfully created a cultural and institutional space that allowed egalitarian relations alongside and within a competitive boxing society and a hierarchical larger society. The results of this study give concrete examples of some of the points brought up by Sabo and Messner (1994) in their 11-point strategy intended to change thinking about sport. The results of this study also, I suggest, point to a need to discuss social issues in sport without reifying gender differences by conforming ideologies and practices to a gender framework or order. Although physical aggression in sport is still a problem for men, it is also increasingly becoming a problem for women. Rather than discussing aggression and the denial of intimacy as immanent in a male model of sport or looking for alternatives only in Oriental or feminist sporting practices, I suggest that we might well focus on the hegemonic ideology of competition and the age- and sex-segregated institution of sport and develop and nurture the egalitarian sporting practices that already exist.

Notes

1. It is difficult to categorize boxers as recreational, amateur, or professional. For example, many former professionals continue to train for fitness and recreation. Many amateurs aspire to become professionals, whereas many others do not. Also, there are so few competitive opportunities that describing someone who trains all year and has one bout as "competitive" fails to reflect the diversity of motivations and experiences.

2. "White-collar sparring" is predominantly engaged in by whites. African Americans and Latinos, even those who box primarily as recreation, rarely participate. However, not all participants are college-educated or employees in professional occupations. That the division falls primarily along lines of race speaks more to the public performance of racial and ethnic identities than to practical differences in sparring.

3. Many Gym members suggested that Latino boxers and trainers took a more aggressive approach to sparring. These allegations, however, are contested by Latino Gym mem-

bers and not conclusively verified. The complexity of this issue requires more space than is possible in this chapter.

4. Women's experiences in the Gym invoke many rhetorical paradoxes. Gender relations in the Gym are complex and varied. Again because of space limitations, women's experiences in the Gym are not fully developed here.

7

Researching Sports Injury

Reconstructing Dangerous Masculinities

KEVIN YOUNG
PHILIP WHITE

In Canada, the systematic sociological study of sports injury was pioneered quite recently by Michael D. Smith (1987, 1991; Weinstein, Smith, & Wiesenthal, 1995), whose research posed preliminary questions about the social, physical, and legal implications of injury. Concomitantly, a body of research literature on aggression, injury, and pain in sport has emerged across North America (Curry & Strauss, 1994; Messner, 1992b; Nixon, 1994a, 1994b, 1996b; Rail, 1990, 1992; Young, 1993; Young, White, & McTeer, 1994), much of it raising critical questions related to gender dynamics. Although we acknowledge the importance of physicality and injury in the lives of female athletes and continue to work in that area (Young, 1997; Young & White, 1995), this chapter examines the physical hazards of hegemonic masculinity codes for male athletes. Specifically, we attempt to show how social processes producing dominant forms of masculinity and popular sports practices interact to systematically produce injury, disability, and even death.

Our analysis begins with a sociological discussion of masculinity and masculinities. Here, we address the debate on masculinities as social constructions, suggesting that relations of power are fundamental to theorizing not just the gender order but also what have been identified in the literature as "hierarchies" of masculinity (Bird, 1996; Connell, 1987, 1995; Hearn, 1992; Kimbrell, 1995; Pyke, 1996; Segal, 1990). From this understanding, we explore the notion of "dangerous masculinities," critically interrogating the extant research on damaged male bodies. Using primary and secondary data sources, we then present evidence for the case that gendered norms in sport often have deleterious consequences for male participants. In arguing our case, we use both quantitative evidence from various Canadian and international sources on the extent and nature of serious injury across different types of sports and draw on our qualitative research on the experiences of seriously injured male athletes in Canada (White, Young, & Gillett, 1995; Young, 1993; Young & White, 1998; Young et al., 1994). We conclude by asking some questions about the need to reconstruct dangerous masculinities and by proposing some directions for future research.

Because it is one of the aims of this volume to underscore the reflexivity that men bring to their lives, we think it important to acknowledge that we arrived at research into sports-related pain and injury, at least in part, through direct experience. We mention this because we have learned that when we raise questions regarding violence, aggression, and sport, a common response by some people (predominantly men) who seem threatened by such challenges often follows the doubtful logic contained in questions such as "Oh, yeah? Have you ever played contact sports? Have you ever been injured?" Fortunately (and unfortunately) for us both, the answer to both of these questions is "Yes." Both authors had prolonged and active careers in soccer and rugby, both have been hospitalized with serious injuries, and both currently endure ongoing physical discomfort directly attributable to injuries suffered when younger. We are also both men. Having said that, of course, our personal biographies hardly count as scientific evidence that males suffer sport injuries more or differently than do females, nor do they identify sports injury as a particularly serious social problem. However, what they do is to acknowledge our complicity in the production of dangerous masculinities that, at the very least, puts us in a nuanced position to speak on these matters. This chapter, then, examines how a combination of dominant forms of masculinity and taken-for-granted ways of playing sport combine to exact a considerable toll on the physical well-being of many males.

Masculine Rules, Masculine Consequences

Hierarchical Masculinities

Current thinking about masculinity ranges from social psychological sex role theory, to feminist models of masculinities under patriarchy, to models based on notions of rediscovered "traditional" masculinity emerging from the "mythopoetic" movement. Kimmel (1992) indicated what has been made clear from this debate:

> Definitions of masculinity are constantly changing. Masculinity does not bubble up into behavioral codes from our genetic makeup, nor does it float in a current of the collective unconscious, waiting to be actualized by any particular man and, simultaneously, all men. Masculinity is socially constructed, changing (1) from one culture to another, (2) within any one culture over time, (3) over the course of any individual man's life, and (4) between and among different groups of men depending on class, race, ethnicity, and sexuality. (p. 166)

To understand how gender is socially constructed, we emphasize the importance of relational processes that are suffused by power differences between women and men, but also between men and other men, and women and other women (Sabo & Gordon, 1995). These processes are dialectical because people both live within and are socially constrained by social structures; they also operationalize human agency in how they experience and construct their gendered lives (Whitson, 1984; Young, 1993).

Hierarchical masculinities have been subject to extensive theorizing in recent gender studies (Connell, 1987, 1995; Hearn, 1992; Morgan, 1992; Rutherford, 1992; Segal, 1990). For example, researchers have attempted to explain the processes through which power and privilege are differentially allocated within and between groups of men. Processes occurring within intermale dominance hierarchies themselves operate within other systems of social stratification, as Sabo and Gordon (1995) observed:

> Some critical feminist approaches are attempting to fill the need for a conceptual scheme that theorizes the varied and shifting dimensions of male domination as they interact with other forms of social domination. The term *multiple systems of domination analysis* has been used to describe these efforts. What we are suggesting is that the adaptation of feminist theory . . . needs to somehow address the differential exploitation of lesser-status, marginalized male subgroups (e.g., men of color, gay men, underclass men) in the changing gender order. (p. 13)

Although, in our view, it is appropriate to acknowledge the existence of multiple masculinities, it is also important to recognize relations between them. In his analysis of the social organization of masculinity, Connell (1995) identified the principal patterns of masculinity as hegemonic, subordinate, complicit, and marginal, but there is likely a kaleidoscope of masculinities beyond them. The relations between these broad configurations collectively form a cultural dynamic that tends toward the reproduction of a gender order that subordinates women and less dominant masculinities.

For our purposes, Connell's (1987) by now familiar concept of "hegemonic masculinity," which refers to an ideological construction that serves and maintains the interests of dominant male groups, is particularly useful. For Connell, a key aspect of the idea of hegemonic masculinity is to reject the notion of a monolithic "maleness." Rather, societies such as Canada are seen to encompass a range of "masculine" possibilities. Some men embrace hegemonic masculinity, others protest it, and others feel more or less comfortable with certain aspects of it. There is, then, no single, homogeneous notion of maleness or manhood that is defined by an essentially endowed set of norms and values.

Despite the complex, diverse, and relational basis of masculinities, within a particular set of historical and social conditions, some types of masculinity are clearly ascendant over others. Some men enjoy more access to power and influence than others; other men suffer from levels of exploitation, marginalization, and abuse that also are experienced by women in the workplace and other areas of society, such as sport. What most men in patriarchal societies share in common, however, is the ability to benefit from their privileged position as a gender class in the form of certain rewards or "patriarchal dividends."

The Rewards of Masculinity:
Patriarchal Dividends

Because hegemonic masculinity is an ideological construct, many men (including many powerful men in an economic, political, or social sense) do not adhere to ideal typical characteristics such as physical toughness or emotional stoicism. It is the legitimacy of domination that is important, and although many men do not conform to the blueprint of hegemonic masculinity, they may nevertheless benefit from it. In this sense, they contribute to the reproduction of hegemonic masculinity, as Connell (1995) argued:

The number of men rigorously practicing the hegemonic pattern in its entirety may be quite small. Yet the majority of men benefit from its hegemony, because they benefit from the patriarchal dividend, the advantage men in general gain from the overall subordination of women. (p. 79)

Feminist and other research has identified gender domination in a number of social arenas. For example, patriarchal dividends are visible in men's domination of the workplace, the media, and the state, men's control over the practices of violence, men's enjoyment of privileges of wealth and income, and a gender ideology that normalizes the objectification and marginalization of women in general (Connell, 1995). As suggested previously, men may be complicit in the process of hegemonic masculinity in a number of ways, as Connell (1995) noted:

> Marriage, fatherhood, and family life often involve extensive compromises with women rather than naked domination or an uncontested display of authority. A great many men who draw their patriarchal dividend also respect their wives and mothers, are never violent towards women, do their accustomed share of the housework, bring home the family wage, and can easily convince themselves that feminists must be bra-burning extremists. (pp. 79-80)

In brief, it may be argued that gender relations generally reproduce social inequalities in status, prestige, and material rewards. As Connell (1995) continued, "In the rich capitalist countries, men's average incomes are approximately double women's average income. . . . Men are vastly more likely to control a major block of capital as chief executive of a major corporation, or as a direct owner" (p. 82). Sociological research clearly shows how men profit from the current gender order. Men enjoy more power, wealth, prestige, and opportunity than do women, a process that, according to Jackson (1990), has even affected men's physical selves:

> Learning that you were naturally entitled to social, legal and financial power over women was translated into learning to hold power over your body— tautening your muscles, holding yourself firm and upright, striding with a cocky strut, throwing out your chest and walking from the shoulders. (p. 54)

But, for all of this, the alliance between men, hegemonic masculinity, and social privilege is undoubtedly strained and precarious. As students of men's health have observed, claims of patriarchal dividends should be made cautiously because, in the words of one antisexist male collective, "Our power in society as men not only oppresses women but also imprisons us in a deadening masculinity which cripples our relationships—with each other, with women, with ourselves" (Achilles Heel, in Segal, 1990, p. 287).

The Costs of Masculinity: Damaged Men

> I gradually have come to realize that I, with every other man I know, have been limited and diverted from whatever our real potential might have been by the prefabricated mold of the male sex role. (Robert Brannon, quoted in Ehrenreich, 1983, p. 124)

> The initial and irrefutable reason for men to transform themselves was not to improve their social status or expand their souls—but to save their lives. No treatise or document of men's liberation, no matter how brief, failed to mention the bodily injuries sustained by role abiding men, from ulcers and accidents to the most "masculine" of illnesses, coronary heart disease. (Ehrenreich, 1983, p. 140)

It may thus be argued that men pay a price for the "privileged" positions they occupy and enjoy, as Kimmel (1995b) reported:

> Most of the leading causes of death among men are the results of men's behaviors—gendered behaviors that leave men more vulnerable to certain illnesses and not others. Masculinity is one of the more significant risk factors associated with men's illness. (p. vii)

For example, to be socialized into most dominant forms of masculinity involves learning and celebrating emotional denial, distance, and affective neutrality, but also the cultural importance of actions that often exact a physical toll (Jackson, 1990). Male prowess often is based on types of physicality that are frequently destructive but that also often involve conspicuous silences around health (Rutherford, 1992). As a result, sensitization to bodily well-being and matters of preventive health in general become viewed as the jurisdiction of women and "ambiguous" men. Cultural prohibitions on health orientations for men outside of sport are, of course, visible in the disproportionate numbers of women found in venues of health care provision (Hearn, 1992). In sum, health care interests tend to be conspicuously absent in the task orientation of men in general.

At almost every age, men die at greater rates than do women and more often from preventable causes (Stillion, 1995). In North America, the leading causes of death among males between the ages of 15 and 19 are car accidents, suicide, and AIDS, all at rates far higher than for females. Among Canadian men aged 20 to 44, 28 per 100,000 die from suicide, followed by car accidents at 21, and AIDS at 18. The corresponding rates for women are 7 suicide deaths, 7 deaths from car accidents, and 1 AIDS death per 100,000. In the 15 to 19 age group, the death rate from suicide was almost four times higher for males than females, although the death rate from car accidents was almost twice as high. Gender differences in both death rates from external causes start to widen following early childhood (Statistics Canada, 1995). By the early teens, accidents become a leading cause of death, but more so for males than for females.

In the American workplace, males constitute more than 90% of those employed in dangerous occupations, and 93% of the 6,000 people killed at work each year (Toscana & Windau, 1994). In Canada, Reasons (1985) and Reasons, Ross, and Patterson (1981) also documented the hazardous nature of a number of workplaces dominated by men, including the asbestos, mining, paper milling, construction, electrical, and chemical industries. Consequently, males have much higher rates of workplace injury than do females, a trend that is not disappearing and that is at least partly attributable to gender processes, as Young (1993) argued:

> Although this differential may be explained in part by the often uneven numbers of men and women involved in dangerous work, it would be a mistake to overlook the explanatory potential of a culture of "masculinism" which tends to accompany male preserves, vocationally and elsewhere. (p. 379)

Put simply, data from the literature on occupational health and safety not only highlight male health and injury issues but underscore an association between these trends and the "culture of masculinism" that seems to encourage risk taking and discourage thoughtful preventive measures.

Other aspects of the workplace are also hazardous for men. For example, it has been suggested that stress now accounts for 10% of all workplace health problems, indicating a huge jump in stress-related problems in the last two decades. For Kimbrell (1995), much of this trend is rooted in structural changes in the nature of work precipitated by "downsizing," restructuring, and "outsourcing" introduced by companies since the early 1980s. Millions of displaced workers, the greater proportion of whom are men, have experienced difficulty regaining employment, have found alternative forms of employment less rewarding and lower paid, and have increasingly had to work at more than one job. Of the members of the workforce who currently hold two or more jobs in the United States, men outnumber women by two to one (U.S. Bureau of Labor Statistics, 1991).

Loss of work and the experience of unemployment also have ramifications for health, again disproportionately among men, who have been more likely than women to lose their jobs in recent years (U.S. Bureau of

Labor Statistics, 1992). Victims of restructuring have included both blue-collar workers in the traditional industries such as automotive manufacturing, mining, and steel production and white-collar workers, often men in their 40s and 50s (Kimbrell, 1995). These long-term shifts have been linked with markedly negative health consequences. Merva and Fowles (1992; see also McLanahan & Glass, 1985), for example, showed that for a large metropolitan area in the United States, a 1% increase in unemployment between 1990 and 1992 was linked to a 5.6% increase in deaths due to heart disease, a 3.1% increase in deaths due to stroke, a 6.7% increase in homicides, a 3.4% increase in violent crimes, and a 2.4% increase in property crimes.

Dangerous Masculinities Related to Sport

There is evidence that the health of many men is compromised during their leisure time and, more specifically, that men are more susceptible than women to sports injury. This is not to suggest that sports injuries are unique to men, especially with regard to high-performance sport (cf. Young & White, 1995). Neither is it true that specific codes of masculinity are alone responsible for injury. It is reasonable to argue that participants in highly intense and/or competitive types of involvement are also vulnerable to injury, regardless of gender. In a similar vein, we also should caution that gender is not necessarily an exclusive predictor of injury in all sport/exercise arenas that celebrate the testing of personal body limits, whether it be, for example, running an ultramarathon, pursuing excellence in dance, or exploring physicality through yoga. In these types of activities, the norms of the sport-specific culture itself may have relatively little to do with gender.

Having said this, there are numerous ways that men, more than women, take risks, endure pain, and suffer ill health through sport and play. Body-building, for example, is a particularly masculinist arena that may, ironically and somewhat paradoxically, foster ill health. As Klein (1995a) suggested, to be a serious bodybuilder is to celebrate the endurance of pain during training and to normalize the use of anabolic steroids. Beyond the confines of the elite gym, however, steroid use has grown to alarming proportions among young people. In Canada, it is estimated that 83,000 males between the ages of 11 and 18 use anabolic steroids either to improve their athletic performances or simply to enhance their appearance (Canadian Centre for Drug-Free Sport, 1993). At the same time, research also shows that the misuse of anabolic steroids is injurious to cardiovascular, hepatic, endocrinologic, and behavioral health (Siegal, 1989).

Overuse injuries are also examples of negative health outcomes that may be associated with dominant forms of masculinity, but not necessarily with sports that involve direct violence to the body. Some male athletes construct alternative ways of masculine identification by focusing more on endurance than aggression. Swimmers, long-distance runners, speed skaters, cross-country skiers, and others rely on the ability to silence pain to establish their allegiance with hegemonic masculinity.

Typically, though, research conducted to date has explored the role of violent, contact, or high-risk sport in the process of masculinization (Curry & Strauss, 1994; Sabo & Panepinto, 1990; Young et al., 1994). As a central experience among school-age boys, sport confirms and consolidates violent physicality as one of the cornerstones of masculinity that "not only defines itself positively through assertiveness, virility, toughness, and independence, but also negatively by defining itself in opposition of what it is not—feminine or homosexual" (Jackson, 1990, pp. 123-124; see also Bryson, 1987; Connell, 1983; Messner, 1990d; Sabo & Panepinto, 1990; White & Gillett, 1994; Young, 1993).

Dominant sport values are often paradoxical. Although violence is often accepted, even celebrated, there is also growing concern about serious sports injury. A recent example of this paradox is that although numerous rules in ice hockey have been changed for the purpose of preventing catastrophic (often cervical) injuries, the popular cultural images and meanings of the sport remain largely unaltered. For example, although the rougher aspects of the sport constitute only a fraction of the overall "action," daily newspapers continue to rely on them to sell copy, often using photographs of crushing hits and fistfights. The same is true of the electronic media (Young, 1990; Young & Smith, 1988-1989). The paradox here lies in how media images and representations ignore the injurious outcomes of aggression and fighting in professional hockey; the latter, it recently has been argued, is a leading cause of games lost in the National Hockey League (Dryden, 1997). In two examples from the 1995/1996 season, fighting resulted in Rob Ray of the Buffalo Sabres having his orbital bones crushed and Bill Berg of the Toronto Maple Leafs breaking his leg. In 1997, Nick Kypreos of the Toronto Maple Leafs suffered a serious concussion in a fight and never returned to the NHL.

In what follows, we present evidence from a variety of sources to help identify the injurious outcomes of the processes whereby physical risk among boys and men is naturalized, promoted, and celebrated. In doing this, we show how this process has become so entrenched and internalized that it is difficult to see beyond, to see that alternative less physical and forceful versions of masculinity seem at face value to be irrational and inappropriate, especially in such a macho setting as sport. In examining these processes, we also point to their insidious consequences for men's health. Just as Bordo (1990) identified how women who are eating-disordered feel more subjectively empowered when they are physically (and objectively) disempowered to the point that they approach severe illness and even death, so men may derive meaning from violent sport practices that at any moment may result in varying degrees of physical damage. The insidiousness of this process lies in the degree to which the inevitability of injury and the physical and emotional pain it implies go largely unproblematized in the world of sport. As Young (1993) argued in his study of masculinist work cultures, including that of professional male athletes, there is currently a significant silence in the culture of male sport about the physical toll exacted on players in the process of sport-related masculinization. This is even true for collectives like players' associations that purportedly are designed to protect players' careers and health.

To better understand the relation between dominant codes of masculinity, male involvement in sport, and injury, we now provide an overview of the research documenting gender differences in injury rates of sport in general and in select sports. The review is not definitive in terms of establishing the size of the problem posed by catastrophic injury. It is not the purpose of this chapter to suggest that sports injuries are epidemic or that all men fall prey to injury-promoting sport norms. To put our evidence in perspective, we should caution that aggregate data from both convenience and national samples show injury rates in the general population to be substantial but not rampant (cf. McCutcheon, Curtis, & White, 1997). We offer, instead, a preliminary step toward understanding how serious sports injuries are socially structured. On the basis of these patterns, we argue that there is need for a better understanding of the gendering of sports injury and for progressive intervention to make future sport practices safer and, arguably, more humane.

Gender Differences in Sports Injury

Catastrophic athletic injuries, although comprising a small percentage of all catastrophic injuries, are tragic events affecting the lives of mostly young healthy individuals. For example, of the 2,500 new cases of paraplegia and the

1,050 new cases of quadriplegia in the United States each year, about 7% (174 paraplegia and 74 quadriplegia) are related to sports injury. Of the 410,000 people who sustain brain injury each year, 17,600 are left with some type of permanent disability. About 10% of brain injuries are the result of sport or recreational activity (Mueller, Cantu, & Van Camp, 1996, p. 1). Between 1989 and 1993, the car accident rate among 15 to 24 year-old males fell from 655 per thousand to 514. . . . Sport injuries overtook car crashes as the leading cause of accidents in that high risk group. (Carey, 1995, p. A3)

Sources from a number of countries show definitive gender differences in patterns of sports injury, variously defined. In the United States, for example, Mueller et al. (1996) reported comparative rates of injury in high school sport.

As the data derived from their research and reported in Table 7.1 show, injury rates were, with only a few exceptions, higher for males than for females. In absolute terms, football was the most common source of injury among males on measures of serious injury, injury resulting in disability, and direct fatality. In relation to numbers involved, ice hockey and gymnastics carried more risk for participants. Females were much less likely to be injured in sport in general, although female gymnasts were relatively at risk.

In Canada, a recent study (Tator, Edmonds, & Lapczak, 1993) reported on 516 incidents causing either death or long-term disablement in 1992 (see Table 7.2). Among those injured or killed, 84.7% were male and approximately one third were 30 years of age or younger. Although another study conducted by Statistics Canada (Statistics Canada, 1995) reported an increase in sport accidents from 1988 to 1993, serious injuries in hockey have declined from 79 in 1986 to 26 in 1992. Nevertheless, hockey accounted for 4.6% of catastrophic injuries in Ontario in 1992, of which 92.3% occurred in males.

Major contributors to catastrophic sports injuries in Ontario were water sports such as boating, canoeing, and fishing—presumably to some extent caused by crashes and drowning rather than by inherent dangers in the activities themselves. Males accounted for 86.5% of those injured in water sports. Motor sports, such as snowmobiling, were also hazardous (22.4% of all injuries), again particularly for males who constituted 89.7% of those injured. Field sports, including football, rugby, soccer, and track and field, accounted for only 2.6% of all serious injuries in Ontario. Almost all of the injuries in field sports were sustained by male athletes. Although not reported in Table 7.2, findings for sport and recreation-related fatalities in

Table 7.1   Injury Rates Per 100,000 Participants in U.S. High Schools by Sport and Gender, 1982-1983 to 1991-1992

	Fatal Injury			Disabling Injury			Serious Injury		
Sport	N	Male	Female	N	Male	Female	N	Male	Female
Fall sports									
Football	48	0.35	0.00	103	0.75	0.00	112	0.81	0.00
Soccer	2	0.10	0.00	0	0.00	0.00	4	0.20	0.00
Winter sports									
Basketball	0	0.00	0.00	2	0.02	0.03	2	0.04	0.00
Gymnastics	1	1.75	0.00	5	1.75	1.28	3	0.00	0.96
Ice hockey	1	0.43	0.00	4	1.73	0.00	2	0.86	0.00
Swimming	0	0.00	0.00	4	0.24	0.24	3	0.36	0.00
Wrestling	2	0.08	0.00	16	0.66	0.00	9	0.37	0.00
Spring sports									
Baseball	3	0.07	0.00	7	0.17	0.00	6	0.15	0.00
Lacrosse	1	0.57	0.00	0	0.00	0.00	0	0.00	0.00
Track and field	9	0.17	0.03	6	0.13	0.00	6	0.13	0.00

Data are taken from Mueller, Cantu, and Van Camp (1996).

Ontario in 1992, numbering 226 in all, also showed a disproportionately heavy toll among males. Males accounted for 62.5% of fatalities in winter sports, 89.5% of fatalities in water sports, and 91.5% of fatalities in motor sports.

In a study of sports injuries among young Canadians (age 5 to 19), males accounted for 68% of the 37,169 recorded treatments in hospital emergency rooms in 1990 and 1991 (Ellison & Mackenzie, 1993). By comparison, only 57.8% of patients treated for nonsport injuries were male. Injured boys outnumbered injured girls at all ages in the sample. For males, ice hockey accounted for the highest proportion of injuries in each age group, although this might be accounted for by the overall popularity of the game rather than by the nature of the game itself. For females, basketball injuries were the most frequent of those reported.

Ellison and Mackenzie (1993) also reported that males tend to incur more severe injuries than do females. At each age, males were more often

Table 7.2 Sport and Recreational Injuries by Sport Type and Gender
in 1992

Sport Type	Gender			
	Male		Female	
	N	Percentage	N	Percentage
Water sports (boating, diving, fishing, water skiing, etc.)	135	86.5	21	13.5
Motor sports (ATV, snowmobiling, etc.)	114	89.7	13	10.3
Bicycling	73	81.1	17	18.9
Winter sports				
Hockey	24	92.3	2	7.7
Alpine skiing	12	80.0	3	20.0
Other	11	44.0	14	56.0
Field sports				
Football	5	100.0	0	0.0
Rugby	3	100.0	0	0.0
Soccer	5	100.0	0	0.0
Track and field	2	100.0	0	0.0
Baseball	18	94.7	1	5.3
Miscellaneous (17 activities, e.g., inline skating, skydiving, hiking)	35	81.0	8	19.0

SOURCE: Data are taken from McLaren (1992).

admitted to the hospital or held for observation as a result of their injuries.
This difference might, in part, be explained by variations in the nature of
injuries experienced by males and females. For respondents over the age
of 10, boys were more likely than girls to have been treated for a bone frac-
ture, a cut or laceration, a concussion, or an abrasion. Females were more
commonly treated for sprains and strains (particularly of the lower ex-
tremities), inflammation, or swelling. These differences possibly reflect

boys' propensities to be more often involved in high-risk sports or physical contact sports and for them to play sports more aggressively than girls (Messner, 1990d; Nicholl, Coleman, & Williams, 1993; Zaricznyj, Shattuck, Mast, Robertson, & D'elia, 1980). Gender differences in sports injury also were examined in a recent study of Finnish athletes (Kujala et al., 1995). Reporting on acute injuries requiring medical treatment, the findings showed gender differences to be more pronounced among athletes aged 20 to 34 than among adolescents, a difference attributed by the authors to adult men having a "rougher style than women" (p. 1467). Among the sports included in the study (soccer, ice hockey, volleyball, basketball, judo, and karate), the highest risks were in judo, karate, and ice hockey, suggesting a positive relation between bodily contact and injury. Interestingly, the authors speculated that catastrophic hockey injuries are less frequent in Finland than in Canada, possibly because of the larger playing surface but also because of the less aggressive European style of play. Both of these possibilities suggest differing cultures of sport between males and females, types of sports, and societies.

Gender also has consequences beyond the physical toll that sports injury exacts on the lives of individual men and women. The risks associated with sport also have economic consequences for the community as a whole. On this issue, Nicholl, Coleman, and Williams (1995) projected that each year in England and Wales there are 29 million sports injury incidents, of which 9.8 million require medical treatment or render the victims unable to take part in their usual activities. Among injury incidents reported in the study, 75% were sustained by males, and more than one third were incurred by men aged 16 to 25 years. Soccer accounted for more than 25% of injuries, or an estimated 8.6 million incidents per year, although the rate of injury in soccer was not as high as for other sports. In relative terms, rugby was more hazardous than soccer and other sports. The risk of injury in rugby was 95.7 per 1000 occasions of participation, about 50% higher than for soccer.

Several studies have offered estimates of the health care costs of managing and treating sport and exercise-related injuries. Nicholl et al. (1993), for example, estimated that the total annual cost of sport and exercise-related injuries in the population aged 16 to 45 in England and Wales was £643 million, with a possible annual cost of £354 million for the treatment of recurring injuries. Given that males participate more than females in physically risky sports, it is likely that they are also more responsible for a higher proportion of health care costs attributable to the treatment and management of sports injuries. As Nicholl, Coleman, and Brazier (1994) reported, "The rates of injury associated with jogging, keep-fit exercising (such as aerobics), and swimming are all less than one-fifth of the rates associated with rugby, soccer, (ice) hockey, and cricket" (p. 118).

Other international studies have included estimates of health care costs of sports injuries, although methodological disparities make comparisons difficult, and few examine gender effects. In the United Kingdom, a Sports Council study (1991) found that 7% of sports injuries resulted in participants taking time off work, resulting in a total of 11.5 million working days lost annually in England and Wales, at a cost of £575 million in production value. In Denmark, Sorensen and Sonne-holm (1980) estimated that the annual cost of treating "acute sport injuries" was £2.3 million. A Swiss study, based on data from the Swiss Accident Insurance Association for the years 1963 to 1973, estimated that the total direct and indirect costs of sport accidents in 1976 were £400 million (1976 prices) (Fasler, 1976). From New Zealand, Hume and Marshall (1994) reported that 15% of the treatments received at the Dunedin Hospital Emergency Department were for sports injuries and that sport accounted for 17% of all injuries compensated by the Accident Compensation Corporation.

In sum, we believe that these aggregate data provide strong support for the position that gender is a key determinant of both sports injury as well as the costs of injury to the individual and to society as a whole.

Rethinking Masculinity:
Directions for Future Research

In his hugely popular book *Iron John: A Book About Men,* Robert Bly (1990) has contended that

> we are living at an important and fruitful moment now, for it is clear to men that the images of adult manhood given by the popular culture are worn out; a man can no longer depend on them. By the time a man is thirty-five he knows that the images of the right man, the tough man, the true man which he received in high school do not work in life. Such a man is open to new images of what a man is or could be. (p. ix)

Although we share Bly's concerns with the unreliability of traditional masculinity codes, and although our earlier research (Young et al., 1994) suggests that some injured male athletes reflect critically on what he calls the "images . . . of the tough man" (p. ix), we do not recognize the sweeping social change in hegemonic masculinity that Bly's writing so cavalierly implies. Indeed, far from "worn out," the evidence that we have reported here and earlier findings on the suppression of sports-related pain suggest an ongoing complementarity between these ascendant codes of masculinity and the sports-related injury process. Rather than the football lineman who revels in the pain he inflicts on his opponents (Young, 1993), the ice hockey player, coach, administrator, or commentator who insists that fist-fighting remains an essential and "honorable" part of the game (Faulkner, 1973; Gillett, White, & Young, 1996), or the downhill skier who remains unreflexive about the implications of his injury-jinxed career for his long-term health (Young et al., 1994), we think it likely that Bly is speaking to still relatively small numbers of males for whom conventional forms of masculinity through sport no longer carry cultural meaning.

There remains a fundamental association, albeit one that is often contested, between sport involvement in boyhood and dominant (and, we might add, heterosexual) masculinity in adulthood. Playing sport, particularly those sports connected with aggression and toughness, distances the participant from the possibility of being labeled a "sissy" or a homosexual. To relinquish the opportunity to participate in the sporting rite of passage, or at the very least to identify with sports heroes or teams, is to risk estrangement from other boys.

In saying this, we do not mean to argue (deterministically) that hegemonic modes of masculine body expression are universal or exhaustive, as we wrote in an earlier article:

> Counter-hegemonic challenges to the hypermasculine body and masculinist physical culture not only exist but are precipitating resistant forms which resonate for thousands of participants. Across Canada, for example, young hockey players, unimpressed by their toothless professional counterparts, are finding new non-contact versions of their favoured pastime both empowering in the pursuit and emancipatory in the avoidance of injury. . . . Elsewhere, gay men continue to resist the compulsory heterosexuality of modern sport organizations and strategically carve out new spaces both within and outside the mainstream . . . while men of colour chip away at the racist foundations of sports apartheid as they construct broader opportunities for participation. (White et al., 1995, p. 174)

Nevertheless, our research suggests that for males to use sport and athletic bodies as key sites for "masculinity verification" (Dubbert, 1979) remains meaningful enough, even when the outcomes may be literally incapacitating.

The preliminary evidence that we have reported here derives from a variety of sources and research methodologies that make gender comparisons between sports difficult. Although our overview of existing data suggests a relation between sports injury, contemporary sports norms, and gender processes, further research is required to more accurately assess the validity of the argument that masculinizing processes within sport contribute to a disproportionate level of damage to athletic bodies. Smith's (1991) observation that circumstantial evidence "allows those who are predisposed to do so to dismiss it as such" (p. 108) reminds us of the preliminary and as yet unsubstantiated nature of our argument.

A number of questions come to mind in terms of fruitful directions for future research. First, as we suggested previously, there is a general paucity of benchmark data on gender differences in rates and types of sports injury. To better understand these issues, future work might profitably introduce controls for levels and types of sport involvement when looking at gender differences in sports injury. Though we believe strongly in the benefits of in-depth qualitative work, this approach would be suited to quantitative methods, such as sample surveys, an approach often relegated to the methodological junkyard in research based on feminist and other critical perspectives. As Lewis (1997) suggested, however, given Bourdieu's (1980; see also Dimaggio, 1982) use of surveys to analyze class and cultural distinction in France, "There is nothing intrinsically implausible about the use of statistics and surveys in cultural studies research" (p. 84).

Second, our use of the notions of "dominance-based" and "forceful" masculinities in this chapter and elsewhere has been useful in helping to open up the area for research consideration. However, these notions may have simultaneously obscured other realities surrounding men, their bodies, sport, and injury. In this regard, our research is only a start, and much remains to be done in exploring processes whereby men and boys involve themselves in activities that are at once pleasurable and thrilling but also extremely hazardous. It remains to be seen, for example, how activities such as heli-skiing, bungee-jumping, skydiving, or the so-called extreme sports are linked to gender processes (if at all), and to what extent such activities are explained by factors beyond gender. To do this, it is crucial that the voices of participants themselves be represented in research to directly tap the key question of meaning. It could be argued that, so far at least, sports injury researchers have been more concerned with saving participants from themselves than with understanding the sources of pleasure and meaning derived from risky pursuits.

Third, most of the existing research has focused on injuries sustained through trauma (sprains, dislocations, fractures, concussions, etc.) among children, youth, and young adults. This limited approach leaves open a plethora of sports injury issues that remain uncharted. For example, little is known about injuries that are sustained through repetitive activity such as that found in swimming, Nordic skiing, and long-distance running. Furthermore, there has been almost no research on the cumulative effects over the life span of intense physical activity and related injuries suffered during youthful athletic careers. Long-term wear and tear on joints, rheumatoid arthritis, and the compounded effects of concussions and the like may only present themselves symptomatically later in life, potentially creating physical, emotional, and financial costs—costs not anticipated during one's youth, when the body seemed vibrant and invulnerable. This brings us back to gendered body norms.

With firmer evidence at hand, discussions addressing interventionist and transformational efforts to improve the safety of sport for both males and females may be more productive. For the moment, however, we conclude from the existing research that the way that sport is played matters for sports injury as much as the game itself. In this regard, males are more likely than females to be socialized into ways of playing that are potentially injurious. If this pattern were challenged, the sparing of only one victim of a catastrophic sport injury would be a resounding step forward.

As suggested in our analysis, gender differences in the economic outcome of sports injuries also have to be considered. The often taken-for-granted relation between exercise, health, and health care cost reduction is, in reality, complex, particularly when age and gender are taken into account. Research needs to be carried out to unravel these complexities. However, on the basis of what we know about gender and injury, it seems plausible to suggest that the balance of costs and benefits for sport and exercise is likely different for women and men because women are less involved in high-risk activities.

Gender influences on the cost-benefit ratio for exercise and health care costs also likely interact with age and class effects. For example, the benefits of exercise for health may be more pronounced for older men who have higher risk for cardiovascular problems (Morris, Everitt, Pollard, Ghave, & Semmence, 1980). On the other hand, it also seems reasonable to postulate that younger men are at higher risk because they have had less of an opportunity, or simply are not ready, to reflect critically on the exploitive and dangerous aspects of the sports process. In a recent related review of the relation between exercise, health, and health costs, gender effects were not reported (Nicholl et al., 1994). Results indicated that for younger adults (aged 15 to 44), the annual medical care costs per person incurred by sport and physical activity involvement exceeded the costs that would have been avoided by the health-promoting effects of exercise. Conversely, among older adults (older than 44), the annual benefits to health care costs resulting from exercising outweigh the costs. Similar conclusions were reached by a Dutch study that noted a reversal of the cost-benefit ratio in the exercise-health relation with aging (Reijner & Veltuijsen, 1989). The evidence that injury in sport tends to be skewed toward the young calls into question broader images of risky behavior among adolescents and young adults. To better understand this process, epidemiological and sport studies might productively be merged. In particular, longitudinal analyses of population-based data could begin to interrogate the place of sport within a range of risky behaviors and their relations with gender. Again, such an approach could be combined profitably with more qualitative procedures to tap the question of the experience and meanings of sport injury.

As it stands, the available evidence suggests that the dividends of what Connell calls hegemonic masculinity paradoxically are accompanied by certain dangers, as indicated by this review of Canadian and international sports injury data, our earlier work on injury (Young et al., 1994), and the disproportionately high morbidity and mortality rates of male athletes. Reverence for risky sport promoted by dominant masculinities is closely linked to disproportionately high and often preventable levels of physical incapacitation. Given various safety awareness campaigns and rule changes addressing particularly hazardous sports practices like spearing in football (i.e., using the helmeted head as a battering ram in the tackle), there are signs of progress and change. But the cultures of some sports continue systematically to produce high injury rates not only because of the financially driven emphasis on winning but also because of the connection between aggression and the process of masculinization. For this reason, if we are correct in our thinking, it is unlikely that rule changes alone will be able to counter the health risks these sports and the dangerous masculinities they represent impart.

8

Domestic Violence and Televised Athletic Events

"It's a Man Thing"

DON SABO
PHILIP M. GRAY
LINDA A. MOORE

Jennifer is a 44-year-old African American woman who has lived with her 36-year-old partner, Charles, for 7 years. Charles played basketball in high school and, later, in a job corps league. Today he is an avid sports fan, watching football and basketball all day on weekends, and betting between $2 and $10 on each game. During games, he drinks beer and liquor and smokes marijuana. Charles first started beating Jennifer after his favorite team, the Buffalo Bills, lost their first Super Bowl championship. As she recalled:

> It was horrible, crazy. He punched me in the mouth, split my lip. I had bruises on my body and the side of my face. This was the worst. Now I know to get out of the house when he starts throwing things. As soon as he starts yelling, my eldest daughter (6 years old) goes for help. The police have come often. Now it happens weekly during football season, then there's a break, and the weekly attacks start up again with basketball [season]. If he understood hockey, it would be even worse.

Is Charles's behavior unique or part of a larger social pattern? Is his violence in any way related to the athletic events he watches on television?

The assertion that televised sporting events can contribute to domestic violence was made as early as June 1981 by counselors attending the seventh national conference on Men and Masculinity at Tufts University. Counselors who worked with men who batter from Boston's "Emerge" and Denver's "Raven" crisis centers claimed that the incidence of men's violence against women climbed during and immediately after major football games like the Super Bowl. Fueled by increasing media attention, public curiosity and lore around the issue grew and, by 1993, journalist Robert Lipsyte had dubbed the Super Bowl the "Abuse Bowl."

Gender theorists in the 1980s began to conceptualize male violence in sport as an expression of masculinity and structural inequalities between men and women. Sport sociologists discussed links between sports, masculinity, and male aggression inside and outside sport (Dunning, 1990; Melnick, 1992; Messner & Sabo, 1990; Sabo & Runfola, 1980). Theory grew faster than research, however, and very little systematic investigation was done to describe or document the purported connections between televised sports and men's violence against women. The lack of research in this area was noted by the outspoken critic of feminism Christine Sommers (1995), who berated radical feminists for exaggerating the problem of domestic violence and mounting an ideological attack on televised sports without solid evidence in hand.

For this study, we conducted in-depth telephone interviews with 18 women who reported that they were regularly beaten by male partners during and/or shortly after televised athletic events. We were not interested in settling the larger sociological debate that regionally or nationally televised athletic events trigger widespread increases in domestic violence. Rather, we accepted the basic clinical claims that in some instances, televised sports can contribute to men's violence against women. To uncover the social-psychological dynamics involved, we developed a descriptive, exploratory approach geared to elicit and analyze women's accounts of such beatings when they did occur. Our approach drew on standpoint epistemology, which "begins with the idea that less powerful members of society have the potential for a more complete view of social reality than others, precisely because of their disadvantaged position" (Nielsen, 1990, p. 10). The insights and interpretations presented here, therefore, grow out of the perceptions and voices of the women we interviewed, along with our own theoretical views on masculinity, violence, and culture.

We begin with a general review of theory and research on the interrelations between sports and men's violence against women. Next, we consider the small body of research that sheds light on possible linkages between televised sports and domestic violence. After discussing our methods and findings, we lay out some interpretations and conclusions.

Sport, Masculinity, and Men's Violence

Given the pervasiveness of sports media, the millions of male sports fans in American culture, and claims that televised sports can provoke aggression among some men, it is surprising that so little systematic research has focused on sport-related male violence in domestic settings (Sabo & Jansen, 1998). The sociological study of synergy among sports, masculinity, and aggression is only recent. Sheard and Dunning (1973) recognized that certain aggressive sport subcultures such as the British rugby tradition and the phenomenon of soccer hooliganism constituted a "male preserve." Sabo and Runfola (1980) argued that sports help some boys learn that a capacity for violence is part of adult masculinity and, furthermore, that the cultural belief in men's propensity for violence that is reinforced by sport legitimates male aggression in other institutional sectors, such as the military or family.

Building on Gramsci's (1971) concept of hegemony, feminist theories, and the work of Connell (1987), critical feminist and cultural studies scholars analyzed sport as a set of masculinizing cultural practices that at once reflects and feeds multiple systems of domination within the gender order (Messner & Sabo, 1990). Similarly, scholars argued that print and electronic sport media are a site for the social construction of hegemonic masculinity that, in the larger gender order, define masculinity in ways that reflect and secure gender differences and men's collective domination of women (Bryson, 1987; Connell, 1987; Hanke, 1992; Hargreaves, 1986b; Messner, 1988; Miller, 1997; Wenner, 1998a). Hegemonic masculinity, which has been a prominent feature of much sports media, is said to valorize and naturalize men's capacity for violence (Messner & Solomon, 1993).

A small but growing body of research on the linkages between sports, masculinity, and violence against women has issued in recent years. Loy (1992) tested the hypothesis that the forms of hegemonic masculinity that emerge within fratriarchal relations of patriarchal (male-dominated) cultures are likely to be associated with higher rates of men's violence against women. Using the Human Relations File as a cross-cultural data base, Loy found that the characteristics of agonal fratriarchies were significantly correlated with higher rates of both intermale violence and gang rape of women. Loy (1995) later observed that athletic teams share the following features in common with other "modern tribal groups" such as fraternities, military groups, and youth gangs: (a) "they are competitive, peer-based, age-graded, segmentally bonded, male-dominated groups that emphasize the pursuit of prestige through physical prowess"; (b) all support "violent performative masculine styles"; and (c) they are involved with intense activities that are felt to be worthwhile for their own sake (pp. 266-267).

A few researchers have focused on male athlete violence against women (Benedict, 1997). Two journalistic accounts have documented what appears to be a high rate of assaults on women by professional male athletes (Brubaker, 1994; "Special Report: Crime and Sports," 1995). A scientific study of 20 NCAA Division I universities found that, although athletes made up only 3.3% of the total student population, they committed 19% of the sexual assaults reported to judicial affairs offices (Crosset, Benedict, & McDonald, 1995). Other researchers have found that college athletes are more likely than their nonathletic counterparts to sexually assault women (Koss & Gaines, 1993; Sanday, 1990). Two recent ethnographic studies of the inner workings of university athlete subcultures revealed that sexual exploitation of women (i.e., ridicule, casual sex, sharing partners, rape, and gang rape) was intricately tied to both individual and group constructions of hegemonic masculinity (Curry, 1996; Harvey, 1996). These studies also uncovered additional factors that were tied to male athlete violence against women, such as alcohol and drug use, male bonding, chauvinism, sexism, predatory sexual attitudes, and the lack of accountability for transgressions.

Although these links between sports spectatorship and men's violence proneness are important to note, in this chapter we are concerned with men who view sports on television. Only one regional analysis has directly tested the contention that men's violence against women escalates during and after televised football games. White, Katz, and Scarborough (1992) discovered a significant correlation between the incidence of female admissions to hospital emergency rooms in northern Virginia after Washington Redskins football team victories. Although this study is flawed because of its indirect measure of domestic violence, it does suggest that mass sporting events may be linked with collective patterns of violence in a community. In contrast, Drake and Pandey's (1996) analysis of statewide data from the Missouri Division of Family Services did not find any associations between days on which professional sporting events were held and rates of child abuse by men.

Some psychological research suggests that the aggressive cues in sport media may trigger violent reactions among some male viewers. Early psychological theory posited that frustration led to aggression that, in turn, produced a cathartic or purging effect that reduced frustration and made the aggressors feel better. Subsequent research, however, showed that the connections between frustration and aggression are more nuanced and convoluted. Researchers now regard frustration as only one of an array of factors that can elicit aggression, and that the presence of "aggression-associated cues" in the environment or associations with unpleasantness also can act as triggers (Berkowitz & Frodi, 1979; Berkowitz & LePage, 1967; Carlson, Marcus-Newhall, & Miller, 1990). Televised sports imagery can be a source of aggression-associated cues or unpleasant stimuli for some men. Rather than experiencing sport spectatorship as a cathartic experience, researchers found that viewing violent athletic events was associated with increased arousal and aggression (Arms, Russell, & Sandilands, 1979; Goldstein & Arms, 1971). Commercials during sports events also might supply aggression-associated cues, such as advertisements for violent television programs and big-screen movies during the 1996 Major League Baseball playoffs (Anderson, 1997).

Compared to females, male viewers may find violent sports imagery more enticing and exciting. Bryant, Comisky, and Zillman (1981) found that male and female college students experienced similar levels of enjoyment while watching football plays of low or intermediate levels of violence. When viewing highly violent plays, in contrast, the males reported higher levels of enjoyment. Wann, Schrader, and Adamson (1996) also studied college students to find out whether they experienced increased cognitive anxiety (e.g., worry) or somatic anxiety (e.g., nervousness, feeling uncomfortable) before, during, and after sporting events. They discovered that anxiety increased as the sporting event approached, with the importance connected to the event, and with the level of identification that fans attached to the sport. Hard-fought wins or losses also were found to be especially anxiety-producing, and somatic anxiety was greater among the highly identified fans. To the extent that men in American culture are more identified with athletics, therefore, it is reasonable to expect that male fans are more likely than female fans to experience mental and bodily anxiety surrounding an athletic event.

Some readers may be reminded here of the research linking exposure to pornography to men's sexual violence against women. Some studies found that long-term exposure to pornography was associated with increased sexual callousness toward women (Zillmann & Bryant, 1982, 1984). Donnerstein and Linz (1986) concluded that it is mainly exposure to "aggressive" images in pornography (not necessarily sexual images) that can desensitize male viewers toward women. In any event, it appears that mediated porn can influence some men's moods, attitudes, and feelings about women.

Finally, Wann (1993) argued that aggression is used by some sports spectators to reestablish their social identity, especially those who see themselves as fans or who highly identify with their team. Simply put, fans draw on sports events and their relationships with certain teams to construct their identities. He identified three "tactics" or "techniques" that sports fans enact to maintain their social identity. Some fans increase their self-esteem by "basking in the reflected glory (BIRGing)" of their team or athletic idols. Other spectators build their self-esteem by "cutting off reflected failure (CORFing)," that is, by dissociating themselves from unsuccessful teams. Here, individuals put psychological distance between themselves and a team's losses or failures. Third, some fans shore up their identity by derogating or putting down the members of an outgroup. Wann (1993) called this "blasting," and he pointed out, "By acting in a negative and/or hostile manner toward outgroups, persons acquire the psychological perception that they are 'better' than others which subsequently leads to increases in self-esteem" (p. 136). Through blasting, fans build themselves up by putting others down.

In summary, the available research does not invite the simple conclusion that "televised sports cause domestic violence." Rather, hegemonic masculinity and gender relations appear to be highlighted within a combination of interrelated cultural, institutional, and social psychological processes that are said to contribute to men's violence.

Method

Eighteen women who self-reported as having been beaten by their male partner during or after viewing a sporting event on television volunteered for this study. The women were recruited through notices placed in the personals section of the regional daily newspaper, *The Buffalo News.* Each notice read, "If you have been beaten during or after a TV sports event, D'Youville College researchers will pay to interview you. Confidentiality is respected. Call Linda Moore at [phone number]."

The average age of the participants at the time of the interviews was 31 (*Mdn* = 29; range = 21-44). Twelve were Caucasian, and 6 were African American, and all had at least a high school degree or its equivalent. They lived in the Niagara Frontier Region of western New York, and most of them (61%, *n* = 11) said they were not sports fans.

The interviewer initially gathered demographic information about the interviewee, the battering partner, and the relationship itself. Next, she asked about the sports-related batterings that had taken place—for example, frequency and timing and social situation. Finally, the women were invited to share their perceptions of their respective partners' behavior, motives, and emotions. Seventeen interviews were conducted by telephone at the interviewer's residence, and one was done in person at the participant's home. To facilitate trust and self-disclosure, confidentiality was assured, and the interviews were conducted by the female researcher. We felt that "woman-to-woman talk" would be more apt to yield more insight and information than cross-gender communication (DeVault, 1990). The interviews lasted about 30 minutes and provided opportunities for clarification, discussion, and sharing sensitive information (Reinharz, 1992).

The interviews were transcribed and analyzed by grouping all responses to each question and looking for differences and commonalities, patterns and themes. We tallied results to develop an overall understanding of the sample characteristics—for example, age, race, rate of alcohol or drug use, length of the relationship, and marital status.

Relationships, Batterers, and Televised Sports

The women we interviewed were generally uninterested in sports. Their male partners, in contrast, were likely to have previous athletic histories, to be involved currently with informal athletic pursuits, and to watch televised games regularly with male friends. Most of the male partners were described as former and/or current athletes. Eighty-one percent of the males had participated in high school sports, and 63% currently participated in pick-up games of basketball and football.

All of the women portrayed their battering partner as a "sports fan" who regularly watched sports on television. The most common sports watched were football, basketball, and hockey, which are forms of contact sport. Many male partners were said to watch sports daily (39%), and half watched during weekends only. The men were said to "switch channels from game to game," to watch "10 hours on weekends," "when he could, all day," or "2 to 3 hours on weekdays."

The Relationships and Beatings

Two thirds of the couples were Caucasians, and one third were African Americans. There were no interracial couples. Only six of the couples were married, and all but one of the remaining couples were cohabiting. At the time of the interviews, most of the relationships were ongoing, and the couples had been together on average for almost 5 years.

The beatings were likely to have begun early in the history of the relationship. Three respondents stated that the beatings began shortly after moving in together, and 1 married woman indicated that battery had been part of their dating relationship. Three interviewees specifically stated that the beatings began after the local team (the Buffalo Bills) lost a Super Bowl. A 44-year-old participant reported that "the first beating happened after the first trip to the Super Bowl. He lost a large sum and he had bet to fix up some financial trouble. He beat me up bad."

All our women participants reported that law enforcement officials had intervened at some point to deal with the beatings. The outcomes of police interventions varied, but we uncovered an overall pattern of reluctance to report beatings or to follow through with legal complaints once made. In 10 cases, there were no charges filed by the battered woman, and in two cases the battered woman dropped charges after filing them. We found three cases in which an order of protection or restraining order had been issued, and two cases where the battering partner was arrested after charges had been filed. It took a lot of misconduct on the part of the battering man before the woman would press for an arrest; for example, one woman acted only after her partner severely beat her, spit on her, and trashed the apartment.

Some of the women participants described the beatings with a flat affect, as though reporting a sequence in a soap opera. For others, their descriptions appeared to stir difficult emotions. As a young Caucasian woman recounted, "We were fighting over losing money. He would hit me. Another time he punched me and threw a pot that split my forehead open. I ended up in the hospital."

A 36-year-old mother of three recalled,

> I had just had a baby. The game was going to be shown at the bar and I didn't want him to leave. He came in after the game angry because of a loss. He was swearing mad because the baby cried, and he beat me up.

The comments of several participants showed that sometimes family members became involved with violent episodes. One 21-year-old African American shared,

One time my mother called when he was watching a game. She teased him because his team was losing. It ended up as a fistfight between us. He picked me up and slammed me into a glass coffee table and broke it.

A mother of two children recalled,

Another time during a preseason football game we were outside fixing a barbeque dinner. He was inside watching the game and friends were over. After [the game] he took the friends home around 1:30 a.m. [When he returned] he crashed something against the wall and pushed me out of the bed when I said I wanted to go back to sleep. After I got away and got the children together, he threw the baby at me. The police came and took him to a friend's house.

Still another participant recounted,

He was drinking and watching a football game. The team lost and when I came home he started yelling at me, slapped me and pulled my hair. When I threw my ring at him, he slapped me. My mother called the police. I spent some time at a woman's shelter but then went back to him. He threatened my life when I was going to court, so I didn't pursue it.

Women's Perceptions of the Beatings

Most participants felt that the beatings were somehow related to sports events. A 25-year-old Caucasian woman indicated,

He was watching hockey at a tavern. The game wasn't going well so he came home. I had gone to bed and he woke me up and blamed it all on me. He said he was going to do to me what was done to the players. He said I deserved it. He split my lip, broke my nose, fractured my ribs. I had bruises all over my upper body, and arms and legs. I was in the hospital for 2 days. I went to [name of shelter deleted] for 3 days, but then went back. Both of us had been drinking.

More than half of our participants (56%, $n = 10$) said that watching sports on television had led their partner to beat them on a regular basis. Three felt that beatings were more likely to occur during specific sport seasons (e.g., hockey, football, and basketball). A young Caucasian woman commented, "Hockey season seemed to be the worst time. Sometimes [I'd get beaten] every weekend." As Jennifer stated at the outset of this chapter, the beatings took place "during football season weekly" followed by "a break," but then with the beginning of basketball season, "the weekly attacks started again."

We discovered that it was not uncommon for beatings to take place in the presence of others. Our preconception that the typical beating took place in a domestic environment in which a solitary man watching TV sports suddenly sets upon his partner proved inaccurate. Other spectators included the batterer's male friends, children, or other extended family members. In three instances, the male friends who were present tried to calm down the battering man or get him to leave the scene. Another woman recounted, "Because his friends were there he became more violent. He punched me, slapped me, and threw me against the wall. His friends pulled him away from me." However, in two other instances, the male bystanders did nothing to intercede in any decisive manner. As one female victim explained, "[His] friends would offer a place to stay, but they never intervened." She recalled, bewilderingly, that although her 11-year-old daughter would call 911 for help, her partner's male friends never tried to help.

Drugs, Alcohol, and Gambling

Our women participants reported that, when the beatings took place, either they or their partner were drinking or using drugs. All the battering men drank alcohol or did drugs while watching TV sports. Although 10 (56%) of the men used only alcohol, 8 (44%) also used drugs. One man used cocaine, and 7 used marijuana. Only 1 woman said that sometimes the sports-related beatings took place without her partner drinking, whereas 2 others pointedly felt that higher levels of violence were tied to higher rates of drinking. The typical pattern was for alcohol to be used alone or in conjunction with other drugs such as marijuana or cocaine. In most cases, it was the battering partner who used drugs and alcohol, and there were only two cases in which both partners used drugs or alcohol. Two women said they avoided drug or alcohol use when their partner was watching televised sports to stay on guard and not lose self-control. As 1 woman stated, "He drinks beer, some hard liquor, and smokes some marijuana. He might drink five 40-ounce bottles in one game. I don't drink [in order] to stay alert." Another woman explained, "I know he gets out of hand [when drinking] so I need to be able to recognize trouble."

Several women participants discussed how gambling fed their male partner's anger and violence. Most of the battering men (78%) regularly bet on sporting events. The wagers were typically small (less than $50) and placed among friends and through football pools at work or in a bar. We uncovered several instances in which beatings occurred immediately after a sport-gambling loss. A 34-year-old Caucasian woman reported, "I would nag him about betting the money. He'd tell me to shut the 'f' up and then slap and punch me." Another woman whose partner had bet on a Buffalo Bills game recalled a recent episode: "Three weeks ago the Bills lost. We were at home and he was swearing. The phone rang and he thought I was talking too loud. He pulled my hair, slapped me, kicked me and punched me all over my body." A 36-year-old African American woman volunteered,

> He went over to a friend's house to watch a football game. He came home mad because he lost a lot of money and he blamed the loss on me. There was screaming and I threw a knife at him. He grabbed the knife and then stabbed me all over my body. I was hospitalized. He was arrested and spent a year in jail and then he was deported [back to his native country].

Two women reported that beatings had occurred due to conflicts over what to watch on television. A college-educated interviewee explained, "He gets angry because I'm not watching the game. It interferes with his enjoyment of it. He has said that I think I'm too good to watch this. Then he starts pushing me around." A young mother stated, "He wanted to watch sports and the children wanted to watch something else. They would come to me and then he'd beat me up for interfering."

Interestingly, only 2 women talked about other nonsport televisual content that triggered violent behavior in their partner. One specified that the well-known violent movies *Reservoir Dogs* and *Falling Down* had instigated a beating. The former is a brutally violent film about a group of criminals who bungle a robbery and suspect one another of being a police informant. The latter film features Michael Douglas in the role of an alienated white-collar man whose anger and confusion around a failed marriage leads to a series of violent episodes. Another woman intimated that her partner had become violent while watching "violent" and "degrading pornography" that she had been forced to watch.

Televised Sports as a Gateway to a "Man's World"

It was evident that the women we interviewed saw their partner's interest in sports as intricately tied to his manly identity. A cluster of their responses pointed to their view that televised sports gave male partners a

way to vicariously identify with masculinity. For example, most participants described violent televised sports as a "man's world" or a "manly activity" that allowed men to shore up or express masculinity. Some pointed
out that televised sports linked boyhood and manhood in their partners. As
one stated, "They're involved since childhood. . . . Fathers bring them up to
be athletes." Another stated pointedly, "It's the way they're brought up.
They learn it's the thing to do." "They're men," another respondent commented, "and that's what men are supposed to do." Another offered that
males learn "to be a man through physical skills" and that televised sports
showcase such skills.

Eleven interviewees felt that men are more interested in sports than are
women. One participant observed, "I like sports, but women can watch
them sensibly. It's just a game. For men, it's the world." Although men
were said to be intensely immersed in sport, women were not. As one
mother who described her partner as "staring into the TV" during sports
events stated, "Women have other things to do—the house and children.
Women look at TV objectively." As another woman put it, "Women enjoy
the socializing, but the men seem to be glued to the screen."

Several responses showed that many women felt that their partners
identified with the male athletes on the screen. As one explained, "He puts
himself into what the athletes do. He becomes the stars he admires. If they
do badly, he feels terribly frustrated, as if it's happening to him."

Another indicated, "Men want to be that athlete up on the pedestal. They
envy this position." Watching sports on TV "defines their manhood for
them," and, as a young woman observed, "He relives his own athletic accomplishments" through the television sports.

Sports and Aggression as a "Guy Thing"

Several women believed that televised sports somehow fed their partner's self-image as an aggressive man. They suggested that their partner
modeled his own masculinity after the aggressive athletes on the screen. A
29-year-old Caucasian woman who described televised sports with the
phrase "It's a guy thing" suggested that "society tells them to be aggressive, to be in control of other people. When they are not in control, they get
mad." Another volunteered, "Aggressive sports allow men to be aggressive. Most batterers have a problem with their masculinity, a macho need
for control. [Televised sport] pumps them up. They like the fighting."

It may be the aggression itself that sparked many men's fascination for
televised sports. One interviewee suggested that men and women differ in

the ways they perceive and experience televised sports violence: "Men seem to enjoy watching the aggressiveness more than women. Women like watching too, but not the same way men do." Another commented that male viewers sometimes fail to distinguish between televised violence and real-life violence: "Sports are really aggressive. Men have to be aggressive to get their point across. They see a football player knock people down and think, 'So can I.' Men have trouble identifying the differences between the game and reality."

Some men were said to be especially preoccupied with televised depictions and commentaries of hits and injuries. They would cheer, leap, or yell in response to brutal action on the screen. As a 44-year-old African American woman put it, "He's very involved with the injuries. He's fascinated with the impacts. Even when he plays his video games, he makes comments about the contact that gets made. . . . If he watched bowling, maybe he wouldn't get so emotional."

Why Do Some Male Fans Batter?

Televised sports were more than a passing fancy for the men described by our participants. Real and Mechikoff (1992) observed that, for many male fans, televised sports function as a "symbolic refuge" in which personal and cultural meanings converge around success and failure, masculinity, winning and losing, pain and sacrifice, struggle and defeat (p. 337). As Nixon and Frey (1996) stated, sports offer fans a type of "fantasyland" or "leisure sanctuary" where they can escape "lives of ambiguity, frustration, anxiety, uncertainty, and contradictions" (p. 55). Although the men described in this study seemed to seek refuge in the symbolic universe of televised sports and its gripping diversion from everyday life, the lines of separation between aggression, frustration, and manly struggle for power on the screen and in the living room seemed to blur and rupture, contributing to the seemingly senseless and brutal attacks on their women partners. Indeed, the men in this study did not find sanctuary in the manly world of televised sport, but rather, there seemed to be connections between the aggression of athletes, the media representations of athletic struggles for dominance, and the male fans' dispositions toward aggression in the domestic setting.

The women we interviewed helped us unearth a variety of factors that seemed to coalesce in ways that triggered domestic violence for some male fans of televised sports. White et al. (1992) observed, "To understand assaults against women one must put these triggers into a context of social-cultural factors conducive to violence against women, and the individual and relational factors that increase the likelihood that certain men will assault women" (p. 168). Subsequently, we discuss several interpretations of our findings that, taken singly or in combination, may offer insight into why some men batter women during or after televised sports events.

The Televised Sports and
Hegemonic Masculinity Hypothesis

The women we interviewed talked repeatedly and insightfully about their male partners' experience of sport as a manly endeavor, a "man's world." Our respondents located their men's intense fascination for televised sports in boyhood athletic experiences and father-son interactions. They observed that their male partners not only talked about and watched sports a great deal, but that they also participated in athletic pastimes. Most significantly, each of these activities was linked to their partner's manly identity or what we would label hegemonic masculinity.

Televised contact sports also appear to have contributed to the construction of hegemonic masculinity by heroizing men's aggression and violence. Masculinity and violence are often symbolically suffused in the televised sports events that were so important to the men in this study, as Katz (1995a) noted:

> Violence on-screen, like that in real life, is perpetrated overwhelmingly by males. Males constitute the majority of the audience for violent films, as well as violent sports such as football and hockey. It is important to note then, that what is being sold is not just "violence," but rather a glamorized form of violent masculinity. (pp. 139-140)

Moreover, the women we interviewed described their male partners' fascination with the aggressive action, physical contact, hitting, and injuries depicted on the television. Many men heroized those athletes known for aggressive play. Finally, respondents repeatedly pointed to the fact that their men were emotionally and physically stimulated by their vicarious involvement with the games, players, and violence on the screen. In short, these men appeared to be engaged by and at the same time (and more dynamically) to be engaging televised sports as a cultural resource that helped them to express, reaffirm, and act out their masculine identity.

We are suggesting that televised sports were used as a vehicle for the men in this study to deploy "manly" aggression to maintain their gender identity and domination of women partners. Televised sports became a cultural site for acting out hegemonic masculinity in ways that pit men against women and, perhaps, the world of "femininity" that women and sometimes babies and children symbolically represent. As Connell (1995) pointed out, when men interrupt women in conversations or boys intrude on girls' spaces in playgrounds, these "enactments of hegemonic masculinity in everyday life" reverberate with the "difference/dominance" dynamics that suffuse gender relations in larger society (p. 232). Whether it is a Buffalo man punching his wife in the chest during a football game or a Japanese businessman groping a schoolgirl on the subway, individual men participate in social choices and cultural practices that reflect and feed hegemonic masculinity and collectively oppress women. Consistent with Wann's (1993) insights that fans draw on sports events to maintain their social identities, we suspect that hegemonic masculinity is being constructed by men who batter during televised sports events.

Our findings suggest that men's battering behavior was not simply an uncontrolled, irrational, or purely emotional outburst, but rather a dramaturgical device used by some men to reestablish their masculine identity and interpersonal dominance. It appeared that battery was a vehicle for "acting out" a primarily masculine agenda, that is, to send messages to female partners about dominance, submission, physical power, ruthlessness, rough anger, and control. The dramaturgical dimensions of the battery were further evident in that the "audience" often included children, extended family members, and male friends. Hence, men's displays of power and domination were not just aimed at partners, but also at friends and family. Here men's violence can be seen as a transaction among men as well as between men and women (Connell, 1995). As in Shakespeare, in some domestic settings there appeared to be a "play within a play," that is, an imitative importation of the televised aggression in sport into the interpersonal dynamics of the domestic scene.

Frustration, Aggression, and Exploding Men

The interviews did not paint a picture of male sports fans happily lounging before the television. The demeanor and behavior of male partners was characterized as reclusive, tense, frustrated, extremely focused, labile, and irritable. In short, these guys did not appear to be having a good time. Indeed, several findings suggest that watching sports was a source of frustration for the men described in this study. Men appeared to "gear up" for the games, experiencing, perhaps, the early stages of cognitive and somatic anxiety that Wann et al. (1996) observed among some college student fans. Several men were easily annoyed by children seeking attention, telephone calls, and especially female partners. We also heard reports of frustration due to lost games and championships, disappointment with their favorite sports heroes, and anger over gambling losses. After all, the hierarchical structures of athletic competition and gambling both produce more losers than winners, that is, only one team ultimately wins the championship, only a handful of bettors wins money.

Many of our interviewees observed that their male partners were emotionally moved by the depictions of injury during games. We wonder if the battery of men's bodies in televised contact sports may give men glimpses into their own vulnerability and victimization, especially poor and working-class men and men of color. The psychodynamic inference might read, "Because the men on the screen are vulnerable and beaten, so am I." McBride's (1995) analysis of the psychodynamics of sacrifice in contemporary patriarchal culture contends that sports provide a cultural theater for men to identify with the victims of violence that, in turn, generates rage and anguish that then gets projected onto the female other. Drawing on the theories of Bataille (1985) and Irigaray (1985), he argued that within the "masculinist psychic economy" of American culture, war, football, and battery are interrelated expressions of men's need for power and control. However, the suppression of men's needs for intimacy necessitated by conformity to hegemonic masculinity results in emotional ambivalence and deep-seated frustrations that, in turn, get channeled individually through battery and collectively through gang rape or war.

In addition, recall that some psychological research has showed that exposure to aggression-associated cues in sports is likely to heighten feelings of frustration and aggression in viewers rather than serve as a vehicle for emotional catharsis. The studies of the relation between exposure to aggressive pornography and aggression against women make this point (Donnerstein & Linz, 1986; Kimmel, 1991). The visual glorification and valorization of athlete aggression that are so common in televised contact sports, therefore, may have heightened the likelihood of explosive violence among the battering men in this study.

Finally, we speculate that the men's use of alcohol and drugs may have brought on feelings of loss of control that frustrated their need to maintain a sense of mastery and masculine adequacy in both the sport and family contexts. All our respondents indicated that their partners' attack was at least partly prompted by alcohol and drug use. It is overly simplistic to infer that alcohol and drug use caused battery to occur. In fact, Ptacek's (1998) interviews with abusive men showed that they commonly used being drunk as an excuse for their violent behavior. However, in light of the psychological research cited earlier in this chapter, it may be that intoxication heightens both the cognitive and somatic anxiety experienced by highly identified sports fans during athletic events. Could drugs and alcohol lower a man's ability to cope with the increased levels of cognitive and somatic anxiety that have been linked to sport spectatorship? It also might be that being drunk or stoned are also likely to make violence-prone men more easily frustrated and agitated by the aggression-associated cues that proliferate in mediated contact sports. Booze and drugs are neither "causes" nor "excuses" in this scheme, but rather elements within a psychosocial and physiological process that feed men's violence.

We wonder about the extent to which cultural synergies were operating between alcohol consumption, the construction of masculinity, and vicarious identification with athlete heroes. Sport media and corporate advertising abound with booze-and-buddy images and cultural equations between manhood and alcohol consumption in mass media (Wenner, 1998a). It is likely that the men in this study made at least some gendered associations between alcohol and masculinity in that children between the ages of 2 and 18 view about 100,000 beer commercials (Postman, Nystrom, Strate, & Weingartner, 1987). Drug and alcohol also might provide a "cover" for batterers to wage their power plays within relationships without being held accountable, that is, "The booze made me do it," or "That was some bad weed. I just lost it."

The Media-Inducement Hypothesis

Our analysis does not support the notion that sport media are a singular "stimulus" to men's violence. Rather, we suggest that televised contact sports operate as a dramatic and meaningful catalyst within a cultural "setting" that can be conducive to domestic violence. Mediated sports appear to function for some men as a cultural site in which a union occurs between psychosocial processes (e.g., boyhood and adult identification with sports and aggression, and interpersonal dynamics in family relationships), psychosomatic excitation, and the adoption of cultural scripts that equate manhood to aggression and domination over women. These dynamics receive highly ritualized expression in much sport media through production practices that often merge glorification of physical power and violent masculinity with video game sound effects and violence motifs that are charged with emotion and drama. Sport media representations of manhood are laced with patriarchal narratives and emotions that flow through the culture and into gender relations. We regard sport media as not so much a "cause" of the violent actions of the men in this study but more as the "carrier" of psychosocial meanings and cultural practices that can be linked to men's collective oppression of women.

Conclusion

Each woman interviewed had a tale of woe to tell, some more horrific and violent than others. Their respective comments about a partner's abuse, or what it was about televised sports that triggered his frustration and rage, came across during interviews as separate statements, fragments of conversation. Their insights into the battery seemed at once hidden yet palpable amid moments of confusion, pain, and anger. Yet, as we analyzed the texts from the 18 interviews, a discernable tapestry took shape. Several theoretical insights emerged that help to explain the interplay between televised sports and spousal abuse.

The respondents placed masculinity in the foreground as a central contributor to their partners' violence. Ironically, it is remarkable that much of the mainline literature on domestic violence does not include discussion or theoretical analysis of masculinity. Masculinity remains implicitly problematic but not explicitly analyzed (Katz, 1995c). Although this study uncovered several factors commonly associated with battery, such as alcohol and drug use, the respondents clearly saw masculinity as a key force behind the battery.

Our findings lend credence to theoretical arguments that sports media can inform the social construction of violent masculinity. Most of the male partners participated in sports in their youth, were currently involved with sports activities, and were immersed in televised sports events. The men described by our participants appeared to be "deep fans" (Real & Mechikoff, 1992), who invested much of their identities in mediated images of athletes and the outcomes of televised games. We can only speculate about the extent to which these men tapped televised sports in the construction of their own homespun brand of violent masculinity.

This study also showed that neither masculine identity nor the preoccupation with televised sports is a sufficient condition for spousal abuse.

Other contributory factors were involved, such as alcohol and drug use, frustration, gambling, and the degree of identification with a team. Finally, we wonder about the accuracy of theoretical formulations that posit mediated sport as a symbolic refuge or sanctuary from everyday reality. If our women participants' perceptions are valid, the mediated messages surrounding sport, manliness, and the need for domination spilled over into the identity, psychology, and behavior of their battering male partners. For some men, fantasy can become identity, aggression on the screen can spill over into violence in the home. Obviously, men vary a great deal in the extent to which they identify with mediated expressions of hegemonic masculinity and gender difference. And many men distance themselves from cultural spectacles of men's aggression in sports. Similarly, pornography plays different roles in the social construction of masculinities. For some boys and men, pornography offers a symbolic diversion from sexual identity and relationships. For others, however, the symbolic landscape of pornography, its visual and erotic thematization of aggression, gender difference, and male domination, can negatively influence boys' and men's constructions of masculinity, sexual practices, and relationships with women (Donnerstein & Linz, 1986; Kimmel, 1991).

Thus, the question is not whether pornography causes sexual assault by men, but rather how the cultural presence of pornography figures into the larger social reproduction of predatory forms of male sexuality. Likewise, our study does not beckon the conclusion that televised sports cause men to beat down their partners. Rather, we found that, for the men reported on here, televised sports aroused emotional and cultural associations with masculinity that, in turn, seemed to combine with aspects of life history, individual psychology, the use of drugs and alcohol, and gambling to produce violence against women.

This qualitative research study is limited by the small number of participants interviewed. Though the results are not generalizable, we hope our findings and interpretations will promote insight, theoretical discussion, and future research. Additional interview studies with women victims could provide more reliable insights into sport-related domestic violence. Future researchers may want to interview men for whom sporting events have been associated with fighting, throwing or smashing things, or battery. We suspect, however, that such an endeavor would be fraught with methodological problems, for example, difficulty with participant recruitment, selectivity bias, and inability to get at authentic and accurate description from male batterers. Finally, surveys of larger male populations also could be done to measure the prevalence of aggressive or antisocial behavior among males during or after televised athletic events.

In closing, the men described in this study gravitated toward televised sports with an emotional and physical intensity. Televised sport was not a distant entry in *TV Guide* or a flickering ensemble of images on a screen; rather, it constituted a cultural drinking fountain that somehow enabled the men under study to define their masculinity in ways that included physical aggression and brutal domination.

9

Athletic Affiliation and Violence Against Women

Toward a Structural Prevention Project

TODD CROSSET

During the mid-1990s, probably no social issue in sport received more media attention than male athletes' violence against women. For example, at this writing, the following athletic figures are the focus of sport media discourse on violence against women: Nate Newton, a member of the Dallas Cowboys and accused rapist; Will Cordero, a power hitter for the Boston Red Sox, on trial for battery; Denis Johnson, former Boston Celtic, also accused of wife battery; and Tom Walsh, the organizer of the 2002 Salt Lake City Olympics who resigned after his wife filed a domestic violence complaint. Journalists augment this list with other athletes whose names have become synonymous with violence against women, such as Mike Tyson (boxing), O. J. Simpson (football), Darryl Strawberry (baseball), Lamar Parrish (basketball), John Daly (golf), Jose Conseco (baseball), Lawrence Phillips (football), and Bobby Cox (baseball). From such lists, many journalists conclude that athletes, and those involved with athletics, have a problem with aggression and women.

The media discourse has shaped the public perception of sport spectators. In a recent poll conducted by ESPN on their web site, 51% of the 1,019 respondents thought athletes are involved in crimes against women more often than is the general population. Only 10% thought they were less likely to be involved in crimes against women than the general population. The results are even more striking given that it is fans who are most likely to visit the ESPN web site and more likely to be tolerant of athletes' misbehavior than are less "invested" observers (ESPN, 1996).

Clearly, the recent media coverage of athletes' violence against women has contributed to this issue being defined as a social problem (Blumer, 1971). The logic of the media, however, is suspect. We also could generate a list of actors, politicians, or schoolteachers who have battered women and make similar claims about men in those and other occupations and their violence toward women.

What do we really know about athletes and violence against women? Like the media, sport sociologists have taken up the issue of athletes' violence against women. Subsequently, I review the current sociological literature on the relation between athletes and violence against women. I begin with early attempts to theorize athletes' violence against women, followed by a review of the empirical research that attempts to validate these theoretical pieces. This review is followed by a brief discussion of the limitations of this research. In the balance of the chapter, I examine some of the more recent research that focuses on the precipitating factors associated with violence against women and sport participation.

This chapter assumes that violence against women is primarily about power and control—men's desire to retain power and control over women and, in some cases, men's desire to demonstrate power to other men. In this respect, athletes' violence against women is no different than non-athlete's violence against women (Kane & Disch, 1993). Given the extent to which women feel threatened by men's violence, this chapter assumes that violence against women is a social issue—a product of a society that supports both male domination and violence. It is impossible to disassociate violence against women from aspects of masculinity. Similarly, it is difficult to discuss masculinity without noting men's use of sport to construct and maintain masculine identities (Bryson, 1987; Glassner, 1988; Messner, 1988, 1990a). Given the primary concern of this chapter—male athletes' violence against women—masculinity is a subtheme that runs throughout. The question that drives this review, however, is how can we use what we know about male athletes' violence against women to reduce the amount of violence perpetrated against women.

The Culture of Violence Explanation

Much of the early sociological writing on athletes and violence against women combined the personal experiences of athletes and the notion of "rape cultures." Peggy Sanday (1981), an anthropologist, coined the term rape culture in her study of rape in tribal communities (Sanday, 1981). She found that the frequency of rape varied substantially from one tribal society to another. Cultures that displayed a high level of tolerance for violence, male dominance, and gender segregation had the highest frequency of rape. Those cultures lacked the social constraints that discourage sexual aggression or contained social arrangements that encourage sexual aggression. More recently, she has employed this concept to explain gang rape in certain college fraternities (1990).

Sport is widely acknowledged to be the most visible cultural display of a masculine culture (Kidd, 1990). Athletes are admired for their attributes of strength, speed, and stamina. They also are praised for their intelligence, will, and courage. In the masculine status hierarchy, athletes reside close to the pinnacle—particularly athletes in contact sports—because their endeavors require them to combine many of these highly regarded masculine attributes. Through sport, as it is often presented to young people, boys are encouraged to ignore pain ("no pain, no gain"), hurt others ("let's see how tough these guys really are"), and separate themselves from women ("stop throwing like a girl"). Coaches and parents argue that sport prepares boys for an adult world (Fine, 1987) and that it rewards men for dominating others ("that's why you get paid the big bucks"), for hiding their fears ("never let them know that you're sweating"), and for distinguishing themselves from women ("he's a man's man").

Popular discourse about sport rarely presents the potentially damaging consequences of a historically masculine culture (Messner, 1992b). One of the consequences of the hypermasculine, violent world of athletics, sport sociologists argue, may be increased violence against women (Coakley, 1997; Nelson, 1994; Sabo & Runfola, 1980). The social world that prepares boys to be successful in masculine culture also encourages them to be violent, as Messner (1990a) wrote:

> Many of our most popular sports [are] predicated on the successful utilization of violence, that is, these are activities in which the human body is routinely turned into a weapon to be used against other bodies resulting in pain, serious injury or death. (p. 205)

Victory and success are associated with this physical domination. Rewarded routinized violence blends with a highly gender-segregated and male-dominant culture in which weakness and femininity are despised. Taken in full, athletic teams are breeding grounds for rape (Warshaw, 1988.

Accounts of rape cases like Bernard Lefkowitz's (1997) detailed examination of the Glen Ridge rape case and Tim Curry's (1996) research into a
university athletic subculture support the contention that some athletic
contexts are rape cultures. Although Lefkowitz and Curry (1996) examined different age groups, the cases are strikingly similar. Both groups
were highly segregated and condoned voyeurism, pornography, excessive
drinking, vandalism, and hostility toward women. Both groups enjoyed
high status in their communities as a result of their sports affiliation, and
both exploited their status to gain sexual favors or to coerce women into
sex. In the end, both groups selected women who seemed particularly vulnerable, a retarded girl in the former case and an elderly homeless woman
in the latter.

Implicit in the "rape culture" hypothesis that connects sport, masculinity, and violence against women is an outline of prevention and intervention programs—the wholesale transformation of the construction of masculinity within the male sports world. One approach to reducing athletes'
violence against women focuses on "raising the consciousness" of male
athletes (Katz, 1997). Athletes receiving a profeminist message, particularly if it is delivered by a high-status athlete, it is assumed, may be less
tolerant of violence and harassment directed toward women.

Athletes and Violence Against Women:
The Empirical Research

Although sociologists hypothesized that athletes would be more likely
to be violent toward women than would nonathletes, empirical research
did not exist to support or deny this claim until the 1990s, when researchers began to test this contention. Empirical research, to a certain extent,
does support the idea that the sports world is a rape culture. For example,
Fritner and Rubinson's (1993) analysis of 925 undergraduate women
found that athletes were overrepresented in reports of sexual assault,
abuse, and intimidation. Crosset, Ptacek, McDonald, and Benedict (1996)
found that athletes were significantly overrepresented in reports of sexual
assault and battery of women to judicial affairs offices at 10 large universities over a 3-year period.

Koss and Gaines (1993) collected self-reported data from students and
found a low but statistically significant relation between athletic participation and sexual aggression on one large university campus, after controlling for alcohol. In a study using self-reported data collected from 477

men, of whom 77 were athletes, Boeringer (1996) found that a higher percentage of athletes than nonathletes reported the use of coercion (60% vs. 53%), drugs or alcohol (28% vs. 21%), or force (15% vs. 8%) in "sexual" encounters with women. Although these findings were directional, none of these differences was statistically significant. Where athletes demonstrated a significant difference from nonathletes was in their responses to the likelihood of forcing a woman to do something sexual that she did not want to do if they could be assured they would not be caught or punished. Athletes expressed a disproportionately greater willingness than nonathletes to use force to coerce a woman into a sexual act.

In another study, using face-to-face interviews, Bloom and Smith (1996) found some support for an association between the culture of hockey and the approval of violence off the ice. This study sampled house players and select players (n = 604) and nonplayers (n = 153). Players at the highest levels of the sport (select players) were less likely to disapprove of violence than were house players and nonplayers. Select players were also more likely to be violent in other sports. These two findings were statistically significant. Although violence directed at women was not tested, this study supports the notion that training for violence "spills over" into other areas of life.

In contrast, other findings suggest athletes are no more violent toward women than are nonathletes. For example, Crosset, Benedict, and McDonald (1995) found no significant difference between athletes and nonathletes in reports to campus police. Schwartz and Nogrady (1996) found no significant difference between college athletes and nonaffiliated students on a number of variables associated with sexual assault. In no study of athletes' violence toward women do male athletes self-report violence against women at a statistically significant higher rate than do nonathletes (Boeringer, 1996; Schwartz & Nogrady, 1996).

The conclusions we can draw from this quantitative research are limited. The research to date, driven by early theoretical understandings of men's violence, is best regarded as incipient. It does not prove that athletic participation is a predictor of violence against women. It does suggest, however, that athletic participation is associated with some other predictors of violence against women, such as rape-supportive beliefs, overrepresentation of athletes in official reports, and women's self-reports of violence. The mixed results of the early empirical research push researchers to question some of the assumptions about the relation between sport, masculinity, and violence against women. A more nuanced theory of men's violence and some multifactorial analyses are needed.

From the Social World of
Sport to Team Cultures

Peggy Sanday (1996a) has been critical of the way some have employed her concept of rape culture to organizations. In her own research on fraternities, she is careful to note that rape culture describes a few fraternities and not fraternities in general. Boswell and Spade (1996), for example, found qualitative distinctions in the settings, interactions, and attitudes of participants of fraternity parties identified by women as low risk for rape from those they identified as high risk for rape. Assuming all fraternities are responsible for the violence against women, Sanday noted, "is unwarranted unless we can show that the same templates for behavior are present in all fraternities" (p. 193) and, by extension, we can add, in all teams and levels of sport. Sport teams are not "culturally homogeneous."

The inconclusive results of the quantitative research may be a product of too broad a use of the concepts "sport subculture" and "rape culture." The results of the earlier studies suggest that variations may exist between teams or sports. For example, Bloom and Smith (1996) found that select hockey players and nonplayers were less violent in their families than were house players. Koss and Gaines (1993) found the association between athletes and sexual assault was most pronounced among "revenue-generating" sports. Crosset et al. (1995, 1996) found that contact sports (football, hockey, and basketball) accounted for a majority of reported assaults. Michael Welch's (1997) review of 100 media reports of NFL perpetrators revealed that running backs and receivers were overrepresented. These findings suggest variations in the experiences of athletes between sports, levels within a sport, and sport organizations. The practice of lumping all sport environments together under the rubric of "athletic affiliation" misses the variations across specific team subcultures and between athletes.

Athletic affiliation is too broad a variable to be useful as a predictor of assault. Early quantitative studies may not have found athletic affiliation to be a significant predictor of sexual assault because they did not take into account the differences between teams and sports and between levels within a sport. Research designs also have not taken into account the possibility that men have a variety of experiences in sport. Furthermore, researchers generally have not taken into account other variables men bring into a sport situation, like attitudes toward women, class, or nonathletic peer groups that may shape their sporting experience.

Koss and Cleveland (1996) questioned the utility of any attempt to demonstrate the link between athletic affiliation and sexual aggression:

> Even if future . . . data support the hypothesis that individuals belonging to fraternities and sports teams, compared with unaffiliated men, have higher levels of sexually assaultive beliefs and behaviors, the findings would not explain where these beliefs and behaviors come from. (p. 186)

Other intervening variables may be far more predictive of violence against women than athletic affiliation. It may be more fruitful to explore how sport affiliation is linked to these other variables, such as alcohol consumption, number of sexual partners, or association with others who have been violent toward women. It is possible that some teams create and foster a climate comfortable for rapists and batterers, a climate conducive to the neutralization of negative attitudes toward rape and battery (Boeringer, 1996).

A Typology of Violence Against Women

Researchers in the area of violence against women have begun to make distinctions between the types of violence against women. Not all rapes are the same, and not all battery is the same. Feminist researchers increasingly distinguish between types of sexual assaults. The context, tactics of the perpetrator, the response of the victim, and the consequences of a typical date rape are very different than those of an acquaintance rape, party rape, or stranger rape. Similarly, the typical patterns associated with party rape shift depending on the relationship between the perpetrator and the victim (Ward, Chapman, Cohn, White, & Williams, 1991). Furthermore, researchers distinguish between domestic battery and separation assault (Mahoney, 1990).

The patterned variation of violent crimes against women enables sociologists to simultaneously narrow their research questions and broaden their theory. Take, for example, Boeringer's (1996) findings that athletes appear to be more likely than fraternity members to use force to coerce women into unwanted sex. Research on fraternity-affiliated perpetrators indicates that they tend to employ drugs and alcohol in party settings to coerce women into unwanted sex. Hence, the likelihood that a larger percentage of athletes appear willing to use force may not be associated, for example, with date rape, but may be linked with incidents of acquaintance rape (Ward et al., 1991). The differences in tactics, combined with differences in the victim's previous knowledge of the perpetrator, may, in turn, have an impact on reporting rates. Women victimized by force, Koss and Cleveland (1993) speculated, may be more likely to report an assault than would women who have been verbally coerced or plied with alcohol or drugs. Athletes' use of forceful tactics may account for the higher rate of reports of athletes as perpetrators (Crosset et al., 1996), without significant differences in the self-report data. The previous discussion suggests that researchers need to distinguish between types of violence against women and focus on particular team dynamics. The earlier attempts to explain athletes' violence against women as a product of the hypersexist sports world both overstated and simplified the relation between sport and athletes' violence against women (Benedict, 1997).

New Understandings of Masculinity, Sport, and Violence Against Women

The general thrust of the current popular debate has been whether athletes commit more violence against women than nonathletes. To me, this debate seems unproductive. Arguing about whether athletes are more or less violent detracts from the fact that some athletes are violent toward women.

More productive discussions (and research questions) may focus on why some positions, some teams, some sports, or some programs are more prone to violence against women than are others. If membership on some teams or levels of sport is associated with certain types of violence against women, we need to understand the dynamics of those organizations. Theories that simply employ sport affiliation or a reified conception of masculinity to explain all the forms of violence against women fail to capture the dynamics of rape-prone organizations. Researchers need to explore how team members, coaches, or people associated with a team promote behavior associated with violence against women or how some programs foster environments in which potential rapists and/or batterers feel comfortable.

Recent conceptualizations of masculinity offer more a nuanced understanding of the ties between masculinity and violence against women, which, in turn, can inform our understanding of athletes' criminal behavior. Messerschmidt (1993), using key concepts from West and Zimmerman (1987; doing gender), Giddens (1976; structuration) and

Connell (1992; hegemonic masculinity) understood men's violence as situationally structured actions that are resources for doing gender. Masculinity is something that is made, and violence against women is one resource for making it. Messerschmidt's (1993) conceptualization of crime is not unlike the recent conceptualizations of sport. Sport is generally understood as a resource through which men do gender (Crosset et al., 1995; West & Zimmerman, 1987) and a means by which they define themselves in contrast to women (Connell, 1995; Kane, 1995; Lorber, 1994). Sporting prowess has become symbolic "proof" for men of their socially constructed "natural" superiority over women (Connell, 1995; Kane & Snyder, 1989). At the same time, sport is contested terrain (Messner, 1988). Women have gained access to sport and, through sport, challenge ideological justifications for men's domination. As such, sport is readily viewed as a cultural resource for maintaining and resisting hegemonic masculinity.

The benefit to Messerschmidt's (1993) theory of men's crime and more recent theories of men's sport is that they incorporate power relations and social structures and allow for variations between situationally distinct men and masculinities. In sport, in which the distinctions between men are so clearly delineated, few men actually achieve top honors. Yet, all male athletes (and, I would argue, female as well) depend on the maintenance of the current masculine hegemony for whatever special status and power they enjoy as a result of their athletic identity and status. This formulation anticipates variations in resources, tactics, and the types of acts between male athletes. Nonetheless, it recognizes that "there are patterned ways masculinity is enacted and represented" that sustain masculine hegemony (Messerschmidt, 1993, p. 83).

Masculinity, then, is a behavioral response to a particular situation. The same man may participate in a variety of masculinities depending on the context: the team, the classroom, a peer group (Messerschmidt, 1993). Power relations (race, class, and sexuality) further define a situation. Athletes' violence against women then can be understood as situationally dependent, structurally encouraged or constrained demonstrations of masculinity.

In the balance of this chapter, I review some of the more recent research avenues that offer insight into athletes' social practices, social occasions, and activities that sustain masculine hegemony and might also structurally encourage assaults on women. By extension, this research suggests alternative ways to deter athletes' violence against women.

Social Learning/Socialization

Pain is part of the everyday social practices of athletes. Placing one's body at risk to impede or hurt others is not a natural act. Athletes must learn to "mix it up," to view victory as more important than personal safety (Sabo, 1994). There are enough accounts in the biographies of athletes coming to understand the rewards of being mean to suggest that athletes learn from coaches and peers to be violent. In the acknowledgments of Tim Green's (1996) collection of essays on life in the NFL, for example, he thanks George O'Leary for teaching him to "bring the dark side [of himself] to every down of football [he] ever played" (p. viii). In Madeline Blais's (1995) account of a girls' high school basketball season, we see how one otherwise caring coach systematically teaches aggressive play. Working with a particularly sweet and demure player, the coach renamed the player, thereby enabling her to disassociate herself from her aggression and to play the game in the persona of her "evil twin."

If we train athletes to be violent through sport, some suggest, it is reasonable to suspect that this training has an impact on the way athletes think and act off the field. Some athletes readily admit that violent sport influences their behavior off the field (Coakley, 1997). There is possibly no more vivid portrayal of the connection between violent athletic training and off-field violence than Elwood Reid's (1997) recounting of his career as a college football player. In his brief article, he offhandedly described party rapes, brutal assaults, and self-inflicted abuse. "In the world of Big Ten football, you feast on inflicting pain—on and off the field. You do it because you can . . . because it's what's expected of you" (Reid, 1997, p. 361).

Some argue that this violence is cultivated in a culture hostile toward women. Examples of coaches employing images of castration and femininity to chastise athletes abound. In the conclusion of their study that found athletic affiliation to be a slight predictor of violence against women, Koss and Gaines (1993) suggested that we pay attention to what coaches say to their athletes. Koss and Gaines alluded to the possibility that the comments and the counsel of coaches may contribute to athletes' hostile attitudes toward women. Are the ways that coaches advocate violent physical domination and promote masculinity supportive of rape attitudes? Research suggests that sexually aggressive men endorse a set of attitudes that are supportive of rape more strongly than do nonaggressive men (Malamuth, 1986; Malamuth, Linz, Hearvey, Barnes, & Acker, 1995; Malamuth, Sockloskie, Koss, & Tanaka, 1991). Do men who learn to enjoy pain in sport project that enjoyment onto women? Men who believe that women enjoy violence or that violence is a legitimate means for men to keep women in line are more likely to commit violent acts against women (Crowell & Burgress, 1996). Clearly, more research needs to be done in this area. But if training practices for violence on the field mix with hostile attitudes toward women and then spill over to violence off the field, sport practitioners will need to investigate ways of promoting aggressive play without promoting hostile attitudes toward women or to explore ways to decrease the level of violence in sport.

Peer Support

Paying attention to what coaches say probably accounts for only a small part of sport's influence on athletes' violence toward women. Attention also needs to be given to the informal world of athletes. In a study of dating violence on college campuses in Canada, DeKeseredy and Kelly (1995) found that peer support of abuse and social ties with abusive peers are predictors of violence against women. Schwartz and Nogardy (1996) argued that the type of affiliation (e.g., fraternity, sport team) will be far less significant than the type of attitudes toward violence held by members and the expressed practice of violence by members of these groups. The more peer support there is for violence against women, the more likely a member of that group will be to engage in violence against women.

If peer support for violence against women is a causal influence, then how might teammates interact to communicate this support? Harvey's research (1996), based on data obtained while he worked as manager of a men's college volleyball team, offers us clues. The following incident took place as he walked into the locker room. The team had surrounded a shy team member Harvey called "Bashful":

> The guys were being very supportive, smiling and giving encouragement. Bashful was looking down at the floor smiling and appearing to psyche himself up to do something. Then out of nowhere, Bashful began to yell . . . things like "fucking bitch, eat pussy, lick twat, suck my balls, do her doggy style, stick my finger in her ass." Harvey noted the anger in Bashful's face as he yelled obscenities. When it was all over, the team cheered, slapped his hand and congratulated him. Bashful seemed proud of his accomplishment. (p. 140)

Episodes like this one are common in sport; older, more experienced team leaders egg on younger players to engage in risk-taking behavior. On one level, these incidents are fairly benign attempts by older athletes to help younger athletes to become men, more competitive, or both. But on some more fundamental level, these informal team rituals are attempts to maintain team norms, in some cases the acceptance of open hostility toward women. Harvey's work (1996), along with other recent descriptive works (Curry, 1996; Lefkowitz, 1997; Reid, 1997), offer researchers and practitioners a window into the cultural and interpersonal dynamics of a team that openly expresses support for violence against women and shows how resistance to these team norms is systematically discouraged.

Institutional Support

Another line of inquiry related to peer support explores the support athlete perpetrators receive after women report a violation. Institutional support for perpetrators tends to blame women and fails to hold athletes responsible for their actions. No case demonstrates this better than the University of Nebraska's handling of the Lawrence Phillips case. Phillips, who brutally beat a former girlfriend (separation assault), was suspended from play temporarily. University officials argued that severing relations with Phillips would be detrimental to the young man in this time of need. The charges against Phillips were dropped and he returned to action in time to play in Nebraska's bowl game. He was subsequently drafted to play in the NFL and faced no significant or lasting repercussions for his brutalization of a fellow student.

The university's support for Phillips's victim was not as generous (Moran, 1996). Kate McKewan, a member of the varsity basketball team, lost her athletic scholarship and was cut from the team as a result of her poor performance following the brutal beating. In the wake of public outcry, the university offered her a nonathletic scholarship. She left the university. Jeff Benedict (1997) investigated a number of cases of athletes' violence against women and, in case after case, he detailed how university and professional teams failed to hold violent athletes accountable for their criminal behavior and actively worked to silence their victims.

The inability of institutions to hold athletes accountable also extends to the court system. As Benedict and Klein (1997) found, the high-status world of sports cuts two ways when athletes are charged with violence against women. First, athletes seem to be brought to trial more frequently than are nonathletes. Benedict and Klein (1997) speculated that prosecutors feel public pressure to bring public figures like athletes to trial to demonstrate that they do not receive special treatment. But athletes bring more resources (financial and otherwise) into the judicial process and are better able to escape punishment for their crimes against women than are nonathletes. The impediments to prosecuting athletes who perpetrate violence against women, real or imagined, may contribute to the likelihood an athlete will commit violence against women.

Alcohol Consumption

Alcohol consumption is associated with violence against women. Obviously, many incidents of violence occur in the absence of alcohol, and many people drink without engaging in violent behavior. Nonetheless, the association between alcohol and violence is quite high, particularly for the perpetrators of the violence (Crowell & Burgess, 1996). Men's consumption of alcohol, particularly binge drinking, is associated with marital violence. This finding cuts across all ethnic groups and social classes (Kantor, 1993). Thus, although alcohol consumption is not a cause of violence against women, social scientists theorize that alcohol consumption plays a complex role in men's violence against women. Alcohol consumption, particularly drinking to get drunk, may impair reasoning and communication that otherwise may militate against some types of rape and battery. Drinking also may be a part of some men's premeditated strategy to coerce women into unwanted sex; it also may be a strategy to be violent and may be a convenient and a socially accepted means by which men can distance themselves from their violence. The strong connection between drinking and sport is suggested in studies of college alcohol abuse. In a Harvard School of Public Health survey of 17,251 students, athletes were the group most likely to self-report binge drinking. Athletes drink, get drunk, and drink to get drunk at a higher rate than do nonathletes (Wechsler et al., 1998).

Alcohol consumption cannot be separated from the party setting. The physical layout of party spaces (Boswell & Spade, 1996; Curry, 1996) may be staged to decrease communication and increase opportunities for men to assault women (or other men) while limiting their risk of being caught or reported. Furthermore, partying and alcohol consumption cannot be divorced from sexual liaisons. Evidence also suggests that some male athletes have a considerable number of partners (Benedict, 1997). These sexual practices often are supported by formal and informal institutional encouragement for "groupies." Like the physical layout of some parties, a high number of sexual partners (Malamuth, 1986) is associated with incidents of rape.

Head Injuries

Another aspect of sport that may contribute to men's violence is the encouraged disregard for men's bodies in contact sports. Head injuries, like alcohol abuse, impair judgment and are associated with violence toward women. The jarring of the brain, which produces concussions, may damage the frontal regions of the brain and impair one's ability to control impulses. There is substantial evidence to suggest that the brain abnormalities caused by head injury are associated with aggression (Crowell & Burgress, 1996). It is not surprising that researchers have discovered that batterers are more likely to have sustained moderate or severe head injuries than nonbatterers (Rosenbaum & Hoge, 1989; Rosenbaum et al., 1996). In Rosenbaum et al. (1996), a history of significant head injury increased the chances of marital violence sixfold. Sport-related injuries were the third most likely type of head injury, behind car accidents and falls, and most of these head injuries occurred prior to age 16.

Many researchers believe that the impaired reasoning or impulse control due to head injury that is associated with violence against women may interact, in turn, with more predictive developmental and environmental factors. Like alcohol consumption, head injury is not the direct cause of violence against women but clearly one that may play a role in some athlete violence against women.

Conclusion: A Crime of Opportunity

It is fruitful to view male athletes' assaults on women as crimes of opportunity. Certain types of violence against women are structurally available for male athletes through which they construct their masculinity. Star athletes, whose mediated images represent an idealized masculinity, and lesser male athletes, by association, enjoy elevated status within the masculine status hierarchy. Athletes can garner considerable access to resources for demonstrating masculinity—including crimes against women. The factors that increase the likelihood that an athlete will perpetrate a crime against a woman may vary depending on his status, class, race, team culture, sport culture, and the level of sport. Researchers have begun to locate some factors and resources that seem to increase the likelihood that some men will commit violent acts against women that are also associated with athletic life.

Effective intervention approaches would address the structural features of athletes' lives to limit opportunities for athletes to assault women or increase the constraints on men's actions. Such a project would combat a number of factors simultaneously. Given the research outlined previously, institutions could work to reduce binge drinking, head injuries, and expressions of physical domination by coaches. Institutional policies could be formulated to charge and discipline violent athletes. In short, programs can address athletes' violence against women by focusing on specific features of athletes' lives. By transforming the structures of athletes' lives, we can reduce the opportunities for athletes to commit crimes against women.

To view violence against women as crimes of opportunity, we need not lose sight of the fact that crimes against women are hate crimes provoked by men's desire to control women. Masculinity is accomplished by a combination of material features (behaviors, experiences, relationships, practices, and appearances) and discursive features (language and relationship discourses; Collinson & Hearn, 1994). These two broad categories are not mutually exclusive. Changes in the material features of masculinity also have the potential to change how men think.

It will not be easy to change the structures of athlete's lives to decrease the opportunities for men to be violent toward women. Attempts to change these structures also will change how male athletes construct their masculinity. Even small pragmatic steps to change the structures of athletes' lives may be felt by athletes as threats to their manhood. The simple and most obvious prevention measures, such as efforts to reduce alcohol abuse, may be felt as a threat to some athletes' masculinity. Consumption of alcohol, particularly beer and hard liquor, is a resource through which men "do gender." In some circles, the ability to drink hard and then perform well athletically is the ultimate demonstration of manliness (Foley, 1990). Drinking, physical disregard of the body, expressions of hostility toward women, and the physical structure of parties all contribute to some men's sense of masculine identity. Therefore, some men who may never be physically violent toward women are likely to resist these efforts.

Solace can be found in knowing that not all activities or qualities associated with the construction of masculine identity need to be dismantled to reduce violence against women. As Connell (1992) noted, efforts to challenge hegemonic masculinity will need to call on the very "qualities hegemonic masculinity exalts—toughness, endurance, determination and the like" (p.182). If done right, we can teach athletes to embrace the very qualities necessary to challenge the hegemonic patterns of masculinity.

10

Booze and Bar Fights

A Journey to the Dark Side of College Athletics

TIMOTHY JON CURRY

A well-known textbook on the sociology of sport summarizes what is know about sport and aggression:

> Research clearly shows that many male athletes in heavy contact sports learn to accept and use violence and intimidation as strategies during competition. But does this learning carry over into the rest of their lives? Does sport participation make them more aggressive? It would seem that most athletes are capable of distinguishing between the playing field and other types of interaction settings. And most realize that the aggressive strategies they use in their sports are not appropriate in the classroom, in a bar, or on the streets. However, the violent off-the-field reputations of some athletes, along with a number of highly publicized court cases involving athletes charged with violent acts, suggests that this is a possibility—especially in the case of athletes in elite, heavy contact power and performance sports. (Coakley, 1998, p. 195)

The author, Jay J. Coakley, went on to state that more research is needed on the question of whether violent strategies learned in sports carry over to the rest of life. He suggested that we need to know more about the social world of sport and the connections between that world and other aspects of community life. The research described in this chapter attempts to get at some of those connections by focusing on the everyday life of college athletes.

Specifically, my focus is on issues related to the group dynamics of sport participation, especially the peer group factors involved in aggression and the masculine identity of athletes. I follow a research trail blazed by others, such as Messner and Sabo (1994), who wrote extensively about sport and masculinity. These authors made the point that many men choose to participate in contact sport because the heavy hitting and violent confrontations of those sports validate cherished images of what it means to "be a man." National surveys have documented that even high school varsity athletes have higher rates of aggression than do nonathletes, and this behavior may generalize to other situations (Rees, Howell, & Miracle, 1993). For instance, in an exploratory survey of 200 male and female athletes at a medium-sized university, Nixon (1997) found that attitudes toward toughness in sport, hurting people in sport, and participating in contact sports were all related to physical aggression outside of sports for male athletes.

As part of my research specialty, I focus on gender issues in deviance. Most recently, I have become concerned with the deviant, undesirable qualities of all-male sport groups. For instance, I am curious to understand the social forces that encourage some elite athletes to demean and humiliate others, even while they are being held up as role models (Benedict, 1997; Bird, 1996; Coakley, 1998; Harvey, 1996; Welch, 1997). To illustrate, why do some athletes target those who threaten their images of masculinity, such as gay males? Why do some athletes aggress against women who admire them? Is such behavior stimulated by the aggression generated by contact sports?

Heavy drinking also has been identified as part of the masculine identity of college and professional athletes (Green, 1996). Although many students participate in drinking, male college athletes have been identified along with fraternity members as having higher rates of alcohol use than nonaffiliated students (Boswell & Spade, 1996; Green, 1996; Koss & Gaines, 1993; Sanday, 1996b). For instance, a survey conducted in 1994 and 1996 of 51,483 students on 125 college campuses (two- and four-year, private and public) found that men on intercollegiate sports teams reported consuming 10 drinks a week; a total of 12 drinks a week was reported by men in fraternities. In comparison, nonaffiliated college men averaged only 6 drinks a week. Nearly two thirds of the male team leaders reported binge drinking, defined as consuming more than 5 drinks in one sitting. Binge drinking also was reported by nearly half of the women team leaders, but female athletes reported only an average of 4 drinks a week, less than half the average for the male athletes (Leichliter, Meilman, Presley, & Cashin, 1998).

Given the aggressive tendencies among some male college athletes, an interesting question comes to mind: What happens when the tendency toward drinking and the tendency toward aggression come together in campus bars and taverns?

Sports Bars and Male Bonding

Social scientists studying masculinity note that a male bond is an affiliation link, but one that is based on activity rather than the expression of emotion, that is, men typically relate to each other through participation in activities rather than through intimate self-disclosures. In fact, men frequently strive and compete for prestige within their peer groups, and such striving may be the basis of the bonds between men (Curry, 1991; Messner & Sabo, 1994; Nixon, 1997). The sports bar, with its combination of alcohol and sport fan activities, provides a safe haven for men to bond with one another and even to open up emotionally (Wenner, 1996). In addition, men may bet on the outcomes of games while in the sports bar, thus giving their interactions with others a familiar competitive edge (Curry & Jiobu, 1995). Yelling, cursing, slamming on tables, fighting, and other instances of rowdy behavior are more acceptable activities in sports bars than they are in other public places, thus giving men an opportunity to display extreme masculine behavior (Eastman & Land, 1997; Wenner, 1996).

Understanding the nature of male bonding provides us with an important perspective on the relationship between male athletes and the women whom they may encounter at the sports bar. Women frequently serve as "props" or objects that men use to gain status from their peers rather than as equal partners. For instance, as drinking supersedes eating as an activity in sports bars, bars become more sexually segregated. As bars become more sexually segregated, women are defined more as outsiders, even if they have apparent interest in being sport fans (Eastman & Land, 1997). Just as there are relatively safe and unsafe fraternity parties for women to attend on campuses, there are relatively safe and unsafe sports bars for women (Boswell & Spade, 1996; Sanday, 1990; Schacht, 1996).

Aggression in the Locker Room

In previous work, I employed qualitative research techniques (described subsequently) to study locker rooms as sites for studying the interaction of college athletes. I gathered fragments of conversation from two locker rooms at a university with an elite "big time" sports program (Curry, 1991). The conversations revealed numerous instances of verbal aggression. For instance, conversational jibes and "put-downs" were frequently heard as athletes attempted to outdo each other to gain status among their teammates, as seen in these illustrations:

- Striving for academic success was treated as a joke, and locker room culture affirmed a rather cynical view of campus life.
- When women were discussed, they were treated as sexual objects and as members of an inferior out-group. Even the coaches joined in.
- Homophobic comments were directed at teammates, and stories were told about the mistreatment of gay males (gay bashing).
- Locker room talk revealed a masculinist ideology that was enacted through heterosexist aggression (a rape culture).

My research did not extend into the activities outside the locker room, and I was curious as to whether these talk fragments were based on interaction or were just "talk." After I published the results of the locker room study, an opportunity arose to find out more fully what lay behind the talk. Ultimately, two related research questions described in this chapter were pursued: (a) What was the connection between what was said in the locker room and behavior outside? (b) What was the role played by campus bars in facilitating aggression by male athletes?

Qualitative Research Methods

Both the locker room research and this case study employ qualitative research methods. Such methods have certain advantages. The advantage of participant observation in gathering talk fragments in the locker room study, for instance, was that it provided a new insight into the emotional behavior of athletes. Clearly, the athletes enjoyed the give-and-take of locker room talk. I, too, enjoyed the jokes and put-downs. Only later, when I analyzed the content of the talk fragments, did I become aware of the negative aspects of culture that were being created (Curry, 1991).

I have used a different qualitative technique, the life history method, in studying behavior outside the locker room. The life history method is used by social scientists to develop an intimate knowledge of the life of one person (e.g., Connell, 1990). Through a long interview or series of interviews, the researcher attempts to discover the essential features, decisive moments, or turning points in a respondent's life. The advantage of this method is that it provides a deep understanding of the subjective meaning of behavior. To illustrate, I used this method in discovering the meaning of pain and injury to an athlete (Curry, 1993). Although this study stayed within the framework of a single athlete's life history, it suggested research questions that had broad theoretical applications. Other researchers explored those questions, enlarging the research basis considerably through survey methods (Nixon, 1996a). Thus, although the life history method is limited in its ability to provide data from vast numbers of respondents, it may focus attention on theoretical issues that have broad scope.

Marcello's Story

Here, I have constructed the life history of a former athlete whom I refer to with the pseudonym of Marcello (see also Curry, 1998). I have known Marcello for several years. I first interviewed him in connection with the locker room study when he was a freshman, and we have stayed in touch in the years since his graduation. Marcello has spoken to my sociology of sport class on several occasions about various issues relating to the competitive pressures of big-time college sport. Over the years, we have built up sufficient rapport and trust to explore some of the deviant aspects of elite sport culture. Marcello provided me with seven taped interviews, ranging from 30 to 90 minutes over a 7-month period. The research agreement I made with the Human Subjects Review Committee concerning these interviews limited my freedom to discuss the actual teams involved. In creating this life history, I have validated independently as many events as possible. Because I had known Marcello for more than 5 years before the interviews began and previously had interviewed some of his brothers, cousins, other relatives, coaches, and teammates, I was in a position to verify much of the information he provided. However, some of the stories he related could not be verified without further enlarging the scope of the study, and I deleted those stories that were not of fundamental importance in understanding the dynamics of behavior of athletes in the campus bar.

Marcello's credentials as an informant are impressive. He comes from a large family that has produced three generations of elite college athletes. Marcello was interested in talking about his experiences because of several traumatic events in his family. He believed that what he termed "the dysfunction" in the family was due in part to its immersion in the culture of sport and alcohol. He was particularly sensitive to how "macho" sport culture had influenced his relationships between his brothers and their relationships to his parents.

Marcello understood "macho" to mean a very competitive and aggressive stance toward one's brothers, teammates, and fellow athletes. He sought a supportive emotional environment from his family and from his coach, whom he tried hard to please. But such emotional support was seldom forthcoming. Wanting to break free from an environment he perceived as negative and hostile, he sought allies among his wife's family, a sister-in-law, and a priest. These alliances gave him the support he needed to create some emotional distance from the sport culture he had grown up with and had been immersed in for most of his life. I believe they also gave him the moral support he needed to discuss what had transpired during his college career.

In discussing his 5 years as a college athlete, Marcello drew a chart that depicted the high and low points of his college career. We then discussed the various events of his life as they related to these high and low points. In structuring the interviews in this way, I was using a standard life history technique in which respondents are asked to focus on the turning points or epiphanies of their lives.

Marcello explained that he lived at home during his freshman year and the following "red-shirt" year (i.e., a year when an athlete does not compete for the team, saving that year's eligibility). During that time, he dated a woman he met in high school. His sophomore and junior years were his peak years of involvement with the social activities of the team. Most of the stories he related took place in his sophomore and junior years. During that time, he shared an apartment with a friend, frequently went out with the guys, and also saw his girlfriend on a regular basis. He had his greatest athletic success in his junior year, and he had great hopes for a strong finish to his career. Unfortunately, his injuries created difficulties for him during his senior year, and he did not perform up to his or the coach's expectations. He felt increasingly alienated from the team during that time.

Once we had finished establishing this framework, we went back over some of the locker room conversations I had collected during his freshman year. I was particularly interested in determining whether the braggadocio in the locker room was merely talk or whether the athletes were referring to actual behavior. At first, Marcello spoke only in generalities, but I pressed him for details, and gradually we constructed the following account of the relation between locker room talk and the behavior outside.

Booze and the Boys

During their freshman year, several athletes on his team lived on the same floor in a dormitory, where they developed a reputation for wild behavior. The following year, they moved out of the dorm and rented one side of a two-story double that provided them convenient access to the campus and to the dozens of bars that lined the main street that flanked the campus. The fellows in this rooming house had a clique of their own. Their leader was a powerfully built athlete, new to the team. Not part of the established leadership structure, he operated as an outsider. Marcello said that he seemed to prefer keeping his distance from the establishments and was not a "stand-up" kind of guy who would struggle for conventional status and position in a new environment. He took pride in cynically defying team rules and regulations and persuaded some of the others that it was "cool" to do so. Those who took their studies seriously, for instance, were derided as "geeks." He developed a following among the younger athletes, who called him by the nickname "King."

King and his roommates lived near the bar district—a blighted, disreputable area on the border of the campus. These bars were very popular among undergraduates, but local authorities were concerned about the problems they brought to the campus community. At the beginning of each year, new students who moved into the dormitories near the area were warned of the high crime rate at the campus bars. To illustrate, during a 6-month period in 1996, police made 536 arrests at these campus bars (approximately 10% were for assault). Several bars eventually lost their liquor licenses as a result of selling liquor to minors and other illegal and questionable activities.

Marcello indicated that as many as 20 of his teammates might gather at one of these bars, especially on a Thursday, Friday, or Saturday night. He explained that the drinking would frequently start after classes on Thursday and continue through most of the weekend, especially during the off-season. Drinking was not as pronounced when the team was traveling, because the coaching staff would monitor their activities.

Unfamiliar with the everyday world of campus bar life, I asked Marcello to explain in some detail what he and his teammates did at the bars. As he described their activities, it became clearer that most of the focus was on drinking, picking up women, and getting into fights.

He began by explaining that most of the time, athletes would not arrive at the bars until around 11 p.m.—"when the women would be there." Several of the athletes might have started drinking several hours earlier in their apartment. They would be joined later by others waiting for the appropriate time to hit the bars. Upperclassmen would have the timing of their entrance down to a fine art, whereas freshmen and sophomores would frequently show up too soon and not have an appropriate audience.

Drinks Are on the House

Knowing that many of the athletes were strapped for cash, I inquired about how they could afford to drink so frequently. The athletes received special attention from the bartenders. Bar owners wanted the athletes to frequent their bar to attract other students, and so the bartenders would provide them free drinks or only charge them for a few of them. Marcello indicated that the going rate for an athlete at that time was seven beers for a dollar. Free or almost-free drinks allowed the athletes to compete among themselves to see who could drink the most. In one case, the bartender set up seven expensive mixed drinks in a row for one of the team's star athletes. These were "Doctor Peppers"—a brew consisting of a 12-ounce beer, an ounce of Amaretto, and a shot of 151-proof hard liquor. The athlete downed all seven, one after the other, and challenged anyone else to top him.

A macho vocabulary supported drinking to excess. Marcello explained that heavy drinking was required to "prove you're not a pussy." The culture supported such attitudes as "Let's see how drunk I can get. Hang in there with your fellows." Better yet was the attitude "Hang in there 2 days in a row." Married guys who had finished their athletic careers would still "hang in there" to be part of the culture. One athlete won some esteem by becoming totally "out of it" on a regular basis, even falling asleep at the bar. These and other stories were exchanged regarding who could or could not hold their liquor: As Marcello explained, "Most of the guys live together. . . . There is always a story. . . . [It] could be about how much you drink or that your buddy couldn't hold that shot."

How to Stage a Bar Fight

As Marcello related, the athletes would try to "own" every bar they frequented. Often, this meant staging bar fights to demonstrate their power. Several of the athletes were good fighters, and they were typically the ones to start the fight. Often, these fighters would pick out a particular victim based on the fact that he "looked queer." The victim need not do anything particularly provocative—sometimes victims were chosen because "they looked like they didn't want to fight." After the first punch was thrown, others in the group would enter in, either throwing punches of their own or attempting to break up the fight. The team always backed up its most aggressive members, so that the victim seldom had much of a chance.

These fights with other males (never members of one's own team) had a way of building team cohesion and expressing masculine courage. There was less risk than one might assume, because the bouncers inevitably would take the side of the athletes and throw the victim and his party out of the bar.

Marcello had been in many such fights, but not as one of the instigators. Usually, his role was to stand behind his teammate and try to separate the fighters once the fight had begun. Typically, the fight was over quickly. As Marcello said, "They beat up a guy, the guy would get kicked out, and they continue to drink. It's a way to rally—rally the troops, get support." But such fighting was by no means harmless. In one case, the athletes jumped a member of another team and broke one of his legs, and, in another case, one of Marcello's teammates was hit with a bottle. Interestingly, Marcello said that the bar was a special place because he felt safe there. Safe from the criticism from the coaches and from the negative comments of teammates, one could count on one's teammates for protection.

I asked Marcello how his teammates could come so quickly to the aid of the athlete who threw the first punch. Wouldn't they stumble over chairs? Marcello and I took a field trip to one of these bars so that I might sketch the layout and resolve this question to my satisfaction. This particular bar was a large wooden structure, one of the oldest bars near campus. It had long been a "hangout" for undergraduates and was decorated with symbols of the campus sport culture—posters, banners, and various sport memorabilia. Inside, it featured a large bar, with several booths, movable tables, and a small dance floor.

Figure 10.1 shows in schematic form the layout of the dance floor in relation to the booths, entranceway, and a narrow corridor that allowed passage between the dance floor and drinking areas. The athletes positioned themselves near the dance floor, where, according to Marcello, they could get a good view of the available women. They kept their beer within easy reach, in buckets placed on the floor. If an athlete wanted to start a fight, it was easy enough to punch someone as they were leaving the floor. Given the proximity of the passageway to the dance floor, the rest of the team members could get involved in the fight immediately—either to put an end to it or to come to the aid of the instigator.

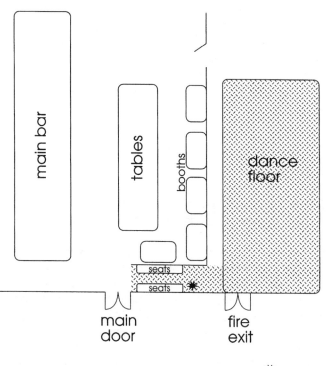

Figure 10.1. Diagram of a Campus Bar

Marcello drew a map of the interior of one of the campus bars he frequented. The map was later redrawn to show more clearly the positioning of his teammates relative to the dance floor. Later in that same year, the bar illustrated caught fire and was destroyed. The university purchased the lot on which it was located in the hope that more desirable uses could be found for the property.

Fighting was one way to create excitement and to show dominance; however, it was not the only way. Some of the athletes also were interested in using the bars as places to pick up women. According to Marcello, "pickups" usually would occur at closing time. An athlete who succeeded in picking up a date would escort her back to the apartment, where some of his teammates would be sitting on the couch waiting to see if anyone scored. If the young woman was a stranger rather than the athlete's regular girlfriend, they would head upstairs at the first opportunity. They would hide in the athlete's room or go to the roof, where they could look into the bedroom through a skylight. The "game" was to get the woman into the upstairs bedroom and into bed and let the other athletes watch the sexual activity take place. I describe such practices in more detail elsewhere, but the point to be made here is that women were being used as objects to gain status and satisfy the sexual curiosity of the young men (Curry, 1998).

The Dark Side

The activities described by Marcello were quite out of character to the public image the athletes presented. Certainly, they were in violation of the university's code of student conduct and in opposition to the values stated by the coaching staff. It was also quite risky behavior. There was risk that a bar fight could get out of hand, and there was risk that such promiscuous sexual activity could lead to sexually transmitted diseases, charges of sexual assault, and other serious problems. In pursuing how the athletes justified such behavior, I asked Marcello to describe in greater detail how his teammates explained their behavior. What was the meaning of these activities to them?

Marcello described a special vocabulary that was adopted by the members of King's clique to characterize their activities. They referred to themselves as members of the "Dark Side," a phrase they apparently gleaned from Star Wars, a motion picture that was popular when they were adolescents. According to Marcello, the rationale they presented for the Dark Side was simply that "you've got to do something bad to cover up for the good stuff." In other words, they took pride in doing outlandish things, things that were contrary to their public demeanor, and then bragging about them later to their teammates. The image of members of the Dark Side was that of the risk taker—someone who would go beyond the limits set by society.

The activities of the Dark Side consisted of a separate subculture, independent but symbolically linked to the conventional sport culture. It was a culture that thrived during off-season and was in the shadows during the regular season. The coaches were never aware of the details of the Dark Side, and, in fact, they would have found it difficult to believe that important members of the team were violating team and university rules purposely.

Occasionally, members of the Dark Side might have a close call. For instance, one of them was almost discovered while cheating on an exam. These close calls made the game even more exciting and were referred to in cryptic comments made in the locker room. In fact, the athletes even had a name for these close calls; they called such occasions "a McGyver"— named after a television character who was forever escaping from seemingly impossible situations. Snyder (1994) reported a similar case in which athletes engaged in deviant activities (mostly theft) to induce risk and generate thrills.

I believe that the imagery of the Dark Side appealed to several fancies of the young men. In part, it was an adolescent version of the antihero or "shadow warrior." The antihero is someone who uses the hero's skills for personal gain without any thought of morality or ethics (Pearson, 1991, pp. 14-17). In other words, antiheroes are people who compromise the basic principles of being a hero to get their own way. At the same time, antiheroes retain some of the strengths of the hero. For instance, athletes on the Dark Side were respected for being fearless, good fighters, and virile. Although the Dark Side was negative, it also was seen as a liberating force, because it removed some of the burdens imposed by being an elite athlete. Like the classic story of Dr. Jekyll and Mr. Hyde, the tales from the Dark Side represented the fascination of the evil side of the personality, hidden from view yet powerful (Pascal, 1992, pp. 122-123).

The concepts of a dark side and the hero/antihero or warrior/shadow warrior are known in many cultures. Jung (1959) thought that such pervasive images were archetypes inhabiting the collective unconscious mind. One does not have to be trained in psychoanalysis to understand or be aware of the image of the Dark Side and the antihero; they have entered popular culture in a thousand different guises through the "warrior myth." The Stars Wars films were simply another retelling of a classic story line (Pearson, 1991).

Regardless of the psychological interpretation one makes of the Dark Side, it is important to stress that from a sociological perspective, the activities on the Dark Side were an abuse of power made possible by an elite status. The athletes would not have been given special favors by the bartenders, and would not have been so attractive to the other undergraduates, if they had just been regular students. Marcello and his teammates who were not members of the Dark Side recognized the abuse of power, and they were both attracted to it and repulsed by it. For instance, the activities of the Dark Side were reported regularly to other team members. Stories were told, legends constructed, as Marcello explained:

You try to get into a situation where you can tell a good story the next day. Get into a fight or screw some bimbo or whatever. How can I get on the Dark Side so I can tell the fellows, "You thought you were so bad, well, look at this one. I've got one for you, this is absolutely crazy."

Conclusion

Marcello's life history and his description of these events provide us with some important insight into the pressures and anxieties of elite sports. They also reveal the significance of the campus bar as a stage for aggressive behavior among college athletes. Aggression and assault in this case were encouraged by campus bars' privileging of male athletes— allowing them to drink for free, taking their sides during fights, giving them an arena in which to operate, and providing them the props necessary to impress others. The bars were very permissive toward athletes, and the athletes took advantage of the situation to prey on others. In return, the athletes attracted attention to the bar and helped to increase its patronage among undergraduates. This symbiotic relationship between athletes and bar owners has gone on for many years. The bar frequented by Marcello and his teammates had been a popular hangout for generations of athletes.

Although fraternities frequently have been researched as institutional supports for male aggression toward women, gay males, and others perceived as outsiders, campus bars that provide similar institutional supports for such aggression have received less notice. Bar culture perpetuates itself through generations, and, if male aggression toward women and other men on campus is to be dealt with more effectively, greater attention must be paid to private drinking establishments. For instance, a bar that provides free drinks for athletes is not contributing to the health and well-being of those athletes, and it is undercutting many of the policies designed to improve the quality of life of athletes and other undergraduates. Such bars should not be tolerated indefinitely by campus authorities.

Marcello's unique life history also reveals continuity between bragging in locker rooms, drinking and fighting in bars, and sexual misconduct in apartments. What is learned about aggression and masculinity in sports carries over to other areas of life, especially those areas in which the peer group reigns supreme. The striving for status in the peer group, fundamental to the motivation of these athletes in sport, easily lent itself to the striving for status in the bar through consumption of alcohol and in the apartment through public display of sexual activity. The camaraderie of the

peer group, in other words, seems focused on issues of hegemonic masculinity, and one's acceptance by the group requires living up to manly standards and protocols set by the group. Unfortunately, the peer group seems
to keep this manly activity at a very sophomoric level. For instance, repeatedly drinking to excess in the middle of the week poses an impossible
burden on establishing a creditable academic record. The better students,
such as Marcello, needed to distance themselves from this culture at some
point if they were to graduate from the university. Similarly, picking fights
with strangers, although defined as manly by the peer group, can lead to
many problems. For instance, one can never assume that a bar fight will
end with a few punches. Some people may decide to "settle the score" later
in the parking lot with knives or guns or later in the courtroom with lawyers and judges.

Similarly, picking up a woman and putting on "a show" for your teammates may be defined by the peer group as a manly display, but it is hardly
the way to learn about romantic encounters. It is particularly destructive
training for developing sexual intimacy with a future spouse, because it relies on performance characteristics of sex and has no positive emotional
content (Stanway, 1993). In the same vein, aggressing against one's teammates, either through verbal attacks against them in the locker room or by
competing with them in drinking contests in the bar, is a way to establish
manly dominance, but it ultimately is an unsatisfying way to build relationships. Such displays prevent deeper friendships from developing
through the sharing of feelings and private thoughts.

In brief, from the perception of the peer group, the Dark Side provided a
boundary separating the "real men" from men who did not measure up and
from women who might threaten the male bond. But in return, it discouraged positive emotional ties between the athletes and more intimate ties
with the women they met.

11

After the War?

Soccer, Masculinity, and
Violence in Northern Ireland

ALAN BAIRNER

As hopes for peace in Northern Ireland rise, there is an urgent need to discuss what kind of society can emerge after almost 30 years of conflict. Will violence persist albeit in a changed context? Or will violent energies be channeled into less harmful activities? One potential outlet is sport although the evidence of the past would suggest that it is as likely to contribute to a continuation of violence as to its eradication. Indeed, I shall argue in this article that, far from playing a role as aggression-displacer, sport in Northern Ireland, and specifically sport spectatorship, feeds hegemonic masculinity which, in turn, can reflect and encourage patterned male violence at large. In particular, there are links, which have gone largely unnoticed, between certain forms of soccer crowd behavior, masculinity, and violence beyond the immediate confines of soccer stadia.

Despite, or arguably because of, the cessation of large-scale terrorist violence resulting from the paramilitary cease-fires of 1994, Northern Ireland has continued to attract extensive academic and media attention. Most of the interest has been in the persistence of sectarian divisions, together with the likelihood, or otherwise, of finding a political solution to

AUTHOR'S NOTE: An earlier draft of this chapter was presented at the annual conference of the North American Society for the Sociology of Sport held in Sacramento, CA, November 1-4, 1995. I thank Peter Shirlow for encouraging me to write on this subject and Don Sabo, Eric Dunning, and Jennifer Hargreaves for their comments on the conference paper. I am also grateful to Jim McKay, Michael Messner, and Don Sabo for their subsequent encouragement and editorial advice.

the problems that have beset the province since 1969. As in the past, other aspects of Northern Irish society, including gender, have been relatively ignored. This article, however, addresses the issue of gender in contemporary Northern Ireland. Specifically, it focuses on the relationship between two groups of men from the Protestant working-class community, namely soccer fans and loyalist paramilitaries. But the discussion is about more than masculinity. It explores a variety of topics, including the organization of sport in Northern Ireland, particularly the culture surrounding the game of soccer; the current political situation; the dynamics of sectarianism; Protestant working-class identity; and, above all, the connections between different categories of violent or aggressive behavior.

Taking Masculinity and Gender Into Account

It is undeniable that gender should be taken into account when assessing the character of Northern Irish society. The concept of masculinity is elusive (MacInnes, 1998). However, as Messner observes, "like it or not, men today must deal, on some level, with gender as a problematic construct rather than as a natural, taken-for-granted reality" (Messner, 1997, p. 2). Writers guilty of ignoring the subject might argue that from 1969 to 1994, sectarianism rather than any other source of division not only dominated the political scene but was also directly responsible for the deaths of well over 3,000 people. The evidence appears to suggest, therefore, that sectarianism has transcended all of Northern Ireland's other cleavages and thus has warranted the greatest amount of academic and media interest. Such a conclusion, however, ignores the irrefutable facts that during almost 30 years of violence, men have done the vast bulk of the killing (as well as a large proportion of the dying); the security forces charged with confronting the civil unrest have been predominantly male; and the politicians who have sought (or in most cases failed to seek) ways out of the political impasse have been men. In contrast, the role of women during this period, although fairly impressive in terms of the overall history of Ireland, often has been limited to involvement in peace groups and cross-community initiatives (Sawyer, 1993). As Sales (1995) observed, "Women in Northern Ireland have been largely excluded from the formal political process" (p. 16).

Feminist writers are correct to complain that this political marginalization of women has been mirrored by academic and media neglect of gender issues in Northern Ireland (Porter, 1998; Sales, 1997). In recent years, however, they have attempted to redress the balance and the role of women is under increasing scrutiny as a result (Roulston, 1997). What remains largely unexplored, however, is the status of men *qua* men in Northern Ireland society. One might argue, of course, that the study of virtually every facet of life in Northern Ireland—its churches, economy, political parties, and paramilitary organizations—is necessarily a study of men. However, the men in question are studied not first and foremost as men but as ministers, priests, industrialists, politicians, terrorists, and so forth. Seldom, if ever, has masculinity per se been a matter for discussion. Thus, issues such as the relation between masculinity and violence have been almost totally neglected.

In a study of domestic violence, McWilliams and McKiernan (1993) examined the specifically Northern Irish aspects of the problem. Their entire emphasis, however, was on how local factors have affected the victims and have influenced societal responses to their suffering. No attempt was made to determine whether local factors may have influenced the behavior of the aggressors. Although this chapter does not examine domestic violence, by looking at two predominantly male domains, it is intended to provide insights into Northern Irish factors that are relevant to the construction of masculinity and to the links between gender and violence.

Writing after the 1994 cease-fires, Archbishop Robin Eames (1995), head of the Church of Ireland, wrote, "We have moved from the culture of actual violence to the culture of uncertainty as we seek to find something better than violence as a means of ordering society" (p. 17). According to Eames, "The vacuum following the cessation of violence has been filled by a peace process which has brought hope, but also uncertainty as people of both traditions have faced new situations" (p. 17). As becomes clear, there is, indeed, considerable indecision about the future, in particular within Protestant working-class communities. Other commentators, however, have been even more alarmist than Archbishop Eames, pointing out that far from simply being replaced by uncertainty, terrorism merely gives way to other forms of violence that may increase or, at best, become more obvious in the absence of the higher profile activities of the paramilitaries. These include punishment beatings and shootings, which are usually the work of the paramilitary organizations, along with domestic violence, child abuse, and muggings (O'Farrell, 1995).

Just as the cease-fires provided some much-needed space for political discussion, so too there has been unprecedented room to study those issues that have been either ignored completely or subsumed within wider analyses of sectarianism. This includes looking at patterns of violence that may have operated independently or, more likely, in conjunction with sectarian division, but that have been disregarded in earlier studies. For example, men's violence is evident not only with regard to terrorist violence but also in other forms of aggression and violence, including soccer hooliganism. However, to date, there have only been tentative steps toward an understanding of this phenomenon (Bairner, 1997).

In discussing the relationship between violence and anti-social behavior at soccer matches in Northern Ireland, this chapter concentrates on male violence within Protestant working-class communities. This is not to suggest that all Protestant working-class men are inclined toward violence. Nor is it to imply that Protestant working-class men alone are, or have been, responsible for the ongoing violence in Northern Ireland. It is to recognize, however, that some Protestant working-class men are violent, that the loyalist paramilitary organizations have recruited primarily from the ranks of the Protestant working class, and that loyalist paramilitarism has had far less prominent female or middle-class involvement than has been the case with armed republicanism. As far as soccer hooliganism is concerned, it is a fact that, despite considerable Catholic interest in the game, the majority of those who follow Irish League teams and the Northern Ireland national side are Protestant, working-class men. The maleness of these soccer fans, however, and also that of the loyalist paramilitaries, seldom has been a matter for analysis.

Although loyalist paramilitarism has been investigated (Bruce, 1992; Nelson, 1984), the gendered composition of organizations such as the Ulster Defence Association (UDA) and the Ulster Volunteer Force (UVF) has provoked little, if any, serious interest. Similarly, the overwhelmingly masculine ambience of soccer fans in Northern Ireland has passed without comment. When the antisocial behavior of these fans has been examined, the analyses have been conducted for the most part within the context of sectarian division (Harvie & Sugden, 1994; Sugden & Bairner, 1988). The overwhelmingly androcentric nature of the protagonists has not been explored, despite the substantial body of literature dealing with the relation between soccer hooliganism and masculinity. In both areas of research, therefore, further work needs to be done. Before turning our attention to these main themes, some general aspects of sport in Northern Ireland, as well as the issue of why sectarianism has tended to dominate discussion in this area of research, need to be discussed.

Sport in Northern Ireland

There have been several detailed investigations of the relation between sport and community relations in Northern Ireland (Bairner, 1994; Cronin, 1997; Harvie & Sugden, 1994; Sugden & Bairner, 1993). Put simply, Northern Irish sports culture consists of three general categories of sporting activity. First, there are sports that arrived as a direct result of British influence and continue to be played primarily in countries that have had historic links with Britain (e.g., cricket; rugby union; and, to a lesser degree, field hockey). Second, there are sports such as football and hurling that are tied to the Irish Gaelic tradition. These were given new life during the late 19th century as a reaction against the growing popularity of foreign (i.e., British) games, thereby becoming important elements in the development of Irish nationalism. Finally, there are those sports that came as a result of British influence but have become so universally popular as to make it nonsensical to describe them as British games (e.g., soccer, track and field, boxing, golf).

The sports in the first category are played mainly by Protestants, whereas Gaelic games are played almost exclusively by Catholics. The sports in the third category, however, might offer some seeds of hope in terms of cross-community reconciliation, because they are played by both denominations. In sum, Northern Ireland provides fascinating material for researchers interested in the relations between sport, sectarianism, and national identity. Nevertheless, by focusing virtually all of their attention on those issues, researchers have ignored that men tend to dominate all three categories of sport. Masculine hegemony is apparent in the three categories of sport—British, Gaelic, and universal—and transcends divisions of social class.

According to Messner (1992b), "Sport is a domain of contested national, class, and racial relations, but the hegemonic conception of masculinity in sport also bonds men, at least symbolically, as a separate and superior group to women" (p. 19). Indeed, Messner suggested that in the United States, gender has become "the central organizing principle" of sport. Although Messner stops short of arguing that gender is the single most important factor in Northern Irish sport, one certainly can find evidence to support Whitson's (1990) assertion that it is "one of the central sites in the social production of masculinity in societies characterized by longer schooling and by a decline in the social currency attached to other ways of demonstrating physical prowess (e.g., physical labour or combat)" (p. 19). Although women take part in a variety of sports in Northern Ireland, there is no denying the relevance of Whitson's claim that "the major games . . . continue as institutions through which the reproduction of hegemonic masculinity, and through this, male hegemony, are actively pursued" (p. 28). Although demands have been made for more equitable access and increased levels of funding for sportswomen, this has had little impact at an institutional level, given the valorization of men's sport and men's domination of sporting organizations. Furthermore, unlike some countries, little or no attempt has been made to challenge the gendered values and symbols that have been institutionalized through sport (Thompson, 1994).

Soccer in Northern Ireland

Although soccer is played and watched by both men and women of all social classes, it is a quintessentially working-class sport. However, this does not mean that working-class people control the game. Although local businessmen have exercised considerable formal control since the game was established toward the end of the 19th century, the social origins of the overwhelming majority of players and supporters have ensured effective working-class "colonization," to use Clarke's expression (1978, p. 42). Moreover, this process has been facilitated by members of both main communities. Unlike those sports that have remained tied either to Britishness or Irishness and have helped to keep Protestants and Catholics apart, soccer has brought members of the two communities together, both on the field and the terraces. Frequently, however, soccer has exacerbated rather than improved intercommunity relations. In addition, any integrative potential that soccer might possess at the grassroots level is seriously undermined by the overwhelmingly Protestant ethos with which it is imbued, particularly at the highest levels of achievement.

Despite the existence of two separate political entities, most sports played in Ireland are organized on an all-island basis. Soccer is unusual in that it reflects the political divisions established by partition. This resulted in the Irish Football Association (formed in 1880 and with its headquarters in Belfast) having overall responsibility for the game in that portion of Ireland, which remains an integral part of the United Kingdom. Despite soccer's British origins, however, it is probably as popular with Catholics as with Protestants. Ultimately, this is reflected in the fact that all of Northern Ireland's semiprofessional soccer teams playing in the Irish League, as well as the national team, contain Catholic players. Nevertheless, there is far less cross-community involvement when one examines support for Irish League teams or for the Northern Ireland side.

Out of 18 Irish League clubs, only Cliftonville, Omagh Town, and Newry Town can claim to have a significant Catholic following. The majority of teams play in the more Protestant eastern half of the province, and all of those that have been most successful in recent years are mainly supported by Protestants. As for international soccer, there has been a marked decline in the number of Catholics who support the Northern Ireland team, regardless of its Catholic players. In fact, most Catholic fans in the north have transferred their allegiance to the team representing the Irish Republic. One reason for this shift in loyalty is the relatively better performances of the Republic's players in recent years. It is fair to say, however, that Catholic disaffection also has been caused by the apparent Protestant hegemony that is exercised over soccer in Northern Ireland. Although this may always have been a feature of soccer's development in the province, given the game's British origins and the resultant opposition to it on the part of advocates of the Gaelic sports movement, the problem has intensified due to a number of specific factors. For example, Northern Ireland's international games are played at Windsor Park, situated in a working-class Protestant area of Belfast and home to Linfield Football Club, traditionally seen as the most Protestant of all Irish League teams. In addition, Catholic involvement in top-level soccer was greatly diminished with the withdrawals from Irish League of Belfast Celtic (in 1949) and Derry City (in 1971), clubs that had large Catholic followings. Finally, the Protestant ethos is manifest most insidiously via the loyalists' songs and chants and anti-Catholic rhetoric that are heard regularly at Irish League grounds. Even when emotions are not running high, the widespread interest at most Irish League grounds in the fortunes of the Glasgow club, the Rangers, so long associated with Protestantism, is a clear indication of the identity of most of those who attend the games. The behavior of a section of these supporters is a major concern of this chapter.

Soccer Crowd Behavior in Northern Ireland

Soccer in Northern Ireland is characterized by the same patterns of male working-class culture as elsewhere in the United Kingdom—heavy drinking, sexism, and profanity. For many fans in Northern Ireland, however, regardless of which team they follow, watching soccer is also intimately bound up with being an Ulster Protestant. For the most part, theirs is a secular or non-Christian Protestantism, which has been described as "a mixture of selective theological dogma, anti-Catholicism and pragmatic loyalism" (Gillespie, Lovett, & Garner, 1992, p. 35). However, despite their lack of religiosity, the commitment of these secular Protestants to their native Ulster is almost spiritual in character. Referring to the importance of sport for the consolidation of national identity, Jarvie (1993) commented, "It is as if the imagined community or nation becomes more real on the terraces or the athletics track" (p. 75). For many Northern Irish Protestants, the imagined community is Ulster, the potent symbolism of which cannot be exaggerated. As Gillespie et al. stated, "One of the overriding patterns to emerge from our discussions with young Protestants is that when they speak of Ulster they are not merely referring to a place" (p. 163). This phenomenon is also explored by Bell (1990), for whom the mythic representation of the Protestant people and their idealized territory, Ulster, is an attempt "to resolve at the level of the imaginary, the real material contradictions confronting the Protestant working-class in contemporary Northern Ireland" (p. 23). In light of this strong commitment to the Protestant way of life, it is hardly surprising that supporting the Northern Ireland (or Ulster) national team or simply a club with a predominantly Protestant support becomes such a passionate affair.

From time to time, this fervor leads to violence either on the terraces or in the streets close to the soccer grounds. Trouble often occurs when the predominantly Catholic Cliftonville plays against teams like Linfield, Glentoran, and Portadown, which are solidly supported by Protestants. The most Protestant of these clubs, Linfield, has played its "away" matches against Cliftonville on its own ground, because of police fears that violence would be difficult to contain if matches were contested at Cliftonville's home field. In addition, during the 1996-1997 season, Cliftonville supporters were prevented from attending two away matches as a result of loyalist demonstrations. It should be added that violence also occurs at games involving two Protestant sides, for example, between the great Belfast rivals Linfield and Glentoran. It would be wrong, however, to create the impression that violent crowd behavior has been a major problem for Irish League football. International matches have been remarkably free of violence, in part, ironically, because of the reluctance of the supporters of visiting teams to travel to such a troubled part of the world.

There are a number of reasons for the relative scarcity of soccer hooliganism in Northern Ireland. First, Irish League games attract fairly small crowds. Second, important and potentially troublesome games have tended to be supervised by large contingents of armed policemen, sometimes supported by the military, who have been concerned less with soccer hooliganism per se than with the possibility that any incidents might escalate into more generalized civil unrest. Third, although soccer crowds in Northern Ireland are made up primarily of working-class men, these men by no means conform to a uniform type. As early as the 1970s, Jenkins (1982, 1983) noted a marked difference between "rough" and "respectable" children living on a working-class Protestant housing estate in Belfast. A significant aspect of this distinction was the influence of churches in Protestant working-class life (Jenkins, 1982, pp. 21-22). Religion continues to play an important role in moderating behavior, including that of many of the young men who go to soccer games. This is not to suggest that boys or young men who go to church or are members of the Boys' Brigade could not become involved in soccer hooliganism. But they are less likely to be protagonists than their peers who have escaped the influence of a variety of Protestant churches. Fourth, violence has not disfigured soccer to the same extent in Northern Ireland as it has in other parts of the United Kingdom, because traditionally, the province has not been a particularly violent place, having had much lower rates of "ordinary" criminal violence than Scotland or England.

Nevertheless, soccer hooliganism consists not only of overt violence but also of a range of antisocial behaviors that are all too apparent at Irish League grounds. Indeed, the thesis developed here is that although hooliganism can be viewed as a problem in itself, it is also closely linked to the broader social problems of sectarianism, sexism, and terrorism. For example, singing loyalist and anti-Catholic songs is commonplace not only during Irish League games involving clubs with mainly Protestant supporters but also at Northern Ireland international matches. The traditional song most frequently heard is *The Sash My Father Wore,* a popular song that refers to the regalia worn by members of the Protestant Orange Order. Almost as popular is the traditional song that begins with the words "Hello, hello, we are the Billy Boys," and contains the lines "We're up to our knees in Fenian blood, surrender or you'll die." This song celebrates the deaths of Catholics and is sung even by supporters of teams like the national side, which contain Catholic players. Indeed, Linfield goals, even if scored by Catholic players signed since the club ended what appeared to be a policy of employing only Protestants in the mid-1990s, are still celebrated with a chorus of this unashamedly sectarian song.

Such refrains, along with accompanying anti-Catholic rhetoric, reach a crescendo during games involving Cliftonville or when Northern Ireland plays the Republic of Ireland at Windsor Park, the home ground of both Linfield and the Northern Ireland national team. "You dirty Fenian bastards" is chanted on the terraces regardless of the fact that the followers are cheering on a club or national side that contains "Fenians."

Sectarian chants also are heard when both opposing groups of supporters are mainly Protestant. Referring to their club's former unofficial policy that maintained all-Protestant players, Linfield supporters used to taunt fellow Protestants who followed Glentoran with a terracing chant containing the words "No Fenians on our team. . . . No not one." In response, Glentoran fans, highlighting the fact that many Linfield supporters live in an area of Belfast that is nowadays home to far more Catholics than Protestants, insulted their rivals with the words, "Gerry Adams is your MP." Or to attest to their own Protestantism, despite the presence of Catholic players at their club, the Glentoran fans (or "Glenmen") claimed as one of their members the notorious loyalist murderer Michael Stone with the words, "Michael Stone's a Glenman, Michael Stone's a Glenman." Evidence of this is sparse, although it is true that Stone grew up in east Belfast, home to Glentoran and most of the club's supporters. In summary, irrespective of which teams are playing and no matter how many Catholic players are on view, anti-Catholic songs and chants abound.

All of this antisocial rhetoric means that Irish League soccer grounds are seldom welcome places for Catholics, who simply want to watch a game without allying themselves to Cliftonville and the particular brand of sectarianism exhibited by the club's supporters. One can scarcely be surprised that Catholics feel uneasy in situations with people who celebrate the activities of the UDA and the UVF, which have been responsible for the deaths of numerous Catholics.

It is not only Catholics, however, who may feel vulnerable at many Irish League grounds. Women are also discouraged from attending soccer games either by the facilities or by the behavior of predominantly male supporters. Some young girls attend with their fathers or girlfriends; some teenage women are encouraged to attend by teenage men who believe there is a close relation between hardness and sexual attractiveness and who thus hope to have opportunities to exhibit their newly acquired sense of masculinity (Canaan, 1991). More commonly, male fans seem eager to exclude women from their preserve. This is certainly evident in the impression created by the sexist comments that they direct at a variety of women, ranging from scantily clad models promoting sponsorship deals to first aid and ambulance workers who are obliged to attend matches. Superficially, to judge from the rhetoric coming from the terraces, sectarianism is a greater problem than sexism, not least perhaps because the men have won the gender battle and thereby ensured that few women enter the grounds. I now turn to the argument that there is a gender dimension to the sectarianism of Protestant working-class soccer fans that may not manifest itself in overtly sexist rhetoric but that is related to questions of masculinity and that, in turn, has helped to create both antisocial behavior at soccer grounds and loyalist paramilitary violence.

Loyalist Paramilitarism

The two organizations whose activities are most commonly celebrated in the songs and chants of Protestant soccer fans are the UDA and the UVF. Acting under their own names or a variety of pseudonyms, these bodies were responsible for around 900 killings between 1969 and 1994. Their ultimate objective has been to defend Northern Ireland's status as part of the United Kingdom in the face of nationalist demands for a united 32-county Irish Republic. Because they regard their violence as being supportive of the constitution, they consistently have rejected the accusation that their behavior is criminal.

Despite the protestations of loyalists, however, the distinction between political violence and ordinary crime has been blurred constantly (Bairner, 1986). A majority of those involved between 1969 and 1994 in paramilitary organizations, both loyalist and republican, also were implicated to some degree in a multiplicity of routine criminal activities, including, on the part of the loyalists, the killing of Catholics who posed no direct threat to the Union as well as armed robberies and racketeering that were used partially, but by no means exclusively, to fund further military operations. In fact, what is most striking about the majority of the paramilitary organization members is their ordinariness and close ties to their local communities. This is particularly true of republicans who have been more obviously sustained by a tradition of unconstitutional violence. As Heskin (1980) suggested, "Although there is a traditional respect for the force of arms in the Northern Protestant tradition, there is no widespread tradition of guerrilla warfare" (p. 85). Yet, he also made another claim:

The behaviour of terrorists [in Northern Ireland] does not differ substantially from the behaviour of men in conflict-oriented groups generally, and that behavior is largely explicable, at a psychological level, in terms of the formalistic and authoritarian structure of conflict-oriented groups and the role requirements of members of such groups. (p. 93)

Heskin (1980) also stated, "Similar behavior can be elicited from ordinary people in the right circumstances" (p. 93). Thus, although the paramilitary organizations have recruited psychopaths more than willing to operate under the flags of convenience provided by organizations such as the UDA and the UVF, most of their members have been attracted to violence because of a set of political circumstances and their own, arguably misguided, response to them and not as a result of some deep psychological flaw. This pattern of enlistment also has been tied to the reproduction of a particular conception of masculinity.

Morgan (1994) proposed, "Of all the sites where masculinities are constructed, reproduced and deployed, those associated with war and the military are some of the most direct" (p. 165). In Northern Ireland, sport has had to operate alongside a militaristic ethos that is particularly prevalent in working-class communities and influential in the construction and reproduction of a certain type of masculinity. The remainder of this chapter considers the extent to which the ordinary men in the loyalist paramilitary organizations and the ordinary men who engage in antisocial behavior at soccer games in Northern Ireland are connected through the construction of masculinities.

Soccer Hooliganism in Northern Ireland:
Between Hooliganism and Terrorism

Although soccer hooliganism as normally defined is not a regular feature of games in Northern Ireland, the rough working-class masculinity of those most often associated with hooliganism elsewhere certainly is. According to Elias and Dunning (1986), "The values which underlie hooligan behaviour at football matches and in match-related contexts are relatively persistent, deeply rooted and long-standing features of the communities of specific sections of the working class" (p. 266). Elsewhere, Dunning, Murphy, and Williams (1988) argued, "The identities of males from the rougher sections of the working class thus tend to be based on what are, relative to the standards dominant in Britain today, openly aggressive forms of masculinity" (p. 210). This section of the working class is characterized by segmental bonding, which is more typical of traditional societies than the functional bonding that is increasingly the norm in industrial societies, and, for a variety of reasons, this segmental bonding appears more conducive to affective masculinity (Elias & Dunning, 1986, pp. 233-234). Thus, young men find themselves in a situation that encourages the sort of aggression that wins them greater respect from their peers. As Elias and Dunning suggested, "Segmental groups in modern society are subjected to restraint *from the outside* but not, to anything like the same extent, *from within*" (p. 243). It is clear that many Protestant working-class communities in Northern Ireland, particularly in Belfast, are characterized by this segmental type of attachment. This may help to explain why these young men react with displays of aggressive behavior (e.g., at soccer matches) when faced with problems emanating from the outside world.

This does not mean that all of the Protestant working-class men who attend soccer games engage in violence or even in anti-Catholic rhetoric. As indicated, regular churchgoers are frequently able to stand apart from this sort of behavior. On the other hand, there is a hegemonic masculinity at work that is capable of drawing in even some of the most resolute unless they are given special dispensation from the hegemonic males. As Robert Hanke describes it, "Hegemonic masculinity . . . refers to the social ascendancy of a particular version or model of masculinity that operates on the terrain of common sense and conventional morality that defines 'what it means to be a man,' thus securing the dominance of some men (and the subordination of women) within the sex/gender system" (Hanke, 1992, p. 190). At many soccer grounds in Northern Ireland, the hegemonic masculinity constructed by young men, who are primarily from rough Protestant working-class districts, demands participation in sexist and sectarian rhetoric, celebration of the deeds of loyalist paramilitaries and, from time to time, engagement in soccer violence. Even if certain young men are able to resist incorporation, it is this hegemonic masculinity that tends to dominate many soccer games.

According to Archetti (1994), soccer "permits a legitimized definition of a bodily practice as eminently masculine, which does not need to be accepted by the entire population" (p. 236). This might explain why some soccer fans have been able to resist the hegemonic masculinity that surrounds the game and develop a fanzine culture that, according to Haynes (1993), "has been able to challenge the male identity which is constructed through soccer, thereby allowing male (and female) fans to derive more productive pleasures from the game" (p. 69). There is little evidence, however, that the fanzine culture has had an appreciable impact on the hegemonic masculinity that pervades soccer grounds in Northern Ireland. It would be nonsensical to suggest that there is no appreciation of the aesthetic delights of soccer in a society that has produced so many talented players. Nevertheless, the fanzine culture has tended to reproduce masculine and sectarian values rather than offer fundamentally different perspectives. Other soccer developments have been equally unsuccessful in changing basic attitudes. Giulianotti (1993) commented on the role of Aberdeen's soccer hooligans as cultural intermediaries in Scottish society:

> Operating in a sporting context in which soccer violence had been hypostatised into an affective, sectarian mundaneness, the ASC [Aberdeen Soccer Casuals] through an active corporeality of violence and style, embodied a new subcultural challenge to Glaswegian hegemonies of violence. (p. 169)

Giulianotti admitted that, for a number of reasons, this counterhegemonic project was bound to fail (p. 178).

Despite the adoption of designer labels and "smart violence" by a minority of fans in Northern Ireland, the intervention of the casuals into the soccer hooligan equation was arguably doomed from the very outset. Violence that appeared unrelated to sectarianism was unlikely to have met with the approval of the paramilitaries, but violence and antisocial behavior that had manifest links, through sectarianism and traditional notions of masculinity, to the parental culture could be tolerated and perhaps even welcomed. In general, therefore, although not totally unaffected by developments elsewhere, the soccer culture of the Northern Irish Protestant working class remained locked in traditional sectarian patterns. To explain how these came to have an impact on crowd behavior, even at games watched almost exclusively by Protestants, it is essential to discuss the issue of masculinity in more detail.

Protestantism and Masculinity

It is possible to identify both an idealist and an essentially materialist approach to the relation between Protestantism and masculinity. For example, Morgan (1992) pointed to the possibility of a strong ideological connection between these two phenomena. Drawing on Weber's discus-

sion of patriarchy, Morgan referred to the separation of home and work
that was necessary for the capitalist deployment of formally free labor:

> Protestantism might have something to contribute to the sharpening definition
> of these constraints. . . . The Protestant world, the capitalist world, is a public
> world and a masculine world, as far removed from the comforts of the home as it
> was from the traditional controls of the church or the monastery. (p. 61)

This process imbued men with a strong sense of responsibility, specifically as breadwinners. Thus, Morgan maintained, "There are strong links,
it would seem, to be made between the domestic ideas of responsibility
and ideas of self-control, discipline and sober rationality" (p. 62). He concluded:

> Different complex societies have a range of masculinities which are more or less
> approved or positively sanctioned and that religion, in this case Protestantism,
> is one part of the process whereby certain masculinities are accented as well as
> shaping the limits of acceptable masculinity within a particular society. (p. 65)

Although these abstract arguments are somewhat removed from the material realities of Protestant working-class life, they are pertinent to perceptions widely held by members of the Protestant working class of the
Protestant work ethic and their own relationship to work and employment.
Implied in this perspective is a negative view about Catholics' attitudes toward work. However, the political economy of Northern Ireland, rather
than a simplistic idealist analysis coupled with popular mythology, offers
clearer insights into the relation between Protestantism, masculinity, and
violence.

According to Segal (1990), "Men's desire for dominance at work is
connected with the preservation of their 'masculine' identity" (p. 209).
Indeed, as Morgan (1992) suggested,

> The impact of prolonged unemployment and redundancy would seem to be a
> fruitful area for the exploration of masculinities for it is here, one might assume,
> that there is a major assault on one of the most fundamental pillars of male iden-
> tity, that of employment and occupation. (p. 118)

Regardless of the stereotype of the lazy Catholic that has been constructed in Protestant mythology, both Catholic and Protestant men and
women are greatly diminished by unemployment. But in terms of rela-

tive deprivation, it could be argued that Protestant working-class men are more affected, and their masculinity questioned more deeply, by the harsh realities of unemployment than Catholic working-class men, who during many years have come to regard long-term unemployment as a fact of life. Coulter (1995) pointed out, "The material foundations of sectarian social relations remain broadly and obstinately in place" (p. 4). For instance, Catholic men are still twice as likely as their Protestant counterparts to be unemployed. As Shirlow and McGovern (1995) observed, however, deindustrialization and the post-Fordist economy responsible for increased unemployment in the heavy engineering sector have affected particularly heavily the Protestant working class:

> The erroneous perception held by sections of the Protestant working class that their economic plight is due to a growth in employment for working class Catholics has led directly to the targeting of Catholic workers in predominantly Protestant workplaces as part of the recent Loyalist paramilitary campaign. (p. 24)

Thus, the intensity of feeling caused by growing unemployment in Protestant working-class areas also may have played a significant part in promoting anti-Catholic rhetoric at soccer games. But because unemployment undermines a certain image of masculinity, it is even a factor in provocative chanting at matches watched exclusively, or mainly, by Protestant coreligionists. A popular song on such occasions refers to the housing conditions in the area in which most of the rival supporters live (e.g., "In your Shankill Road slums" or "In your east Belfast slums"). The meaning is obvious—you are not manly enough to have nice homes. By extension, you are not manly enough to get decent jobs and to be able to afford to move to a more salubrious area. Even the more directly sectarian chants carry similar messages. You let Catholics play for your football team. You let Catholics move into your area. What sort of men are you?

Bell (1990) pointed out the extent to which unemployment among young Protestant working-class men has led many of them to embrace the culture of the marching bands (linked to the Orange Order and to loyalism more generally) as a means to assert their masculinity. Following certain soccer clubs, and, indeed, the national team provides a similar outlet, not least when the manner in which the support is expressed can be linked to the parental loyalist culture of the fans who are involved. Again, this provides an opportunity to assert an aggressive form of masculinity. Furthermore, not so far removed are the loyalist paramilitaries (also linked to the parental culture), almost exclusively men who have reacted to political and economic threats, real and imagined, in extremely violent ways. To what extent, then, can the antisocial behavior of the soccer fans and the murderous campaign of the loyalist paramilitaries legitimately be equated? Also, to what extent does the hegemonic concept of masculinity permit such an equation to be made?

Conclusion

In the modern world, it is reasonable to describe athletes as "proxy warriors" (Hoberman, 1984, p. 6) who represent towns, cities, nations, and ethnic groups; in return, the public salutes them. Northern Irish soccer fans regard their soccer teams in this way, but they also use soccer matches as the occasions to salute their other combatants, who are actual warriors as well. The precise relationship between the fans and these warriors has a number of dimensions.

First, it is conceivable that there is some degree of overlapping membership between the two groups. It is unlikely, of course, that leading members of the UVF or the UDA would wish to draw attention to themselves by chanting sectarian slogans or getting involved in violence at soccer games. In addition, it would be wrong to suggest that everyone who utters anti-Catholic rhetoric at a soccer game is on the fringes of the loyalist paramilitary organizations. On the other hand, one suspects that most members of these organizations will have served a form of apprenticeship on the terraces of certain Irish League grounds.

Second, even if the idea of coinciding affiliation is to exaggerate the links between the two groups, some degree of personal contact is inevitable, as the terrorists and the soccer fans come mainly from the same communities.

Third, and most important, a mutual support system operates, whereby the chants of the fans appear to sanction the actions of the terrorist, who, in return, provides the fans with an added sense of male hardness in communities where this is a prized commodity. Many, perhaps most, of the fans who chant the names of the paramilitary organizations do not really condone their violent excesses. Nevertheless, they are clearly influenced by the type of hegemonic masculinity that permeates the crowds and elicits antisocial behavior, including the celebration of terrorist violence. By their actions and regardless of their innermost feelings, fans thus help to maintain a climate of aggressively masculine sectarianism that legitimizes the possibility of a return to terrorist violence on the part of the paramilitaries. Meanwhile, the soccer fans strut to games buoyed with the sense that they are connected to the real hard men, not only on the soccer field but, more sinisterly, in the hidden trenches of a terrorist struggle. One cannot be certain of the extent that this continuum of violence, linking fans and terrorists, is rooted in a "crisis" of masculinity in Protestant working-class areas. However, Segal (1990) suggested, "There are links between the prevalence of violence in our society and men's endeavors to affirm 'masculinity'" (p. 269). Economic and cultural factors at the macro level may have affected masculinity at the micro level, resulting in antisocial behavior at soccer games, which, although very different in kind from terrorist violence, is part of the same continuum. Numerous authors have sought to comprehend the linkages between young men (especially working-class young men) and violence. Horrocks (1994), for example, suggested, "These male youths are expressing their utter frustration and their feeling that they aren't wanted except as factory-fodder, if they are lucky enough to get a job" (p. 144). Unemployment, coupled with a perceived threat to the political identity of Protestants in general, has certainly been an important factor in determining the character of hegemonic masculinity in Protestant working-class areas, which then finds expression in the sectarian chants of soccer fans or the violence of the paramilitaries. This is not to look at the men in question as merely unfortunate victims of external pressures (Coltrane, 1994). Other men grow up in the same circumstances and they neither engage in anti-Catholic (or sexist) rhetoric at soccer matches nor join the ranks of the loyalist paramilitaries. But the masculinity of those who do react in these ways remains a necessary matter for investigation.

In no way does this chapter attempt to explain in a definitive manner the intricate relationship between masculinity and violence in Northern Ireland. Rather, the intent has been to underline that there is important work to be done in this area. The ceasefires of 1994 and the peace process more generally provided the opportunity to explore corners of Northern Irish society, such as domestic violence, that were once unvisited. It is ironic to think that as we begin to explore these dark recesses, we may ultimately be able to shed more light on those subjects, including sectarianism, which have previously attracted almost all of the academic comment. As far as the behavior of soccer crowds is concerned, it could be assumed that, with levels of loyalist paramilitary violence much diminished, sectarian rhetoric now serves only to provide an outlet for lingering animosities. As such, it might be characterized as playing a civilizing role. In contrast, however, here we have argued that the sectarian behavior of soccer crowds remains inextricably linked to other forms of sectarianism, including sectarian violence. Indeed, there is little evidence to date that the relationship between masculinity and violence is any closer to being broken or even dissipated. Engaging in violent rhetoric at a soccer game may be inherently more civilized than shooting an "enemy" or battering a wife or child, but it unfolds along an interconnected and uncivilized continuum consisting of men behaving badly. As Northern Ireland looks toward a more peaceful future, it will be imperative that strategies are devised to ensure that all forms of violence, and not merely political violence, are eradicated. Among other things, that will involve even more detailed research into the links between violence and masculinity.

12

Conceptions of Masculinity and Gender Transgressions in Sport Among Adolescent Boys

Hegemony, Contestation, and the Social Class Dynamic

SUZANNE LABERGE
MATHIEU ALBERT

Cases of women venturing into men-dominated fields and of men venturing into women-dominated ones constitute rich social facts that can shed light on key issues about the dynamics peculiar to the construction of gendered social life and gendered identities. Various social processes are particularly enacted in these experiences, such as (a) the complex interaction between patriarchal culture, gendered social organization, and gender identity; (b) the asymmetry of gender relations; and (c) the dynamics of change and resistance in a given social order. Modernization, the progression of capitalism, and the feminist movements that marked the first quarter of the 20th century led to a mass entry of women into "male pre-

AUTHORS' NOTE: This research was supported by the Social Sciences and Humanities Research Council of Canada. We thank the editors for their constructive comments. We also are indebted to Michael Gilson and Yvan Girardin for their invaluable help in editing the English version of this chapter. Address correspondence to Suzanne Laberge, Department of Kinesiology, Université de Montréal, P.O. Box 6128, Station Centre-Ville, Montréal (Québec), CANADA H3C 3J7; phone: (514) 343-7934 (office); fax: (514) 343-2181; e-mail: suzanne.laberge@umontreal.ca

serves" (Dunning, 1986; Theberge, 1995), such as the workplace and sport, thereby fostering the study of gender relations with a particular focus on the integration of women in "nontraditional" domains. Hence, feminist scholars scrutinized many social processes that previously had gone unchallenged or were only marginally questioned, such as men's oppression of women (patriarchal power) and the sexual division of labor. The upheavals in social organization and the turbulence in gender ideologies that eventually occurred fueled the gender self-consciousness and "crisis" then experienced by some men (Kimmel, 1987b) and influenced the rise of scholarship on masculinity. The primary concerns of these scholars were mainly oriented toward deconstructing and theorizing masculinity, that is, discovering the sociohistorical construction of masculinity and its cultural and internal differentiations (Brod, 1987; Carrigan, Connell, & Lee, 1985; Connell, 1993; Kimmel, 1987a; Hearn & Morgan, 1990; Morgan, 1992). It is only somewhat recently that we have witnessed a growing number of empirical studies addressing the issue of men venturing into nontraditional occupations (e.g., Poole, 1996) or into so-called women's sporting activities (Adams, 1993; Davis, 1990). We believe that this avenue can provide a fruitful means to further our understanding of the internal differentiation of maleness and the dynamics of gender relations.

This chapter seeks to explore and interpret (a) the various meanings that male adolescents give to masculinity, intermale tensions, and oppositions; and (b) their differential and contradictory appraisals of men who participate in so-called women's sports—that is, men who transgress the rules of the gender order in sport. The chapter aims ultimately to identify and understand the links and the contradictions between conceptions of masculinity and expressed judgments of men's transgressions of the gender order. Particular attention is paid to how conceptions of masculinities and judgments of men's transgressions interact with the structure of social classes.

Conceptual Framework

Some of the main research questions were inspired by the theorizing of Harding (1986) regarding the social construction of gender. According to Harding, gendered social life is produced through three distinct processes. First, there is *gender symbolism,* which refers to "assigning dualistic gender metaphors to various perceived dichotomies that rarely have anything to do with sex differences" (p. 17). Cultural expressions of gender symbolism are to be found in the binary oppositions masculine/feminine and the various gender stereotypes (e.g., delicate/sturdy, gracious/powerful, sensitivity/toughness) that are quite illusive and exclude a majority of men and women. The process *gender structure* consists of "appealing to these gender dualisms to organize social activity" (p. 17); this results in social interactions that are constructed according to a dualistic division of activities based on gender. The third process, which Harding calls *individual gender*, refers to "a form of socially constructed individual identity only imperfectly correlated with either the 'reality' or the perception of sex differences" (p.18). In this chapter, we consider the understandings of masculinity expressed by adolescents as an interaction between individual gender and gender symbolism. We attempt to discern the extent to which they personally integrate or contest masculine stereotypes or dominant symbols of masculinity. We conceptualize sport as a gender structure that is organized according to a dualistic understanding of gender. We also examine agency by addressing individual reactions to gender symbols (personal opinions about masculinity) and individual beliefs about gender transgressions in sport.

Our analysis relies heavily on Connell's (1995) conceptualization of masculinity as "simultaneously a place in gender relations, the practices through which men and women engage that place in gender, and the effects of these practices in bodily experience, personality and culture" (p. 71). We believe that his approach meshes well with Harding's (1986) formulation, because both stress that genders are simultaneously cultural forms, structures of social activities, and identities. Following Connell (1987), we distinguish between the local or microlevel dimensions of gender relations (e.g., in sport, religion, work, the state, the media, family life), which he calls "gender regimes," and the abstract or macrolevel "gender order," which refers to "the structural inventory of an entire society" (pp. 98-99, 111). We also employ recent feminist and profeminist research that emphasizes the need to acknowledge the existence of multiple masculinities and the complex intersections and tensions among gender, class, race, and sexuality (Brod, 1987; Carrigan et al., 1985; Connell, 1993, 1995; Hearn & Collinson, 1994; Messner, 1990b, 1993).

Method

This chapter reports on the qualitative portion of a larger study on coeducation, somatic culture, and gender relations undertaken among Québec adolescents. The qualitative part of the research was designed to address the following questions:

1. What are the current referents for masculinity and femininity among male and female adolescents? To what extent do they reproduce, resist, or transform dominant gender symbols or stereotypes?
2. What are adolescents' judgments vis-à-vis transgression of a gendered social activity like sport? Is the acceptance or discrediting gender-symmetric?
3. Is there a relation between conceptions of masculinity and femininity and the approval or stigmatization of gender transgression?
4. What do the previously stated processes suggest regarding the reproduction or the transformation of gender hierarchies?

In previous research, we noted that it was difficult to get adolescents to articulate their genuine opinions in face-to-face interviews. Adolescents are often reticent to express themselves, either because they are afraid that they might give a wrong answer, or because they feel uncomfortable in this artificial form of interaction. As a result of informal talks with some adolescents, we decided that essays on an issue of concern to their age-group would be a more suitable strategy for eliciting responses. Accordingly, we asked students in three French secondary 5 grade schools (i.e., 15- to 16-year-olds) in the Montréal area to write essays. We included students from two public high schools, one in a working-class (WC) district and the other in a middle-class (MC) suburb, as well as another group from a private high school in an affluent neighborhood (UC).

At our first meeting, the students were asked to write an essay about gender and sport. They were encouraged to think about their compositions and to discuss them with their friends. The essay was presented as an opportunity to express their opinions on a debatable subject. They were told that their essays would be handled in a confidential manner and that their anonymity would be preserved. They were given four topics that were presented in colloquial language and in ways that stressed there was no right or wrong answer and that they should feel comfortable about expressing their highly personal opinions. Students also were encouraged to relate any of their own sport experiences that were relevant to the following four topics:

1. Describe what a "masculine" or a "virile" boy means to you, if such a category exists. How would you characterize a person who is said to be masculine? In other words, how would you define masculinity?

2. Describe what a "feminine" girl means to you, if such a category exists. How would you characterize a person who is said to be feminine? In other words, how would you define femininity?

Assuming that men's sports are those mainly played by men (e.g., football, boxing, ice hockey) and women's sports are those primarily participated in by women (e.g., figure skating, aerobic dance, ringette[1]).

3. How would you perceive a man who plays a women's sport? In your opinion, does this make him less masculine?
4. How would you perceive a woman who plays a men's sport? In your opinion, does this make her less feminine?

A few days after our first meeting, we returned and allowed students a full class period (usually 75 minutes) to write the essays. They were asked to write about half a page on each topic and to indicate their gender and their country of origin at the top of the page (there were quite a few immigrants in the MC and WC schools). This research strategy exceeded our expectations, as the students were surprisingly expressive in their opinions and appraisals of our questions.

We undertook a content analysis of the essays using a computer program called *Content Analysis Tool,* designed especially for this study by a computer technician using Macintosh HyperCard language. After rejecting a dozen essays either because the handwriting was illegible or because the text was incomprehensible, we ended up with a total of 354 valid essays, 174 by boys and 180 by girls, which were quite evenly issued from the three social milieus (see Table 12.1).

In this chapter, we examine only the boys' essays and only the sections that contained their ideas about masculinity (Topic 1) and about men's transgressive behavior (Topic 3). The boys' appraisals of girls' transgressions and the girls' appraisals of boys' trespasses are briefly considered to highlight the significance of the findings.

Our analysis is composed of three sections. We begin by exploring conceptions of masculinity (Topic 1), using Connell's (1990) concept of hegemonic masculinity, which refers to the "culturally idealized form of masculine character," which associates masculinity with "toughness and competitiveness," the "subordination of women," and "the marginalization of gay men" (pp. 83, 94). We also relate this approach of hegemonic masculinity to Connell's (1995) triad of *reproduction, resistance, and transformation* (pp. 76-77). The second part focuses on judgments of

Table 12.1 Type of School Students Attended, by Gender

Type of School Attended	Boys	Girls
Public school in working-class neighborhood	55	63
Public school in middle-class neighborhood	54	63
Private school in affluent neighborhood	65	54
Total	174	180

men's transgression, to find out whether boys endorse or critique the gendered organization of sport. Finally, we look into possible links or contradictions between conceptions of masculinity and appraisals of men's transgressions of the gender regime of sport.

Results

Conceptions of Masculinity

Reproducing hegemonic masculinity. The boys' understandings of masculinity approximated the hegemonic form, as they stressed physical and moral strength, seductive power, heterosexuality, control over one's own emotions, leadership, and masculine display. The following quotation[2] is typical of the form of masculinity exalted by a significant proportion of boys from the three social milieus:

> A virile guy is one who is tall, has wide shoulders, and who, above all, is strong. He plays a lot of sports, mainly men's sports such as ice hockey and football. He's got to be macho[3] because if he isn't, he will not be successful with girls. Usually, a virile guy is successful with all the girls because, whether we like it or not, girls like manly guys. He is also someone who impresses others and commands respect. He is not afraid of others. (UC, No. 03532)

This type of masculinity also was expounded in relational terms, with a great many boys positioning masculinity in opposition to femininity and/ or other types of men—typically, physically smaller, "low-profile" men, or homosexuals:

A normal guy, a real guy, is a guy who has character, who won't be henpecked by a girl. (WC, No. 43212)

A virile guy, a "real one," can be any guy that is really built or who rides around on a Harley-Davidson. Not necessarily a Hell's Angels. A guy like Arnold or Sylvester Stallone, who are strong physically and also mentally. A real man has few feminine manners. Thus, he can't be too soft. Or, not too timid or a loner. They are not "fags." A gay is neither a man nor a woman, he is garbage, waste. He may be muscular, but, he is surely a sado-masochist, therefore not a "real man." (MC, No. 27022)

In summary, boys' descriptions of maleness consistently articulated hegemonic principles such as domination over women and the subordination and marginalization of men who did not possess their masculine ideals.

Class Background Hegemonic Masculinity

Further examination showed that the boys' understandings of hegemonic masculinity differed according to their class milieus. For example, leadership and sociability were more exalted among boys in the private high school:

A virile guy is a guy that is not shy, who is the "leader" of his group, who expresses his opinions, without being ridiculous, who is not embarrassed to talk to anybody. He distinguishes himself from others because he imposes himself much more. (UC, No. 08732)

Boys from the public school in an MC suburb extolled intelligence and sociability: "[A virile guy] is an intelligent person, who has self-confidence and high self-esteem. A man who respects others, and expects others to respect him" (MC, No. 32022). Insouciant bravado, male chauvinism, and masculine showing-off were more exalted among the boys from the public school in a WC district:

A virile guy is physically fit, is tall enough and has a deep voice. He must look "cool" when he walks. He must look good to be noticed when he wanders about in the street. Sometimes, he is a "showoff." He is always ready to fight to show he is the strongest. . . . He should have a knack with girls. Also, a real man should have many women because it is inconceivable that a man have only one woman. (WC, No. 19712)

To understand these differences, we need to look into the differential living conditions under which they arise and assess what is at stake for members of the various classes. Conceptions of masculinity are shaped by the range of possibilities, interests, and the experiences of everyday life. UC boys are most often socialized with the aim of occupying management or leadership positions in the labor force. Thus, to become a man means developing the qualities that characterize a future position associated with administering people. Their class position means that they are unlikely to aspire to occupations requiring physical strength, thereby lessening the importance of physical sturdiness in the evaluation of maleness. For the MC boys, upward social and economic mobility is one of their major goals; thus, a diploma and academic capital are perceived as the major means available for achieving that end. This possibly explains the emphasis they placed on intelligence in their descriptions of a "real man." The masculine showoff and the perceived necessity of being fearless associated with maleness in the WC boys' essays is consonant with the violence that often surrounds their lives. Most telling in this regard was the statement of one of them:

> For me a real guy is someone athletic, someone who is not afraid to be hurt and not afraid to protect his girlfriend. A real guy is also someone who can go out late at night and come back home without any harm. (WC, No. 21612)

This class-distinctive valorization of "fearless" persona among the WC boys also was evidenced by Goodey (1997), as seen in his study on adolescents and crime:

> At its extreme, "fearlessness" can be expressed as physical aggression among working-class boys in their attempt to assert their masculinity. In comparison, middle-class boys, while also having to take on the masculine criteria of fearlessness, are able to and tend to project their masculine hegemony through different channels, such as academic success. (p. 410)

Hondagneu-Sotelo and Messner (1994) and Messner (1990b) shed light on this hypermasculine style. On the basis of their study of Mexican immigrant men, they found, "Marginalized and subordinated men tend to overtly display exaggerated embodiments and verbalizations of masculinity that can be read as a desire to express power over others within a context of relative powerlessness" (1994, p. 214). They share, with Collinson's (1988) understanding of the sexually aggressive and misogynist humor of Australian male blue-collar workers, and with Majors and Billson's (1992) reading of the "cool pose" of young black men, the insight that subordinated men tend to use specific masculine displays as a way to resist, at least symbolically, the various forms of oppression that they face within hierarchies of intermale dominance. Hypermasculine style thus can be read as a gender-class affirmation and an oppositional politics to the "discreet masculine charm" favored by men of the bourgeoisie. For instance, one boy from the UC milieu enunciated, with a certain contempt, his stereotyped representation of WC masculinity:

> Listen, for me, a virile man is the typical worker with big arms working in the factory all week long to provide for his family, who plays hockey with his buddies on Wednesday night, who goes to get drunk with them on Saturday night at the corner pub, who loves his wife but he does not let her know very often because he doesn't know how, who lives a rather boring life that makes him happy. In short, as cliché as it may seem, that is my definition of a virile man. Please note, this is not the type of man I admire. (UC, No. 12932)

In sum, we suggest that hegemonic conceptions of masculinity are oriented toward dominance over women and the subordination of other configurations of masculinity. We also submit that the exercise of power is culturally produced through the strategic use of signifiers associated with this form of masculinity. Furthermore, we have argued that hegemonic masculinity interacts with class background, as a component of class politics.

Contesting hegemonic masculinity. Although hegemonic, the mode of masculinity just discussed also was contested and confronted strongly with alternative versions among the adolescents. Indeed, the content analysis of the writings relating to the first topic showed two opposing tendencies: one that endorsed the hegemonic form of masculinity (the reproduction process presented previously) and others that critiqued or challenged it (resistance process), sometimes with a call for alternative versions to it (transformation process). Although the aim here is not to count heads, we present in Table 12.2 the findings that emerged from the content analysis according to the categories of reproduction, resistance, and transformation of hegemonic masculinity within each social milieu. As we can see, reproductive elements were prominent in all three social groups. However, nearly equal numbers of respondents enunciated resistant or transformative views.

Table 12.2   Boys' Conceptions of Hegemonic Masculinity, by Type of
School Attended (in Percentages)

	Conceptions of Hegemoic Masculinity		
Type of School Attended	Reproductive	Resistant	Transformative
Public school in working-class neighborhood (n = 55)	55	27	18
Public school in middle-class neighborhood (n = 54)	48	19	33
Private school in affluent neighborhood (n = 65)	54	21	25
Total (N = 174)	52	23	25

Resisting hegemonic masculinity. Recalcitrant views were roughly similar across social class. Many boys criticized overt and exaggerated masculine displays and also strongly voiced their own oppressive experiences:

A virile guy is a guy who always shows that he is not scared and who always takes up challenges of force and who always shares his sexual adventures with his friends. He walks like a "showoff" and he is not himself. Guys like that bug me! (MC, No. 37922)

In a manner similar to that seen in the writings endorsing hegemonic forms of masculinity, oppositional stances had some class-specific links. UC and MC boys usually challenged hegemonic masculinity, theoretically by advocating a disruption of gender categories:

A virile guy is a stereotype. . . . The important thing is to be well-balanced, not virile nor feminine. We must attain a balance between our feminine and our masculine sides. To feel well within ourselves. Not be stuck in a stereotype or make up stories. We shouldn't constantly try to distinguish ourselves from girls. Between the two sexes, there are similarities. After all, we are all human. There are also some differences, and here too, there is no harm. (UC, No. 01732)

By contrast, WC boys tended to critique the social problems that hege-monic masculinity raised for them in everyday life (e.g., violence, rejec-tion of school, family problems):

> A virile guy or a real guy, I believe is a person who is somewhat stuck up. It is a guy who thinks of his image a lot. It is someone who may also wear tattoos on his body to show his "tough" side. He has long hair and a pretty "tough" look. A virile guy is also someone who doesn't care about others nor about school. He always wants to party. (WC, No. 19812)

A kind of resigned oppositional politics vis-à-vis the breadth sway of heg-emonic masculinity was also evident in some of the WC boys' writings:

> Virility is a behavior that has always existed, only recently have we begun to abolish this behavior. . . . Being virile is playing for the gallery, showing off. I do not like virility because in my mind, it leads to violence. My grandfather was a "virile man," he could not show his emotions towards my mother. Instead of showing his love for her, he was harsh and behaved like a man raised by wolves. Virile men are well accepted in society's lower classes but they will never make it with normal people because as soon as a person is slightly more intelligent and refined, he becomes humane, has emotions, and has actions which are more thought-out than simply scratching one's balls. I say "up yours" to all macho guys. (WC, No. 43612)

This young man bitterly expressed the dual oppression that he, like many others in his environment, suffered as a result of hegemonic mascu-linity and class oppression. We speculate that oppositional politics to the hegemonic form of masculinity would be more difficult to sustain in the working class due to more overt masculine displays, the threat of violence that might be encountered, and the comprehension that possibilities for upward social mobility are very slight. On the other hand, these boys are also the most common victims of other men's violence and exploitation, so they have a material basis for opposing hegemonic masculinity.

Transforming hegemonic masculinity. A significant proportion of all boys (about 25%) communicated transformative views about hegemonic masculinity in their essays. Such tendencies usually were related to hav-ing the capacity to develop intimate and respectful relationships with others, particularly with women:

What is a virile guy? An intelligent guy who knows how to use his brains. A polite guy who knows how to be discreet. A sociable guy who knows how to weigh his words. A guy who knows how to court a lovely young woman without rushing her. A romantic guy. Not too much of a boaster. (MC, No. 29822)

We again found differences across the three social classes. Thoughtfulness, peacefulness or nonviolence, and respect for women were emphasized among some WC boys, who asserted an oppositional politics to the prevailing style of hegemonic masculinity:

He is an understanding guy with whom we can have fun. A guy who does not have [a] macho style. . . . He is rather the kind of guy who likes to mingle with good people, who, instead of using his muscles, will use his head and think before acting. He is the type of guy that a girl will say of him, he is decent, he has never harmed me in any way or done anything I did not want. (WC, No. 23812)

The larger proportion of MC boys (33% as opposed to 25% overall) explicating new definitions of the "real man" should be viewed cautiously, because many of them showed some ambivalence, especially with regard to gender equality. Although they advocated equality between the sexes, they also insisted on the necessity of maintaining differences and, furthermore, refrained from granting too much liberty:

A virile guy is a guy who can express his feelings and not physical strength. Because a man's real strength is not in his muscles but in his heart . . . and he lets girls assume the place they deserve, *without however allowing them too much freedom*. (MC, No. 31822, italics added)

One possible explanation for this ambivalence or apparent contradiction concerning gender relationships may come from the impression that women represent a threat to boys' longing for social advancement, especially because MC girls often do better in school than their male classmates (Bouchard & St-Amand, 1996). Because social and economic achievement are key factors in the construction of their masculine identity, the egalitarian values of the MC boys are mitigated by fear of competition from MC girls.

Emotional expressivity and greater concern for family life were more often advanced by UC boys (a masculine pattern often labeled "*homme rose*" [pink men] in the Francophone community):

He is a sensitive and affectionate guy; he can easily express his feelings. He respects people of his sex as well as those of the opposite sex. . . . He has much respect for women without being afraid of them. Family is very important for him. He respects his parents and pays attention to the advice of his friends (males and females). . . . He solves all his problems without physical intervention. . . . He must be faithful to his girlfriend. (UC, No. 15132)

On one hand, it is possible that such expressions signify that a genuine shift is occurring among some of these boys in appraisals of what it is to be a man. On the other hand, it is feasible that their statements are merely an attempt to appear "politically correct." For instance, Hondagneu-Sotelo and Messner (1994) and Messner (1993) argued that recent emotionally expressive manifestations of masculinity are not a sign of counterhegemonic gender politics, but rather

a shift in personal styles and lifestyles of privileged men that eliminate or at least mitigate many of the aspects of "traditional masculinity" that men have found unhealthful or emotionally constraining. . . . These shifts in styles of masculinity do little, if anything, to address issues of power and inequality raised by feminist women. (Messner, 1993, p. 728)

This interpretation is apposite to our UC group, although it would be necessary to conduct an in-depth field study of the boys' everyday practices to verify this thesis. Thus, we would concur with Messner's (1993) observation:

[Some men] would like to stop paying the "cost" of the hegemonic form of masculinity, but it does not necessarily signal a desire to cease benefiting from what Connell (1995) calls the "patriarchal dividend." Because the new, softer symbols of masculinity do not substantially address issues of gender inequality and men's power over women, it would rather suggest they represent a "modernization of hegemonic masculinity" (Carrigan et al., 1985, p. 596) rather than a real desire for transformation in the structure of power. (p. 730)

In this first section, we have explored the symbols or signifiers that adolescents from different social classes associate with masculinity. A content analysis based on the categories of reproduction, resistance, and transformation of the hegemonic masculinity has shown that the gender symbols of masculinity are contradictory and that the differing conceptions of maleness serve as ground for oppositions and power relations between the adolescent boys. Moreover, we found that social class and gender interacted. Indeed, distinctive emphases on particular signifiers of masculinity showed different stakes according to social class and diverse positions in the power structure.

Transgressing the Gender Regime of Sport

This section focuses on the second process identified by Harding (1986), gender structure. The gendered structure of sport is conspicuously evident in "sport typing" (Kane, 1995), by which some activities are defined as exclusively male (e.g., football, boxing) or female (e.g., synchronized swimming, rhythmic gymnastic), or, within the same sport, different rules or modalities of play are set up (e.g., tennis, figure skating).What happens when this dualistic gender structure is challenged, as in the case of men venturing into so-called women's sports and vice versa? To what extent does overstepping gender boundaries contest or transform the binary structure of sport and eventually erode gender stereotypes? The third and the fourth topics suggested for the student essays were aimed at investigating such issues. We first examine the boys' appraisals of men participating in women's sports to ascertain whether they believe that transgressions of the gender regime affect masculinity. Second, we contrast their judgments about men's transgressions with their beliefs about women's trespasses. Third, we briefly consider the girls' appraisal of men's transgressive acts. Finally, we examine connections between the opposing conceptions of masculinity and the contrasting appraisals of transgressions. This allows us to analyze the links between gender symbolism and gender structure, as well as the internal contradictions that surround masculinity.

Boys' Judgments of Men's Transgressions

To highlight the wide range of stances with regard to men playing a women's sport, we classified the boys' comments into those that were perceived to be threatening and nonthreatening to masculinity. The argument most frequently used to support perceived threats to masculinity was that participating in a women's sport prevented men from developing their inherent physical prowess:

> A guy who plays women's sports looks less virile. A real guy must be sturdy and strong. He cannot develop these characteristics in the majority of sports for girls. Strength is THE characteristic of men, while beauty is THE characteristic

of the feminine girl. . . . For me, a guy who plays football or ice hockey will always be more virile than one who figure skates or does aerobic dance. Figure skating is a very nice and difficult sport; however, guys who play it look less virile. (UC, No. 16832)

Similarly, other boys felt that it was simply unnatural for men to engage in such unorthodox behavior:

But I cannot deny that they are less virile since they are more gracious and less "brutal." We try to get rid of stereotypes and that is why we do sports of the other sex. *However, we forget that these stereotypes were created by nature which has made guys larger and more sturdy and girls smaller and more gracious.* (UC, No. 05732, italics added)

Moreover, men who crossed over gender boundaries were assigned an inferior status:

When I see a guy who figure skates, I have ideas much more pejorative than when I see a guy who dances. I don't know why it is like that but in general, *I have a tendency to treat men who do women's sports as inferior to others.* (UC, No. 14332, italics added)

With regard to the nonthreatening stance to masculinity, two main arguments were invoked. First, men participating in women's sports were nonetheless perceived to display physical prowess:

A guy who figure skates is a virile guy because he must be in as good a shape as a guy who plays ice hockey, and maybe more because when he has a partner, he must be careful not to drop her when he "throws" her in the air: A lot of power is needed to catch her. I find seeing this quite fantastic. It is very virile. (MC, No. 36722)

Second, some boys claimed that each individual has the right to do what he wants:

It does not mean that because he is involved in a sport "reserved" for girls, that he does [it like] a girl. I do not find him more "queer" than me or than another guy because it is what he likes to do and I do not have the right to stop him from doing what he likes to do, like he does not have the right to stop me from mountain biking. (MC, No. 32422)

Table 12.3   Boys' Judgments of Men's Transgressions in Sport as a Threat to Masculinity, by Type of School Attended (in Percentages)

	Judgments of Men's Transgressions in Sport as a Threat to Masculinity	
Type of School Attended	Threatening	Nonthreatening
Public school in working-class neighborhood (n = 55)	67	33
Public school in middle-class neighborhood (n = 54)	48	52
Private school in affluent neighborhood (n = 65)	46	54
Total (N = 174)	53	47

Table 12.3 shows that there are class differences between stances of the WC, MC, and UC boys toward transgressive acts, with two thirds of the WC boys believing that involvement in women's sport threatens masculinity, whereas MC and UC boys were split almost equally between a positive and a negative appraisal.

Two out of three of the WC boys considered women's sports to be inappropriate for men. The main reasons given for this view were that these sports either did not require physical strength or did not have competitive objectives:

A guy who does women's sports looks totally ridiculous. When I watch him in action, I cannot stop laughing at him. If we take, for example, aerobic dance, this type of sport does not work for guys as girls do this sport to maintain their figure or to look pretty. (WC, No. 24312)

The dominant logic here was that men participating in a women's sport were associated with women, "queers," or "fags":

For me, a guy who participates in women's sports is a fag who cannot express himself in men's sports like ice hockey where one must use one's physique. Women's sports are for girls and guys who take part in them look less virile because a virile guy is one who has character and physical strength, and who would never dare play a women's sport where there is hardly any physical contact or challenge. (WC, No. 24112)

A guy who plays women's sports is less virile because he ruins his male image. For me he is only a fag and he disgraces our reputation. (WC, No. 19712)

WC boys expressed a considerable amount of verbal violence against homosexuals. This might be due to the fact that their previously noted hypermasculine style makes breaches of gender boundaries in sport particularly formidable for them. We also might speculate that (as Messner, 1992b, has demonstrated) the social significance that men attach to sport varies by social class, so it is possible that sport plays an especially potent role in the construction of masculinity among WC boys.

Despite some boys' endorsement of a dualistic gendering of sport, about half of the MC and the UC boys asserted that masculinity was not affected by transgressive acts in sport. However, the reason most frequently put forward was different for the two social groups. MC boys usually gave a "freedom of choice" account:

I believe a guy who likes his sport (whatever it may be) has the right to play it without being called a homosexual. In fact, he is not less virile, because a sport is a sport and anybody who wants to play it may do so without being finger pointed. (MC, No. 29222)

This statement suggests a desire to depart from the conventional gender dualism in sport. Yet, it might also constitute what some feminists have termed "a liberal 'gloss' on a generally more conventional outlook" (Kraus, as quoted in Messner, 1993, p. 726), as Hearn and Morgan (1990) contend:

Even when men are developing a consciousness of their gender identity and a desire to challenge gender ideologies, the basis of these desires often appears to be more in terms of abstract principles or general political programmes than direct experience. (p. 15)

Because the boys' open-mindedness does not seem to lie within the scope of the feminist project of social transformation, we would be more inclined to interpret it as a liberal veneer that does not seriously challenge the status quo between men, and between men and women in the gender structure.

The main argument supporting men's transgressive behavior among UC boys consisted of connected ideas about corporeal and moral strength:

> Fag, wimp, sissy are only some of the insulting names that guys practicing women's sports must sustain. Figure skating, gymnastics, and aerobic dance are sports that are physically demanding. I support a hundred percent the guys who have the courage to undertake those sports. It is only machos who laugh at the men who play these sports. I would like to see them doing only half of what the others do. (UC, No. 03832)

These accounts suggest a kind of "ideological recycling" of symbols associated with hegemonic masculinity. Moral strength (in this case for facing stigmatization and discrediting by peers) and physical prowess are used as proof of masculinity, thereby "legitimating" transgressive behavior. This reinforces rather than contests the hierarchical and dualistic gender configuration of sport, as men are still considered both different and superior even when they are involved in a traditionally women's arena. Moreover, the reference to physical and mental strength to support a positive appraisal of transgressions may be construed as a strategy for the members of the dominant class to overcome the paradox of maintaining and reconstructing their cultural and structural dominance over women while preserving their image of gender equality promoter. Once again, boys' assessments of transgressions demonstrate that social class contributes to the construction of various masculinities: The strong stigmatization of transgressions among WC boys is congruent with the hypermasculine style prevailing in this milieu; the "neutral-safe" rhetoric of the MC boys is consonant with a logic of individual rights; and the ideological recuperation of traditional markers of hegemonic masculinity by the UC respondents is congruent with their affirmation of greater gender equality while still clinging to the status quo.

Boys' Judgments of Men's and Women's Transgressions

As noted, we also compared (a) the boys' appraisals of men participating in women's sports with their evaluations of women taking part in men's sports and (b) the boys' and girls' assessments of men's transgressions. Because of space limitations, we give only a brief account of these two new sets of data.

Sixty percent of the boys indicated that transgressive sportswomen did not threaten femininity, compared with 47% who claimed that transgres-

Table 12.4 Symmetry/Asymmetry in Boys' Judgments of Men's and
Women's Transgressions in Sport, by Type of School
Attended (in Percentages)

	Judgments of Men's and Women's Transgressions in Sport			
Type of School Attended	Positive for Men and for Women	Negative for Men and for Women	Positive for Men/Negative for Women	Negative for Men/Positive for Women
Public school in working-class neighborhood (*n* = 55)	27	47	6	20
Public school in middle-class neighborhood (*n* = 54)	43	26	9	22
Private school in affluent neighborhood (*n* = 65)	43	23	11	23
Total (*N* = 174)	38	31	9	22

sive men threatened masculinity (see Table 12.4). Arguments supporting
women's transgressions included items like "She is as feminine as any
other woman"; "She will even be more sexy, because she will be in better
shape"; "It's OK if she's still feminine after playing sports"; and "She has
the right to do what she wants, without any harm to her femininity." Forty
percent of the boys considered women's transgressions to be a threat to
femininity, compared with 53% who believed that transgressions by men
threatened masculinity. Arguments against women transgressors were
mainly posed in terms of "It's not their place," "They behave like men," "It
depends on the sport," and outright sexism.

Because the judgements on men and on women may not necessarily be
symmetric for the same individual, we examined the symmetry/asymme-
try within each boy's writing in more depth. Table 12.4 indicates that,
overall, a higher percentage (22%) were asymmetric in being negative for
men and positive for women, compared with only 9% asymmetry in the
reverse sense. Lamar and Kite (1998) found similar asymmetry in men's
attitudes toward gay men and toward lesbians, the former being more negative than the latter.

The following comments were typical of boys from all three social
classes:

Men's transgression: A guy who plays a women's sport is not a "real" guy. Women's sports are finesse sports mostly based on movement. Men's sports are mostly rough, with physical contact and strategy. A guy who plays a women's sport is, therefore, weak, a weakling who does not want to hurt himself. He is less virile than others. . . . Men's sport is contact, strategy, fast thinking. Therefore, I believe that a guy who does women's sports is less intelligent.

Women's transgression: A girl who does men's sports is not the same. She is less feminine but there is a place for them. . . . *Girls can dare participate in men's sports because they are weaker than boys but guys cannot do women's sports. This is degrading oneself!* (MC, No. 27022, italics added)

This gender asymmetry in the boys' appraisal of sportive transgressions highlights their valorization of so-called men's sports and their trivialization of so-called women's sports. Men's transgressions would signify an erosion of male superiority, whereas women's transgressions would signify transcending women's weakness. This logic contributes largely to the resistance to a "degendering" (Connell, 1995; Harding, 1986) process among men and is a crucial issue in the politics of changing men.

One shortcoming of some feminist claims for equity is that they ask women to "exchange major aspects of their gender identity for the masculine version—without prescribing a similar 'degendering' process for men" (Harding, 1986, p. 53). Promoting a degendering process among men in sport would have to be effected via an undermining of the cultural supremacy of men's sports and of the forms of bodily practices associated with hegemonic masculinity, while enhancing the status of women's sports and of bodily practices associated with femininity. Indeed, masculine hegemony is not simply a product of the things men do but also of the meanings their activities acquire through unequal social interactions.

Boys' and Girls' Appraisals of Men's Transgressions

There were striking differences between the boys and girls, especially in attending the school in the WC district, with respect to how men's transgressions affected masculinity (see Table 12.5).

Following is a girl's telling expression of valorization of men's participation in women's sports:

As far as I am concerned, there is no difference between boys who play women's sports and those who play men's sports. It's great if, in spite of the various preju-

Table 12.5 Boys' and Girls' Judgments of Men's Transgressions in Sport as a Threat to Masculinity, by Type of School Attended (in Percentages)

Type of School Attended	Judgments of Men's Transgressions in Sport as a Threat to Masculinity	
	Threatening	Nonthreatening
Public school in working-class neighborhood		
Boys (n = 55)	67	33
Girls (n = 63)	36	64
Public school in middle-class neighborhood		
Boys (n = 54)	48	52
Girls (n = 63)	26	74
Private school in affluent neighborhood		
Boys (n = 65)	46	54
Girls (n = 54)	22	78

NOTE: The gender difference was statistically significant at $p < .001$.

dices, a boy has a positive attitude in this regard. I would be proud of him, and I would be proud to show to the other guys that he is not a "sissy" because he wants to engage in a women's sport. We need equality between genders, and to obtain it we [need to] begin by involving men in our sports. (WC, No. 40511)

The greater openness displayed by girls in all three schools toward men's transgressions represents what Bourdieu (1979/1984) terms a "logic of equality" commonly found in subordinated groups.

Interestingly, in a survey we conducted within the current research program, we also found a stronger positive attitude among the girls toward coeducation in physical education classes (Laberge, 1996). Although gender integration in sport is still a controversial issue among feminist scholars (Birrell, 1984; Kane, 1995), we speculate that it can constitute a worthwhile avenue for the degendering of sport and other gendered bodily practices, as well as for the transformation of unequal gender relations.

Nonetheless, we cannot ignore the substantial proportion of girls in every school (36%, 26%, and 22%, respectively) who believed that men's participation in women's sports affected masculinity in a negative fashion,

Table 12.6 Boys' Judgments of Men's Transgressions in Sport, by
Their Conception of Masculinity (in Percentages)

	Judgment of Men's Transgressions in Sport as a Threat to Masculinity	
Conception of Hegemonic Masculinity	Threatening	Nonthreatening
Reproductive (n = 91)	69	31
Resistant (n = 39)	33	67
Transformative (n = 44)	39	61
Total (N = 174)	53	47

NOTE: The relation was statistically significant at $p < .001$.

thereby contributing to the maintenance of hegemonic masculinity in sport. The reconstruction of the larger gender order depends to some extent on the collusion of certain women with hegemonic masculinity and their endorsement of dualistic gender stereotypes. In this regard, women, like other dominated groups, sometimes actively participate in their own subordination.

Relationships Between Boys' Conceptions of Masculinity and Men's Transgressions

In the final stage in our analysis, we explore a possible connection between the boys' different conceptions of masculinity and their opinions of men's transgressions. As expected, there were relatively strong differences with respect to how "reproductive," "resistant," and "transformative" boys viewed the threats that men's transgressions posed to hegemonic masculinity (see Table 12.6).This may indicate the intimate connections between the processes of gender symbolism and gender structure that construct gendered social life. But this pattern does not seem to be systematic within individuals, as there were differences among the boys.

In the case of the boys who endorse hegemonic masculinity, just fewer than one third claimed that transgressions did not threaten masculinity. Closer scrutiny of their appraisals revealed that physical and moral strength were the two main arguments that they invoked:

For me, that has nothing to do with virility, because I know that most so-called "women's sports" are at least as demanding as the so-called "men's sports." For example, ballet dancing is one of the most demanding sports at the muscular level, and so are figure skating and gymnastics. I, myself, did some aerobic dance and believe me, when I started, I found it as exhausting as the physical conditioning I had done for football. (UC, No. 08732)

A guy who does women's sports is as masculine as he would be if he practiced men's sports. In fact, he could even be more masculine than the other guys who participate in men's sports because he must have a strong character in order to play a women's sport because other guys could see him as "inferior." (UC, No. 13432)

As noted, this appeal to physical and moral strength is in line with the hegemonic form of masculinity, thereby suggesting an "ideological recycling" with regard to gender politics. Therefore, the contradiction found here seems to be more apparent than substantive.

However, the data also showed a contradiction among the boys who either mentioned resisting or transforming hegemonic masculinity and their claims that men's transgressions threatened masculinity (33% and 39%, respectively). For the boys who showed some resistance to hegemonic masculinity, this contradiction appeared more frequently in the WC group:

I find that guys that do women's sports are not respected by the other guys. It's true, they look less virile. So what? It is their choice. They have the right to do as they wish, they must learn not to listen to what other guys tell them, like for example, when they are called fag, idiot, girlie. (WC, No. 22312)

This ambivalent appraisal shows both a denunciation of prejudices, alongside a relative compliance with the gender regime that fosters these prejudices. Although the boy believes that this sport practice makes the boys "look less virile," he also seems to approve of, and encourage, boys' participation in women's sports, the latter view being more in line with his contestation of the hegemonic form of masculinity. Given the hypermasculine ethos of the working class, participation in women's sports is unlikely to be viewed as an enticing proposition for men.

For the boys who sought a transformation of hegemonic masculinity, this contradiction appeared more often in the MC and UC groups. In reading the following excerpts, one should keep in mind that the boys did propose counterhegemonic interpretations of masculinity in previous lines of their essays:

Writing high-class moral principles would be very nice, very elegant, but would be very hypocritical. Excuse the expression, but a guy who does women's sports is a fag, a queer, a brown pusher. Why? I find it impossible to explain. This idea was instilled in me by the people in my social environment; society carved it in my head. For a long time, this idea has been deeply carved in my skull and the worst part of it is that I really believe that a guy who does a women's sport is a faggot; what can I say! The power of society's pressures on us! Incredible but true! (UC, No. 03132)

I do not want to be sexist, but I will not perceive as virile a guy who plays women's sports; it is my first impression. If I had known a guy for a long time and he started to do women's sports, I would ask myself some questions but I would respect his choice. (MC, No. 36422)

These tensions suggest that (a) gendered practices, particularly bodily ones, are more resistant to change than are gender symbols; and (b) gendered practices play a pivotal role in the construction of social life.

Gender symbolism works at a general and abstract level, whereas gender structure immediately affects the meanings of one's experience and one's social interaction. Moreover, these findings attest to the complexity of the articulation of gender symbolism and gender structure within individual subjectivity and the contradictory layerings of an individual's gender identity.

Conclusion

This study has shown that the construction of hegemonic masculinity is neither seamless nor unproblematic but a relational and conflictive process that is marked by differences, power relations, and ambivalence. In summing up, we emphasize two major points.

First, the differences and tensions we observed among the three groups of boys suggest that class milieus interweave with gender at both the symbolic and structural levels. Beyond a core of similarities, the images of hegemonic masculinity propounded by the three groups revealed nuances that were closely linked to the specific material conditions in which they arose: Leadership was valued more highly in the UC setting, sociability was more important for MC boys, and hypermasculine displays were prominent in the WC group. Reciprocally, gender symbolism was found to contribute to class politics, in that class-specific signs of hegemonic masculinity were used by the UC boys to reassert their cultural dominance. Likewise, resistance to hegemonic masculinity was shaped by intraclass gender politics, as the UC and MC boys stood mainly on classic liberal grounds, and the WC group was more concerned with deploring the social problems caused by hegemonic patterns of masculinity in their daily lives. Neither did the purportedly transformative and progressive versions of masculinity escape class influences—their emphases were congruent with specific class interests and intraclass gendered power relationships.

Appraisals of transgressions of the gender regime of sport showed the interaction between class and gender more conspicuously. For instance, the pronounced stigmatization of transgressions by the WC boys is congruent with the hypermasculine style that prevails in this context. Although MC and UC boys showed comparably greater openness to men's transgressions in sport, their reasonings were based on a distinctive social logic that was clearly grounded in class interests. The liberal stance that generally predominates in the middle class likely inspired the boys' stronger appeal to individual rights in support of their positive assessment of men's transgressions, a position that is not at odds with their concern for social and economic mobility. As for the UC group, the ideological recycling of the symbols of hegemonic masculinity, which legitimized men's transgressions, points to their contradictory stakes as a dominant group—maintaining the status quo in gender and class relations while adopting the image of gender equality promoter.

Our findings confirm the contribution that a materialist analysis can make to the understanding of the social construction of gender. As Messner (1996) put it, "[M]aterialist analysis reveals how differential access to resources, opportunities, and different relationship to structural constraints shape the contexts in which people think, interact and construct political practice and discourse" (p. 228). It must be stressed that we are not privileging class over gender in our analysis. To the contrary, we are advocating a nonhierarchical theorizing, one "that allow[s] us to conceptualize varied and shifting forms of domination in such a way that we do not privilege one at the expense of distorting or ignoring the others" (Messner & Sabo, 1990, p. 10). In this regard, it seems important to examine how interactions between gender and other hierarchical symbols and structures (e.g., race, ethnicity, and sexuality) shape our beliefs and practices about gender. This approach might cast light on the complexity observed in the gender-class dynamic and, hence, provide further evidence against a theory that would advocate the autonomy of gender relations.

A second key finding relates to the boys' appraisal of men's transgressive behavior in sport. The strong negative appraisal of men's transgressions appeared both in their contrasts with women's transgressions and via those boys who contested hegemonic masculinity but perceived men's transgressions as a threat to masculinity. These results point to the boys' reluctance toward degendering and, hence, the development of any meaningful transformative potential.

Nonetheless, we concur with Connell (1995) and Harding (1986), and with many feminist scholars, in asserting that a strict degendering strategy may involve important flaws—one being that it means sameness and the loss of positive elements of both men's and women's culture. Degendering also could result in the disparagement of transgressors and a failure to dismantle either the binary opposites of gender hierarchies or the intramale pecking order. To counter the first shortcoming, Connell (1995) proposed a "degendering-recomposing" strategy that is intimately linked to a project of social justice (p. 234). Another shortcoming of a simplistic degendering strategy, given how many boys (and significant numbers of girls) held negative attitudes toward men who participated in women's sports, is that it can underplay the crucial importance of "meaning" in gender politics. As we have stressed, masculine hegemony is not simply a product of men's practices but is closely linked with the connotations their activities acquire through unequal social interactions.

Thus, we argue that a necessary condition for a degendering strategy to work in a transformative fashion in sport is for it to be grounded in a collective project that contests naturalized assumptions about sportsmen's alleged superiority and sportswomen's purported inferiority. Moreover, we believe that a degendering strategy inspired by a "politics of meaning" must be implemented not only at the symbolic and structural levels but also, and perhaps primarily, at the level of the body, the material basis of individual identity—"the ground chosen by defenders of patriarchy, where the fear of men being turned into women is most poignant" (Connell, 1995, p. 232). In this regard, sport practices may represent a powerful site of contestation. Ultimately, what is at stake in a degendering strategy is power in a context of inequality. Indeed, to the extent that genders structure our perceptions and organize social life, they also serve to distribute power, that is, differential control over, and/or access to, material and symbolic resources.

Notes

1. Ringette is a relatively recent sport that originated in Ontario and was designed as an alternative to ice hockey for girls. Although it was played almost exclusively by girls, there is now a growing interest among boys to try the game.

2. All quotations have been translated from French. Because most of the essays were written in vernacular language, close attention has been paid to ensuring that the students' comments correspond as closely as possible to their original meaning.

3. The term *macho* has long been part of the vernacular French of Québec, although its users are not necessarily familiar with its ethnic reference to Latino and Latin American men. It has become a hackneyed word whose referent varies greatly among users. However, it generally conforms to Klein's (1995b) definition: men's propensity to "dominate and control through sexuality, fighting, and other forms of competitive behavior" (p. 371).

13

Homosexuality and Sport

Who's Winning?

BRIAN PRONGER

In this chapter, I attempt to situate the intersections of homosexuality and sport within larger developments in lesbian and gay culture over the last three decades.[1] I analyze these developments in the light of debates in lesbian, gay, and queer theories of sexuality and their correlative visions of liberation and freedom, as well as within the empirical context of histories of the lesbian and gay liberation movement.

I confine my comments to social developments in Canada and the United States. This is not to suggest that what I am saying is necessarily inapplicable to other national domains, especially Holland, Germany, the United Kingdom, Australia, and New Zealand, as well as further reaches of globalized "late" capitalist culture (Jameson, 1984). But sexual politics still are constituted differently in different parts of the world. It would be a mistake to try to homogenize sexual cultures even in the Untied States and Canada, where they are significantly varied by other cultural influences, such as ethnicity, class, language, and physical location. Indeed, I hope the arguments offered here suggest that the homogenization of desire is deeply problematic. More to the point, I suggest that the explicit mingling of homosexuality and sport over the last 10 to 15 years reflects the homogenization of sexual diversity in North American culture and the consequent tempering of the emancipatory potential of homosexual desire.

Gay Cultures and Mainstream Sports

Without question, much has happened in lesbian and gay culture over the last 30 years. Same-gender desire emerged from the silence and shadows of North American cultures: The love that formerly dared not speak its name, as Oscar Wilde's paramour Lord Alfred Douglass called his desire for men, has become "the love that won't keep its mouth shut," according to a much-quoted editorial in the *New York Times*. A gay liberation movement that 30 years ago (before the hallmark Stonewall Inn riots in New York's Greenwich Village, widely considered to mark the beginning of contemporary lesbian and gay political culture) was made up of a number of small cells of homophile activists has become a noticeable political presence in governments, commerce, entertainment, arts, and letters. In most jurisdictions in Canada, discrimination on the basis of sexual orientation is prohibited by human rights legislation. There are also some jurisdictions in the United States with protection on the basis of sexual orientation. However, as Urvashi Vaid (1995) said at the beginning of her book on the fate of gay liberation in the United States,

> On one level, our movement has been a staggering, if controversial success; yet on another level, gay and lesbian people remain profoundly stigmatized, struggling against the same crises—in health, violence, discrimination, and social services—that have plagued us for decades. Hundreds of thousands of gay and lesbian Americans are openly integrated into our communities, families, and workplaces. Yet the vast majority of our people remain closeted, still unwilling to openly acknowledge their sexual orientation. A backlash against gay rights swells at the same instant we witness the widest cultural opening gay and lesbian people have ever experienced. Public opinion is deeply divided about how to respond to our emergence from the shadows.

Similarly, in sport there has been success. Twenty years ago, only one athlete with a public profile was openly gay (NFL player David Kopay); there were few lesbian and gay community sports clubs in North America; there had not been a major gay sporting event such as the Gay Games; and lesbians and gay men in gyms and recreation centers for the most part did everything they could to keep their sexuality invisible. Twenty years later, there are more openly lesbian and gay athletes with public profiles; gay sports groups in many urban centers are the largest gay community organizations; the Gay Games are an international event that by 2002 will have been held on three continents (North America, Europe, and Australia, with an estimated 15,000 participants at the 1998 Amsterdam games); and overtly gay presence in urban gyms is virtually a cliché. Where sport was formerly a hostile environment for gays and lesbians, it has in some respects become a haven. That one could participate in sports as an expression of gay pride, as is the case with many lesbian and gay athletic events, was unthinkable two decades ago.

Thus, it could be argued that progress has been made in the quest for lesbian and gay liberation: Athletes who are public figures are coming out, "breaking the silence," and claiming space for gays and lesbians in mainstream sport;[2] in the lesbian and gay community, sport has been transformed from its history of systematic oppression and is now a vehicle for liberating lesbian and gay expression. But considering that across North America in the last 20 years, fewer than two dozen high-performance athletes have declared their homosexuality publicly, and only a few of them have had significant public profiles (e.g., Martina Navratilova and Greg Louganis), and that very few of that already small number have continued in their athletic careers once they have come out, it is clear that the effect that out gay athletes have had in making mainstream sport a sexually liberated environment is negligible. At the time of writing, most studies of lesbians and gays in mainstream sport document the fearful extent of homophobia in sport (Burton-Nelson, 1994; Cahn, 1994b; Griffin, 1998; Lenskyj, 1986, 1992a; Pronger, 1990; Rogers, 1994). I am aware of no scholarly research that shows mainstream sport to be a significantly welcome environment for sexual minorities.

The fact is that mainstream sports continue to be overwhelmingly hostile to explicit lesbian and gay presence. This situation in sport is parallel to Urvashi Vaid's (1995) observation that mainstream North American culture in general, despite the increased visibility of lesbian and gay people in it, continues to be overwhelmingly homophobic. She argued, moreover, that lesbian and gay freedom is equivocal, completely contingent on the transitory will of various judicial and legislative bodies—the bleak fate of the rights of lesbians and gays in the military under the regime of a "pro-gay" American president being a recent and landmark case in point.[3] It is similar in mainstream commercial sport: The already minimal tolerance of lesbian and gay athletes is completely dependent on the whims of the sports entertainment marketplace of the moment. Furthermore, although most jurisdictions in Canada and several in the United States have legislation and case law that militate against discrimination on the basis of sexual orientation (albeit of widely varying rigor)—a fact that could be cited as proof that some progress has been won in society in general—the dominance of the closet in the world of sport is actually proof of the limited reach of the law and of the defeat of lesbian and gay liberation in sports culture. Indeed, the very suggestion that there has been significant progress for lesbians and gays in sport (or, for that matter, in society in general) is an ironic expression of the low expectations of a deeply homophobic consciousness. In mainstream noncommercial sport (intercollegiate, intramural, recreational), tolerance depends on the strength of the relevant organizations's nondiscrimination and sexual harassment policies and enforcement practices, if they even have them. In such a framework, lesbian and gay liberation is contingent on the expectations and good will of the overwhelmingly homophobic culture of sport. Vaid said that such contingency means that lesbian and gay freedom is nothing more than "virtual" and will remain such unless there are deeper social transformations that eradicate the dependency of the freedom of sexual minorities on their tolerance by the mainstream, which is to say, only in a society in which there is true openness to sexual diversity, only where the body and sexuality are no longer tied to larger programs of social and economic control, will human freedom and equality be possible.[4] We are very far from such a world.

Gay Sports Cultures

Although mainstream sport still may be overwhelmingly homophobic and sexist, it could be argued that the development over the last 20 years of extensive networks of lesbian and gay community sporting activities signifies progress for sexual minorities in the arena of physical activity. One's position in this regard depends on one's erotic and political aspirations for the cultures of sport and sexuality. It depends on whether one wants sport as a bodily cultural practice to continue essentially unchanged, but to be more inclusive of people with marginalized sexual identities, or whether one wants sexuality to disrupt or even transform the very foundations of sport as a bodily practice. I argue that gay community sports have made "progress" in the former sense and have failed in the latter. Following Vaid, I suggest that the progress of lesbian and gay community sports, seen in the light of the socially transformative ambitions of some of the historical streams of the gay and lesbian liberation movement, has been more about dominant sociocultural systems (including sports) appeasing, coopting, indeed diffusing the transformative possibilities of the sexual margins than it has been about increasing human freedom.

The historical development of gay sporting cultures is related to the development of lesbian and gay political cultures from the 1950s to the present. Since the early years of the "modern gay liberation movement," there have been tensions between gay conservative and radical critiques of society and agendas for political action (Adam, 1995; Duberman, 1993; Vaid, 1995). Since the Second World War, the homophile movement, which later became known as the gay liberation movement, has had radical leftist factions. In Canada and Great Britain, these were fairly influential until the early 1970s; they continue now on the margins. In the United States, however, they always have been marginal to lesbian and gay politics. The traditional American hatred of socialism (which continues to be expressed in the widely popular embargo of Cuba as well as in deep-seated distrust of social welfare programs, such as Medicare) was and continues to be a powerful presence in American gay politics. The leftist elements of the lesbian and gay political movements tend to seek the total transformation of society, economically, culturally, and sexually. For leftists, the political agenda is not so much to give homosexual people a piece of the (bourgeois consumer capitalist) pie by focusing on gay rights as it is to participate in the liberation of all forms of oppression. The left-leaning gay and lesbian liberationists envision not just the end of lesbian and gay oppression but the transformation of all sexual and other categories that limit the fullness of human potential. Moreover, they see sexual oppression as deeply related to other dynamics of oppression: capitalism, racism, sexism, classism, ethnocentrism, ablism, and so on. This increasing breadth is the product of historical struggles in the radical lesbian, gay, and queer activist movements and is far from being a coherent *fait accompli*. Nevertheless, I think it is fair to say that most radicals see the pursuit of sexual freedom as a "window of opportunity" that can, in the context of a radical political culture, foster an appreciation of and resistance to multiple dynamics of oppression. Sexual freedom, then, is not understood as a self-sufficient point of departure for transformative politics but as one way of engaging in complex, highly fragmented, and often contradictory sets of political projects.[5] Sexual liberation, in this context, is not conceived as a single struggle but as intricately related to other struggles for dignity and freedom. Moderate liberal and conservative elements of lesbian and gay movements, on the other hand, tend to be satisfied with the fundamentals of modern capitalism and many of the social formations that function within it, and they strive to stop discrimination against lesbian- and gay-identified individuals so that they can participate more fully in mainstream economics and culture. Urvashi Vaid (1995) characterized this tension between radicals and liberals/conservatives as the tension between commitments to lesbian and gay "legitimation" versus "liberation." The liberal tendency toward legitimation seeks tolerance and acceptance in the mainstreams of society: It proposes doing so by a process of educational and legislative reform that stresses that homosexual people are human beings, essentially no different from everyone else except by virtue of their preference of sexual partners. Liberals thus pursue single-issue politics, that is, the end of discrimination and the protection of lesbian and gay rights. Radical liberation politics seeks the larger transformation of society and sees sexuality as one way of joining in that larger pursuit.

For the remainder of this chapter, I argue that the lesbian and gay cultural embrace of sport has been for the most part a liberal strategy of legitimation—liberals are essentially satisfied with the fundamentals of sport as a bodily practice and do not seek basic changes to the practices and rules of sport. On the whole, gay community sports have not pursued a radical strategy of liberation that would see the gay engagement with sport as an opportunity to transform sport's cultural conservatism, an opportunity to refigure the construction of sport as conservative culture of desire, which could in turn contribute to the critique and transformation of oppressions that are perpetuated by conservative political cultures more generally.

Theoretical Perspective:
The Philosophy of the Limit[6]

I situate my analysis within the continental critical path that often has gone by the name "deconstruction" and about which there has been considerable scholarly and political debate. Given that this chapter is specifically about homosexuality and sport and not about methodology, it would be inappropriate to engage in a lengthy discussion of this analytical trajectory. But I hope that in the few words that follow I am able to clarify my analytical framework and give some justification for it.

A frequent critique of deconstruction has been that it is preoccupied with taking apart the play of language and thus slides into a dangerous and elitist ludic idealism. Deconstruction, it is claimed, fails to "grasp" material reality, the "real" lives of people who suffer from the material organization of life that perpetuates privileges of hierarchical minorities in the context of class, race, gender, sexuality, ethnicity, and so on, the reality of which can be grasped by sociologists who engage in "materialist conceptions of social structure" (Messner, 1996, p. 228). Deconstructionists reply by attempting to show how the confident, positive assertions that social scientists make about the material structure of social life are, in fact, systematic attempts to control and limit scholarly and political discourse. The unreflective mobilization of concepts such as materialist conceptions of social structure, they would say, facilitates the author's attempt to impose his or her own conceptual system and political aspirations on material reality. In this way, antideconstructionist social scientists contribute to the reification and perpetuation of the very social structures they are trying to critique. It is precisely such political maneuvering that deconstruction tries to expose.

Jacques Derrida (1978), among the most influential practitioners of deconstruction, says that systems (be they linguistic, musical, visual, athletic, sexual, economic, or sociological conceptions of social structure) impose limits on the power to appreciate material reality, which thus preclude the possibility of engaging in deeply ethical relationships with material reality, which in turn undermines the political power to formulate alternate constructions of reality. The point of Derridadian deconstruction is to expose the insensitivity to the power of limitation that is part of any operative system and to show that this insensitivity precludes the possibility of ethical relationships with anybody or anything that is other—other either to the operators of the system or other to the system itself. Deconstruction seeks to reveal what is left out and to show how such exclusions prohibit just, ethical relations. A deconstruction of lesbian and gay sports culture, therefore, aims to expose what is left out by that culture and what that marginalization indicates about the true nature of the culture.

Deconstruction, by the seeming negativity of the word itself, is sometimes confused with a kind of cynical, nihilistic reductionism—take apart the constructs and you are left with nothing. Some sociologists, philosophers, and political activists, thinking that because deconstruction reduces everything to a cynical and unreconstructable litter, believe that political action is rendered impossible (Dews, 1987; Ebert, 1996; Habermas, 1983). To counteract such misunderstanding, the feminist legal philosopher Drucilla Cornell (1992) suggested renaming the project "the philosophy of the limit." Questioning limits has been the source of many politically active liberation movements—feminists questioning the limits of gender, antiracists the limits of racism, postmodernists the limits of modernity (Game, 1991; Gray, 1995; Hutcheon, 1989; Jameson, 1984; Lyotard, 1984; Miller, 1993), the handicapped the limits of ablism, gays the limits of homophobia, queers the limits of gay culture (Champagne, 1995; Kipnis, 1993; Warner, 1993), and postqueers the limits of queer (Simpson, 1996). All of these have engaged in some philosophy of the limit, questioning the ways in which social, economic, cultural, and bodily systems construct the limits of human possibilities. Clearly, there are activist political agendas in them all. Simply put: What limits are operative?

How can they be justified? Where and how might it be wise to dismantle them? The questions of limits are often most poignant for those who find themselves outside them; which is why deconstruction is so popular with deviants like homosexual academics. It may be that those whose personal lives are mostly consonant with the limits of white, patriarchal, middle-class, straight, sporting social structures have a relatively shallow experience of their own otherness to those social structures and prefer to work within them politically, the point being to include more people. In such situations, deconstruction would not have much personal appeal.

Derridadian deconstruction interrogates the limits of systems as such. Although there is much to this metacritique, for the purpose of this chapter, I briefly call attention to three important and related elements that are particularly apt for the question of homosexuality and sport: *the logics of parergonality, secondness,* and *alterity.* Derrida (1987) coined the expression the logics of parergonality to name the way in which the establishment of any system as a system suggests a beyond to it, that is, that which the system excludes, by virtue of what the system cannot comprehend, or by what it prohibits to accomplish its systematic objectives. The philosophy of the limit asks: What lies beyond a particular system by virtue of its existence as a system? What are the system's limits? In the context of this chapter's interrogation of homosexuality and sport, the question becomes: How does sport as a system limit sexuality?

Cornell (1992) also drew on what Charles Peirce, in his critique of Hegelian idealism, called secondness, which is "the materiality that persists beyond any attempt to conceptualize it. Secondness, in other words, is what resists. Very simply, reality is not interpretation all the way down" (Cornell, 1992, p. 1). The philosophy of the limit, then, asks about what realities resist and persist beyond systems of interpretation. Here is a much more robust materialism than "materialist conceptions of social structure." It does not suggest that social systems do not exist, nor that they do not exercise considerable power over human beings. Rather, it does suggest that there is material reality that resists systematic conceptual reductions and control. Moreover, the materiality of secondness is significant, not only by virtue of its marginalization and therefore exclusion from the benefits the system bestows on those included or, alternatively, the benefits that freedom from the system might bestow, but also by virtue of what the exclusion says about the reality that is being produced in the system. In other words, one often understands more about what is in a system by looking at what is left out. Where the system happens to be a dominating force like the formal and informal rules for the conduct of sport and sexuality, the realities that either succumb or resist inside and outside a given system are extremely important. What material realities in sport, for instance, resist the system of sport? What realities in homosexual desire resist gay culture and gay identity? Even more important, how do those systems either foster the potentialities of secondness or attempt to control or erase them?

By alterity, Cornell (1992) referred to an ethical philosophy that remains open, indeed committed, to fostering the ways in which the other is differentiated from and inaccessible to systems of interpretation and social organization. Derrida says that for the other to be appreciated of itself, it must remain other to the system: "For Derrida, the excess to the system cannot be known positively [by the system]. . . . We must try, if we are to remain faithful to the ethical relationship, to heed [the other's] otherness to any system of conventional definition" (Cornell, 1992, p. 2). Cornell grounded the philosophy of the limit in the ambitious ethical quest to engage the other and otherness nonviolently:

> The entire project of the philosophy of the limit is driven by the ethical desire to enact the ethical relation . . . the aspiration to a nonviolent relationship to the Other and to otherness more generally, that assumes responsibility to guard the Other, against the appropriation that would deny her difference and singularity. (p. 2)

The politics of inclusion, which tries to bring the other into a system while requiring them to manifest themselves within the structure of the system, appropriates the other's otherness. This is what I will shortly argue that gay community sports does: It includes gay men in sport by eliding their potential otherness, requiring them to work within the established system of sport. The ethics of alterity, on the other hand, is characterized not by inclusion but by openness, openness to otherness in a way that allows the other to deconstruct the system, to call into question the system's limits, particularly in its appropriation of their otherness.

The philosophy of the limit does not suggest some simple eradication of limits. Life, of course, would be impossible if there were no limits. The traditional etymological definition of philosophy is that it is the love of wisdom. The philosophy of the limit is the love of wisdom about limits. What are wise ways of constructing limits? How can limits be constructed with an ethics of alterity? So, the ethical question becomes: What wisdom is there in the ways that interpretive systems and social organizations, such as sport, limit the potentialities for difference and otherness? This makes the question for the lesbian and gay cultural embrace of sport: How and to what degree does gay community sport foster or erase the possible otherness of homosexuality?

The Limits of Gay Community Sports Culture

The philosophy of the limit (or deconstruction) is particularly germane for the question of homosexuality and sport because homosexuality traditionally has been organized as decidedly, negatively, indeed prohibitively other to sport (Burton-Nelson, 1994; Cahn, 1994a, 1994b; Lenskyj, 1986, 1990, 1992a; Rogers, 1994), and sport was traditionally beyond the limits of male homosexuality (Pronger, 1992). How has the lesbian and gay cultural embrace of sport effected limits vis-à-vis the logics of parergonality, secondness, and the ethics of alterity? How has the insinuation of sport in gay culture "appropriated and denied the difference and singularity" of homosexual ways of being?

My appraisal is complicated by the fact that the lesbian and gay cultural embrace of sport has not been singular. There are, for instance, many pockets of those cultures in which sport continues to have no interest or appeal, just as there are many realms of mainstream culture in which sport is irrelevant. Moreover, sport is taken up in different lesbian and gay communities in different ways; some, for instance, have made concerted attempts to downplay the importance of competition and to structure sport as a purely friendly, even cooperative, practice. Others have tried to develop gay sport as a highly competitive alternative to mainstream sport. Some have attempted to reconfigure the traditional sexist formulations of sport by making it coeducational. Many gay community sports groups have gone out of their way to stress inclusiveness, regardless of ability, age, gender, race, class, and sexual orientation. To date, there has been little scholarly empirical research on the social and political organization of lesbian and gay community sports. I attempt to analyze trajectories that are being followed but whose prevalence still needs to be documented empirically.

Gay community sports organizations have made concerted efforts to change the social organization of sports so they are more inclusive of lesbians and gay men. The concern has been to remove the barriers that can prevent lesbians and gay men from participating in traditional competitive sports forms: hockey, baseball, track and field, swimming, curling, soccer, bodybuilding, figure skating, gymnastics, and so on. Lesbians and gay men who have an interest in sport often have avoided it because of the dominance of heterosexism and homophobia. The creation of specifically lesbian and gay community sports has been influential in fostering environments that are inclusive. The quadrennial Gay Games are by far the largest example of such gay community sports. Inclusion is the watchword of the Gay Games. Great care is taken to encourage gender parity, to foster coeducational competitions, to provide opportunities for disabled athletes, to create opportunities for people regardless of their ability, and so on. In many ways, the Gay Games is a model for inclusiveness in sport. Most smaller gay community sports organizations also do most everything they can to take down barriers to participation. It is fair to say that virtually all lesbian and gay community sports organizations do not discriminate on the basis of sexual orientation and, like the Gay Games, welcome all who support their inclusive and "gay-positive" culture. Gay sports culture is the very model of liberal, inclusive lesbian and gay politics and aspirations. Because of that, it is a very popular form in mainstream gay culture.

One of the reasons it is such a popular form is that it expresses the dominant gay liberal philosophy: Lesbians and gays are just like anybody else: We shop, we eat, we have families, we play sports. The only real difference between us and everyone else is that we have sex with people of the same gender. Lesbians and gay men are essentially "normal" human beings. Although our sexuality and experience of marginality make us especially sensitive to issues of inclusion, in the final analysis, we are the same: Gay community sports proves our normality. When I was at the Gay Games in Vancouver in 1990, time and again, I heard the organizers proclaim that the fact that lesbians and gays do sports and do it in the same way that anyone else does is testimony to the normality of lesbians and gay men. And many lesbian and gay sports events are now sanctioned by mainstream sports governing bodies, conducted under the rules of the particular sport, with duly appointed officials. This is seen as important because it legitimizes the event as sport: Records and results become "official" because the competition was held in accordance with the rules of the sports governing body. Officially sanctioned events prove that lesbian and gay sports are conducted in strict accordance with the norms of sport. Toby Manning (1996) pointed out that a photo caption for the New York Gay Games in 1994 said that the Games were "an affirmation of the human spirit" (Manning, 1996, p. 100). This suggests that what is important in the Gay Games is the humanity that the participants have in common with all human beings; sexuality is secondary. The Dutch sexuality scholar Gert Hekma noted that the organizers of the 1998 Amsterdam Gay Games downplayed the sexuality of gay culture by stressing "friendship" rather than sex; the official slogan of the Games was "Friendship through Culture and Sports."[7] Such avoidance of sexuality is especially ironic for Amsterdam, given that it is quite rightly world-famous for its explicit and readily available sexual culture, homosexual and otherwise. Such a strategy, again, stresses the normality and respectability of homosexuality as just another version of normal friendliness.[8] Lesbian and gay "friendship" does not threaten the heterosexism, homophobia, and sex phobia of dominant culture in the way that lesbian and gay sexuality does.

Homosexual culture is thus constituted as a minor variation on an essential sameness. The effect of this sporting legitimation is the erasure of lesbian and gay difference. Homosexuality is not a challenge to the status quo, because it fits in so well. As Vaid (1995) amply documented, such liberalism has become the dominant political agenda of lesbian and gay politics in North America. Part of the success of lesbian and gay community sport has been its ability to promote the liberal agenda. From a deconstructionist and liberationist point of view, however, I would say that although this has made life easier for lesbians and gay men whose greatest ambition is to join the dominant discourse, it has foreshortened the transformative promise of the more radical sexual political movements. The effect of gay community sport has not been the transformation of sporting life but merely has included homosexual people in the established practices of sport. Sport, I argue, has played a role, perhaps not the leading one, but a role nevertheless in the appropriation, control, and perhaps ultimate erasure of the otherness of homosexuality and thus of its transformative power. From a legitimizing liberal perspective, this has been a good thing. The problem with homosexuality was its position as deviant, perverse, abnormal, and disturbingly invisible. Once it is no longer conceived as different from heterosexuality, once it no longer poses a threat, once it is respectably visible, the battle is over, and lesbians and gays can simply enjoy the privileges of normality, if they are middle-class, white, English-speaking supporters of globalizing consumer capitalism.

From a more radical liberationist transformationist perspective, the gay embrace of sport marks the end of the rather short era in which homosexuality provided a window of opportunity for the deeper transformation of society. Early radical gay liberationists saw the emancipation of homosexuality as a tool for the emancipation of all forms of sexuality and ultimately as an important contribution to liberation from other forms of oppression—gendered, racial, and economic. It shared much of the politics of Herbert Marcuse (1969) and Norman O. Brown (1966). Indeed, many have argued that the liberation of homosexuality could lead to the end of all exclusive and restrictive forms of sexuality. The most recent version of this political agenda is found in postmodern "queer" politics, which suggests that desire, not just homosexual or heterosexual, indeed not just sexual desire, but the desire to move and be at all, needs to be freed from restrictive cultural forms that limit the potential for individual and collective human creativity. That is decidedly not the agenda of gay community sports or of the rest of mainstream gay culture, which seeks only the admission of gays and lesbians into the mainstream culture. That tendency is also evident in the targeting of the gay market as just another consumer niche—this is made blatantly obvious in virtually all gay media, as well as in the highly commercialized spectacle of the Gay Games and enthusiastically documented by Lukenbill (1995) and criticized by Manning (1996). Urvashi Vaid (1995) documented extensively the end of transformational politics in the American gay political scene, calling it "mainstreaming of gay and lesbian liberation." As Tatchell (1996) stated,

> Most lesbian and gay men, if they ever had any vision of sexual emancipation, have long ago lost it. The idealism of the immediate post-Stonewall lesbian and gay liberation movement has been swamped by a short-sighted, short-termist *Realpolitik*. Few homos aspire to anything more than assimilating into the hetero status quo. They happily conform to the straight system. The battle cry is gay rights, not queer emancipation. (pp. 46-47)

Lesbian and gay sport has been instrumental in that process of assimilation. The problems in this are exposed by appealing to the philosophy of the limit. I argue that the gay embrace of sport has reproduced systemic limits on desire that undermine the ethics of alterity. Both homosexuality and sport are socially constructed systems that regulate desire, which means that both are subject to historical processes. In the last two decades, the radical and transformative potential of homosexuality has been undercut by its mainstreaming. That process has changed the meaning of homosexuality. Gay community sport has contributed to the process by separating homoeroticism and its radical potential from sports practice, preferring that sports be played out strictly within the rules that regulate bodies in mainstream sports.

Sport and Desire

The word "sport" obviously refers to a vast array of activities, institutions, and often contested sociocultural practices, and this makes it very difficult to speak of it generically. Nevertheless, there are some elements to competitive sport, ways in which it organizes the body that are preponderant and relatively stable. Following Foucault's analysis of penal institutions (1979) and sexuality (1980, 1985), I suggest that sport is a disciplinary practice that organizes the body and desire in time and space. All sports have rules that dictate how, when, and where the body can move, which is to say there are rules that dictate how the body's flow of energy is supposed to manifest itself.

Gilles Deleuze and Felix Guattari (1987) have developed a theory of the body that shows how the body's power to move, its power to connect with other bodies, is socially organized. Desire, they say, is the very essence of the body's being. Many writers have suggested that the control of desire is the primary occupation of any society.[9] Obviously, there are many historically contingent ways of dealing with the issue of desire, or what Turner (1984) called "the problem of the body." As Deleuze and Guattari (1987) stated, "To code desire—and the fear, the anguish of decoded flows—is the business of the socius [i.e., any particular social ordering]" (p. 139). These codes organize the body such that there are socially appropriate and inappropriate functions of body parts, correct and incorrect pairings for the interpenetrations of bodies, their surfaces, their holes. The codes of traditional patriarchal heterosexuality, for instance, are meant to determine the "correct" insertions of bodies, to ensure that the "right" organ gets inserted into the "correctly sexed" holes, which is to say: man and woman, penis and vagina, top and bottom.

For Deleuze and Guattari (1987), desire is not at all confined to "sexuality." In fact, sexuality is one particular codification of desire that institutes systems of control by making distinctions, such as the sexual and nonsexual, licit and illicit, homosexual and heterosexual. It is such a codification of desire that suggests there is a proper distinction between "sex" and "sport" and that attempts to maintain these as essentially different activities. The codification of desire in the institutions of sport legislates the way that bodies may connect with each other. In some sports, for instance, physical contact is against the rules; in others, only some kinds of contact are permitted. The economic expenditure of energies, such as when, where, and how one can move, is codified by sport. The codification of desire and ensuring that desire does not break lose and undermine the social system thus codified is the very purpose of the rules and institutional practices of sport. Many questions follow: How is the body/desire/energy-flow controlled in modern sport? What is the philosophy of the limit in sport? How would a radical sexual liberationist philosophy of the limit seek to reconstruct those limits? How does gay community sport construct these limits?

Sport brings people together so that the desire to move and connect with others can be expressed. Just as much as sexual activity, sport clearly involves the exertions of the body and always in reference to the exertions of others. The body is on display: locker rooms, showers, on the playing field, in the swimming pool, on the court, around the track, even sitting on the bench. Some sports more than others, and especially nowadays, use very revealing clothing (or lack thereof, as in swimming). There are many sports in which actual contact between bodies is at the center of the affairs (e.g., rugby, American football, wrestling, boxing). The vast majority of sports have limited the interplay of bodies, segregating them by gender; they require that desire be expressed homo-sexually, that is, only between men or between women. There are very few sports that allow hetero play. There are strict codes of behavior that govern how, when, and where bodies can move. Anyone who has tried to teach sport to little children has seen the tension between regulated and unregulated desire. Two codified domains that are particularly germane here are those that regulate (a) forms of erotic expression and (b) libidinal logic of domination.

The reproduction of orthodox heterosexual masculinity is central to the culture of mainstream men's and boys' sport. As I argued at length in *The Arena of Masculinity* (1990, 1992), there are homoerotic undercurrents in sport, regardless of the sexual identity of the participants. The bodily interactions between players are prohibited from becoming overtly homoerotic. The only place that happens is in gay pornography, and, not insignificantly, it is a fairly common theme.[10] Men's sport is particularly homophobic because of the omnipresence of implicit homoeroticism in a cultural practice that is supposed to build heterosexuality—homophobia helps to prevent what is implicit from becoming explicit. Sporting homophobia is part of the system of men's sport that regulates the flow of desire by codes of suppression. Homophobia operates within sport's logic of parergonality, systematically producing homoeroticism as an excess to the domain of sport as an arena of orthodox, heterosexual masculinity. Homoeroticism is maintained as an excess to the system by a comprehensive, unwritten, but well-known and closely adhered-to set of rules that govern the nature of caresses, hugs, and kisses on the playing field, not to mention the display of erections, erotic massage, masturbation, fellatio, and buggery in locker rooms, showers, washrooms, sleeping accommodation, or at team socials. By following these rules for the governance of intermale desire, sportsmen (and boys) can play with each other's bodies in highly erotic and intimate ways without that desire becoming other to the system of masculinist hetero-normativity that sport reproduces. That logic of parergonality thus renders explicit homoeroticism a material reality that is "second" to the system, marginalized but not extinguished. In this way, sport reflects the logics of parergonality that form the social construction of heterosexual identity, in which the possibilities of homosexual commerce are made excessive to the system of exclusive heterosexuality that prohibits same-gender erotic interests. In sport, in which homoeroticism is rendered second to the system, homoeroticism nevertheless maintains some material reality, albeit a restricted one, in that realm of intermale bodily/erotic interactions that the codes allow in the locker room, for instance: look but do not caress, control erectile tissue, make sure that hugs and slaps do not linger, give massages for purely therapeutic reasons, and so on.

The most important code pertains to the playing field itself: Engage only in body contacts that are functional to the official libidinal logic of the game: winning.[11] I call the desire to win "libidinal," especially in sport, because it is the mobilization of the desire for human bodily interaction, which is a bodily, erotic way of coming to presence, of exchanging energy with other human beings. Essential to this libidinal logic is the logic of domination: The only way to score a point is by depriving one's opponent of the same by dominating them. The production of hierarchical difference is at the heart of competitive sport. Of course, there are many friendly strategies for downplaying the psychic impact of this production of hierarchy, for example, the opponents going for a convivial beer after the game, with the winner buying. Yet, the inner libidinal logic of domination remains intact. Sporting desire does not work if there is no desire to overcome one's opponent.[12] The parergonality is evident in that competitive sport systematically structures desire for the production of hierarchical difference, setting strict limits on the way that people connect with each other. Love of the other, specifically as the other is constructed as an opponent, is excluded from this system of desire production. In loving desire, one does not seek victory over the beloved by taking something away from him or her. The loving desire to give to the other what the other desires is rendered second in this libidinal logic. In fact, one does everything one can to withhold what the other desires, to selfishly guard it for oneself. Love, at the very least, is generous. Although loving generosity is sometimes encouraged among teammates, by definition it is never encouraged between "opponents." Sport limits the expression and experience of love between people. Indeed, it makes a game out of it, for taking success from the other is supposed to be fun. This is a profoundly unethical construction, one that is fostered among men and boys to "build character." It goes against the ethics of alterity in which I have grounded my argument, an ethical imperative that is deeply opposed to appropriative, aggressive, and violent relations to the other. The sporting logic of parergonality that sets the limits on love reflects the larger version of the same in patriarchal capitalism, that is, the desire to accumulate wealth and status are considered more important than the sacrifice of the same in the name of love.

The celebration of love and the radical potential that it could have in undoing all kinds of oppressions and ugly human relations were core values of the radical lesbian and gay liberation movement, which sought the free expression of love and the deconstruction of hierarchical differences in every aspect of life. Leftist liberationists tied the politics of emancipatory love to very ambitious personal, political, social, and cultural projects: the dismantling of patriarchy, capitalism, consumerism, racism, ageism, ablism, sexism, monogamy, the bourgeois family, as well exclusionary sexualities, such as homo- and heterosexuality (Hekma et al., 1995). The mode for this pathway to emancipation is the subversion of the sex phobia (not just homophobia) of contemporary culture (Tatchell, 1996, p. 48). In the field of sport, the agenda would be the emancipation of sport as highly regulated erotic desire, transforming it into a freer field of erotic possibilities, neither homo nor hetero; it would be eros opened by the possibilities of alterity. At the cynical beginning of this millennium, such ambitious desires may seem foolish. But their alternative—the acceptance and reproduction of those oppressive discourses—remains just as unethical as it was in the 1960s.

Homosexual Transformation of Sport?

Radical lesbian and gay liberationists are not for the most part a sporty bunch. Nevertheless, some have tried to promote physical activities that were in line with their larger political and cultural agendas by trying to reinvent sporting forms that avoided the homophobia and libidinal logic I have described. For example, in Toronto, the Not-So-Amazon (women's) softball league tried to develop this form of play and spent as much time debating the politics of the game as they did playing it. But just as radical transformative agendas have been unseated by the process of mainstreaming in the wider lesbian and gay political culture since the 1970s, so too radical visions of physical activity have been mostly supplanted by mainstream versions of sport in lesbian and gay sports culture. Admittedly, some pockets of gay culture have continued to resist this mainstreaming tendency. Deconstructing specific gay community sports organizations and events in terms of their control of explicit homoeroticism and libidinal logic would reveal the degree to which they have been able to resist, or indeed subvert, the limits of sport.

Some of the peripheral aspects of lesbian and gay community sports do look different from their mainstream counterparts. There is much greater parity between men's and women's sports events at the Gay Games than at the Olympics, for instance. The explicit and ambitious agenda of inclusion, which I summarized previously, differentiates gay sport from some mainstream sports—although the workers' sports movement of the early part of this century (Kidd, 1996; Kruger & Riordan, 1996), much of the masters sports movement, disabled sports, as well as ethnically based sports groups, also have had ambitious inclusionary agendas. Gay sensibilities have had an effect on some sports; for example, gay swim meets almost always include the "Pink Flamingo Relay," which is a gay camp extravaganza. As I said earlier, all of this has made it easier for lesbians and gays to participate. It has done so because it has engaged in the politics of inclusion, which is to say it takes down the barriers to participation in established sporting cultural forms. But I have yet to see any significant developments in gay community sports that deconstruct logics of parergonality and pursue the ethics of alterity that I suggest are part of radical lesbian, gay, and queer agendas. The actual sporting practices of lesbian and gay sport are no different from mainstream practices. Indeed, it seems that the whole point of gay community sports is to show the world and gay people themselves that they are part of the mainstream and offer no challenge to the construction of desire in hierarchical, capitalist, patriarchal culture.

Competitive gay community sports reproduce the mainstream libidinal logic I have just described (many even import officials from mainstream sport to guarantee that there are no disruptions in the libidinal rules). Perhaps more surprisingly, they also reproduce the parergonal homophobia of mainstream sport as well, as I now argue.

Over the last 100 years, Western male homosexuality has had a rich history of illicit sexuality in parks, washrooms, locker rooms, dormitories, barracks, jails, alleyways, bathhouses, gyms, YMCAs, summer camps, churches, and choirs. Radical gay liberationists brought these activities out of secrecy and pressed them into public celebrations of disruptive sexuality.[13] Public promiscuous homosexuality was strategic to unseating the propriety of sex that restricted it to the parergonality of monogamy, privacy, and the bedroom. It also was championed as challenging the cultural dominance of competitive and hierarchical relations between men: Far better for men to make love with each other in public than to compete and distance themselves in public spectacles such as sport and warfare. It is a poignant sign of a culture that for most of its people it is more acceptable to see men in parks, on television, or in movies aggressively taking things from each other, be it points in a game or life itself (in the case of violent movies), than to see them lovingly probe each others' bodies with hands, tongues, mouths, and penises. Radical gay liberationists were and still are aware of this and have promoted public homosexuality as a disruptive, transgressive alternative to more violent and unloving expressions of intermale desire. Toby Manning (1996) pointed out, "In contrast to [mainstream, liberal] gay culture, a transgressive culture operates outside the mainstream's rules, jettisons its rationales, and rejects its bourgeois morality, as part of a broader, oppositional movement of outsiders" (p. 109). It is such a transgressive culture that radicals have tried to organize around public, promiscuous homosexuality. This upset many adherents of straight culture, including many lesbians and gays who prefer that homosexuality fit within the dominant organization of society rather than challenge it. The disruptive potential of homosexuality is thus best hidden in the privacy of the bedroom and confined within the rules of monogamy, which exert considerable control over the expression of desire. Such a strategy, of course, renders homosexuality not very disruptive at all.

One of the great fears that circulated during the debates about gays in the U.S. military was the fear that homosexuality would become overt, which is to say that the military disciplines of the body that construct desire as the power to kill rather than to love would be undermined, and the joys of easy and accessible erotic commerce would become so attractive that they would distract soldiers, sailors, and airmen from the discipline of their primary purpose. There has not yet been a similar public debate about overt homosexuality in sport. Interestingly, the issue has barely arisen in gay community sports. Although at Gay Pride Day celebrations in major cities in North America, there are usually heated debates about public nudity and explicit expressions of homosexual desire (SM displays, men masturbating and having sex in public, and so on), these issues do not even arise in gay community sports. Straight sexual respectability reigns both on the playing fields and in the locker rooms and showers of gay community sports. With the exception of the odd affectionate peck on the cheek or the occasional holding of hands and lingering hugs, gay community sports are the same as mainstream sports. Anecdotally, I have observed that mainstream sports facilities, such as those at my university or the YMCA or some private health clubs, have a more robust sexual commerce than any gay sporting event I have attended. It is as though gay men are "on their best behavior" when they are in gay sports settings. The opening and closing ceremonies of the Gay Games are so "respectable" that they could easily be mistaken for a mainstream event. The official slogan of the Gay Games in Amsterdam, which I mentioned earlier, focuses on friendship rather than sex and further indicates the desire for asexual respectability.

The sexual freedom that can be found readily in many other facets of gay culture is not part of the gay construction of sport. Certainly, gay men meet each other in gay sport settings and pursue sexual liaisons, but this is always peripheral to the practice of the sport itself, in which virtually the same rules about erotic conduct apply as in straight sports.[14] From a radical perspective, gay sports is part of the gentrification of homosexuality; it straightens out homosexuality, making it more palatable to, indeed more like, conservative taste. This is an important historical political development in gay culture, because it undermines the transgressive, transformative potential of homosexuality. Although this is no doubt attractive to liberal mainstream gay sensibilities, from a radical perspective it perpetuates the parergonality of the traditional sporting construction of desire. In short, people with gay identities are welcome to participate in sport, but they should leave homosexuality out of it. Ironically, then, gay community sports, although inclusive of gay identities in the peripherals of sport, continue to marginalize homosexuality from the activity. Here, the politics of inclusion are not the politics of alterity—you can join my game but you must play by my rules.

In *The Arena of Masculinity* (1990, 1992), I suggested that the ethical promise of homosexuality comes from its power to transgress oppressive, violent norms of masculinity, refiguring intermale desire as an expression of love. The gay embrace of the libidinal logic of domination in sport defuses this positive ethical promise by incorporating homosexual desire within the mainstream construction of sporting desire. It has the important political effect of reforming homosexuality as a minor variation of heterosexuality, which has been the liberal agenda all along.

Conclusion

Since the Stonewall Inn riots in New York City in July 1969, much has happened to homosexual culture(s). In some jurisdictions, there are laws that prohibit discrimination on the basis of sexual orientation. Homosexuality is an accepted theme in some parts of the entertainment industry, in movies, music, and visual arts. And there are now hundreds of thousands of lesbians and gay men who live their homosexual lives openly and some who are even able to incorporate their homosexuality in their professional work, as is the case with some academics, such as myself. The Governments of Amsterdam and Holland enthusiastically supported the Gay Games: All major public buildings sported Gay Games banners; even the trams were all flying Gay Games flags. These things were impossible 30 years ago. Nevertheless, the vast majority of homosexual people continue to live in fear of exposure and in the shadow of homophobic violence. Any progress remains contingent on the will and whim of mainstream culture, legislation, and economics. Very little progress has been made in mainstream sport. This equivocal success is largely the effect of a gay liberation movement that has contented itself with the single-issue struggle for legitimation through lesbian and gay rights (which has been a dubious success, at best) rather than the more fundamental liberationist struggle for the transformation of society.

Although lesbian and gay community sports have created friendly and inclusive environments for homosexual people who like to play sports, they have not, on the whole, taken up the liberationist challenge to transform social and interpersonal relations in sport. Most lesbian and gay community sports simply have reproduced dominant sporting practices for homosexual people by making them more accessible, thus emphasizing the liberal lesbian and gay political agenda, which is not to challenge fundamental sociocultural structures but to give lesbians and gay men the opportunity to conform to those structures.

Notes

1. Because this volume is about men and sport, I focus my attention on men. Where I use the words "lesbian and gay" in reference to culture and sport, I do so because the reality to which I am referring is constituted as such and not as exclusively gay male. I use the word "homosexual" as an adjective in reference to people who have same-gender erotic imaginations, fully aware that this might actually be everybody, to some degree. I use the word

"homosexuality" as a noun in reference to the phenomenon of same-gender erotics. When I use the word "gay," I refer to persons and cultures that are part of homosexual cultures that have developed over the last 30 years and that tend to be labeled or call themselves "gay."

2. For discussions of homosexualities and spatial organization, see Ingram, Bouthilette, and Retter (1997).

3. Arguments made later in this chapter would suggest that the specter of liberated homosexual people in the U.S. military (the hierarchical, patriarchal, violently forceful arm of American capitalist imperialism) is profoundly at odds with the goals of the socially transformational side of the gay and lesbian liberation movement—and that there is therefore a certain logic to their exclusion, which, fully considered, would rightly be self-exclusion. On the other hand, the U.S. military, especially in so-called peacetime, can be understood as a work-for-welfare program that keeps vast segments of the poor out of the ranks of the "unemployed." As an economic welfare program, therefore, it is unfair that lesbians and gay men would be denied the opportunity to benefit from it.

4. Foucault (1979, 1980, 1983) has called this control "biopolitics." Many other sociologists, philosophers, and anthropologists have documented the importance of the control of the body and sexuality to modern social order. The body has become a major subject of social analysis. A short list of works on the subject (in chronological order) would include Deleuze and Guattari (1983); Turner (1984); Levin (1985); Deleuze and Guattari (1987); Gallagher and Lacqueur (1987); Probyn (1987); Gallop (1988); Bordo (1989a, 1989b); Butler (1990); Featherstone (1991); Haraway (1991); Harvey and Sparks (1991); Shilling (1991); Stone (1991); Currie and Raoul (1992); Deleuze (1992); Abelove, Barale, and Halperin (1993); Bordo (1993); Harwood, Oswell, Parkinson, and Ward (1993); Kipnis (1993); Shilling (1993); Warner (1993); Braidotti (1994); Falk (1994); Goldberg (1994); Kirk (1994); Kirk and Spiller (1994); Sinfield (1994); Balsamo (1995); Champagne (1995); Featherstone and Burrows (1995); Gray (1995); Halperin (1995); Hekma, Oosterhuis, and Steakley (1995); Jordan (1995); Pronger (1995a, 1995b); Rail and Harvey (1995); Vertinsky (1995); Weinstein (1995); Herdt (1996); Morton (1996); Duberman (1997); Haraway (1997); Pronger (1998); Andrews (in press).

5. Shane Phelan (1994) has articulated these politics particularly well in a postmodern perspective.

6. I have developed this theoretical approach similarly in Pronger (1999), "Outta My Endzone: Sport and the Territorial Anus," *Journal of Sport and Social Issues, 23*(4), 373-389.

7. Hekma made these comments in his unpublished keynote address at the conference titled "Queer Games? Theories, Politics, Sports" at the University of Amsterdam immediately prior to the 1998 Gay Games.

8. It should be noted that increasingly the Gay Games has included a significant "cultural" festival. At Amsterdam, the cultural festival was for the first time a major part of the program, with more "cultural" events than sporting events, 58 and 29, respectively. The "cultural" events often included explicit representations and discussions of sexuality. There was also a more explicitly politically critical dimension to the "cultural" events—the conference "Queer Games?" for instance, questioned the sexual politics of the Gay Games. An empirical comparative study of the sport and "culture" elements of the Games could present a fascinating profile of contemporary lesbian, gay, and queer politics.

9. For a fuller treatment of this statement, see Turner (1984, 1991) and Shilling (1993).

10. The rarity of mixed-gender sports precludes much in the way of heteroerotic undercurrents.

11. Activities such as shinny hockey and basketball hoop shooting are not competitive sports, both because scores are not kept and there is no real opponent. These activities, therefore, have libidinal logics that are rather different from competitive sports.

12. I believe this argument about production of hierarchical difference also holds for the increasingly popular quest for personal bests, in which case one attempts to differentiate oneself hierarchically from one's former self.

13. More conservative gay liberationists argued that surreptitious and promiscuous homosexual activity in public places was "caused" by the oppression of gay men who were denied the "advantages" of legitimate sexual relations that were accorded to heterosexuals. It was often argued that once homosexual men had the opportunity to construct "respectable" relations, they would confine their activities to the privacy of the bedroom, just like straight people. This has not proven to be the case. Backrooms in bars, bathhouses, parks, washrooms, and gyms are flourishing in cities such as Toronto and New York, where being gay is in many ways broadly legitimized.

14. There are homosexual wrestling clubs that make sexual intercourse part of the sport—these are not part of "legitimate" wrestling, and this activity is not part of the lineup for the Gay Games or any other public gay sports events.

14

Panic Sport and the Racialized Masculine Body

DAVID ROWE
JIM McKAY
TOBY MILLER

The Politics of Sporting Bodies

With the advent of consumer capitalism and what might loosely be called postmodern culture, human bodies have become an increasingly visible locus of personal needs and desires. By the manipulation of general appearance, adoption of fashion codes, bodily adornment, calculated nutrition, physical conditioning regimes, and so on, the projection of body images into the social realm has taken on renewed (although hardly unprecedented) importance (Featherstone, Hepworth, & Turner, 1991; Kirk, 1993; Shilling, 1993). Human bodies also constitute a site of struggle over symbolic and material rewards between dominant and subordinate groups. Ultimately, social control is exercised through direct bodily coercion or the threat of it, or by training bodies to "discipline" themselves (Bartky, 1988; Bordo, 1990). Bodies are, then, both social subjects and objects, phenomena that are constantly in action and also acted on.

The sociohistorical development of bodies is, according to Shilling (1991), a dialectical process by which "people make their bodies through labour, sport and play, but they do not make them in circumstances of their own choosing" (p. 665). In this chapter, we are concerned with this process of "body-making" through sport which, especially in its mass mediated form, is one of the principal institutions through which disciplined bodies are activated and displayed. The physical, psychic, and representational forms of bodies (Gatens, 1988) are made meaningful through what Grosz (1987) called "corporeal subjectivities" articulated under conditions in which "there is no monolithic category 'the body' . . . only particular kinds of bodies" (p. 9), although we maintain that there are material limits to signifying and discursive processes and practices (Ebert, 1992-1993; Hall, 1985). We concentrate on the constructed, black male body—a configuration with a peculiarly strong attachment to the institution of contemporary sport. We do not wish to rehearse here our arguments concerning the strengths and weaknesses of postmodern theory (McKay & Rowe, 1997; Miller, 1993) but instead to use selected elements of postmodern insights to help inform the analysis of sport, gender, and race.

This chapter considers the dual role that media representations of sport play in constituting symbolic and material struggles over bodies, especially those that are heavily masculinized and racialized. Sport is deeply implicated in discourses of the body, in that it is a cultural form productive of various bodily dispositions—exertion, force, rule-bound activity, physical competition, and so on (Andrews, 1993; Cole, 1993; Gruneau, 1991; Heikkala, 1993). Hargreaves (1986a) described the body as "an emblem of society" (p. 13) over which there is a struggle for control, so that the corporeal arena of sport is of necessity a key site of social and cultural contestation (see also Messner, 1988; Trujillo, 1991). Sport, particularly in its elite, commercial form, has both reflected and projected a worldwide body crisis—or, in postmodern terms, "body panic" (Kroker, Kroker, & Cook, 1989). The subversion of traditional gender-bound body images; the continued expansion of bodily surveillance, modification, and manipulation; and the "dis-ease" of AIDS have all problematized bodies in new ways, and in a manner that has placed sport in the foreground. To illustrate this argument, we analyze how some recent media scandals have dwelt on the meanings of specific sporting bodies in the elaboration of contentious ideological positions. Such discourses of celebrity (Marshall, 1997; Rowe, 1997) provide fertile ground for the practice of contemporary cultural critique and politics.

Gendered and Racialized Sporting Bodies

Traditionally, sport has been a potent symbol of commonsense ideas about masculine superiority, as Messner (1990d) argued:

> Football, based as it is on the most extreme possibilities of the male body, . . . is clearly a world apart from women, who are relegated to the role of cheerleaders/sex objects on the sidelines. . . . In contrast to the bare and vulnerable bodies of the cheerleaders, the armored bodies of the football players are elevated to

mythical status, and as such, give testimony to the undeniable "fact" that here is at least one place where men are clearly superior to women. (p. 213)

However, the capacity of sport to legitimize ideologies of masculine superiority has been increasingly destabilized as females have struggled to gain greater access to sport. The "gender gap" in the sporting performances of males and females has gradually narrowed, and some women have outperformed men in certain (usually endurance) events. Increasing numbers of women are competing in traditionally masculine sports like power-lifting, bodybuilding, the martial arts, rugby, and ice hockey. The entry of women into this customary male preserve illustrates the "double movement of containment and resistance" characteristic of all cultural struggles among dominant and subordinate groups (Hall, 1981). On the one hand, the presence of vigorous and robust women athletes demonstrates that sporting prowess is not "naturally" masculine, whereas on the other hand, the presence of physically powerful female bodies poses a threat to hegemonic masculinity, thus precipitating male "hysteria" and attempts by men to contain women's aspirations and resistance (Disch & Kane, 1996; McKay, 1992; Ndalianis, 1995; White & Gillett, 1994). There is a paradox at work in these "intrusions." Women traditionally have suffered restrictions on their access to sport via biologistic claims that their bodies are unsuited to athletic activities. Now these old scientistic arguments partially function in reverse, thanks to female superiority in certain endurance events. But just as the antiquated scientism was vitally connected to power relations between the sexes, so the latter-day biological "truth" is deeply encrusted with social politics in terms of access to facilities, training, and prestige.

Sport, especially at the elite level, plays an integral role in the assemblage and projection of engendered and sexualized postmodern bodies. For instance, in an analysis of photographs of the Olympic Games, Duncan (1990) argued that women were represented as subordinate and sexually inviting, whereas men were represented as dominant. Similarly, Wright (1991) showed that although Olympic gymnastics may inscribe bodily meanings onto women that countenance highly circumscribed kinds of beauty and femininity, it also may present a sustained challenge to limiting and limited accounts of women's physical abilities. The competitive nature of international sports has of necessity extended the form and rigor of exercise beyond polite gender divisions. As a result, activities previously restricted to male gymnasts are incorporated into female routines, thereby equating strength with grace as a sign of competence in the public performance of femininity. All of this, however, occurs in an additionally contradictory manner, with juvenile female competitors being taught to flirt with an audience in the quest for judge and crowd appeal. Messner, Duncan, and Jensen's (1993) study of American basketball and tennis revealed that commentators marked women athletes and women's sports as "other" by infantilizing them and by ambivalently framing their achievements. In an analysis of the entry of Renee Richards, a constructed-female transsexual, into the women's professional tennis circuit, Birrell and Cole (1990) highlighted how journalists constructed and normalized gender/ sex and sexuality through narratives based on conventional binary oppositions. McKay and Huber (1992) demonstrated how specific "technologies/techniques of gender" anchor images of men's and women's bodies in ways that naturalize the technological and sporting superiority of men, and marginalize, contain, and incorporate visions of women. Similarly, Schulze (1990) argued that representations of women bodybuilders are implicated in a "recuperative strategy" that repositions women within permissible spaces.

As noted, the recent literature on bodies stresses their centrality as sites for articulating specific gender identities and practices. Connell (1990; see also Connell, 1995), for example, argued that male identity is both complex and polyvalent, with no singular set of qualities consistently marked as masculine. Masculinity and men's bodies (here symbolically conceived as unitary) are shown to be contested sites fraught with contradictions. In an in-depth interview with an Australian sporting professional who is seemingly the (literal) embodiment of hegemonic masculinity, Connell's respondent is asked about the meaning of being a man. He replies in negative terms: To be a man is to "not be a gay." This exclusion of male desire for other men from the definition of masculinity occurs in the context of all-male competition and single-gender affinity on and off the sporting field. Connell observed a profound contradiction in "the articulation of self and body" here: The body is invested with a narcissistic social currency as an object for professional improvement and success, but this narcissism is unstable and can never be satisfied. The commoditized body is in constant need of self-surveillance and renewal if it is to remain competitive and hence marketable to sponsors. In a similar vein, Miller (1990) showed how the media stitch together an awkward combination of apparently rebellious individualism with highly orchestrated managerial practice among men in Olympic swimming and coaching. Sporting bodies, then, are produced under sociopolitical conditions that simultaneously reinforce and subvert existing structures of power in a manner that militates against secure and consistent gender identities. In summary, sporting bodies can be viewed as a terrain on which power relations are activated, tested, and contested at a number of points in the social formation.

We have argued previously that sport has been one of the most significant means by which gender boundaries have been marked and their meanings extended to propose an ineluctable difference between men and women, especially where that difference entails an assumption of inherent male superiority. If male identity and superiority in sport have been problematized from the outside in recent times, there are also internal fissures within masculinity that have further undermined it. As suggested previously (and discussed subsequently), the idea of male sporting excellence coexisting with homosexuality has been difficult for many men (and also women) to accept, because command of sport has been one of the defining characteristics of heterosexual masculinity. The second area of unease concerns race, because if sex or gender unites white men and men of color, race and racism also socially divide them (Sabo & Jansen, 1998). The appeal to "natural superiority" that men make in regard to women is compromised in the history of white racist ideology because closeness to "nature" is also what makes black men "inferior" to their white counterparts. The capacity to transcend nature and the limitations of the bodily world that white racist masculinity champions is occluded in the corporeally dominated realm of sport (and also sex). It is here that black men not infrequently claim genetic superiority, and white men counter with assertions of mental and moral domination. Hence, the practice of "stacking" in sport (Anderson, 1993), whereby certain roles are distributed by assumed racial characteristics, is an attempt to reinstitute a sporting hierarchy on other than strictly corporeal grounds (Anderson, 1993; Brooks, Alhouse, & Tucker, 1996-1997; Davis, 1995).

One of the remarkable features of contemporary sports culture is the domination of the image of the black male sporting body, especially through its massively successful circulation in the promotion of sports goods produced by companies like Nike and Reebok (Boyd, 1997b; McKay, 1995). The iconic ascendancy of Michael Jordan (Andrews, 1996a, 1996b; Andrews, Carrington, Mazur, & Jackson, 1996), in particular, has produced the contradictory outcome that the black male body is simultaneously celebrated when associated with sport and feared and denounced when connected with violent crime. It has resulted in the projection of the potent image of the "black superstud sportsman" (Rowe, 1994) at a time when systemic racism stimulates "million man marches" and other expressions of the subordination of African American men. We probe these fault lines in sport in an attempt to understand how sports and masculinities are in transition and how changes in one sphere may have corresponding effects in the other. We proceed by examining a series of "panic instances" and provocations concerning the black male sports body, seeking to illuminate their exemplary cultural and ideological roles.

Big Bad Ben on Steroids

One of the biggest media sport scandals of the late 20th century occurred in 1988 when the Canadian sprinter Ben Johnson broke the world record in the 100 meters at the Seoul Olympics but was subsequently disqualified and banned for using anabolic steroids. In the massive controversy concerning the use of performance-enhancing drugs that followed, including a state-funded inquiry, such practices were found to be not only widespread but, in many cases, routine and officially tolerated (Jackson, 1998a, 1998b; Jackson, Andrews, & Cole, 1998; Simson & Jennings, 1992). Hence, the biomedical order of power in sport was revealed to be profoundly contradictory, resting on a notion of "clean bodies" that was being systematically undermined by institutionalized bodily "contamination." Kroker et al. (1989) described these events as the "Panic Olympics," an "age of sacrificial sports" where

> the Olympics, under the pressure of the mass media, re-enter the dark domain of mythology. No longer ... about athletic competition, but [as] *postmodern* sports now fascinating only because the athlete's body is a blank screen for playing out the darker passions of triumph and scapegoatism. (p. 172)

Of course, it was modernity that first enabled Johnson's disgrace to become a global phenomenon. The 19th century British model of competitive sport had, Goldlust (1987) stated, "swept all before it and emerged as a truly universal modern cultural form" (p. 53), constructing in the process a global means by which bodies could be interpreted and disciplined. Modernization, in the form of military, cultural, and media imperialism, disseminated competitive sport across the globe, and so created the conditions for the international emergence of the postmodern condition, with its attendant crisis of the body. This crisis is produced by the simultaneous commoditization of the body and its subjection to instrumental technique, surveillance, and invasion (Fitzclarence, 1990). Sport is particularly significant in symbolizing body panic because of its tendency to present elite

athletes as productive machines whose activities are intensively monitored by the media, even as they are supposed to embody "natural" capa-
bilities. Professional (and, increasingly, semiprofessional and amateur)
athletes are now routinely subjected to bodily invasive techniques of training, physical conditioning, and proscribed drug detection.

Johnson's subsequent life ban (imposed in 1993 after he again tested
positive for steroids) served to confirm the depth of a panic now unrelieved
even by the comforting narrative of detection, exposure, retribution,
remorse, and redemption. The Canadian media quickly attenuated his
"Canadian-ness" by placing his Jamaican origins in the foreground. As his
body plainly shrunk to presteroid proportions, much was made of his figu-
rative as well as literal diminution. The Ben Johnson story suggested two
lessons—that the elite sporting body is susceptible to manipulation, and
that such interventions may be performatively effective, if strictly unethical. This loss of innocence provoked a deeper anxiety about the threat to
corporeal integrity posed by high-performance sport, an ontological inse-
curity produced by the schizophrenic implosion of self and other. Yet,
such uncertainties also are seen to be licensed by the "caring professionals" dedicated to the maximization of corporeal efficiency, whose training
regimens are complicit with the systematic invasion of sporting bodies
(McKay, 1991). The "scandal" of performance-enhancing drug detection
is seen to lie not in the intrusion of the public gaze into the realm of the private and personal, which is a traditional concern of civil liberty, but rather
in the public revelation of the private and personal activities of celebrities
in a postmodern universe in which public/private and surface/depth distinctions have been, if not entirely dissolved, then certainly obscured.
Hence, the detection of recreational (i.e., non-sport-related) drug use has
been of greater widespread concern than the invasion of privacy occa-
sioned by the naming of players and their conduct.

So, the Ben Johnson affair is instructive in relation to the general biomedical struggle over the bodies of athletes. Yet, it also had its specific dimensions. Much of the focus of condemnations of the use of performance-
enhancing drugs in sport concerns its breaching of sex and gender
boundaries. Hence, Chinese female swimmers are pejoratively described
as "men" by some commentators, and much is also made of the feminizing
effects on men of steroid use. In the case of Johnson, Simson and Jennings
(1992, p. 195) noted the consternation among his entourage when it was
discovered "that after years of hormone drug doping he had developed an
enlarged left breast. He was turning into a woman!" Johnson can be seen,
therefore, to have engaged in two transgressions. The first is to be caught

taking drugs, thereby compromising his "natural" attributes (accentuated by his blackness) by using "artificial" and "synthetic" substances. The second is to problematize his masculinity (again, accentuated by his blackness) by ingesting female hormones. (Ironically, as Simson & Jennings pointed out, a "cover story" for Johnson in the case of detection was that he was using the drug probenecid—a well-known steroid "masking" agent—to enhance the effectiveness of penicillin in the treatment of gonorrhea; p. 169.) The sexual and racial anxiety provoked by Johnson, as a successful black man (Mercer, 1992) at the peak of his career, was to some degree discharged by his fall from grace. This phenomenon was also evident following the announcement of the HIV-positive status of the National Basketball Association (NBA) superstar Earvin "Magic" Johnson.

"Magic," HIV/AIDS, and (Hetero)sexual Athletics

When in November 1991 one of the most prominent sportsmen in the United States called a press conference (to preempt a move by the popular media) to announce that he was HIV-positive, the reaction in that country was of similar intensity to that which characterized the Ben Johnson affair 3 years earlier (King, 1993; Rowe, 1994). In this case, corporeal jeopardy did not stem from the calculated injection of drugs but from the unwitting transmission of a virus through sexual contact. The "globalizing panic" (O'Neill, 1990) resulting from HIV/AIDS is, according to Williamson (1988), an acute anxiety about the breakdown of social and bodily systems:

> What seems particularly threatening about AIDS is that it is linked to the breakdown of boundaries. The virus threatens to cross over that border between Other and Self: The threat it poses is not only one of disease but one of dissolution, the contamination of categories. (p. 5)

Attempts by the media to control the ensuing heterosexual panic have resulted in an "epidemic of signification" about HIV/AIDS (Treichler, 1987). The association between virus/syndrome and athletes is particularly problematic because sporting prowess is derived from symbolic and physical transcendence. In the case of Magic Johnson, the virus was apparently transmitted as a result of the heterosexual male "promiscuity" conventional in elite American sporting culture. For this reason, it was a crisis of gender as well as of race and sexuality. The "shock" of the announcement was quickly followed by speculation about the future of

Johnson's contracts to endorse corporate products and the possibilities of infection on the basketball court. The interpenetration of capital and the body thus produced simultaneous panics of capital accumulation, of viral contagion, and of gendered and racialized sexuality. In media narratives, Johnson's disclosure of his HIV-positive status was framed within preexisting channels of hegemonic masculinity, homophobia, and misogyny. For instance, a pervasive theme was Johnson's unselfish "accommodation" of the female groupies who allegedly preyed on him (Crimp, 1993; McKay, 1993). In a *Sports Illustrated* article cowritten with journalist Roy Johnson, Magic stated that he was certain he was infected by a woman who carried the virus but could not specify the time or place, because it was "a matter of numbers" given that "after I arrived in L.A., in 1979, I did my best to accommodate as many women as I could—most of them through unprotected sex" (p. 22). He then pleaded with other athletes and entertainers who also had been "out there" to get tested and to start practicing safe sex, the clear assumption being that "promiscuous" male celebrities are recipients rather than transmitters of the virus, the origin of which was traced to insatiable female desire:

> It doesn't matter how beautiful the woman might be or how tempting she might sound on the telephone. I know that we are pursued by women so much that it is easy to be weak. Maybe by getting the virus I'll make it easier for you guys to be strong. (Johnson & Johnson, 1991, p. 22)

The male athlete-as-victim of female predators (Gmelch & San Antonio, 1998) also emerged in coverage of other basketball players and sports. A syndicated report from the *New York Times* titled "Hockey Teams' Bad Dreams" opened with a statement to that effect:

> Across Canada yesterday, players, coaches and fans of professional ice hockey anxiously struggled to come to terms with the disclosure by two Montreal doctors that a young woman who died of AIDS two years ago contended she had sex with 30 to 70 National Hockey League Players. ("Hockey Teams' Bad Dreams," 1991, p. 7)

In the issue of *Sports Illustrated* in which Johnson made his disclosures, E. M. Swift (1991) described the "Dangerous Games" that male athletes played, including one NBA player "who estimates that he has slept with 2,500 different women, and counting" (pp. 40-43). An article by John Elson (1991) in *Time* titled "The Dangerous World of Wannabes" stated,

"Magic Johnson's plight brings fear into the locker rooms across the U.S. and spotlights the riskiest athletic perk: promiscuous sex," a hazard graphically if improbably illustrated by "Hall of Famer [the late] Wilt Chamberlain [who] boasts of having slept with 20,000 women—an average of 1.4 a day for 40 years" (Elson, 1991, pp. 59-60). Although two NBA players were quoted as saying that players had to take responsibility for their sexual behavior, a considerable portion of the text and graphics concentrated on the "Annies," "buckle bunnies," and "wannabes" who "beguiled" baseball players, rodeo riders, and other male athletes.

The crisis of the sexualized body here is presented as that of the male besieged by "fatal attractors." This is not a wholly novel phenomenon—images of women as "gold diggers" and "*femmes fatales*" are familiar ones, and Treichler (1988) cited the work of historian Allan A. Brandt in demonstrating that "venereal diseases have typically been assigned a female identity" (p. 220). The idea of a global, invasive virus carried by sexually aggressive women and infecting reluctant, passive men gives, however, a new twist to traditional sexual stigmatization. In Magic Johnson's case, it also functioned to override conventional white male fantasy-fears about black male sexual potency by writing sexual difference over racial difference. This racial indifference was long a part of Johnson's blinding mystique as an ideal male citizen. As he put it in describing his rivalry with Larry Bird, who is white: "It's hard to look at a white man and see black, but when I looked at Larry, that's what I saw" (Ryan, 1992, p. 46). Magic Johnson was routinely described as open and friendly with the press and possessed of "the embodiment of Showtime with his million-dollar smile" (Ryan, 1992, p. 49). He also epitomized the kind of fastidious, economic patriarchal obeisance that middle American culture celebrates: "After God and my father, I respect Larry Bird more than anyone" (Ryan, 1992, p. 55).

Male sports reporters demonstrated little professional skepticism about the assumptions that Magic Johnson's infection had come from packs of sexually marauding women. There was virtually no concern for the women who had been in sexual contact with Johnson (apart from his wife, Cookie, with whom he had a socially sanctioned liaison) and other "promiscuous" sportsmen, and so may have been placed at risk by them. By drawing on semantic discourses that celebrate heterosexual men and denigrate women (Schultz, 1975; Spender 1980; Stanley, 1977; Thorne & Henley, 1985), male journalists articulated the body panic surrounding HIV/AIDS and sport in ways that framed heterosexual women as the virulent agents and heterosexual men as the "innocent" victims. These accounts are readily accepted because they are embedded in a gender order that privileges heterosexual male "promiscuity" and devalues, pathologizes, or criminalizes other forms of sexuality (Dworkin & Wachs, Chapter 4, this volume). Thus, the compassion and admiration initially articulated by journalists were not simply because Magic was a venerated athlete who became one of the "chance" victims of HIV infection, but also because he was a (hetero)sexual athlete. The possibility that Magic—or any other male athlete—could have had sex with other men was simply unthinkable.[1]

This favorable media treatment of Magic Johnson (which would have been unlikely if he had "confessed" to homosexual transmission or if he had presented a "queer" public persona like that of Dennis Rodman) enabled him later to come out of retirement to play on the "Dream Team" that won the gold medal at the 1992 summer Olympics and then to return to the NBA. Johnson's decision to play in the Olympics precipitated further unease when some Australian athletes indicated that they were afraid of being infected by him and might not compete against the United States if Johnson played. The resultant U.S. nationalist outburst put the body panic temporarily into reverse. Some American players and journalists responded with outrage and warned that they would hand Australia a severe defeat if the two teams met at the Games. Hundreds of protesting phone calls and some bomb threats allegedly were made to Australia's diplomatic missions in the United States. Australia's Minister for Foreign Affairs publicly rebuked the Australian team's medical director, who had recommended that players should not compete against Magic and called for boycotts against any games in which he participated (Hole, 1992, pp. 1-2). This "reprieve" may be seen as a triumph of national chauvinism and international trade *Realpolitik* rather than of sexual health enlightenment. In November 1992, Johnson again retired after some club opponents (including Olympic teammate Karl Malone) expressed concern about being infected when he bled slightly after vigorous body contact during a preseason NBA game. Even Johnson, one of the most revered idols in the American sporting pantheon, could not overcome the AIDS panic and remain a professional basketball player, instead devoting himself to education campaigns for safe sex (including a book *Safer Sex: What You Can Do to Avoid AIDS*) and higher levels of research funding. For this activity, a *New York Times* journalist described Johnson as "our greatest celebrity leper" (Araton, 1992, p. 30). In the ensuing period, Magic Johnson has returned as a player and retired again, then coached and even toured with his all-star team, in one instance being refused entry into a country on account of his "medical condition."

Media narratives of the HIV/AIDS body panic in sport, in this instance, were anchored by archetypes of male "superstuds" and female "supergroupies." So rhetorically effective was this framing device that no attention was paid to the sexual norms and practices of elite sportswomen and their interaction with "fans." Sportsmen engaging in successions of one-night stands were depicted as being put at risk and undermined, because they "accommodated" licentious women. The only crime of the "victims," as Treichler put it in related context, was to behave like "real men" (Treichler, 1991, p. 191). In a classic scenario of "sin-and-redemption," women were framed as the cause of the HIV/AIDS problem and men were absolved of due responsibility for their actions (Messner & Solomon, 1993). In the case of Magic Johnson, it seems, the particular version of black maleness he represented deflected a racialized discourse of power toward that of gender. "Symbolic" violence was perpetrated against the sportsman through consensual sex with a stigmatized Other—the "promiscuous" woman (also often presented in media accounts as predominantly black or Hispanic). The Magic affair, therefore, can be distinguished from and yet parallels another sport scandal involving the sports star first as rapist and then as "cannibal."

The Fall and Fall of "Iron Mike"

In 1992, Florida police investigated a woman's charge that three New York Mets players raped her, and later in the year former heavyweight champion Mike Tyson was convicted of rape. Reporter John Durie commented on these incidents, as well as on Magic Johnson, Wilt Chamberlain, the rape trial of William Kennedy Smith (the only white male discussed), and the U.S. Senate committee hearings on charges of sexual harassment against Clarence Thomas:

> Baseball players . . . are notorious for accepting the advances of the groupies who mob them in team hotels after the game. This baseball season starts this month and, with spring training in Florida, this is the first chance for the groupies to make friends with a baseballer. It is not the last chance because the six-month season often splits players from their families. Players felt they were

being victimized because they were rich, said Mr. Jesse Barfield, a Yankees outfielder. He noted that, "after this Tyson thing we have to be careful, we are easy targets." (Durie, 1992, p. 10)

After Tyson was sentenced, male reporters and lawyers began raising concerns about the fairness of the trial and Harvard law professor Alan Dershowitz launched an appeal, which invoked themes in the media that were strikingly similar to the Magic Johnson case. Russell Miller (1992), for example, described Dershowitz (the successful defense lawyer depicted in the Hollywood film *Reversal of Fortune* and later a member of O. J. Simpson's "dream team" of defense lawyers) as "a fearless champion of civil liberties" who has earned the enmity of "radical feminists" (p. 3) for claiming that rape should be categorized into degrees of criminality. Miller went on to question the credibility both of the plaintiff, Desiree Washington, and of the jury, alleging that Tyson could not have received a fair trial because "events had conspired significantly against him" in the wake of the publicity surrounding William Kennedy Smith and Clarence Thomas. Finally, Miller queried the motive for the victim's legal action: "Was it because she had been raped, or was it because she had been treated like a cheap groupie?" He quoted Dershowitz's contention that Washington took legal action not because she was raped, but because she was affronted by Tyson's suggestion that she either walk or take a limousine home after consenting to sexual intercourse:

> This woman came on as a groupie. Everybody knows what the rules are for groupies who hang around famous athletes and rock stars. They get 15 or 20 minutes of not very good sex, no kiss goodnight, no telephone number, no appreciation. All they get are bragging rights—"I slept with the champ." (Miller, 1992, p. 3)

In this way, it is Washington, not Tyson, who is positioned as guilty and aggressive. Miller noted that Dershowitz and one of Tyson's associates consider him to be "sweet, soft-spoken and intelligent . . . a very bright guy" (p. 3). Like Johnson, Tyson is portrayed as a victim of female rapacity:

> [Tyson] . . . is not finding it easy in jail. He is terrified of being set up, having drugs planted on him or getting into a fight by someone wanting to make a name for himself. . . . "He is a man in a lot of pain," says Dershowitz. . . . "He doesn't

understand why she did this to him. He understands that she might have been upset, but that's no excuse for destroying a man's life and career." (p. 3)

In this way, the body of Tyson is repositioned to acquire characteristics of "feminine" vulnerability from the now implicitly "masculinized" bodies of women who take the sexual initiative, so reversing the direction of "normal" corporeal power. The functional connection between the basketball groupie who infected Magic Johnson and the boxing groupie who undid "Iron Mike" is made clear in such statements. Causality and culpability are carefully attributed within a gendered discourse that represents the valorized body of the elite male athlete (and, by extension, the male body per se) as devalued through hazardous exchange with the debased bodily currency of the sexually compromised female. This case, like the Clarence Thomas confirmation hearings, is further overdetermined by the competing affinities of gender and race (Kimmel, 1995a). The defense of Tyson, like that of Magic Johnson, was conducted by drawing on the image of racialized and sexualized sports black masculinity and transmuting its symbolic invincibility into vulnerability by invoking another discourse of power—"active" female sexuality. In this way, the body of the black male elite athlete is protected from racist discourses that seek to reduce it to no more than blind sexual urges—only by projecting such identity onto the bodies of women. It can be seen, however, that such strategies are not always successful. Mike Tyson did go to jail, but in less than half a decade he was back in the ring, having converted to Islam (but in other ways apparently unchanged). In June 1997, during a fight with Evander Holyfield, he bit off a portion of the lower ear lobe of his opponent, incurring widespread condemnation for such "savagery." This assault sealed Tyson's fate as incapable of control both in and outside the ring, thereby leaving him open to traditional white racist distrust of black male bodies.

As in the later O. J. Simpson trial discussed subsequently, there are troubling and competing explanations according to the invocation of either gendered or racial discourses. Tyson is reported to have said, "I like to hurt women when I make love to them. I like to hear them scream and see them bleed. It gives me pleasure" (from Callahan, quoted in Sloop, 1997, p. 112). His defense, in seeking to rebut an intentional rape charge, made much of the great difficulty he had in relating to women in a "normal" way. Yet, as Sloop argues (see also Jefferson, 1997, 1998; Lule, 1995), the routine portrayal of Tyson as a "man-beast-machine" and a corresponding distantiation of Desiree Washington from negative images of black women produced a highly racialized prima facie supposition of Tyson's guilt:

> Playing into the myths of the black male and the black athlete, it becomes only logical that Tyson is guilty. Again, the crime is seen as all the more unforgivable once we consider the repositioning of Desiree Washington as something other than the stereotypical black. Washington, given the subject position of the college student and Sunday school teacher, is able to effectively shed the myths of the stereotype of the promiscuous African American female and is enabled to become the sexually naive and innocent debutante, whitened to such a degree that Tyson's inevitable rape is both more predictable and all the more unforgiving. (Sloop, 1997, p. 112)

The difficulty of disentangling assumptions of guilt or innocence of an appalling sexual crime from preexisting racist and sexist discourses—not to mention the knowing exploitation of those discourses by both prosecution and defense—reveals the extent to which ideologies of power are ever-present in the practice of everyday life and in the conduct of cultural politics (Barak, 1996; Chancer, 1998; Morrison & Brodsky Lacour, 1997).

The Ben Johnson, Magic Johnson, and Mike Tyson "affairs" all invoke myths of the black male's inherent physical advantage, translated into white conceptions (and fears) of sporting and sexual prowess (Cashmore, 1990; Dyson, 1993; Wallace, 1991). The image of the black male sporting body, like that of the black male pop star, is a heavily sexualized one. There is no absolute correspondence here between mythos and interpretation, of course. For example, in the case of black tennis player Arthur Ashe, who died in 1993, primary reference was to his medical acquisition of HIV/AIDS. Nonetheless, the generally idealized sexual capacity of the black male does readily serve to reinforce the symbolic potency of these narratives of sexual manners and body panics, whereby even the most heroically formidable embodiments of heterosexual masculinity are overcome by a sexualized, feminized disorder. In a manner similar to British boxer Frank Bruno (Carrington, 2000), Ashe represented "the acceptable face of Black masculinity."

The mythicized downfall of the "black superstud" (Wallace, 1991) also can be placed in the service of a full-blown, multifaceted body panic. Wells (1991), for instance, in a facetious attack on the control and mooted banning of tobacco sponsorship of sport, invents a letter from a David D. (presumably standing for white racist would-be politician David Duke) of

Louisiana to an Australian named Fred. The article, couched in the language of bigotry, represents athletes' bodies as subject to fascist control:

> See the links? Smoking-sport-in-the-dark-races-sex-AIDS-fags? I tell you, when I read that book of Roland Fishman's you sent me, and then heard about Magic Johnson, I wished I was back with the Klan.
>
> So the Australian cricketers went off to the West Indies and Fishman tells us that there was so much skirt chasing going on that it was no wonder that your boys couldn't perform during the day.[2]
>
> And are we supposed to believe that it was only the white ladies your boys were fooling around with?
>
> Then Magic Johnson announces that he has AIDS. And that he got it from a woman. And he sure hasn't been ignoring those black mommas all these years.
>
> If Magic Johnson has AIDS then who knows what is going on in cricket? Or the Olympics, where the athletes of all colours don't seem to be able to keep their hands off each other. Ban sport Fred! (p. 70)

Wells's rhetoric is a perfect expression (following Kroker et al., 1989) of panic sport—the control of tobacco promotion masking an agenda to ban sport and to suppress polymorphous pleasure. It is, however, not an instance of playful postmodernist irony but a right-wing, populist exploitation of the connotative linkages between sport and diverse physical practices. In this instance, the sexuality of Magic Johnson (and, in a more diffuse way, of the Australian men's cricket team) is used to symbolize corporeal freedom. In this way, it can be seen that the image of racialized sports sexuality can be placed in the service of many discourses, but that they are rarely progressive, and, if appearing so, absolve the implied "guilt" of one subordinate group by transferring it to another.

Conclusion

We have argued in this chapter that the combination of sport, race, and masculinity has great popular ideological and discursive power. Our three "case" studies each highlighted different deployments and outcomes, and it is clear that the figure of the black sporting male retains its positive and negative valences. Contested images of black sportsmen continue to emerge and occupy vast tracts of politico-cultural space. On the negative side, the O. J. Simpson trial, for example, afforded an extended opportunity for the interrogation of the black male sports body on and off the field of play (Barak, 1996; Chancer, 1998; McKay & Smith, 1995; Morrison &

Brodsky Lacour, 1997; Rowe, 1997). More positively, the ubiquitous image of Michael Jordan continues to posit highly attractive signs of black masculinity in the entertainment media against its extremely negative meanings in the news media. Somewhere in between is the transgressive, ambiguous body of the black sportsman, best symbolized currently by Dennis Rodman. In both of his books to date, *Bad As I Wanna Be* (1996, with Tim Keown) and *Walk on the Wild Side* (1997, with Michael Silver), Rodman's body is to the fore inside and outside the covers. On the front of *Bad As I Wanna Be,* for example, he is naked astride a motorcycle, gazing directly back at the gazer as the reader's eyes are drawn to his multicolored hair and tattoos, and inside there are images of his cross-dressing. The text makes provocative statements (suitably bolded, often in upper case or different typefaces): **"Fifty percent of life in the NBA is SEX. The other fifty percent is MONEY."** (p. 179); **"MENTALLY, I probably am bisexual."** (p. 216); and **"IF MAGIC HAD A GAY RELATIONSHIP, THAT'S HIS BUSINESS"** (p. 198). On the cover of *Walk on the Wild Side,* he is painted in "animal" mode, with the back cover "blurb" reading, "I have this fantasy that I can live my life like a tiger in the jungle—eating whatever I want, having sex whenever I want, and roaming around butt naked, wild and free." Rodman, it can be seen, is consciously playing on and with discourses of black male sports sexuality, simultaneously exploiting and subverting prevailing readings of the heterosexual "super" body. He also appeared as a front-cover feature in *The Advocate,* a gay and lesbian magazine, in which he detailed his sexual interests and enunciated his libertarian position. Rodman's history as one of the "hard men" of the NBA, via his relationship with the championship Detroit Pistons teams, which engaged in an aggressive style of play, and his legendary rebounding exploits, sit disconcertingly with his love of feather boas. He truly destabilizes the mainstream media discourse that sport is inherently masculine, by showing that there is no necessary correspondence between maleness, physique, and conduct.

From Benton's (1991) "cautious welcome" to the reconceptualization of the relation between modern biology and social science, to Featherstone et al.'s (1991) postmodern reinstatement of bodies in social process, to Falk's (1994) reexamination of corporeality and consumption, it is apparent that bodies are again an integral concept in theoretical analysis. As Loy, Andrews, and Rinehart (1993) noted, "The sporting body is a key site for studying the dynamic relationship between power, knowledge, and corporeal existence" (p. 75). The sporting body, in its postmodern multiplicity of formations, operates, we have argued, as an effective vehicle for the enunciation of the recurrent body panics evident in contemporary life. The welter of discursive practices of "body policing" in sport constitute these bodies as a terrain of struggle, resistance, and subjection. In this chapter, we have attempted to show how the relationships of sporting bodies to gendered, sexualized, racialized, and biomedical orders of power are relayed by the mass general and sports media. Any acquaintance with such politics of the body cannot ignore the crucial role of sport in relaying and problematizing the meanings of gender, sexuality, and race. Social and cultural analysts need to be sufficiently well versed in these popular manifestations of body politics to turn their knowledge of specialized theory and research into effective interventions in the discourses of everyday life. The racialized masculine sports body, now as pervasive in the world of promotional culture (Wernick, 1991) as it is lodged in the collective unconscious, presents a consummately complex and ambivalent phenomenon for those seeking to understand contemporary masculinities.

Notes

1. This attitude is reminiscent of the reaction of a man interviewed by *USA Today* about Rock Hudson's death: "I thought AIDS was a gay disease, but if Rock Hudson can get it, anyone can" (cited in Treichler, 1988, p. 205).

2. The reference is to a journalistic exposé that Fishman (1991) wrote about the off-field sexual behavior of some members of the Australian men's cricket team during a tour of the West Indies.

15

Dennis Rodman—
Do You Feel Feminine Yet?

Black Masculinity, Gender Transgression, and
Reproductive Rebellion on MTV

MICHELLE D. DUNBAR

On August 21, 1996, Dennis Rodman, an African American basketball player with the National Basketball Association (NBA), created a media event that shut down the daily fast-paced movement of New York City for a few hours when he showed up to his book signing in a horse-drawn carriage, wearing a white wedding gown and escorted by female "usherettes" dressed in tuxedos. Music Television (MTV) captured the event and the behind-the-scenes creation of "the nervous bride" for its then-upcoming program titled the *Rodman World Tour.* When MTV aired the episode months after the event, Dennis Rodman proclaimed as an introduction to the show, "When I'm not stroking myself, I'm stroking the media." In the text of the show, the audience is privy to the entire makeup process, fitting session, and the thoughts that were going through Rodman's head as he prepared for his "wedding day." Throughout the step-by-step preparation of the bride, a female member of Rodman's production staff repeatedly prompted Rodman to share his feelings: "Does it make you feel feminine? . . . How do you feel now (after putting the dress on)? . . . Do you feel feminine? . . . You've got your makeup on, you got that dress on. . . . When are you going to feel feminine?"

The questions fired at Rodman during this episode get to the heart of changing gender relations in American society. Contemporary media culture plays an enormous role in this process because of the mass audience that it serves. Therefore, the images and messages sent through popular entertainers such as Dennis Rodman serve an important function in how gender (and race) gets constructed and how the current gender and racial orders get reproduced. As witnessed previously, Rodman regularly pushes the boundaries of gender and sexual conventions, obtaining mass media attention in the process. What effect does Rodman's mediated gender and sexual play have on representations of gender and race in society? Do his media displays represent a potential challenge to prevailing notions of race and gender? In short, is Rodman's image disruptive of the current race/gender system?

To explore these questions, I employed ethnographic content analysis (Altheide, 1996) to look at conventions of gender construction used by MTV's *Rodman World Tour*. Episodes were videotaped from the first season the show aired, running from December 1996 to April 1997. All efforts were made to obtain every episode, in the end missing no more than three (12 out of 15 episodes). To obtain a random sample of shows for qualitative analysis, each of the episodes was catalogued by topic, after which each topic was written on a piece of paper, and 7 were randomly chosen from the possible 12 for inclusion in the data. I decided on 7 episodes because it represents approximately half of the total shows that were aired (15), even though I was only able to tape-record 12 episodes.

Once the sample was chosen, I watched each of the shows and began coding procedures. Because of the new terrain mapped out by the complexity and ambiguity of the images included in the *Rodman World Tour,* I did not develop preexisting categories for analysis. Rather, I approached the text with broad topics in mind and sought to determine how the show handled such topics. These topics included masculinity, sport, cross-dressing, and sexuality and were informed by my knowledge of Rodman's media image prior to the show, my familiarity with the *Rodman World Tour* (which I often watched while video-recording the episodes), and my preliminary review of the pertinent literature. With these broad topics in mind, I allowed the particular categories to emerge from the data. In this process, the following categories became codes that I subsequently used for analysis: athlete, aggression, natural self, badness, body, penis, objectification of women, heterosexuality, homosexuality/homoeroticism, cross-dressing, and "femininity."

Masculinity and the Black Male Athlete

With the increasing role that mediated sports play as mass entertainment, athletes become ever more important actors in the construction/

reproduction of masculinity. The extent to which sports figures such as Dennis Rodman embody and represent black masculinity determines the role they play in the ongoing construction of both gender and race in contemporary society. This study seeks to determine the role that the particular embodiment of black masculinity within the mediated representation of Dennis Rodman plays in this process of gender and race construction. As such, it necessitates a theoretical framework that addresses the popularly disseminated image of black masculinity, its relation to structural and political factors, as well as the agency with which popular media figures such as Rodman take part in enacting and deploying that image.

Sports offer a cultural site where social notions of masculinity are enacted and reproduced. Connell (1987) distinguished between hegemonic masculinity and subordinated masculinities, arguing that hegemonic masculinity is constructed in relation to women and subordinated masculinities (p.186). Sport scholars have illustrated the ways in which sports take part in the construction of hegemonic masculinity, focusing on the exclusion and debasement of women as well as the homophobia that permeates the cultural site (Messner, 1992b; Messner & Sabo, 1994). Throughout history, African American male athletes, in particular, have played an important role in the construction of hegemonic masculinity. Whereas pioneer black athletes challenged racial and class barriers among men by breaking through segregated professional sports, today's black athletes increasingly stabilize hegemonic masculinity as mediated figures in televised spectator sports (Messner, 1992b). According to Messner, black athletes offer middle-class white male spectators a symbolic identification with a shared concept of their "naturalized" superiority over women while at the same time serving as the racialized "'other' against whom privileged men define themselves as 'modern'" (p. 170). This dual role is particularly poignant within basketball, where black male athletes are at once dominant as players and yet socially subordinate as black men.

John Hoberman (1997) goes so far as to argue that it is the prominence of African Americans in sports that has kept them socially subordinate in other realms of society. Arguing that a large part of the African American community accepts the notion that black success in the arena of sports represents a significant overall success for blacks in a racist society, Hoberman asserted that the community (especially black intellectuals) are in complicity with their own "relegation" to the arena of sports (p. 4). Rather than challenging the racism that continues to inhibit African American economic success in business, academia, and industry, the black community, by embracing sports as a viable career choice, accepts racist beliefs about the physical superiority and intellectual inferiority of African Americans (p. 53). Although black athletes often seek "status, respect, empowerment and upward mobility through athletic careers" in response to racial and class constraints, their choice to do so within the venue of sports reproduces the very racist notions they are fighting against (Dworkin & Messner, 1999, pp. 4-5). The tension between black men's subordinate status in relation to white men and their wide acceptance of notions that define hegemonic masculinity, especially through the institution of sport, is an important part of the emerging scholarship on black masculinity even beyond the venue of sports.

Scholarship on black masculinity recently has become a contested terrain, as black feminist scholars challenge traditionally sexist notions embedded within black masculinity discourse. Early in the literature, Robert Staples (1982) identified elements of what he called compulsive masculinity that characterize lower-class black males: crime, violence, sexual promiscuity, and procreation. According to Staples, these characteristics evolved out of the economic and racial subordination of black males that has excluded them from so-called legitimate means to attain and prove their manhood (as deemed by the hegemonic definition of masculinity). Staples's model of compulsive masculinity is challenged by black feminist scholar bell hooks (1992), who criticized Staples for ignoring the widely diverse experiences of masculinity among African American males (p. 98). hooks offered a feminist critique of Staples's assumption that African American men uniformly accept the sexist goals of hegemonic masculinity and merely find various means to attain those goals.

Breaking Staples's theory of compulsive masculinity into its two (sexist) components of patriarchal and phallocentric masculinities, hooks explained that the phallocentric model emerged as a form of masculinity to which all men, regardless of race, had access by virtue of their penis, regardless of their ability to provide for their family as required by the patriarchal model (p. 94). Although arguing that not all black men have accepted and internalized white society's hegemonic notion of patriarchal masculinity, hooks importantly recognized the extent to which patriarchal, and increasingly phallocentric, masculinity is displayed within black popular culture. She explained the ease with which such views make their way into the popular media that relies so much on cultural hegemony:

> Without documentation of [the] presence [of "individual black men who critiqued normative masculinity"], it has been easier for black men who embrace

patriarchal masculinity, phallocentrism, and sexism to act as though they speak for all black men. Because their representations of black masculinity are in complete agreement with white culture's assessment, they do not threaten or challenge white domination, they reinscribe it. (hooks, 1992, p. 98)

hooks indicted public figures in the entertainment industry such as "Eddie Murphy, . . . Spike Lee, and a host of other black males [who] blindly exploit the commodification of blackness and the concomitant exotification of phallocentric black masculinity" (p. 102). For hooks and other cultural theorists, prevailing ideas about black masculinity largely come from the images and messages disseminated through the mass media, no matter the diverse experiences that may exist among individual African American men.

Todd Boyd's (1997a, 1997b) cultural approach to the study of black masculinity articulated more fully the consumerist nature behind black popular culture, focusing on the elements that present a unique black male image to a mass audience. According to Boyd (1997a), black popular culture represents an "excessive image" of African Americans in an attempt to sell products to an increasingly consumerist society (p. 5). African Americans are particularly susceptible to buying and selling these images because they have been excluded from traditional methods of economic consumption for so long. The increasing role that spectacle plays in the "ever-expanding visual space" (p. 5) of mass media accounts, in part, for the excessive image of the black male, illustrated most clearly by the emphasis on style that characterizes black popular culture.

The importance of style in the embodiment of black masculinity has been pointed out by a number of scholars (Boyd, 1997a; Majors, 1992; Majors & Billson, 1992). Owing to the tenuous experience of "winning" among African American males in a white male-dominated world in which the rules of the game can change at any moment, many black males have opted to focus on style as an element over which they have control (Boyd, 1997a, pp. 109-110). Richard Majors (1992) found that what he calls "cool pose" is a "signature of survival" among African American men who mistrust the dominant society (p. 132). Majors explained that acting "cool" portrays images of control, toughness, and detachment that are often elusive to black males in American society. Boyd paid similar attention to style in his analysis of basketball as the embodiment of contemporary blackness (1997a, 1997b). He compared basketball with jazz of the 1940s to the 1960s, focusing on the improvisational nature of contemporary basketball that has its roots in black oral culture (1997a, p. 111).

Bringing elements of street basketball to the professional courts, African Americans have transformed the traditional "textbook" NBA style of play into a fast-paced, highly stylized game (1997a, p. 115).

This sense of style, combined with elements of phallocentric masculinity as pointed out by hooks (1992), creates a unique form of black masculinity that integrates elements of hegemonic (sexist) masculinity into the subordinated status of black masculinity as it is articulated and represented in culturally mediated forms, such as sports, music, and entertainment. Images of homophobia, the objectification and degradation of women, the emphasis on the phallus, and the articulation and embodiment of violence and aggression characterize much of the popular forms of black entertainment in contemporary society, including spectator sports in their mediated and commodified forms. Although this is the prevailing notion of black masculinity that permeates American media culture, hooks (1992) contended that much more diverse experiences of masculinity exist. Is Rodman's experience with masculinity as portrayed in his media image an example of one such different experience? Does his embodiment of masculinity offer us a new model of masculinity, one that critiques normative ideas of masculinity in general and/or black masculinity in particular?

The "Real" Dennis Rodman and Commodified Rebellion

The commodification of athlete/entertainer Dennis Rodman centers on his public representation of always "being himself" rather than constructing an image that society (and particularly the NBA) might expect from him. Like the current street slang popular among black youth, Dennis Rodman embraces the phrase "keepin' it real," promoting the idea that he stays "true" to himself and does not let "the system" keep him down. Having adopted this image, Rodman "talks the talk" and "walks the walk" in his autobiography, on the basketball court, during public appearances and interviews, as well as on his new MTV show, the *Rodman World Tour.* Rodman's public performance "as himself" (and perhaps his willingness to play the role of black man as ridiculous court jester) has made him a hot commodity deemed worthy of commercials for Carl's Junior restaurants, Kodak cameras, Victoria's Secret lingerie, and Converse All Star sneakers.

Before acquiring such recent commercial endorsements, Dennis Rodman was already a mediated personality by virtue of his sports star status. Ever since he began the various actions that defined him as "unusual" on the basketball court (dyeing his hair, piercing his body, getting tattoos), he clearly articulated these actions as "being his real self." This is the central theme of his autobiography *Bad As I Wanna Be* (1996), in which he began the book with the story of how he was about to commit suicide because he could no longer be the person that was expected of a professional basketball player:

> **I couldn't continue to be the person everyone wanted me to be.** I couldn't be what society wanted an athlete to be. I couldn't be the good soldier and the happy teammate and the good man off the court. . . . **I was two people: ONE PERSON ON THE INSIDE, another person on the outside.** The person I wanted to kill was the person on the outside. The guy on the inside was fine, he just wasn't getting out much. . . . I came up with an idea: . . . *Why not just kill the guy on the outside and let the other one keep living?* (pp. 4-8)

Since that time, Rodman has become known for his public displays of cross-dressing that accompany his wild hair colors and growing body art in the form of tattoos and piercings.

Although Rodman actively takes part in the construction of his own visual image, the nature of his agency must be explored. Because his image rests so centrally on his idea of "being himself" by rebelling against "the system" and prevailing expectations about gender norms, we must analyze critically the role that his location within a corporate context plays. If Rodman claims to be resisting dominant norms that are largely defined within consumer media culture, is his agency truly resistant if he gets paid for his so-called rebellion? The monetary rewards that Rodman receives for his transgressions shed light on the possibility that Rodman is appropriating resistance discourse that does not necessarily resist oppressive structures of society, such as race and gender relations.

Because Rodman is situated quite squarely within this consumerist context, Dworkin and Messner's (1999) theoretical model is used to analyze Rodman's agency and its potential for resistance. Dworkin and Messner distinguished between *resistant agency,* which allows for empowerment to change oppressive institutions, and *reproductive agency* "expressed as identification with corporate consumerism" (p. 11), which contributes to and stabilizes oppressive social institutions. Rather than effect real social change, reproductive agency merely offers consumers an image of resistance and/or rebellion with which they may identify but that is appropriated from any real revolutionary potential to sell a product. Different from collective action, individual acts of transgression that leave institutional structures of power intact are reproductive because they stabilize, rather than disrupt, the status quo. Therefore, although there may be potential for meaningful resistance in media images and messages, the consumer context must be evaluated for its limiting effect on that resistance.

Focusing on the potential for resistance, queer theories suggest that the scrambling of codes of masculinity and femininity such as that deployed by Rodman has the potential to offer a challenge to mainstream notions of gender and sexuality (Hawkes, 1995, p. 269). Gail Hawkes (1995) wrote of the importance of disrupting "the one-way causal processes between gender, sexuality and appearance" (p. 266) in an effort to challenge and resist the fixed notions of society through dress as performance. Hawkes implied that by challenging the binary models of gender and sexuality, there is a potential for radical resistance. However, Hawkes failed to place such blurring of the binaries within the contemporary context of commodified popular culture, in which figures such as pop diva Madonna have made the blurring of gender and sexual boundaries fashionable and "vogue" (Bordo, 1993; hooks, 1992; Rubey, 1991). Rodman's own style of cross-dressing may blur the boundaries of gender, but it also leaves room for Rodman to deploy feminine codes of dress without being labeled effeminate.

Contrary to female impersonators such as entertainer RuPaul, Rodman does not cross-dress into clearly feminine attire. Rather, he incorporates elements of women's clothing styles into his own fashion, creating a pastiche of ambiguous gender codes. His inclusion of facial makeup in these instances is what signifies his most apparent transgression from masculine codes of dress. Often, he wears feminine shirts along with jeans or other pants. For example, in one episode in which Rodman attended an L.A. club, he wore white pants with a gold, fuchsia, and purple satin shirt, a black puffy hat, and makeup with hues of fuchsia to complement his shirt. In a scene with actress Tracey Ullman, we saw Rodman wearing a silver sequin top with everyday blue jeans, his hair blonde with blue-green circles and wearing frosty gold lipstick. When Rodman appeared on David Letterman's show, he wore black lace pants and a matching shirt, opened to his waist, and black sunglasses. Although the pants and open shirt are general codes of masculinity, their lace fabric includes a touch of female-coded style. While appearing on *The Tonight Show* with Jay Leno, Rodman entered the stage while music with the words "I'm every woman" played over the studio. He wore what first appeared to be a generally masculine outfit, a long black leather coat over black leather pants, a black sheer top tied at the waist, black combat boots, and a cowboy hat. On closer appearance we, along with Leno, realized he actually was wearing a long skirt when he sat down and his legs became visible through the skirt's slit. Leno asked him if it was a skirt, apparently not noticing at first either.

Rather than offer a radical resistance through gender bending (Hawkes, 1995), Rodman's particular style of dress as performance seems to follow the pattern of masculine uses of cross-dressing. Research has found that men often use cross-dressing as a testimony to their social dominance through the parody of symbols of feminine sexuality (Foley, 1990; Garber, 1992). For example, one study found that male football team members play the role of cheerleaders in burlesque fashion while females attempt a serious game of football during a South Texas high school's annual ritual powder-puff game (Foley, 1990, p. 119). In this way, a man's physical and social dominance gives him the power to play with female codes of sexuality; he is "so much a man" that he is even a man while wearing women's clothing. Rodman's particular appropriation of feminine dress in limited ways suggests that Rodman may be invoking such a meaning rather than employing resistant agency against rigid gender rules.

MTV's Rodman World Tour

Rodman's position both in the NBA and in his newer venue of MTV places him in the center of consumer culture. The increasing commercialization of the NBA has been documented by scholars (Cole & Denny, 1994; McDonald, 1996) and experienced by all who watch television, whether or not they are spectators of the sport itself. MTV, in its own right, has been deemed the quintessential embodiment of consumerism for consumerism's sake—creating music videos that consume our attention until we can go out and buy the music that they have sold to us through television, as Kaplan (1987) explained:

> TV's strategy is to keep us endlessly consuming in the hopes of fulfilling our desire. MTV's programming strategies embody the extremes of what is inherent in the televisual apparatus. The channel hypnotizes more than others because it consists of a series of extremely short . . . texts that maintain us in an excited state of expectation. (p. 4)

Rodman's show follows the same strategies as MTV's signature videos, incorporating a free-flowing text in a nonlinear, fast-paced format that bombards the audience with complex imagery and sound. Using a sound-track of contemporary music, the show juxtaposes visual clips from various news sources and other television programs on which Rodman has appeared with footage shot specifically for the MTV show. Organizing the clips without regard to chronology, the show resembles the pastiche style of MTV's music videos.

MTV's *Rodman World Tour* capitalizes on Rodman's preexisting reputation with the NBA in an attempt to provide the audience with a peek into the superstar's "real" life. In the *Rodman World Tour,* MTV allows the audience to "hang out" with sports star Dennis Rodman as he "hangs out" with other celebrities, carries out everyday tasks, parties on the town, and makes celebrity appearances in public and on other television shows. To define the show as unquestionably real, Rodman constantly seeks to solidify his credibility as always "being himself." The show takes place in various "natural" settings rather than in a studio set, and the focus is on capturing Rodman in his natural element. The raw footage that serves as material for the final product consists of Rodman's various appearances during his book tour (signings and talk show appearances), the filming of his feature film *Double Team* with actor Jean Claude Van Damme, and numerous days on which Rodman is scheduled to "hang out" with different celebrities in various settings. Dispersed between raw footage is Rodman introducing or reflecting on the events, as well as "expert" commentary by various sports writers, coaches, a fashion designer, and even "sex doctor" Ruth Westheimer. Due to the mature nature of Rodman's show, the program aired in a time slot during which young children would not be prone to see it—Sunday nights at 10:00 p.m. After the first of the year (1997), television networks instituted the television rating system. Rodman's show was rated "TV 14," suggesting that it is inappropriate for anyone under age 14.

As a postmodern cultural product, the *Rodman World Tour* blurs the distinction between reality and fictional entertainment, creating a hyperreal atmosphere (Goldman, 1996) that relies on "spontaneous" moments while highlighting the construction process of the show's production. The blurring of reality and fiction is particularly important to the creation of Dennis Rodman's media image as "real" because his own commodification as a consumer product revolves around his self-proclaimed ability to "be himself" rather than merely an image created by the NBA. This conflation of reality and fiction on the *Rodman World Tour* becomes particularly clear in the way the show is constructed as a window to reality while at the same time allowing the audience to see the constructed nature of the show. The audience's constant awareness of the camera and production crew's presence as Rodman interacts with them in the context of the show further validates the theme of "realness." At the same time, the invisible element of its construction remains in the editing room, where deliberate and conscious choices have been made to present a particular version of "the reality" that was captured on film.

Bad As I Wanna Be

As articulated in Rodman's autobiography and during the numerous public appearances he made in the last few years, Rodman's public image centers on his "badness" that serves as one element of his rebellion discourse. From the very first episode of MTV's *Rodman World Tour,* in which the focus was on Rodman's personal history and his rise to fame on the basketball court, Rodman highlighted his "badness" in an opening monologue that described his recent accomplishments, his upcoming movie, and his MTV show. He asked the audience via the camera,

> And you wonder how did this all transpire? . . . I called up MTV and said, "I want my own show, and I won't take no for an answer. If you say no I'm gonna kick your ass, I'm gonna kick her ass, his ass, and the owner's ass"; I mean literally kick some ass because I really wanted it. And I can do that, you see, because, you know, *being king, number one, uno,* is, um, pretty good.

Later on the same episode, we saw Rodman clarify what this all meant when he looked directly into the video camera during a photo shoot and said, "I'm a bad boy." The badness theme was also worked into the textual elements of the show. In one instance, an on-screen title deemed Rodman "Dennis the Menace." In another recurring instance, one of the segments that regularly was used to cut to commercial breaks had a woman's voice singing "He's sooo bad!" as the camera panned down the backside of Rodman's naked body.

Rodman first acquired his "Bad Boy" status from his initial position with the Detroit Pistons. Their aggressive style of play rejected expected norms of professional sportsmanship and made them a liability to the image-conscious NBA, despite their championship titles (Boyd, 1997a, p. 110). Cole and Denny (1994) attributed the image consciousness of the NBA today to lagging public support for professional basketball that plagued the NBA during the early 1980s. During that period, the NBA was tarnished by the "stigmatized black aesthetic" of the game combined with bad publicity about black athletes using cocaine (Len Bias's death, for example) and living dangerous lifestyles (Cole & Denny, 1994, p. 129). Since that time, the NBA has orchestrated a successful marketing campaign that has contained the image of so-called out-of-control black athletes largely through the nice guy images of Magic Johnson initially (Cole & Denny, 1994, p. 129) and Michael Jordan currently (McDonald, 1996). With the contained image of black masculinity that the NBA has achieved, it has become safe for the association to accept some improvisational elements of urban street basketball (such as slam dunks and 3-point shots) that have increased their marketability by creating superstar athletes (Boyd, 1997a, p. 114). In spite of this adaptation, negative elements of street ball such as physically aggressive play and trash talk remain formally unacceptable because of the black underclass connotation they carry. Issues of class now concern the NBA and its image because race has been normalized by the dominance of African American players (Boyd, 1997a, p. 120) and the successful containment of their threatening black masculinity (Cole & Denny, 1994).

This lower-class, street style of "playing dirty" is exactly the element that Rodman brings to the NBA, prompting Boyd (1997a) to place him "squarely in the middle of the debate surrounding the 'nigga mentality' and the NBA" (p. 122). This "nigga mentality," as defined by Boyd, encompasses Rodman's open defiance of the NBA rules and norms of sportsmanship, but it has its historical roots in the image of the "bad nigger" who rebelled against white society by refusing to live by its rules (Boyd, 1997b). The racial subtext by which black masculinity represents a threat to white society is upheld by the fact that Rodman is a black athlete in a sport owned and managed by white elites (Sabo & Jansen, 1994; Shropshire, 1996). However, contrary to the NBA's "bad niggers" of the early 1980s, Rodman as bad boy represents merely a symbolic threat to the NBA's carefully guarded image because it can be contained within the workings of that image while it is used to increase revenues. To this end, Rodman's transgressions of both image and unacceptable levels of aggression are contained within the already managed image of the NBA through official reprimanding in the form of suspensions and fines (during the 1996-1997 season, Rodman received the second-longest suspension in league history—11 games—after kicking a courtside cameraman in his groin).

Importantly, Rodman is a skillful rebounder (holding six consecutive rebounding titles) and is matched with Chicago Bulls teammate Michael Jordan, who represents the center of the NBA's current managed image

(McDonald, 1996). If Rodman represents the "bad nigga" of the NBA, then Jordan's image provides the counter "good nigga" representation against which Rodman can stabilize his image, and vice versa. As Cole and Denny (1994) pointed out, the NBA's campaign success of the late 1980s was due to the "marketing of particular players' personalities" (Magic Johnson and Larry Bird) that served to "reorder and manage" the black masculinity that was closely associated with the sport (Cole & Denny, p. 129). Today, Rodman and Jordan play a similar role in the NBA's marketing machine, as suggested by former Detroit Pistons coach Dick Versace in one episode of the *Rodman World Tour:*

> The NBA is an image-conscious league and I think they try to control the image [of Rodman] as much as they can. . . . I think they watch Dennis. . . . *They love the marketing he does for the league,* but then they think they have to *keep him under control.* [italics added]

Rodman's transgressive but contained image is beneficial to the NBA in the form of increased revenues (attendance at games, Rodman merchandise, etc.). The league gets the best of both worlds: It reaps the benefits of Rodman's marketability and it is able to maintain its image by targeting him as the "one bad apple" in the bunch. Rodman knows this and articulates it within his discourse of being "bad." In one episode of his show, Rodman asserted, "There's not that many athletes who can go out there and do what the (bleep) [fuck] he wants to and so *I'm just challenging the system.*"

The system that Rodman claims to be challenging is the image-producing "star system" of the NBA that gives certain players (i.e., Jordan) enormously lucrative contracts and fails to "recognize" hard-working rebounders like Rodman with equally lucrative contracts. In his autobiography, Rodman wrote about his frustration over what he interpreted as this economic injustice as well as the targeting that he has "suffered" over the years by the NBA. He accused the NBA's "system":

> I'm an easy target. Too easy. They point to me as the bad guy, and the public accepts it. They've come to expect that Dennis Rodman is going to be the bad boy of the NBA. . . . The NBA decides who's going to be the chosen ones. (1996, p. 66)

Importantly, it is the very basis of this accusation that has enabled Rodman to find his own lucrative niche within the NBA. By enacting the bad boy in increasingly diverse and outrageous ways and claiming that it is his "true self," Rodman has achieved the stardom, fame, and fortune to which he aspired. Playing off of Jordan's "everybody's all-American" image (McDonald, 1996) and naming the NBA the "oppressive system" that has "kept him down," Rodman fills the marketing niche that appeals to the rebellious Generation X youth that make up MTV's primary audience. In such a way, Rodman, Jordan, and the NBA marketing machine take part in a mutually beneficial cycle of "antagonism" (perhaps feigned), through which each party gains monetarily. Given the economic end that Rodman's rebellion discourse seems to be supporting, it appears as though the agency with which Rodman enacts his bad boy image is largely reproductive rather than resistant.

Persistent Heterosexual Masculinity

Dennis Rodman's gender and sexual play in the media takes center stage on MTV's *Rodman World Tour.* Even as Rodman pushed the boundaries of gender and sexuality in the media (on both MTV and other venues depicted on the show), the show framed Rodman's behaviors within a limited realm of transgression, consistently invoking codes of hegemonic masculinity in the form of heterosexuality and the objectification of women's bodies.

In a telling moment from the show, Rodman's identity as an athlete becomes central in the framing of an instance in which Rodman was getting made up for a night on the town in Las Vegas. The scene was Rodman's hotel room on one side of a split television screen. The other side showed various women walking through the hotel on their way to Rodman's room. The first on-screen title led the audience with the implicit notion of sport: "Let the games begin." The next title that immediately followed maintained masculine notions, even though it referred to Rodman getting made up. It read, "applying *war* paint," and the camera (on the half screen) cut to Rodman getting makeup on his eyes and face and having his nails polished. We continued to see the women on their way up to Rodman's room on the split screen. The next text read, "Game Plan," and Rodman explained the plan: "All the girls up, so I can interview them, so I can weed in/ weed out." Finally, the audience learned that "the goal" (on-screen text) of the evening was "to have a grrreat time," as Rodman said, exaggerating his speech. Rather than fully resist dominant notions of masculinity,

Rodman's masculine identity was maintained here by implicit references to sport and heterosexuality even as he transgressed the male gender boundary by wearing women's makeup.

Rodman's minor transgressions were further balanced with reproductive images of masculinity through explicit references to Rodman's heterosexuality and his objectification of women. In the next segment, Rodman interacted sexually with the women and related to their bodies as if they were primarily sexual objects. When the women arrived, Rodman visually surveyed them from head to toe, focusing on their bodies. At one point, Rodman consulted with his cameraman (in a private, male-bonding moment) about which ones he should choose, identifying one of the women by her "big" breasts as he makes hand gestures cupping imaginary breasts in front of his own chest. Later, he explicitly told one of the women, "Your chest looks good," as he stared openly at her breasts. Once Rodman had chosen his female entourage for the evening (he takes five of the six women, all white, and "weeds out" the only black woman who was invited), he was ready for his night on the town. Having five women escort him for the evening itself serves to visually mark Rodman as hyper-heterosexual, thus validating his masculinity. As the evening progressed (we saw an edited version) and the group became increasingly intoxicated, the audience saw the escalation of sexual interaction between both the women and Rodman and between the women themselves. The evening culminated in a private dance party for Rodman in his suite as he sat watching the women dance together provocatively. This scene was interspersed with "expert" commentary from "sex doctor" Ruth Westheimer explaining that men (implying heterosexual men) enjoy watching two women together because they have fantasies about being with two women. This expert testimony served to further mark Rodman's heterosexuality.

In other instances, women were objectified by the camera and through Rodman's eyes for the viewing audience. Rodman went "girl watching" at the beach, where the camera took time to give close-up camera shots of two separate sets of bikini-clad women, panning up their bodies from foot to head (in that order). Rodman told the camera crew, "There's the guns boys [pointing], there's the guns." Taking a moment to verbalize his heterosexuality along with these visual indicators, Rodman also announced, "There's a prospect," as he walked past a sunbather and the camera followed his gaze. In another segment from an episode in which Rodman is at the L.A. club The Viper Room, the audience witnessed three consecutive instances of Rodman's gaze close up on women's torsos (we failed to ever see their faces): bare midriffs, a spandex-covered pelvis, breasts in a bra-like top. The audience was able to participate vicariously with Rodman as he interacted with the body parts, dancing closely behind and running his hands along them. The scene concluded with the camera catching Rodman looking directly at a dancing crotch at his eye level (the woman is on a table), then back to the camera sharing his gaze with the viewers. The fact that the audience was encouraged to participate in objectifying the women's bodies along with Rodman suggests a shared understanding of Rodman's heterosexuality that exists because it reproduces prevailing notions of masculinity that dominate American culture.

The objectification of women that is such a defining part of hegemonic masculinity goes hand-in-hand with implied sexuality. Rodman adheres to masculine conventions that make women's bodies passive objects of men's desire, thus solidifying notions about his own heterosexuality that he brings with him by virtue of his basketball star status. Sexuality, sport, and masculinity are intricately tied together in important ways. Sports represent a homosocial environment in which the negation of homosexuality is necessary to define locker room relations between athletes as masculine and not "too close" (Messner, 1992b, p. 36). When Rodman deploys dress and behavior coded as homosexual in the media, he puts himself in a compromising position regarding his teammates. In a revealing comment by Chicago Bulls' coach Phil Jackson, we get a glimpse of the mental compromise that has taken place by the team with reference to Rodman and his ambiguous gender play in the arena of sport. Juxtaposed with a clip of the fashion designer "expert" posing the question "I just wonder about [Rodman] in the locker room. What do the guys think?" Jackson said, "As long as he keeps his clothes on, he'll be fine." Given the function of a locker room where athletes change clothes and shower, this is obviously a metaphorical comment by Jackson. Rather than literally refuse to allow Rodman to change his clothes, the coach is suggesting that Rodman stay within the boundaries of accepted and expected gender and sexual behavior in the locker room. With such rigid sexual codes that define sport, Rodman is careful with his transgressions. Even as he plays with his sexuality on the *Rodman World Tour,* such instances are contained by explicit markers of heterosexuality. This managed image thus neutralizes the destabilizing potential of Rodman's hair, nails, makeup, and clothes.

Although there are numerous innuendos and visual depictions that signify Rodman flirting with homosexuality in his MTV show, two very revealing episodes clearly depict the ambiguity of Rodman's sexual trans-

gressions, as they are immediately contained by behavior coded as heterosexual. The first instance occurred at The Viper Room during a performance by the male disco band "Bootie Quake." In the segment of the show
that recapped the evening's events, the first clips shown clearly were
coded as heterosexual, with Rodman dancing closely with various
women, touching their bodies, and looking at specific parts of their bodies
shown in close-ups for the camera audience (such as their buttocks and
crotches). The first homoerotic image showed a clip of Rodman on the
stage dancing closely behind a white male, helping him take off his shirt
and then running his (Rodman's) hands along the man's chest. Rodman
then embraced the man in a hug from behind as he said something closely
into his ear. Immediately, the camera cut to the lead singer saying into the
microphone, "Hey, you can't come in here and take all our women," followed by a clip of the lead singer alluding to Rodman's penis size in a commentary to the audience: "Are you all ready to get funky? . . . Go Dennis,
go Dennis. . . . *Big hands, big feet. You know what that means.*" Although
the audience saw Rodman transgress sexually, we were told of his heterosexual behaviors and reminded of his penis size, thus serving to couch his
transgression within heterosexual masculinity.

Although the message of contained transgression seems to dominate the
construction of the show, there is, at the same time, room for alternative
readings by diverse audiences. As a cultural product aimed at revenues,
the *Rodman World Tour* satisfies mainstream desires for spectacle within
accepted limits while simultaneously offering the space for different interpretations by more marginalized audiences, thereby increasing the audience base. In this particular example, some audience members may catch a
more nuanced reference to homoeroticism. For example, the comment
about "taking all our women" when Rodman is clearly hugging a man can
be interpreted by members of gay subcultures as homosexual, with the
male in the traditionally "female" position being referred to as a "woman."
Similarly, preoccupation with penis size is certainly not the sole territory
of heterosexual men, and the reminder about Rodman's endowment could
be of just as much significance to homosexual viewers. Indeed, it is possible that some homosexuals may place even more importance on the penis
as a way of "proving" one's manhood in spite of the choice to have a male
sexual partner. These various levels of interpretation embedded within the
text are an important part of the attempt to appeal to diverse audiences and
enjoy greater commodity success in the marketplace. Although the show
leaves room for readings resistant to mainstream ideas, the primary goal of
selling a commodity to a mass audience limits the amount of resistant

agency that can be deployed by Rodman, and his agency remains largely reproductive of mainstream gender and sexual expectations.

In another example of Rodman's sexual transgression, Rodman kissed female impersonator RuPaul full on the lips while appearing on his talk show. Bringing up the topic of Rodman's sexuality, RuPaul asked Rodman, "You've never been with another man before, right?" Rodman, stuttering over his words, replies, "No, I've, I've . . . I've kissed men before." RuPaul then asked Rodman, "Would you kiss me right now?" Rodman looked to the studio audience as if asking, "Do you want me to?" and the audience clapped in response. They both stood up and kissed on their closed lips, lingering a bit before separating. Afterward, Rodman looked at the audience with a smirk and shrugged his shoulders twice while RuPaul smiled widely and laughed, exclaiming, "Oh my god, Dennis Rodman! Ooohh your lips are so big and juicy!" The footage that followed included scenes of Rodman in his studio reflecting on the kiss, as well as he and RuPaul after the RuPaul show reflecting on the kiss together. Meanwhile, a split screen replayed the kiss in slow motion, much like the instant replay strategy of sports media.

Once the kiss scenario was played out, the camera cut back to footage from the RuPaul show in which Rodman was directing a question toward an audience member. He said to RuPaul as he pointed toward the audience, "She's got to have some skeletons in her closet, she's got to [directing his question toward the audience member]. You got a black boyfriend?" We hear the unseen woman ask, "Huh?" and Rodman rephrased his question, "You have any black in you?" She responded, "Uuuh, no," to which Rodman asked, "You want some?" [closing his eyes as if he can't believe he said it, as if it just slipped out]. The studio audience went wild with applause and laughter as RuPaul said to Rodman, "Oh my god, you are **scandalous!**" This classic interracial pickup line suggests both heterosexual sex and the image of the black man's penis during sexual intercourse, "putting some black into" the white sexual partner. Rodman's deployment of this image at that moment reestablished his heterosexual black masculinity in lieu of his transgression (the kiss) that could be interpreted as homosexual. Like the series of clips from The Viper Room, the order in which these images appeared from the RuPaul show only allowed Rodman to transgress so far, quickly reminding the audience that he is a black heterosexual man who clearly likes to have sex with women. The potential resistance embodied in the transgressive kiss therefore was contained and appeared to be more reproductive than resistant.

Rodman's Fetishized Body

As a black male, Rodman is defined by a heightened form of masculinity that historically has been identified by the black male body. This is compounded by the focus on the body in sport, subjecting Rodman to a hypermasculine identity. The hypermasculinity already granted to Rodman via his identity as a black athlete continues to characterize his identity, even as he takes part in gender play. Regardless of the gender play that Rodman deploys via makeup and dress, he is seen as, and highlights the fact that he has, a gendered body that is male.

Central to Rodman's image is his highly sculpted, athletic male body that he displays quite regularly throughout his show. In the introduction of the show, Rodman's headless, naked torso is shown as the camera pans down his body, and we see numerous pairs of women's hands stuffing dollar bills into his spandex pants. In a recurring segment that takes the show to commercial breaks, Rodman's naked body is seen lying on a bed as the camera again pans down his bare back, landing just above his buttocks, where a simulated tattoo of the show's logo appears. In another similar segment that is used when returning from commercial breaks, Rodman's full, animated, naked body is shown from the rear, posing with his hands in the air. Again the camera pans to a close up of his animated buttocks as women's voices sing "Welcome back to the *Rodman World Tour.*" In addition, Rodman's live butt becomes the object of the camera's close-up gaze more than once within the sampled shows.

Although such ongoing objectifications occur throughout the show by both the producer's decisions (such as the segments used during commercial breaks) and by Rodman's actions himself, the most telling moment of Rodman's self-objectification occurred during his appearance on *Late Night With David Letterman.* Letterman brought up the topic of Rodman's then-new book, held up the book, and placed it on his desk in front of the camera for the audience to see. The front cover depicts a naked Rodman sitting on a motorcycle, a basketball covering his lap as he looks into the camera. Rodman reached over Letterman's desk and turned the book around, setting it back in place with the back cover now facing the camera. He said as he did this, "That's better." The back cover shows Rodman's full naked body from the rear view, legs standing shoulder width apart and arms extended upward in a "Y" shape holding two basketballs. This image can be interpreted as phallic, with the upheld balls representing testicles and Rodman's lean, tall body suggesting the phallus. The fact that

Rodman prefers the back cover to the front suggests that he indeed is an agent in his own self-objectification, unlike the women in earlier described segments who had little choice in how their bodies were portrayed on Rodman's show. Further illustrating Rodman's view of his body as object, he later explained to Letterman why he was not chosen to be on the Olympic Dream Team: "Look at me. They don't want *something like this* representing the United States" (italics added).

The most clear examples of Rodman's self-objectification and body fetishizing come in the way of references to his penis. Implicit references to Rodman's penis were the most numerous of all the themes that were found throughout the sampled shows (15 compared with 9 references to "badness" and 9 instances of objectification of women). Although the penis is a symbol of masculinity, it also represents biological maleness that seems to be consistent with Rodman's focus on his sculpted male body. The prominence of penis references and consistent body fetishizing indicates Rodman's concern with invoking biological maleness as his essence and thereby solidifying his masculinity regardless of what clothes he wears. The phallocentrism of such tactics supports hooks's (1992) analysis of prevailing ideas about black masculinity in American culture rather than suggests that Rodman is providing a new idea about masculinity.

As early as the show's introduction, the fact that Rodman's penis is an intended focus of the show is illustrated. The camera pans down Rodman's naked torso and shows female hands stuffing dollar bills into his pants; the camera lands on Rodman's groin as a female voice says "Oh My!" To make sure the viewer knows where the focus of this comment lies, a computer-generated, animated spiral effect (similar to that used to change scenes in the old televised Batman show) emerges from Rodman's spandex-covered penis and cuts to a new animated scene. Throughout the show, we see numerous instances where Rodman himself "spontaneously" highlights his penis during the taping of the footage that becomes the show's contents. In one instance, Rodman explained why he does not like to wear underwear, deploying the image of his long penis hanging loose: "Its too confining. I like to *free fall* every once in a while, you know. . . . I like to be loose. I like to be free, you know, *I like to hang totally free— tall—long*" (italics added). In another episode, Rodman explained to the camera audience that he likes to "stroke" himself as he introduces us to "the two most important women in [his] life," Monique and Julie—his hands further marking him as heterosexual.

Although Rodman takes part in highlighting his penis, it is also significant that others on the show do the same thing. On more than one occasion in the sampled shows, women referred to Rodman's penis, declaring, "I saw IT!" with nervous excitement. One woman is a middle-aged member of Rodman's costume crew who, while helping him into his wedding dress for his book signing appearance, inadvertently saw his penis. In the scene, Rodman's penis was not the subject of any conversation, yet when she made her declaration referring to his penis as "it," she implied that "it" has been the topic of ongoing discussions among the production crew. In another significant scene in the back of a convertible limousine, Jenny McCarthy (who, importantly, is a blonde, white woman viewed as a "sex symbol") brought up the topic of Rodman's penis in an allusive way. As Rodman told McCarthy, "I'm gonna be as bad as I wanna be, as good as I wanna be. . . ." McCarthy interrupted him saying, "As hot and as [her eyes look down at Rodman's lap exaggeratedly] large as you wanna be." Later in the same scene, McCarthy exclaimed, "Oh my god, I saw it, Oh my god I saw it. . . . Ohhh my gooood [clasping her hands in her hair in astonishment]." For further emphasis, this scene also was replayed in a clip during Rodman's appearance on Scott Furrell's talk radio sports show. Before the Las Vegas convertible ride with McCarthy was over, she made yet another allusion to Rodman's penis. In the closing scene of the segment, Rodman and McCarthy were both giving the camera the two thumbs up sign when McCarthy turned toward Rodman and said, "We have three thumbs," as she again looked down at his groin. Rodman laughed, moved both his thumbs down on his lap near his penis and said, "Three thumbs."

Rodman's concern with making his penis visible through language and McCarthy's seeming obsession with Rodman's penis deploy the stereotypical focus on black men's (and particularly black male athletes') sexual prowess embodied in the symbol of the phallus. This hypersexuality assigned to the black male is but one part of the hypermasculinity that is encoded in the figure of the black male athlete. Historically, the black phallus has served as the object of "white fear and fascination" in racist American society (Hoch, 1979; Mercer & Julien, 1988). Citing Franz Fanon, Mercer and Julien pointed out that myths about black men's aggressive sexuality were created by the "white master to allay his fears and anxieties as well as provid[e] a means to justify the brutalization of the colonized" black male (p. 134). This white fear and fascination is embodied perfectly in the scene with Jenny McCarthy. Because she is a white female, the interaction between Rodman and her (as well as all the other white women with whom Rodman has been interacting in sexually implicit ways) may conjure up racist concerns about black male sexuality and its imposed threat to the white female. Clearly, these instances reproduce sexist notions of male essentialism as well as racist notions of black male sexuality, failing to offer resistance to these powerful ideas that have structured American race and gender relations since the founding of the country.

Conclusion

The themes that emerged from MTV's *Rodman World Tour* illustrate the fact that potential acts of resistance are limited when they appear within a consumer context. Although Rodman flirts with homosexuality, wears makeup, and dons sequin tops and even a wedding dress, he also embraces the hyper-(heterosexual) masculinity that is encoded on his black male athletic body. Rodman consistently marks his heterosexuality through his objectification of women and invokes his biological maleness through his fetishized self-objectification, with particular attention paid to his penis. The phallocentrism that dominates Rodman's image reproduces the same sexist black masculinity that has prevailed over popular culture and theory alike (hooks, 1992).

The deployment of resistance discourse through Rodman's proclamation of "being bad" in fact supports a corporate, profit-driven end and reifies black masculinity. Being "bad" allows Rodman to invoke the symbolic threat imbued in his black masculinity, much like that of the phallus to which he is constantly referring. In fact, the hypermasculinity to which black men are subject largely accounts for Rodman's ability to transgress such gender boundaries without becoming completely marginalized. In these ways, Rodman's image mostly works to reproduce the current race and gender system rather than offer resistance to it. Much like the so-called resistance to racism that black athletic success purports to represent while, in fact, helping to reproduce the racist notions that relegate black males to sports in the first place (Hoberman, 1997), Rodman takes part in reproducing racist and sexist ideas that had a hand in his own steering toward a career in sports (Rodman was homeless for a time and even landed in jail for theft before he suddenly grew from 5'11" to 6'8"when he was 19; see Rodman, 1996, pp. 15-20).

Reproductive agency such as Rodman's exists within a consumer context and merely offers an individualized rebellious style that appeals to some consumers. Resistant agency takes the form of action against corporate consumer culture to disrupt oppressive institutions. Rather than constitute resistance, individualized agency such as Rodman's is part of the process of hegemony whereby dominant norms and relations become accepted by a mass society through consent backed by the threat of force or sanction. In analyzing television, Todd Gitlin (1987) explained how the functioning of hegemony allows for alternative and sometimes oppositional ideology by absorbing it into the mainstream (p. 242). The commodification of Rodman's so-called rebellion and transgressive gender play on MTV provides an astute example of such absorption. In addition, Rodman is situated visually and ideologically opposite Michael Jordan, the ideal image of post-Reagan ("colorblind" and equal opportunity) America (McDonald, 1996). As Jordan embodies the quintessential commodification of an athlete, Rodman's location as his foil serves to stabilize Jordan's image, sell the numerous products that he endorses, and thereby support the image of America that Jordan sells to America. In spite of the fact that Rodman's image is one of rebellion against "the system," his containment within this consumer context actually may serve to reproduce the current gender and racial order.

The prominence of Rodman's disruptive image (a professional athlete wearing a wedding dress certainly disrupts on some level) in the media, however, does leave room for some potential resistant agency by audiences, regardless of Rodman's own failure to resist oppressive social structures on a material level. Further research on audiences needs to explore the diverse ways that people read texts such as the *Rodman World Tour* to determine how Rodman's potentially disruptive image affects them and their social environment. Is Rodman more likely to influence audiences to take part in action that challenges oppressive structures (such as fighting for gender equity in society, gay rights, or domestic partnership laws), or do they merely engage in individual acts of symbolic rebellion similar to Rodman's own (such as buying Converse All Star sneakers and "Chicago Bulls 91" jerseys)? These questions need to be studied to understand fully the impact of popular culture on everyday social relations.

References

Abelove, H., Barale, M. A., et al. (Eds.). (1993). *The lesbian and gay studies reader.* Boston: Routledge & Kegan Paul.

Adam, B. (1978). *The survival of domination: Inferiorization and everyday life.* New York: Elsevier North-Holland.

Adam, B. D. (1995). *The rise of the lesbian and gay liberation movement.* New York: Simon & Schuster.

Adams, M. L. (1993). To be an ordinary hero: Male figure skaters and the ideology of gender. In T. Haddad (Ed.), *Men and masculinities* (pp. 163-181). Toronto: Canadian Scholars Press.

Adler, P., Kless, S. J., & Adler, P. (1992). Socialization to gender roles: Popularity among elementary school boys and girls. *Sociology of Education, 65,* 169-187.

Albert, E. (1991). Riding a line: Competition and cooperation in the sport of bicycle racing. *Sociology of Sport Journal, 8,* 341-361.

Altheide, D. L. (1996). *Qualitative media analysis.* Thousand Oaks, CA: Sage.

Anderson, C. (1997). Violence on television commercials during nonviolent programming: The 1996 Major League Baseball playoffs. *Journal of the American Medical Association, 278,* 1045-1046.

Anderson, D. (1993). Cultural diversity on campus: A look at collegiate football coaches. *Journal of Sport and Social Issues, 17,* 61-66.

Andrews, D. (1993). Desperately seeking Michel: Foucault's genealogy, the body, and critical sport sociology. *Sociology of Sport Journal, 10,* 148-167.

Andrews, D. (Ed.). (1996a). Deconstructing Michael Jordan: Reconstructing post-industrial America [Special issue]. *Sociology of Sport Journal, 13*(4).

Andrews, D. (1996b). The fact(s) of Michael Jordan's blackness: Excavating a floating racial signifier. *Sociology of Sport Journal, 13,* 125-158.

Andrews, D. (in press). All-consumed bodies: Baudrillard, hyperreality, and the cybernetic construction of the postmodern body. In C. Cole, J. Loy, & M. Messner (Eds.), *Exercising power: The making and remaking of the body.* Albany: State University of New York Press.

Andrews, D., Carrington, B., Mazur, Z., & Jackson, S. (1996). Jordanscapes: A preliminary analysis of the global popular. *Sociology of Sport Journal, 13,* 428-457.

Araton, H. (1992, January 2). Shameful: How corporate America dumped Magic. *The Sydney Morning Herald,* p. 30.

Archetti, E. (1994). Masculinity and football: The formation of national identity in Argentina. In R. Giulianotti & J. Williams (Eds), *Game without frontiers: Football, identity and modernity* (pp. 225-243). Aldershot, UK: Arena.

Arms, R. L., Russell, G. W., & Sandilands, M. L. (1979). Effects on the hostility of spectators of viewing aggressive sports. *Social Psychology Quarterly, 42,* 275-279.

Baca Zinn, M. (1975). Political familism: Toward sex role equality in Chicano families. *International Journal of Chicano Studies Research, 6,* 13-26.

Baca Zinn, M. (1982). Chicano men and masculinity. *Journal of Ethnic Studies, 10*(2), 29-44.

Baca Zinn, M., & Dill, B. T. (1996). Theorizing difference from multiracial feminism. *Feminist Studies, 22,* 321-331.

Bairner, A. (1995, November). *Soccer, masculinity and violence in Northern Ireland: Between hooliganism and terrorism.* Paper presented at the 16th annual meeting of the North American Society for the Sociology of Sport, Sacramento, CA.

Bairner, A. (1986). The battlefield of ideas: The legitimation of political violence in Northern Ireland. *European Journal of Political Research, 14,* 633-649.

Bairner, A. (1994). The end of pitched battles. The peace process and sport in Northern Ireland. *Causeway, 1*(3), 62-66.

Balsamo, A. (1995). Forms of technological embodiment: Reading the body in contemporary culture. *Body and Society, 1,* 215-238.

Barak, G. (Ed.). (1996). *Representing O. J.: Murder, criminal justice and mass culture.* New York: Harrow & Herston.

Bartky, S. L. (1988). Foucault, femininity, and the modernisation of patriarchal power. In I. Diamond & L. Quimby (Eds.), *Feminism and Foucault: Reflections on resistance* (pp. 61-85). Boston: Northeastern University Press.

Bartky, S. (1998). Foreword. In T. Digby (Ed.), *Men doing feminism* (pp. xi-xiv). Boston: Routledge & Kegan Paul.

Bataille, G. (1985). *Visions of excess: Selected writings, 1927-1939* (A. Stoekl, Ed.; A. Stoekl, C. R. Lovitt, & D. M. Leslie, Trans.). Minneapolis: University of Minnesota Press.

Bell, D. (1990). *Acts of union. Youth culture and sectarianism in Northern Ireland.* New York: Macmillan.

Bem, S. (1974). The measurement of psychological androgyny. *Journal of Consulting and Clinical Psychology, 42,* 155-162.

Bem, S. (1975). Sex role adaptability: One consequence of psychological androgyny. *Journal of Personality and Social Psychology, 31,* 634-643.

Benedict, J. (1997). *Public heroes, private felons: Male athletes and crimes against women.* Boston: Northeastern University Press.

Benedict, J., & Klein, A. (1997). Arrest and conviction rates for athletes accused of sexual assault. *Sociology of Sport Journal, 14,* 86-94.

Benton, T . (1991). Biology and social science: Why the return of the repressed should be given a (cautious) welcome. *Sociology, 25,* 1-30.

Berkowitz, L., & Frodi, A. (1979). Reactions to a child's mistakes as affected by her/his looks and speech. *Social Psychology Quarterly, 42,* 420-425.

Berkowitz, L., & LePage, A. (1967). Weapons as aggression-eliciting stimuli. *Journal of Personality and Social Psychology, 7,* 202-207.

Bird, S. (1996). Welcome to the men's club: Homosociality and the maintenance of hegemonic masculinity. *Gender and Society, 10,* 120-132.

Birrell, S. (1978). Achievement related motives and the woman athlete. In C. Oglesby (Ed.), *Women and sport: From myth to reality* (pp. 143-172). Philadelphia: Lea & Febiger.

Birrell, S. (1984). Separatism as an issue in women's sports. *Arena Review, 8,* 21-29.

Birrell, S., & Cole, C. (1990). Double fault: Renee Richards and the construction and naturalization of difference. *Sociology of Sport Journal, 7,* 1-21.

Birrell, S., and Richter, D. (1994). Is a diamond forever? Feminist transformations of sport. In S. Birrell & C. Cole (Eds.), *Women, sport, and culture.* Champaign, IL: Human Kinetics.

Blais, M. (1995). *In these girls hope is a muscle.* New York: Atlantic Monthly Press.

Bloom, G., & Smith, M. (1996). Hockey violence: A test of the cultural spillover theory. *Sociology of Sport Journal, 13,* 65-76.

Blumer, H. (1971). Social problems as collective behavior. *Social Problems, 18,* 298-306.

Bly, R. (1990). *Iron John: A book about men.* Reading, MA: Addison-Wesley

Boeringer, S. D. (1996). Influences of fraternity membership, athletics, and male living arrangements on sexual aggression. *Violence Against Women, 2,* 134-147.

Bordo, S. (1989a). The body and the reproduction of femininity: A feminist appropriation of Foucault. In S. Bordo (Ed.), *Gender/Body/Knowledge* (pp. 13-33). New Brunswick, NJ: Rutgers University Press.

Bordo, S. (1989b). *Gender/Body/Knowledge.* A. Jaggar. New Brunswick, NJ: Rutgers University Press.

Bordo, S. (1990). Reading the slender body. In M. Jacobus, E. F. Keller, & S. Shuttleworth (Eds.), *Body/Politics: Women and the discourses of science* (pp. 83-111). Boston: Routledge & Kegan Paul.

Bordo, S. (1993). *Unbearable Weight: Feminism, Western culture, and the body.* Berkeley: University of California Press.

Boswell, A., & Spade, J. (1996). Fraternities and collegiate gang rape: Why are some fraternities more dangerous places for women? *Gender & Society, 10,* 133-147.

Bouchard, P., & St-Amand, P. (1996). *Garçons et filles: Stéréotypes et réussite scolaire* [Boys and girls: Stereotypes and academic success]. Montréal, Canada: Les Editions du remue-ménage.

Boulton, M., & Smith, P. (1992). The social nature of play fighting and play chasing: Mechanisms and strategies underlying cooperation and compromise. In J. Barkow, L. Cosmides, & J. Tooby (Eds.), *The adapted mind: Evolutionary psychology and the generation of culture* (pp. 429-450). New York: Oxford University Press.

Bourdieu, P. (1980). The aristocracy of culture. *Media, Culture, and Society, 2,* 225-254.

Bourdieu, P. (1984). *Distinction: A social critique of the judgement of taste* (R. Nice, Trans.). Cambridge, MA: Harvard University Press. (Original work published 1979)

Boyd, T. (1997a). *Am I Black enough for you? Popular culture from the 'hood and beyond.* Bloomington: Indiana University Press.

Boyd, T. (1997b). The day the niggaz took over: Basketball, commodity culture, and black masculinity. In A. Baker & T. Boyd (Eds.), *Out of bounds: Sports, media, and the politics of identity* (pp. 123-144). Bloomington: University of Indiana Press.

Boyle, M., & McKay, J. (1995). You leave your troubles at the gate: A case study of the exploitation of older women's labor and leisure in sport. *Gender & Society, 9,* 556-576.

Brackenridge, C. (1997). "He owned me basically ...": Women's experience of sexual abuse in sport. *International Review for the Sociology of Sport, 32,* 115-130.

Brackenridge, C., & Kirby, S. (1997). Playing safe: Assessing the risk of sexual abuse to elite child athletes. *International Review for the Sociology of Sport, 32,* 407-418.

Braidotti, R. (1994). *Nomadic subjects: Embodiment and sexual difference in contemporary feminist theory.* New York: Columbia University Press.

Brandes, S. (1980). *Metaphors of masculinity: Sex and status in Andalusian folklore.* Philadelphia: University of Pennsylvania Press.

Brod, H. (Ed.). (1987). *The making of masculinities: The new men's studies.* Boston: Allyn & Bacon.

Brooks, D. D., Alhouse, B., & Tucker, D. (1996-1997). African American male head coaches: In the "red zone," but can they score? *Journal of African American Men, 2,* 93-112.

Brown, N. O. (1966). *Love's body.* New York: Random House.

Brubaker, B. (1994, November 20). Violence against women poses problem for NFL, its players. *The Buffalo Evening News,* p. A-10.

Bruce, S. (1992). *The red hand: Protestant paramilitaries in Northern Ireland.* New York: Oxford University Press.

Bryant, J., Comisky, P., & Zillman, D. (1981). The appeal of rough-and-tumble play in televised professional football. *Communication Quarterly, 29,* 256-262.

Bryson, L. (1987). Sport and the maintenance of masculine hegemony. *Women's Studies International Forum, 10,* 349-360.

Burton-Nelson, M. (1994). *The stronger women get, the more men love football: Sexism and the American culture of sports.* Orlando, FL: Harcourt Brace.

Butler, J. (1990). *Gender trouble: Feminism and the subversion of identity.* Boston: Routledge & Kegan Paul.

Butler, J. (1993). *Bodies that matter: On the discursive limits of "sex."* Boston: Routledge & Kegan Paul.

Cahn, S. K. (1994a). *Coming on strong: Gender and sexuality in twentieth century women's sport.* New York: Free Press.

Cahn, S. (1994b). Crushes, competition, and closets: The emergence of homophia in women's physical education. In S. Birrell & C. Cole (Eds.), *Women, sport, and culture* (pp. 327-340). Champaign, IL: Human Kinetics.

Canaan, J. (1991). Is "doing nothing" just boys' play? Integrating feminist and cultural studies perspectives on working-class young men's masculinity. In S. Franklin, C. Lury, & J. Stacey (Eds.), *Off centre: Feminism and cultural studies* (pp. 109-125). New York: HarperCollins.

Canadian Centre for Drug-Free Sport. (1993). *Final report of the National School Survey on Drugs and Sport.* Ottawa: Fitness and Amateur Sport Canada.

Carey, E. (1995, Nov. 21). Youths' drinking accidents dip: Study. *Toronto Star*, p. A3.

Carlson, M., Marcus-Newhall, A., & Miller, N. (1990). The effects of situational aggressive cues: A quantitative review. *Journal of Personality and Social Psychology, 58*, 622-633.

Carrigan, T., Connell, B., & Lee, J. (1985). Toward a new sociology of masculinity. *Theory and Society, 14*, 551-604.

Carrington, B. (2000). Double consciousness and the black British athlete. In K. Owusu (Ed.), *Black British culture and society* (pp. 133-156). Boston: Routledge & Kegan Paul.

Cashmore, E. (1990). *Making sense of sport.* Boston: Routledge & Kegan Paul.

Champagne, J. (1995). *The ethics of marginality.* Minneapolis: University of Minnesota Press.

Chancer, L. (1998). Playing gender against race through high-profile crime cases: The Tyson/Thomas/Simpson Pattern of the 1980s. *Violence Against Women, 4*, 100-113.

Chase, S. E. (1988). Making sense of "the woman who becomes a man." In A. Todd & S. Fisher (Eds.), *Gender and discourse: The power of talk* (pp. 275-295). Norwood, NJ: Ablex.

Clarke, J. (1978). Football and working class fans: Tradition and change. In R. Ingham (Ed.), *Football hooliganism: The wider context* (pp. 37-60). London: Inter-Action Imprint.

Coakley, J. (1993). Sport and socialization. *Exercise and Sport Science Reviews, 21*, 169-200.

Coakley, J. (1994). *Sport in society* (5th ed.). St. Louis, MO: C. V. Mosby.

Coakley, J. (1997). *Sport in society: Issues and controversies* (5th ed.). New York: McGraw-Hill.

Coakley, J. J. (1998). *Sport in society: Issues and controversies* (6th ed.). New York: McGraw-Hill.

Cole, C. (1993). Resisting the canon: Feminist cultural studies, sport, and technologies of the body. *Journal of Sport and Social Issues, 17*, 77-97.

Cole, C. L., & Andrews, D. L. (1996). Look, it's NBA Showtime! A Research Annual. *Cultural Studies, (1)*, 141-181.

Cole, C. L., & Denny, H., III. (1994). Visualizing deviance in post-Reagan America: Magic Johnson, AIDS and the promiscuous world of professional sport. *Critical Sociology, 20*(3), 123-147.

Cole, C. L., & Hribar, A. (1995). Celebrity feminism: Nike style post-Fordism, transcendance, and consumer power. *Sociology of Sport Journal, 12,* 347-369.

Cole, C., & King, S. (1998). Representing Black masculinity and urban possibilities: Racism, realism and *Hoop Dreams.* In G. Rail & J. Harvey (Eds.), *Sport and postmodern times: Gender, sexuality, the body and sport* (pp. 49-86). Albany: State University of New York Press.

Collins, P. H. (1990). *Black feminist thought: Knowledge, consciousness, and the politics of empowerment.* New York: HarperCollins.

Collins, P. H. (1999). Moving beyond gender: Intersectionality and scientific knowledge. In J. Lorber, M. M. Ferree, & B. Hess (Eds.), *Revisioning gender* (pp. 261-284). Thousand Oaks, CA: Sage.

Collinson, D. L. (1988). Engineering humor: Masculinity, joking and conflict in shop-floor relations. *Organization Studies, 9,* 181-199.

Collinson, D., & Hearn, J. (1994). Naming men as men: Implications for work, organization and management. *Gender, Work and Organization, 1,* 2-22.

Coltrane, S. (1994). Theorizing masculinities in contemporary social science. In H. Brod & M. Kaufman (Eds.), *Theorizing masculinities* (p. 60). Thousand Oaks, CA: Sage.

Condit, M. (1989). The rhetorical limits of polysemy. *Critical Studies in Mass Communication,* 103-133.

Connell, R. (1983). *Which way is up? Essays on sex, class, and culture.* Sydney, Australia: Allen and Unwin.

Connell, R. W. (1987). *Gender and power: Society, the person, and sexual politics.* Stanford, CA: Stanford University Press.

Connell, R. W. (1990). An iron man: The body and some contradictions of hegemonic masculinity. In M. Messner & D. Sabo (Eds.), *Sport, men, and the gender order: Critical feminist perspectives* (pp. 83-96). Champaign, IL: Human Kinetics.

Connell, R. W. (1992). Sport and war: Rites of passage in male institutions. In M. Kimmel & M. Messner (Eds.), *Men's lives* (pp. 176-182). New York: Macmillan.

Connell, R. W. (1993). The big picture: Masculinities in recent world history. *Theory and Society, 22,* 597-625.

Connell, R. W. (1995). *Masculinities.* Berkeley: University of California Press.

Cornell, D. (1992). *The philosophy of the limit.* Boston: Routledge & Kegan Paul.

Coulter, C. (1995, February). *Class, ethnicity and political identity in Northern Ireland.* Paper presented at the Contemporary Protestantism in Ireland conference, Queen's University, Belfast, Northern Ireland.

Crimp, D. (1990). *AIDS demographics.* Seattle, WA: Bay.

Crimp, D. (1993). Accommodating Magic. In M. Garber, J. Matlock, & R. Walkowitz (Eds.), *Media spectacles* (pp. 255-264). Boston: Routledge & Kegan Paul.

Cronin, M. (1997). Which nation, which flag? Boxing and national identities in Ireland. *International Review for the Sociology of Sport, 32,* 131-146.

Crosset, T. (1990). Masculinity, sexuality, and the development of early modern sport. In M. Messner & D. Sabo (Eds.), *Sport, men and the gender order: Critical feminist perspectives* (pp. 45-54). Champaign, IL: Human Kinetics.

Crosset, T. W. (1995). *Outsiders in the clubhouse: The world of women's professional golf.* Albany: State University of New York Press.

Crosset, T., & Beal, B. (1997). The use of "subculture" and "subworld" in ethnographic works on sport: A discussion of definitional distinctions. *Sociology of Sport Journal, 14,* 73-85.

Crosset, T., Benedict, J., & McDonald, M. A. (1995). Male student athletes reported for sexual assault: Survey of campus police departments and judicial affairs offices. *Journal of Sport and Social Issues, 19,* 126-140.

Crosset, T., Ptacek, J., McDonald, M., & Benedict, J. (1996). Male student athletes and violence against women: A survey of campus judicial affairs offices. *Violence Against Women, 2,* 163-179.

Crowell, N., & Burgress, A. (Eds.). (1996). *Understanding violence against women.* Washington, DC: National Academy Press.

Currie, D. H., & Raoul, V. (Eds.). (1992). *The anatomy of gender: Women's struggle for the body.* Ottawa, Canada: Carleton University Press.

Curry, T. J. (1991). Fraternal bonding in the locker room: A profeminist analysis of talk about competition and women. *Sociology of Sport Journal, 8,* 119-135.

Curry, T. (1993). A little pain never hurt anyone: Athletic career socialization and the normalization of sports injury. *Symbolic Interaction, 16,* 273-290.

Curry, T. (1996, November). *Beyond the locker room: Sexual assault and the college athlete.* Presidential address at the annual meeting of the North American Society for the Sociology of Sport, Birmingham, AL.

Curry, T. (1998). Beyond the locker room: Campus bars and college athletes. *Sociology of Sport Journal, 15,* 205-215.

Curry, T., & Jiobu, R. (1995). Do motives matter? Modeling gambling on sports among athletes. *Sociology of Sport Journal, 12,* 21-35.

Curry, T., & Strauss, R. (1994). A little pain never hurt anybody: A photo-essay on the normalization of sport. *Sociology of Sport Journal, 11,* 195-208.

Davies, B. (1989). *Frogs and snails and feminist tales: Preschool children and gender.* Sydney, Australia: Allen and Unwin.

Davies, B. (1993). *Shards of glass.* Cresskill, NJ: Hampton.

Davis, L. (1987). A postmodern paradox? Cheerleaders at women's sporting events. *Arena Review, 4*(2), 124-133.

Davis, L. R. (1990). Male cheerleaders and the naturalization of gender. In M. Messner & D. Sabo (Eds.), *Sport, men and the gender order: Critical feminist perspectives* (pp. 153-161). Champaign, IL: Human Kinetics.

Davis, L. R. (1997). *The swimsuit issue and sport: Hegemonic masculinity in* Sports Illustrated. Albany: State University of New York Press.

Davis, P. (1992). Ethical and moral issues in boxing. *Journal of the Philosophy of Sport, 20-21,* 48-63.

Davis, T. (1995). The myth of the superspade: The persistence of racism in college athletics. *Fordham Urban Law Journal, 22,* 615-698.

DeKeseredy, W., & Kelly, K. (1995). Sexual abuse in Canadian university and college dating relationships: The contribution of male peer support. *Journal of Family Violence, 10,* 41-53.

Deleuze, G. (1992, Winter). Postscript on the societies of control. *October, 59,* 3-7.

Deleuze, G., & Guattari, F. (1983). *Anti-Oedipus: Capitalism and schizophrenia.* Minneapolis: University of Minnesota Press.

Deleuze, G., & Guattari, F. (1987). *A thousand plateaus: Capitalism and schizophrenia.* Minneapolis: University of Minnesota Press.

Derrida, J. (1978). *Writing and difference.* Chicago: University of Chicago Press.

Derrida, J. (1987). *The truth in painting.* Chicago: University of Chicago Press.

De Vault, M. L. (1990). Talking and listening from women's standpoint: Feminist strategies for interviewing and analysis. *Social Problems, 37,* 701-721.

Dews, P. (1987). *Logics of disintegration: Post-structuralist thought and the claims of critical theory.* London: Verso.

Dimaggio, P. (1982). Cultural entrepreneurship in 19th century Boston: The creation of an organizational base for high culture. *Media, Culture, and Society, 4,* 194-211.

Disch, L., & Kane, M. J. (1996). When a looker is really a bitch: Lisa Olsen, sport, and the heterosexual matrix. *Signs: Journal of Women in Culture and Society, 21,* 278-306.

Donnerstein, E., & Linz, D. (1986). Mass media, sexual violence, and male viewers: Current theory and research. *American Behavioral Scientist, 29,* 601-618.

Drake, B., & Pandey, S. (1996). Do child abuse rates increase on those days on which professional sporting events are held? *Journal of Family Violence, 11,* 205-218.

Dryden, S. (1997, February 28). Editorial. *The Hockey News,* p. 2.

Dubbert, J. (1979). *A man's place: Masculinity in transition.* Englewood Cliffs, NJ: Prentice Hall.

Duberman, M. (1993). *Stonewall.* New York: Plume.

Duberman, M. (Ed.). (1997). *A queer world: The Center for Lesbian and Gay Studies reader.* New York: New York University Press.

Duncan, M. C. (1990). Sports photographs and sexual difference: Images of women and men in the 1984 and 1988 Olympic Games. *Sociology of Sport Journal, 7,* 22-42.

Duncan, M. C., & Hasbrook, C. A. (1988). Denial of power in televised women's sports. *Sociology of Sport Journal, 5,* 1-21

Duncan, M. C., Messner, M. A., & Jensen, K. (1994). *Gender stereotyping in televised sports: A follow-up to the 1989 study.* Los Angeles: Amateur Athletic Foundation.

Dunning, E. (1986). Sport as a male preserve: Notes on the social sources of masculinity and its transformations. In N. Elias & E. Dunning (Eds.), *Quest for excitement: Sport and leisure in the civilizing process* (pp. 267-283). Oxford, UK: Basil Blackwell.

Dunning, E. G. (1990). Sociological reflections on sport, violence and civilization. *International Review for the Sociology of Sport, 25,* 65-82.

Dunning, E. (1994). Sport as a male preserve: Notes on the social sources of masculine identity and its transformations. In S. Birrell & C. Cole (Eds.), *Women, sport, and culture.* Champaign, IL: Human Kinetics.

Dunning, E., Murphy, P., & Williams, J. (1988). *The roots of football hooliganism. An historical and sociological study*. Boston: Routledge & Kegan Paul.

Dunning, E., & Sheard, B. (1979). *Barbarians, gentlemen and players*. New York: New York University Press.

Duquin, M. (1978). The androgynous advantage. In C. A. Oglesby (Ed.), *Women and sport: From myth to reality* (pp. 89-106). Philadelphia: Lea & Febiger.

Durie, J. (1992, March 21-22). Safe sex eludes rich and famous. *The Weekend Australian*, p. 10.

Dussart, F. (1992). The politics of female identity: Walpiri widows at Yeundumu. *Ethnology, 31*, 337-350.

Dutton, K. (1995). *The perfectible body: The Western ideal of male physical development*. New York: Continuum.

Dworkin, S. L., & Messner, M. A. (1999). Just do . . . what? Sport, bodies, gender. In J. Lorber, M. M. Ferree, & B. Hess (Eds.), *Revisioning gender* (pp. 341-364). Thousand Oaks, CA: Sage.

Dworkin, S. L., & Wachs, F. L. (1998). "Disciplining the body": HIV positive male athletes, media surveillance, and the policing of sexuality. *Sociology of Sport Journal, 15*, 1-20.

Dyson, M. E. (1993). Be like Mike? Michael Jordan and the pedagogy of desire. *Cultural Studies, 7*, 64-72.

Eames, R. (1995, May 17). Free to open new doors. *Guardian*, p. 17.

Early, G. (1994). *The culture of bruising: Essays on prizefighting, literature, and modern American culture*. Hopewell, NJ: Ecco.

Eastman, S. T., & Land, A. M. (1997). The best of both worlds: Sports fans find good seats at the bar. *Journal of Sport and Social Issues, 21*, 156-178.

Ebert, T. (1992-1993). Ludic feminism, the body, performance, and lab or: Bringing *materialism* back into feminist cultural studies. *Cultural Critique, 23*, 5-50.

Ebert, T. (1996). *Ludic feminism and after: Postmodernism, desire, and labor in late capitalism*. Ann Arbor: University of Michigan Press.

Edwards, H. (1973). *Sociology of sport*. Belmont, CA: Dorsey.

Ehrenreich, B. (1983). *The hearts of men: American dreams and the flight from commitment*. New York: Doubleday.

Eisenstein, Z. (1994). *The color of gender: Reimaging democracy*. Berkeley: University of California Press.

Elias, N., & Dunning, E. (1986). *Quest for excitement: Sport and leisure in the civilizing process*. Oxford, UK: Basil Blackwell.

Ellison, L., & Mackenzie, S. (1993). Sports injuries in the database of the Canadian hospitals injury reporting and prevention program—An overview. *Chronic Diseases in Canada, 14*, 96-104.

Elson, J. (1991, November 25). The dangerous world of wannabes. *Time*, 59-60.

ESPN. (1996, November). *ESPNET Sports Zone Showdown topic: Athletes and violence against women*. Bristol, CT: Author.

Falk, P. (1994). *The consuming body*. Thousand Oaks, CA: Sage.

Fasler, S. (1976). Sport accidents: 1963-1973 statistics. *Praventivmedizin, 21*, 296-301.

Faulkner, R. R. (1973). On respect and retribution: Toward an ethnography of violence. *Sociological Symposium, 9*, 17-36.

Featherstone, M. (1991). The body in consumer culture. In M. Featherstone, M. Hepworth, & B. S. Turner (Eds.), *The body: Social processes and cultural theory* (pp. 170-197). Newbury Park, CA: Sage.

Featherstone, M., & Burrows, R. (1995). Cultures of technological embodiment: An introduction. *Body and Society, 1*(3-4), 1.

Featherstone, M., Hepworth, M., & Turner, B. (Eds.). (1991). *The body: Social processes and social theory.* Newbury Park, CA: Sage.

Felshin, J. (1974). The triple option for women in sport. *Quest, 17,* 36-40.

Fine, G. A. (1987). *With the boys: Little League baseball and preadolescent culture.* Chicago: University of Chicago Press.

Fine, G., & Sandstrom, K. L. (1988). *Knowing children: Participant observation with minors.* Newbury Park, CA: Sage.

Fishman, R. (1991). *Calypso cricket: Inside story of the 1991 Windies tour.* Sydney, Australia: Margaret Gee.

Fiske, J. (1994). *Media matters: Everyday culture and political change.* Minneapolis: University of Minnesota Press.

Fitzclarence, L. (1990). The body as commodity. In D. Rowe & G. Lawrence (Eds.), *Sport and leisure: Trends in Australian popular culture* (pp. 96-108). Orlando, FL: Harcourt Brace.

Flax, J. (1987). Postmodernism and gender relations in feminist theory. *Signs: Journal of Women in Culture and Society, 12,* 621-643.

Foley, D. (1990). The great American football ritual: Reproducing race, class, and gender inequality. *Sociology of Sport Journal, 7,* 111-134.

Foucault, M. (1979). *Discipline and punish: The birth of the prison.* New York: Vintage.

Foucault, M. (1980). *The history of sexuality: Vol. I. An introduction.* New York: Vintage.

Foucault, M. (1983). The subject and power. In H. Dreyfus & P. Rabinow (Eds.), *Michel Foucault: Beyond structuralism and hermeneutics* (pp. 208-226). Chicago: University of Chicago Press.

Foucault, M. (1985). *The uses of pleasure: The history of sexuality.* New York: Vintage.

Fritner, M. P., & Rubinson, L. (1993). Acquaintance rape: The influence of alcohol, fraternity membership and sports team membership. *Journal of Sex Education and Therapy, 19,* 272-284.

Gallagher, C., & Lacqueur, T. (1987). *The making of the modern body.* Berkeley: University of California Press.

Gallop, J. (1988). *Thinking through the body.* New York: Columbia University Press.

Game, A. (1991). *Undoing the social: Towards a deconstructive sociology.* Toronto, Canada: University of Toronto Press.

Garber, M. (1992). *Vested interests: Cross-dressing and cultural anxiety.* New York: HarperCollins.

Gatens, M. (1988). Towards a feminist philosophy of the body. In B. Caine, E. Grosz, & M. de Lepervanche (Eds.), *Crossing boundaries* (pp. 59-70), Sydney, Australia: Allen and Unwin.

Ghaill, M. (1994). *The making of men.* Philadelphia: Open University Press.

Giddens, A. (1976). *New rules of sociological method.* New York: Warner.

Gilder, G. (1973). *Sexual suicide.* New York: Quadrangle.

Gilder, G. (1986). *Men and marriage.* Gretna: Pelican.

Gillespie, N., Lovett, T., & Garner, W. (1992). *Youth work and working class youth culture. Rules and resistance in west Belfast.* Buckingham, UK: Open University Press.

Gillett, J., White, P., & Young, K. (1996). The prime minister of Saturday night: Don Cherry, the CBC, and the cultural production of intolerance. In H. Holmes & D. Taras (Eds.), *Seeing ourselves: Media power and policy in Canada* (pp. 59-72). Orlando, FL: Harcourt Brace.

Gilmore, D. (1990). *Mankind in the making: Cultural concepts of masculinity.* New Haven, CT: Yale University Press.

Gitlin, T. (1987). Television's screens: Hegemony in transition. In D. Lazere (Ed.), *American media and mass culture: Left perspectives* (pp. 240-265). Berkeley: University of California Press.

Giulianotti, R. (1993). Soccer casuals as cultural intermediaries. In S. Redhead (Ed.), *The passion and the fashion: Football fandom in the new Europe* (pp. 153-205). Aldershot, UK: Avebury.

Glasser, A. (1992). Men and muscles. In M. Kimmel & M. Messner (Eds.), *Men's lives* (pp. 287-297). New York: Macmillan.

Glaser, B., & Strauss, A. (1967). *The discovery of grounded theory.* Hawthorne, NY: Aldine.

Gmelch, G., & San Antonio, P. M. (1998). Groupies and American baseball. *Journal of Sport and Social Issues, 22,* 32-45.

Goffman, I. (1959). *The presentation of self in everyday life.* New York: Doubleday.

Goldberg, J. (Ed.). (1994). *Reclaiming Sodom.* Boston: Routledge & Kegan Paul.

Goldlust, J. (1987). *Playing for keeps: Sport, the media and society.* Melbourne, Australia: Longman Cheshire.

Goldman, R. (1996). *Sign wars: The cluttered landscape of advertising.* New York: Guilford.

Goldman, R., & Papson, S. (1998). *Nike culture.* Thousand Oaks, CA: Sage.

Goldstein, J. H., & Arms, R. L. (1971). Effects of observing athletic contests on hostility. *Sociometry, 34,* 83-90.

Goodey, J. (1997). Boys don't cry: Masculinities, fear of crime and fearlessness. *British Journal of Criminology, 37,* 401-418.

Gorn, E. J. (1986). *The manly art: Bare-knuckle prize fighting in America.* Ithaca, NY: Cornell University Press.

Gorn, E. J., & Goldstein, W. (1993). *A brief history of American sports.* New York: Hill & Wang.

Gray, C. H. (Ed.). (1995). *The cyborg handbook.* Boston: Routledge & Kegan Paul.

Green, T. (1996). *The dark side of the game.* New York: Warner.

Greendorfer, S. (1978). The role of socializing agents in female sport involvement. *Research Quarterly, 48*, 304-310.

Griffin, P. (1998). *Strong women, deep closets: Lesbians and homophobia in sport.* Champaign, IL: Human Kinetics.

Grosz, E. (1987). Notes towards a corporeal feminism. *Australian Feminist Studies, 5*, 1-16.

Gruneau, R. (1991). Sport and "esprit de corps": Notes on power, culture and the politics of the body. In F. Landry, M. Landry, & M. Yerles (Eds.), *Sport: The third millennium* (pp. 168-185). Laval, Canada: Les Presses de L'université Laval.

Gruneau, R., & Whitson, D. (1994). *Hockey night in Canada: Sport, identities and cultural politics.* Toronto, Canada: Garamond.

Guthrie, S. R., & Castelnuovo, S. (1992). Elite women bodybuilders: Model of resistance or compliance? *Play and Culture, 5*, 378-400.

Gutmann, M. (1996). *The meanings of macho in Mexico City.* Berkeley: University of California Press.

Habermas, J. (1983). Modernity: An incomplete project. In H. Foster (Ed.), *The anti-aesthetic: Essays on postmodern culture* (pp. 3-15). Seattle, WA: Bay.

Halbert, C. (1997). Tough enough and woman enough: Stereotypes, discrimination, and impression management among women professional boxers. *Journal of Sport and Social Issues, 21*, 7-36.

Hall, M. A. (1978). *Sport and gender: A feminist perspective on the sociology of sport* (Sociology of Sport Monograph Series). Ottawa: Canadian Association of Health, Physical Education and Recreation.

Hall, M. A. (1988). The discourse on gender and sport: From femininity to feminism. *Sociology of Sport Journal, 5*, 330-340.

Hall, S. (1981). Notes on deconstructing "the popular." In R. Samuel (Ed.), *People's history and socialist theory* (pp. 227-240). Boston: Routledge & Kegan Paul.

Hall, S. (1985). Signification, representation, ideology: Althusser and the post-structuralist debates. *Critical Studies in Mass Communication, 2*, 91-114.

Halperin, D. M. (1995). *Saint Foucault: Towards a gay hagiography.* New York: Oxford University Press.

Hanke, R. (1992). Redesigning men: Hegemonic masculinity in transition. In S. Craig (Ed.), *Men, masculinity and the media* (pp. 185-198). Newbury Park, CA: Sage.

Hanna, J. L. (1988). *Disruptive school behavior.* New York: Homes & Meier.

Haraway, D. (1991). *Simians, cyborgs and women: The reinvention of nature.* London: Free Association Books.

Haraway, D. (1997). *Modest_Witness@Second_Millennium.FemaleMan Meets_OncoMouse: Feminism and Technoscience.* Boston: Routledge & Kegan Paul.

Harding, S. (1986). *The science question in feminism.* Ithaca, NY: Cornell University Press.

Harding, S. (1998). Can men be subjects of feminist thought? In T. Digby (Ed.), *Men doing feminism* (pp. 171-196). Boston: Routledge & Kegan Paul.

Hare, N. (1973). The occupational culture of the black fighter. In J. Talamini & C. Page (Eds.), *Sport and society: An anthology.* Boston: Little, Brown.

Hargreaves, J. (1986a). *Sport, power and culture.* Cambridge, MA: Polity.

Hargreaves, J. (1986b). Where's the virtue? Where's the grace: A discussion of the social production of gender through sport. *Theory, Culture and Society, 3,* 109-121.

Hargreaves, J. (1994). *Sporting females: Critical issues in the history and sociology of women's sport.* Boston: Routledge & Kegan Paul.

Hargreaves, J. (1997). Women's sport, development and cultural diversity: The South African experience. *Women's Studies International Forum, 20,* 191-209.

Harris, D. V. (Ed.). (1972, August). *Women and Sport: Proceedings from the national research conference* (Pennsylvania State University HYPER Series No. 2). Pennsylvania State University.

Harris, S. M. (1992). Black masculinity and same sex friendships. *Western Journal of Black Studies, 16,* 74-81.

Harvey, J., & Sparks, R. (1991). The politics of the body in the context of modernity. *Quest, 43,* 164-189.

Harvey, S. J. (1996). The construction of masculinity among male college volleyball players. *Journal of Men's Studies, 5,* 131-151.

Harvie, S., & Sugden, J. (1994). *Sport and community relations in Northern Ireland.* Jordanstown, Ireland: University of Ulster.

Harwood, V., Oswell, D., et al. (Eds.). (1993). *Pleasure principles: Politics, sexuality and ethics.* London: Lawrence & Wishart.

Hassrick, R. (1962). *The Sioux: Life and customs of a warrior society.* Norman: University of Oklahoma Press.

Hawkes, G. L. (1995). Dressing-up—Cross-dressing and sexual dissonance. *Journal of Gender Studies, 4,* 261-270.

Haynes, R. (1993). Every man (?) a football artist: Football writing and masculinity. In S. Redhead (Ed.), *The passion and the fashion: Football fandom in the new Europe* (pp. 55-76). Aldershot, UK: Avebury.

Hearn, J. (1992). *Men in the public eye: The construction and deconstruction of public men and public patriarchies.* Boston: Routledge & Kegan Paul.

Hearn, J., & Collinson, D. L. (1994). Theorizing unities and differences between men and between masculinities. In H. Brod & M. Kaufman (Eds.), *Theorizing masculinities* (pp. 97-118). Thousand Oaks, CA: Sage.

Hearn, J., & Morgan, D. (1990). Men, masculinities and social theory. In J. Hearn & D. Morgan (Eds.), *Men, masculinities and social theory* (pp. 1-18). Winchester, MA: Unwin Hyman.

Hearn, J., & Parkin, W. (1995). *"Sex" at "work": The power and paradox of organisation sexuality* (Rev. ed.). New York: St. Martin's Press.

Hearn, J., Sheppard, D. L., Tancred-Sherrif, P., & Burrel, G. (Eds.). (1989). *The sexuality of organization.* Newbury Park, CA: Sage.

Heikkala, J. (1993). Discipline and excel: Techniques of self and body and the logic of competing. *Sociology of Sport Journal, 10,* 397-412.

Hekma, G., Oosterhuis, H., et al. (Eds.). (1995). *Gay men and the sexual history of the political left.* New York: Harrington Park Press.

Herdt, G. (Ed.). (1996). *Third sex, third gender: Beyond sexual dimorphism in culture and history.* New York: Zone.

Heskin, K. (1980). *Northern Ireland, a psychological analysis*. New York: Macmillan.

Heywood, L. (1998). *Bodymakers: A cultural anatomy of women bodybuilders*. New Brunswick, NJ: Rutgers University Press.

Hoberman, J. (1984). *Sport and ideology*. Portsmouth, NH: Heinemann.

Hoberman, J. (1997). *Darwin's athletes: How sport has damaged black America and preserved the myth of race*. Boston: Houghton Mifflin.

Hoch, P. (1979). *White hero black beast*. London: Pluto.

Hochschild, A. (1979). Emotion work, feeling rules, and social structure. *American Journal of Sociology, 85*, 551-575.

Hochschild, A. (1983). *The managed heart: Commercialization of human feeling*. Berkeley: University of California Press.

Hockey teams' bad dreams. (1991, December 6). *The Sydney Morning Herald* (syndicated from *The New York Times*), p. 7.

Hole, J. (1992, January 25). Outrage as basketballers shun Magic. *The Sydney Morning Herald*, pp. 1-2.

Hondagneu-Sotelo, P. (1992). Overcoming patriarchal constraints: The reconstruction of gender relations among Mexican immigrant women and men. *Gender and Society, 6*, 398-415.

Hondagneu-Sotelo, P., & Messner, M. A. (1994). Gender displays and men's power: The "new man" and the Mexican immigrant man. In H. Brod & M. Kaufman (Eds.), *Theorizing masculinities* (pp. 200-218). Thousand Oaks, CA: Sage.

hooks, b. (1992). *Black looks: Race and representation*. Boston: South End.

Horrocks, R. (1994). *Masculinity in crisis: Myths, fantasies and realities*. New York: Macmillan.

Hume, P., & Marshall, S. (1994). Sports injuries in New Zealand: Exploratory analyses. *New Zealand Journal of Sports Medicine, 22*, 18-22.

Hutcheon, L. (1989). *The politics of postmodernism*. Boston: Routledge & Kegan Paul.

Ingram, G. B., Bouthillette, A.-M., et al. (Eds.). (1997). *Queers in space: Communities, public spaces, sites of resistance*. Seattle, WA: Bay Press.

Irigaray, L. (1985). *Speculum of the other woman* (G. C. Gill, Trans.). Ithaca, NY: Cornell University Press.

Isenberg, M. (1988). *John L. Sullivan and his America*. Urbana: University of Illinois Press.

Jackson, D. (1990). *Unmasking masculinity: A critical autobiography*. Winchester, MA: Unwin Hyman.

Jackson, S. (1998a). Life in the (mediated) Faust lane: Ben Johnson, national affect and the 1988 crisis of Canadian identity. *International Review for the Sociology of Sport, 33*, 227-238.

Jackson, S. (1998b). A twist of race: Ben Johnson and the Canadian crisis of racial and national identity. *Sociology of Sport Journal, 15*, 21-40.

Jackson, S., Andrews, D., & Cole, C. (1998). Race, nation and authenticity of identity: Interrogating the "everywhere" man (Michael Jordan) and the "nowhere" man (Ben Johnson). *Journal of Immigrants and Minorities, 17*(1), 82-102.

Jameson, F. (1984). Postmodernism or the cultural logic of late capitalism. *New Left Review, 146,* 53-92.

Jardine, A., & Smith, P. (1987). *Men in feminism.* New York: Methuen.

Jarvie, G. (1993). Sport, nationalism and cultural identity. In L. Allison (Ed.), *The changing politics of sport* (pp. 58-83). Manchester, UK: Manchester University Press.

Jefferson, T. (1997). The Tyson rape trial: The law, feminism and emotional "truth." *Social and Legal Studies, 6,* 281-301.

Jefferson, T. (1998). On muscle, "hard men," and "Iron" Mike Tyson: Reflections on desire, anxiety and the embodiment of masculinity. *Body and Society, 4,* 77-98.

Jenkins, R. (1982). *Hightown rules. Growing up in a Belfast housing estate.* Leicester, UK: National Youth Bureau.

Jenkins, R. (1983). *Lads, citizens and ordinary kids: Working-class youth life-styles in Belfast.* Boston: Routledge & Kegan Paul.

Jhally, S. (1989). Cultural studies and the sports/media complex. In L. A. Wenner (Ed.), *Media, sports, and society* (pp. 41-57). Newbury Park, CA: Sage.

Johnson, E., & Johnson, R. (1991, November 18). I'll deal with it. *Sports Illustrated,* 22.

Jones, R. (1997). A deviant sports career: Toward a sociology of unlicensed boxing. *Journal of Sport and Social Issues, 21*(1), 37-52.

Jordan, E., & Cowan, A. (1995). Warrior narratives in the kindergarten classroom. *Gender and Society, 9,* 727-743.

Jordan, T. (1995). Collective bodies: Raving and the politics of Gilles Deleuze and Felix Guattari. *Body and Society, 1*(1), 125-144.

Jung, C. (1959). *The archetypes and the collective unconsciousness: Collected works* (R. F. C. Hull, Trans.). New York: Pantheon.

Kane, M. J. (1988). Media coverage of the female athlete before, during, and after Title IX: *Sports Illustrated* revisited. *Journal of Sport Management, 2,* 87-99.

Kane, M. J. (1995). Resistance/transformation of the oppositional binary: Exposing sport as a continuum. *Journal of Sport and Social Issues, 19,* 191-218.

Kane, M. J. (1996). Media coverage of the post Title IX athlete: A feminist analysis of sport, gender, and power. *Duke Journal of Gender Law and Policy, 3,* 95-127.

Kane, M. J., & Disch, L. J. (1993). Sexual violence and the reproduction of male power in the locker room: The "Lisa Olsen incident." *Sociology of Sport Journal, 10,* 331-352.

Kane, M. J., & Lenskyj, H. (1998). Media treatment of female athletes: Issues of gender and sexualities. In L. Wenner (Ed.), *MediaSport: Cultural sensibilities and sport in the media age* (pp. 186-201). Boston: Routledge & Kegan Paul.

Kane, M. J., & Snyder, E. (1989). Sport typing: The social "containment" of women in sport. *Arena Review, 13,* 77-96.

Kantor, G. K. (1993). Refining the brushstrokes in portraits on alcohol and wife assaults. In *Alcohol and interpersonal violence: Fostering multidisciplinary perspectives* (NIAAA Monograph No. 24, NIH Publication No. 93-3496, pp. 281-290). Rockville, MD: U.S. Department of Health and Human Services.

Kaplan, E. A. (1987). *Rocking around the clock: Music television, postmodernism, and consumer culture.* Boston: Routledge & Kegan Paul.

Katz, J. (1995a). Advertising and the construction of violent white masculinity. In G. Dines & J. M. Humez (Eds.), *Gender, race and class in media: A text reader* (pp. 133-141). Thousand Oaks, CA: Sage.

Katz, J. (1995b). *The invention of heterosexuality.* New York: Penguin.

Katz, J. (1995c). Reconstructing masculinity in the locker room: The Mentors in Violence Prevention project. *Harvard Educational Review, 65*(2), 163-174.

Katz, J. (1997, May). *Scoring points: Current programs and policies.* Paper presented at the conference The Rise of the Sports Hero: Tackling the Issue of Violence Against Women, Bentley College, Waltham, MA.

Kidd, B. (1990). The men's cultural centre: Sports and the dynamic of women's oppression/men's repression. In M. Messner & D. Sabo (Eds.), *Sport, men and the gender order: Critical feminist perspectives* (pp. 31-44). Champaign, IL: Human Kinetics.

Kidd, B. (1996). *The struggle for Canadian sport.* Toronto, Canada: University of Toronto Press.

Kimbrell, A. (1995). *The masculine mystique: The politics of masculinity.* New York: Ballantine.

Kimmel, M. S. (1987a). *Changing men: New directions in research on men and masculinity.* Newbury Park, CA: Sage.

Kimmel, M. S. (1987b). Men's responses to feminism at the turn of the century: 1880-1920. *Gender and Society, 1,* 261-283.

Kimmel, M. (1990). Baseball and the reconstitution of American masculinity, 1880-1920. In M. Messner & D. Sabo (Eds.), *Sport, men and the gender order: Critical feminist perspectives* (pp. 55-66). Champaign, IL: Human Kinetics.

Kimmel, M. S. (Ed.). (1991). *Men confront pornography.* New York: Meridian.

Kimmel, M. (1992). Reading men: Men, masculinity, and publishing. *Contemporary Sociology, 21,* 162-171.

Kimmel, M. (1995a). Clarence, William, Iron Mike, Tailhook, Senator Packwood . . . and us. In M. Kimmel & M. Messner (Eds.), *Men's lives* (3rd ed., pp. 497-506). Boston: Allyn & Bacon.

Kimmel, M. (1995b). Series editor's introduction. In D. Sabo & D. Gordon (Eds.), *Men's health and illness: Gender, power, and the body* (pp. vii-viii). Thousand Oaks, CA: Sage.

King, S. (1993). The politics of the body and the body politic: Magic Johnson and the ideology of AIDS. *Sociology of Sport Journal, 10,* 270-285.

Kipnis, L. (1993). *Ecstasy unlimited: On sex, capital, gender, and aesthetics.* Minneapolis: University of Minnesota Press.

Kirk, D. (Ed.). (1993). *The body, schooling and culture: A reader.* Geelong, Australia: Deakin University Press.

Kirk, D. (1994). Physical education and regimes of the body. *Australian and New Zealand Journal of Sociology, 30*(2).

Kirk, D., & Spiller, B. (1994). Schooling the docile body: Physical education, schooling and the myth of oppression. *Australian Journal of Education, 38*(1), 78-95.

Klein, A. (1991). *Sugarball: The American game, the Dominican dream.* New Haven, CT: Yale University Press.

Klein, A. (1993). *Little big men: Bodybuilding subculture and gender construction.* Albany: State University of New York Press.

Klein, A. (1995a). Life's too short to die small. In D. Sabo & D. Gordon (Eds.), *Men's health and illness: Gender, power, and the body* (pp. 105-120). Thousand Oaks, CA: Sage.

Klein, A. (1995b). Tender machos: Masculine contrasts in the Mexican baseball league. *Sociology of Sport Journal, 12,* 370-388.

Klein, A. (1996). Borderline treason: Nationalisms and baseball on the Texas-Mexican border. *Journal of Sport and Social Issues, 20,* 296-313.

Klein, A. (1997). *Baseball on the border: A tale of two Laredos.* Princeton, NJ: Princeton University Press.

Koss, M., & Cleveland, H. (1996). Athletic participation, fraternity membership and date rape: The question remains—Self selection or different causal processes? *Violence Against Women, 2,* 180-190.

Koss, M., & Gaines, J. (1993). The prediction of sexual aggression by alcohol use, athletic participation, and fraternity affiliation. *Journal of Interpersonal Violence, 8,* 94-108.

Kroker, A., Kroker, M., & Cook, D. (1989). *Panic encyclopedia: The definitive guide to the postmodern scene.* New York: Macmillan.

Kruger, A., & Riordan, J. (Eds.). (1996). *The story of worker sport.* Champaign, IL: Human Kinetics.

Kujala, U., Taimela, S., Antii-Poika, I., Orava, S., Tuominen, R., & Myllynen, P. (1995). Acute injuries in soccer, ice hockey, volleyball, basketball, judo, and karate: Analysis of national registry data. *British Medical Journal, 311,* 1465-1468.

Laberge, S. (1996, September). *La mixité dans les cours d'éducation physique au secondaire: Un contexte émancipatoire ou aliénant pour les adolescentes* [Coeducation in high school physical education classes: An emancipating or alienating context for adolescent girls]. Paper presented at the International Symposium on Feminist Research, Université Laval, Québec, Canada.

Lafrance, M. (1998). Colonizing the feminine: Nike's intersections of postfeminism and hyperconsumption. In G. Rail & J. Harvey (Eds.), *Sport and postmodern times: Culture, gender, sexuality, the body and sport* (pp. 281-300). Albany: State University of New York Press.

Lamar, L., & Kite, M. (1998). Sex differences in attitudes toward gay men and lesbians—A multidimensional perspective. *Journal of Sex Research, 35,* 189-196.

Lancaster, R. (1992). *Life is hard: Machismo, danger, and the intimacy of power in Nicaragua.* Berkeley: University of California Press.

Lasch, C. (1979). *The culture of narcissism.* New York: Norton.

Lefkowitz, B. (1997). *Our guys: The Glen Ridge rape and the secret life of the perfect suburb.* Berkeley, CA: University of California Press.

Lehne, G. (1980). Homophobia among men: Supporting and defining the male role. In M. Kimmel & M. Messner (Eds.), *Men's lives* (pp. 120-132). Boston: Allyn & Bacon.

Leichliter, J. S., Meilman, P. W., Presley, C. P., & Cashin, J. R. (1998). Alcohol use and related consequences among students with varying levels of involvement in college athletics. *Journal of American College Health, 46,* 257-262.

Lenskyj, H. (1986). *Out of bounds: Women, sport and sexuality.* Toronto, Canada: Women's Press.

Lenskyj, H. (1990). Power and play: Gender and sexuality issues in sport and physical activity. *International Journal for Sociology of Sport, 25,* 236-245.

Lenskyj, H. (1992a, November). *I am but you can't tell.* Paper presented at the North American Society for the Sociology of Sport, Toledo, OH.

Lenskyj, H. (1992b). Sexual harassment: Female athletes' experiences and coaches' responsibilities. *Science Periodical on Research and Technology in Sport, 12,* 1-5.

Lenskyj, H. (1992c). Unsafe at home base: Women's experience of sexual harassment in university sport and physical education. *Women in Sport and Physical Activity Journal, 1,* 19-33.

Leonard, G. (1974). *The ultimate athlete: Re-visioning sports, physical education, and the body.* New York: Viking.

Levin, D. M. (1985). *The body's recollection of being: Phenomenological psychology and the deconstruction of nihilism.* Boston: Routledge & Kegan Paul.

Lewis, J. (1997). What counts in cultural studies? *Media, Culture, and Society, 19,* 83-97.

Lewis, O. (1961). *The children of Sanchez: Autobiography of a Mexican family.* New York: Vintage.

Lipsyte, R. (1993, January 31). Violence translates at home. *New York Times,* p. S5.

Lorber, J. (1994). *Paradoxes of gender.* New Haven, CT: Yale University Press.

Lorber, J., & Farrell, S. (1991). Principles of gender construction. In J. Lorber & S. Farrell (Eds.), *The social construction of gender* (pp. 7-11). Newbury Park, CA: Sage.

Loy, J. (1992, November). *The dark side of agon: Fratriarchies, performative masculinities, sport involvement and the phenomenon of gang rape.* Presidential address at the annual meeting of the North American Society for the Sociology of Sport, Toledo, OH.

Loy, J. (1995). The dark side of agon: Fratriarchies, performative masculinities, sport involvement and the phenomenon of gang rape. In K. H. Beffe & A. Ruffen (Eds.), *International Sociology of Sport: Contemporary issues* (Festschrift in honor of Gunther Luschen, pp. 69-81). Stuttgart, Germany: Verlag Stephanie Naglschmid.

Loy, J., Andrews, D., & Rinehart, R. (1993). The body in culture and sport. *Sport Science Review, 2,* 69-91.

Lukenbill, G. (1995). *Untold millions: Positioning your business for the lesbian and gay consumer market.* New York: Harper Business.

Lule, J. (1995). The rape of Mike Tyson: Race, the press and symbolic stereotypes. *Critical Studies in Mass Communication, 12,* 176-195.

Lyotard, J.-F. (1984). *The postmodern condition: A report on knowledge.* Minneapolis: University of Minnesota Press.

MacAloon, J. (1992). The ethnographic imperative in comparative Olympic research. *Sociology of Sport Journal, 9,* 104-130.

Mahoney, M. (1990). Legal images of battered women: Redefining the issue of separation. *Michigan Law Review, 90,* 1-93.

Majors, R. (1990). Cool pose: Black masculinity in sports. In M. Messner & D. Sabo (Eds.), *Sport, men and the gender order: Critical feminist perspectives* (pp. 109-114). Champaign, IL: Human Kinetics.

Majors, R. (1992). Cool pose: The proud signature of black survival. In M. S. Kimmel & M. A. Messner (Eds.), *Men's lives* (pp.131-134). New York: Macmillan.

Majors, R., & Billson, J. M. (1992). *Cool pose: The dilemmas of black manhood in America.* Lexington, MA: Lexington Books.

Malamuth, N. (1986). Predictors of naturalist sexual aggression. *Journal of Personality and Social Psychology, 50,* 953-962.

Malamuth, N., Linz, D., Hearvey, C. L., Barnes, G., & Acker, M. (1995). Using the confluence model of sexual aggression to predict men's conflict with women: A ten year follow up study. *Journal of Personality and Social Psychology, 69,* 353-369.

Malamuth, N., Sockloskie, R., Koss, P., & Tanaka, T. (1991). Characteristics of aggressors against women: Testing a model using a national sample of college students. *Journal of Consulting and Clinical Psychology, 59,* 670-681.

Mandell, N. (1988). The least-adult role in studying children. *Journal of Contemporary Ethnography, 16,* 433-467.

Manning, T. (1996). Gay culture: Who needs it? In M. Simpson (Ed.), *Anti-gay* (pp. 98-117). London: Cassell.

Marcuse, H. (1969). *Eros and civilization.* London: Sphere.

Marshall, P. D. (1997). *Celebrity and power: Fame in contemporary culture.* Minneapolis: University of Minnesota Press.

McBride, J. (1995). *War, battering, and other sports: The gulf between American men and women.* Atlantic Highlands, NJ: Humanities.

McChesney, R. W. (1989). Media made sport: A history of sports coverage in the United States. In L. A. Wenner (Ed.), *Media, sports, and society* (pp. 49-69). Newbury Park, CA: Sage.

McCutcheon, T., Curtis, J., & White, P. (1997). The socio-economic distribution of sport: Multivariate analyses for the general Canadian population. *Sociology of Sport Journal, 14,* 57-73.

McDonald, M. G. (1996). Michael Jordan's family values: Marketing, meaning and post-Reagan America. *Sociology of Sport Journal, 13,* 344-365.

McKay, J. (1991). *No pain, no gain? Sport and Australian culture.* Englewood Cliffs, NJ: Prentice Hall.

McKay, J. (1992). Sport and the social construction of gender. In G. Lupton, T. Short, & R. Whip (Eds.), *Society and gender: An introduction to sociology* (pp. 245-266). New York: Macmillan.

McKay, J. (1993). "Marked men" and "wanton women": The politics of naming sexual "deviance" in sport. *Journal of Men's Studies, 2*(1), 69-87.

McKay, J. (1995). "Just do it": Corporate sports slogans and the political economy of "enlightened racism" discourse. *Discourse: Studies in the Cultural Politics of Education, 16,* 191-201.

McKay, J. (1997). *Managing gender: Affirmative action and organizational power in Australian, Canadian, and New Zealand sport.* Albany: State University of New York Press.

McKay, J., & Huber, D. (1992). Anchoring images of technology and sport. *Women's Studies International Forum, 15,* 205-218.

McKay, J., & Rowe, D. (1997). Field of soaps: *Rupert v. Kerry* as masculine melodrama. *Social Text, 50,* 69-86.

McKay, J., & Smith, P. (1995). Exonerating the hero: Frames and narratives in media coverage of the O. J. Simpson story. *Media Information Australia, 75,* 57-66.

McLanahan, S., & Glass, J. (1985). A note on the trend in sex differences in psychological stress. *Journal of Health and Social Behavior, 26,* 329.

McWilliams, M., & McKiernan, J. (1993). *Bringing it out in the open: Domestic violence in Northern Ireland.* London: HMSO.

Melnick, M. (1992, May-June). Male athletes and sexual assault. *Journal of Physical Education, Recreation and Dance,* 32-35.

Mendoza, V. (1962). El machismo en México [Machismo in Mexico]. *Cuadernos del Instituto Nacional de Investigaciones Folklóricas* (Buenos Aires), *3,* 75-86.

Mercer, K. (1992). Skin head sex thing: Racial difference and the homoerotic imaginary. *New Formations, 16,* 1-23.

Mercer, K., & Julien, I. (1988). Race, sexual politics and black masculinity: A dossier. In R. Chapman & J. Rutherford (Eds.), *Male order: Unwrapping masculinity* (pp. 97-164). London: Lawrence & Wishart.

Merva, M., & Fowles, R. (1992). *Effects of diminished economic opportunities on social stress: Heart attacks, strokes, and crime.* Washington, DC: Economic Policy Institute.

Messerschmidt, J. W. (1993). *Masculinities and crime: Critique and reconceptualization of theory.* Lanham, MD: Rowman & Littlefield.

Messner, M. A. (1988). Sport and male domination: The female athlete as contested ideological terrain. *Sociology of Sport Journal, 5,* 197-211.

Messner, M. (1990a). Boyhood, organized sports and the construction of masculinities. *Journal of Contemporary Ethnography, 18,* 416-444.

Messner, M. A. (1990b). Masculinities and athletic careers: Bonding and status differences. In M. Messner & D. Sabo (Eds.), *Sport, men and the gender order: Critical feminist perspectives* (pp. 97-108). Champaign, IL: Human Kinetics.

Messner, M. (1990c). Men studying masculinity: Some epistemological questions in sport psychology. *Sociology of Sport Journal, 7,* 136-153.

Messner, M. (1990d). When bodies are weapons: Masculinity and violence in sport. *International Review for the Sociology of Sport, 25,* 203-218.

Messner, M. (1992a). Like family: Power, intimacy, and sexuality in male athletes' friendships. In P. Nardi (Ed.), *Men's friendships.* Newbury Park, CA: Sage.

Messner, M. A. (1992b). *Power at play: Sports and the problem of masculinity.* Boston: Beacon.

Messner, M. A. (1993). "Changing men" and feminist politics in the United States. *Theory and Society, 22,* 723-737.

Messner, M. (1994). Women in the men's locker room? In M. Messner & D. Sabo (Eds.), *Sex, violence and power in sport* (pp. 42-52). Freedom, CA: Crossing.

Messner, M. A. (1996). Studying up on sex. *Sociology of Sport Journal, 13,* 221-237.

Messner, M., Duncan, M. C., & Jensen, K. (1993). Separating the men from the girls: The gendered language of televised sports. *Gender and Society, 7,* 121-137.

Messner, M. A., Duncan, M. C., & Wachs, F. L. (1996). The gender of audience-building: Televised coverage of women's and men's NCAA basketball. *Sociological Inquiry, 66,* 422-439.

Messner, M. A., & Sabo D. (Eds.). (1990). *Sport, men and the gender order: Critical feminist perspectives.* Champaign, IL: Human Kinetics.

Messner, M. A., & Sabo, D. (Eds.). (1994). *Sex, violence and power in sports: Rethinking masculinity.* Freedom, CA: Crossing.

Messner, M. A., & Solomon, W. S. (1993). Outside the frame: Newspaper coverage of the Sugar Ray Leonard wife abuse story. *Sociology of Sport Journal, 10,* 119-134.

Miller, K. E., Sabo, D., Farrell, M. P., Barnes, G. M., & Melnick, M. J. (1998). Athletic participation and sexual behavior in adolescents: The different worlds of boys and girls. *Journal of Health and Social Behavior, 39,* 108-123.

Miller, R. (1992, September 5-6). Can Tyson beat the rape rap? *The Weekend Australian Review,* p. 3.

Miller, T. (1990). Sport, media and masculinity. In D. Rowe & G. Lawrence (Eds.), *Sport and leisure: Trends in Australian popular culture* (pp. 74-95). Orlando, FL: Harcourt Brace.

Miller, T. (1993). *The well-tempered self: Citizenship, culture and the postmodern subject.* Baltimore: Johns Hopkins University Press.

Miller, T. (1997). Sport and violence: Glue, seed, state, or psyche? *Journal of Sport and Social Issues, 21,* 235-238.

Mirandé, A. (1982). Machismo: Rucas, chingasos, y chingaderas [Machismo: Songs, ballads, and singers]. *De Colores, 6*(1), 17-47.

Mirandé, A. (1988). Que gacho es ser macho: It's a drag to be a macho man. *Aztlan, 17*(2), 63-89.

Mirandé, A. (n.d.). *Latino masculinity:* Machos, hombres, y chingones. Boulder, CO: Westview.

Moore, H. (1994). *A passion for difference.* Bloomington: Indiana University Press.

Moran, M. (1996, April 19). Athletic aid ending for Phillips victim. *New York Times,* pp. B11, B16.

Morgan, D. (1981). Men, masculinity, and the process of sociological enquiry. In H. Roberts (Ed.), *Doing feminist research* (pp. 83-113). Boston: Routledge & Kegan Paul.

Morgan, D. (1992). *Discovering men.* Boston: Routledge & Kegan Paul.

Morgan, D. (1994). Theater of war: Combat, the military, and masculinities. In H. Brod & M. Kaufman (Eds.), *Theorizing masculinities* (pp. 165-182). Thousand Oaks, CA: Sage.

Morris, J., Everitt, M., Pollard, R., Ghave, S., & Semmence, A. (1980). Vigorous exercise in leisure time: Protection against coronary heart disease. *Lancet, 2,* 1207-1210.

Morrison, T., & Brodsky Lacour, C. (1997). *Birth of a nation 'hood: Gaze, script, and spectacle in the O. J. Simpson case.* New York: Pantheon.

Morton, D. (Ed.). (1996). *The material queer: A LesBiGay Studies reader.* Boulder, CO: Westview.

Mueller, F., Cantu, R., & Van Camp, S. (1996). *Catastrophic injuries in high school and college sports.* Champaign, IL: Human Kinetics.

Ndalianis, A. (1995). Muscle, excess and rupture: Female bodybuilding and gender construction. *Media Information Australia, 75,* 13-23.

Nelson, M. B. (1994). *The stronger women get, the more men love football: Sexism and the American culture of sports.* Orlando, FL: Harcourt Brace.

Nelson, S. (1984). *Ulster's uncertain defenders.* Belfast, Northern Ireland: Blackstaff.

Nicholl, J., Coleman, P., & Brazier, J. (1994). Health and health care costs and benefits of exercise. *Pharmaco Economics, 5,* 109-122.

Nicholl, J., Coleman, P., & Williams, B. (1993). *Injuries in sport and exercise.* London: Sports Council.

Nicholl, J., Coleman, P., & Williams, B. (1995). The epidemiology of sports and exercise-related injury in the United Kingdom. *British Journal of Sports Medicine, 29,* 232-238.

Nielsen, J. M. (1990). Introduction. In J. M. Nielsen (Ed.), *Feminist research methods: Exemplary readings in the social sciences* (pp. 1-37). Boulder, CO: Westview.

Nixon, H. L. (1994a). Coaches' views of risk, pain, and injury in sport with special reference to gender differences. *Sociology of Sport Journal, 11,* 79-87.

Nixon, H. L. (1994b). Social pressure, social support, and help seeking for pain and injuries in college sports networks. *Journal of Sport and Social Issues, 13,* 340-355.

Nixon, H. L., II. (1996a). Exploring pain and injury attitudes and experiences in sport in terms of gender, race, and sports status factors. *Journal of Sports and Social Issues, 20,* 33-41.

Nixon, H. L. (1996b). The relationship of friendship networks, sports experiences, and gender to expressed pain thresholds. *Sociology of Sport Journal, 13,* 78-87.

Nixon, H. L., II. (1997). Gender, sport, and aggressive behavior outside sport. *Journal of Sport and Social Issues, 21,* 379-391.

Nixon, H. L., & Frey, J. H. (1996). *A sociology of sport.* Belmont, CA: Wadsworth.

Oates, J. (1995). *On boxing.* Hopewell, NJ: Ecco.

O'Farrell, J. (1995, May). The long road home. *Fortnight,* p. 339.

Oglesby, C. A. (Ed.). (1978). *Women and sport: From myth to reality.* Philadelphia: Lea & Febiger.

O'Neill, J. (1990). AIDS as a globalizing panic. In M. Featherstone (Ed.), *Global culture: Nationalism, globalization and modernity.* Newbury Park, CA: Sage.

Ortner, S. (1996). *Making gender: The politics and erotics of culture.* Boston: Beacon.

Padilla, R. (1991). *Qualitative analysis with HyperQual.* Chandler: Author.

Paredes, A. (1967). Estados Unidos, México, y el machismo [The United States, Mexico, and machismo]. *Journal of Inter-American Studies, 9*(1), 65-84.

Parker, R. (1991). *Bodies, pleasures, and passions: Sexual culture in contemporary Brazil.* Boston: Beacon.

Pascal, E. (1992). *Jung to live by: A guide to the practical applications of Jungian principles for everyday life.* New York: Warner.

Patton, C. (1990). *Inventing AIDS.* Boston: Routledge & Kegan Paul.

Paz, O. (1961). *The labyrinth of solitude* (L. Kemp, Trans.). New York: Grove.

Pearson, C. S. (1991). *Awakening the heroes within: Twelve archetypes to help us find ourselves and transform our world.* San Francisco: Harper San Francisco.

Phelan, S. (1994). *Getting specific: Postmodern lesbian politics.* Minneapolis: University of Minnesota Press.

Phillips, S. P., & Schneider, M. S. (1993). Sexual harassment of female doctors by patients. *New England Journal of Medicine, 329,* 1933-1939.

Poole, M. (1996). Being a man and becoming a nurse: Three men's stories. *Journal of Gender Studies, 5,* 39-47.

Probyn, E. (1987). The anorexic body. In A. M. Kroker (Ed.), *Body invaders: Panic sex in America* (pp. 201-212). Montreal, Canada: New World Perspectives.

Pronger, B. (1990). *The arena of masculinity: Sport, homosexuality, and the meaning of sex.* New York: St. Martin's Press.

Pronger, B. (1992). *The arena of masculinity: Sport, homosexuality, and the meaning of sex.* Toronto, Canada: University of Toronto Press.

Pronger, B. (1995a). Eros, thanatos: The emerging body in a postmodern psychology of science. In B. Babich, D. Bergoffen, & S. Glynn (Eds.), *Continental and postmodern perspectives in the philosophy of science* (pp. 247-253). Aldershot, UK: Avebury.

Pronger, B. (1995b). Rendering the body: The implicit lessons of gross anatomy. *Quest, 47*(4), 1-20.

Pronger, B. (1998). Post-sport: Transgressing boundaries in physical culture. In G. Rail & J. Harvey (Ed.), *Sport and postmodern times: Culture, gender, sexuality, the body and sport.* Albany: State University of New York Press.

Ptacek, J. (1998). Why do men batter? In R. K. Bergen (Ed.), *Intimate violence* (pp. 181-195). Thousand Oaks, CA: Sage.

Pyke, K. D. (1996). Class-based masculinities: The interdependence of gender, class, and interpersonal power. *Gender & Society, 10,* 527-549.

Rail, G. (1990). Physical contact in women's basketball: A first interpretation. *International Review for the Sociology of Sport, 25,* 269-285.

Rail, G. (1992). Physical contact in women's basketball: A phenomenological construction and contextualization. *International Review for the Sociology of Sport, 27,* 1-27.

Rail, G., & Harvey, J. (1995). Body at work: Michel Foucault and the sociology of sport. *Sociology of Sport Journal, 12,* 164-179.

Ramazanoglu, C. (1992). What can you do with a man? Feminism and the critical appraisal of masculinity. *Women's Studies International Forum, 15,* 339-350.

Ramos, S. (1962). *Profile of man and culture in Mexico* (P. Earle, Trans.). Austin: University of Texas Press.

Real, M. R., & Mechikoff, R. A. (1992). Deep fan: Mythic identification, technology, and advertising in spectator sports. *Sociology of Sport Journal, 9,* 323-339.

Reasons, C. (1985). Ideology, law, public opinion, and worker's health. In D. Gibson & J. Baldwin (Eds.), *Law in a cynical society* (pp. 42-61). Calgary, Canada: Carswell.

Reasons, C., Ross, I., & Patterson, C. (1981). *Assault on the worker: Occupational health and safety in Canada.* Toronto, Canada: Butterworth.

Rees, C. R., Howell, F. M., & Miracle, A. W. (1993). Do high school sports build character? A quasi-experiment on a national sample. In A. Yiannakis, T. D. McIntyre, & M. J. Melnick (Eds.), *Sport sociology: Contemporary themes* (4th ed., pp. 420-428). Dubuque, IA: Kendall/Hunt.

Reid, E. (1997, September). My body, my weapon, my shame. *GQ,* pp. 361-367.

Reijner, J., & Veltuijsen, J. (1989, November). Economic aspects of health through sport. In *Sports, an economic force in Europe* (Conference proceedings, pp. 76-90). UK: Lilleshall.

Reinharz, S. (1992). *Feminist methods in social research.* New York: Oxford University Press.

Robinson, L. (1998). *Crossing the line: Sexual assault in Canada's national sport.* Toronto, Canada: McLelland & Stewart.

Rodman, D. (with Keown, T.). (1996). *Bad as I wanna be.* New York: Dell.

Rodman, D. (with Silver, M.). (1997). *Walk on the wild side.* New York: Bantam.

Rogers, S. F. (1994). *Sportsdykes: Stories from on and off the field.* New York: St. Martin's Press.

Rosaldo, R. (1993). *Culture and truth: The remaking of social analysis.* Boston: Beacon.

Rosenbaum, A., & Hoge, S. K. (1989). Head injury and marital aggression. *American Journal of Psychiatry, 146,* 1048-1051.

Rosenbaum, A., Hoge, S. K., Adelman, S., Warnken, K., Fletcher, K., & Kane, R. (1994). Head injury in partner-abusive men. *Journal of Consulting and Clinical Psychology, 62,* 1187-1193.

Roulston, C. (1997). Gender, nation, class: The politics of difference in Northern Ireland. *Scottish Affairs, 18,* 54-68.

Rowe, D. (1994). Accommodating bodies: Celebrity, sexuality and "tragic Magic." *Journal of Sport and Social Issues, 18,* 6-26.

Rowe, D. (1997). Apollo undone: The sports scandal. In J. Lull & S. Hinerman (Eds.), *Media scandals: Morality and desire in the popular culture marketplace* (pp. 203-221). Cambridge, MA: Polity.

Rowe, D., & McKay, J. (in press). Sport: Still a man's game. *Journal of Interdisciplinary Gender Studies.*

Rubey, D. (1991). Voguing at the carnival: Desire and pleasure on MTV. *South Atlantic Quarterly, 90,* 871-906.

Rutherford, J. (1992). *Men's silences: Predicaments in masculinity.* Boston: Routledge & Kegan Paul.

Ryan, B. (1992, December 14). The two and only. *Sports Illustrated,* 46.

Saal, F. E., Johnson, C. B., & Weber, N. (1989). Friendly or sexy? It may depend on whom you ask. *Psychology of Women Quarterly, 13,* 263-276.

Sabo, D. (1994). Pigskin, patriarchy and pain. In M. Messner & D. Sabo (Eds.), *Sex, violence and power in sports: Rethinking masculinity* (pp. 82-88). Freedom, CA: Crossing.

Sabo, D. (1997). *The Women's Sports Foundation gender equity report card: A survey of athletic opportunity in American higher education.* East Meadows, NY: Women's Sports Foundation.

Sabo, D. (1999). *Understanding men's health: A gender sensitive and woman-centered approach.* Working paper prepared for the Gender and Health Equity Workshop, Global Health Equity Initiative. Cambridge, MA: Harvard Center for Population and Development Studies.

Sabo, D., & Gordon, D. (1995). Re-thinking men's health and illness. In D. Sabo & D. Gordon (Eds.), *Men's health and illness: Gender, power, and the body* (pp. 1-22). Thousand Oaks, CA: Sage.

Sabo, D., & Jansen, S. C. (1994). Seen but not heard: Black men in sports media. In M. Messner & D. Sabo (Eds.), *Sex, violence and power in sports: Rethinking masculinity* (pp. 169-184). Freedom, CA: Crossing.

Sabo, D., & Jansen, S. C. (1998). Prometheus unbound: Constructions of masculinity in sports media. In L. Wenner (Ed.), *MediaSport: Cultural sensibilities and sport in the media age* (pp. 221-232). Boston: Routledge & Kegan Paul.

Sabo, D., & Messner, M. (1994). Changing men through changing sports: An eleven-point strategy. In M. Messner & D. Sabo (Eds.), *Sex, violence and power in sports: Rethinking masculinity.* Freedom, CA: Crossing.

Sabo, D., & Panepinto, J. (1990). Football ritual and the social reproduction of masculinity. In M. Messner & D. Sabo (Eds.), *Sport, men and the gender order: Critical feminist perspectives* (pp. 115-126). Champaign, IL: Human Kinetics.

Sabo, D., & Runfola, R. (1980). *Jock: Sports and the male identity.* Englewood Cliffs, NJ: Prentice Hall.

Sage, G. (1990). *Power and ideology in American sport: A critical perspective.* Champaign, IL: Human Kinetics.

Sales, R. (1995, February). *Gender and Protestantism in Northern Ireland.* Paper presented at the Contemporary Protestantism in Ireland conference, Queen's University, Belfast, Northern Ireland.

Sammons, J. T. (1988). *Beyond the ring: The role of boxing in American society.* Urbana: University of Illinois Press.

Sanday, P. (1981). The socio-cultural context of rape: A cross-cultural study. *Journal of Social Issues, 37,* 5-27.

Sanday, P. (1990). *Fraternity gang rape: Sex, brotherhood, and privilege on campus.* New York: New York University Press.

Sanday, P. (1996a). Rape-prone versus rape-free campus cultures. *Violence Against Women, 2,* 191-208.

Sanday, P. (1996b). *A woman scorned: Acquaintance rape on trial.* New York: Doubleday.

Sawyer, R. (1993). *"We are but women": Women in Ireland's history.* Boston: Routledge & Kegan Paul.

Scannell, V. (1967). Boxing. In R. Slovenko & J. Knight (Eds.), *Motivations in play, games and sports* (pp. 496-502). Springfield, IL: Charles C Thomas.

Schact, S. P. (1996). Misogyny on and off the "pitch": The gendered world of male rugby players. *Gender & Society, 10,* 550-566.

Schultz, N. (1975). The semantic derogation of woman. In B. Thorne & N. Henley (Eds.), *Language and sex: Difference and dominance.* New York: Newbury House.

Schulze, L. (1990). On the muscle. In J. Gaines & C. Herzog (Eds.), *Fabrications: Costume and the female body.* (pp. 59-78). Boston: Routledge & Kegan Paul.

Schwartz, M., & Nogrady, C. (1996). Fraternity membership, rape myths, and sexual aggression on a college campus. *Violence Against Women, 2,* 148-162.

Scraton, S., Fasting, K., Pfister, G., & Bunuel, A. (1999). It's still a man's game? The experiences of top-level European women footballers. *International Review for the Sociology of Sport, 34,* 99-111.

Segal, L. (1990). *Slow motion: Changing masculinities, changing men.* New Brunswick, NJ: Rutgers University Press.

Sheard, K., & Dunning, E. (1973). The rugby football club as a male preserve. *International Review of Sport Sociology, 3-4,* 5-21.

Sherrod, D. (1987). The bonds of men: Problems and possibilities in close male friendships. In H. Brod (Ed.), *The making of masculinities* (pp. 89-102). Boston: Allyn & Bacon.

Shilling, C. (1991). Educating the body: Physical capital and the production of social inequalities. *Sociology, 25,* 653-672.

Shilling, C. (1993). *The body and social theory.* Newbury Park, CA: Sage.

Shirlow, P., & McGovern, M. (1995, February). *Post-Fordism, sectarianism and the political economy of Ulster loyalism.* Paper presented at the Contemporary Protestantism in Ireland conference, Queen's University, Belfast, Northern Ireland.

Shropshire, K. L. (1996). *In black and white: Race and sports in America.* New York: New York University Press.

Siegal, A. (1989). The effects of anabolic steroids. *Your Patient's Fitness, 2,* 7-12.

Simpson, M. (Ed.). (1996). *Anti-gay.* London: Cassell.

Simson, V., & Jennings, A. (1992). *The lords of the rings: Power, money and drugs in the modern Olympics.* New York: Simon & Schuster.

Sinfield, A. (1994). *Cultural politics—Queer reading.* Philadelphia: University of Pennsylvania Press.

Sloop, J. M. (1997). Mike Tyson and the perils of discursive constraints: Boxing, race, and the assumption of guilt. In A. Baker & T. Boyd (Eds.), *Out of bounds: Sports, media, and the politics of identity* (pp. 102-122). Bloomington: Indiana University Press.

Smith, M. (1987). *Violence in Canadian amateur sport: A review of literature* (Report for the Commission for Fair Play). Ottawa: Government of Canada.

Smith, M. (1991). Violence and injuries in ice hockey. *Clinical Journal of Sports Medicine, 1,* 104-109.

Snyder, E. (1994). Interpretations and explanations of deviance among college athletes: A case study. *Sociology of Sport Journal, 3,* 231-248.

Sommers, C. (1995). *Who stole feminism?* New York: Touchstone/Simon & Schuster.

Sontag, S. (1989). *AIDS and its metaphors.* New York: Farrar, Straus & Giroux.

Sorensen, C., & Sonne-holm, S. (1980). Social costs of sport injuries. *British Journal of Sports Medicine, 14,* 24-25.

Special report: Crime and sports. (1995, December 27). *Los Angeles Times,* pp. A1, A12, C3-C10.

Spender, D. (1980). *Man made language.* Boston: Routledge & Kegan Paul.

Sports Council. (1991). *Injuries in sport and exercise.* London: Author.

Spradley, J. P. (1980). *Participant observation.* New York: Holt, Rinehart & Winston.

Stanley, J. (1977). Paradigmatic woman: The prostitute. In D. Shores & C. Hines (Eds.), *Papers in language variation.* Tuscaloosa, AL: University of Alabama Press.

Stanway, A. (1993). *The art of sexual intimacy.* New York: Carroll & Graf.

Staples, R. (1982). *Black masculinity: The black male's role in American society.* San Francisco: Black Scholar Press.

Statistics Canada. (1995). *Accidents in Canada.* Ottawa: Author.

Stillion, J. M. (1995). Premature death among males. In D. Sabo & D. Gordon (Eds.), *Men's health and illness: Gender, power, and the body* (pp. 46-68). Thousand Oaks, CA: Sage.

Stockdale, M. S. (1993). The role of sexual misperceptions of women's friendliness in an emerging theory of sexual harassment. *Journal of Vocational Behavior, 42,* 84-101.

Stone, A. R. (1991). Would the real body please stand up: Boundary stories about virtual culture. In *Cyberspace first steps.* M. Benedikt.

Strathern, A. (1971). *The rope of Moka.* Cambridge, UK: Cambridge University Press.

Sugden, J. (1987). The exploitation of disadvantage: The occupational sub-culture of the boxer. In J. Horne, D. Jary, & A. Tomlinson (Eds.), *Sport, leisure and social relations.* Boston: Routledge & Kegan Paul.

Sugden, J., & Bairner, A. (1988). Sectarianism and soccer hooliganism in Northern Ireland. In T. Reilly, A. Lees, K. Davids, & W. J. Murphy (Eds), *Science and football* (pp. 572-78). London: Spon.

Sugden, J., & Bairner, A. (1993). *Sport, sectarianism and society in a divided Ireland.* Leicester, UK: Leicester University Press.

Swift, E. M. (1991, November 18). Dangerous games. *Sports Illustrated,* 40-43.

Synnott, A. (1993). *The body social: Symbolism, self and society.* Boston: Routledge & Kegan Paul.

Tatchell, P. (1996). It's just a phase: Why homosexuality is doomed. In M. Simpson (Ed.), *Anti-gay.* London: Cassell.

Tator, G., Edmonds, V., & Lapczak. (1993). *Ontario catastrophic sports: Recreational injuries survey, July 1-June 30, 1992.* Toronto, Canada: Toronto Hospital, Toronto Western Division.

Theberge, N. (1987). Sport and women's empowerment. *Women's Studies International Forum, 10,* 387-393.

Theberge, N. (1994). Toward a feminist alternative to sport as a male preserve. In S. Birrell & C. Cole (Eds.), *Women, sport, and culture.* Champaign, IL: Human Kinetics.

Theberge, N. (1995). Gender, sport, and the social construction of community: A case study from women's ice hockey. *Sociology of Sport Journal, 12,* 389-403.

Theberge, N. (1997). It's part of the game: Physicality and the production of gender in women's hockey. *Gender and Society, 11,* 69-87.

Thompson, S. (1994). Challenging the hegemony: New Zealand women's opposition to rugby and the reproduction of a capitalist patriarchy. In S. Birrell & C. Cole (Eds.), *Women, sport, and culture* (pp. 213-220). Champaign, IL: Human Kinetics.

Thompson, S. (1999). *Mother's taxi: Sport and women's labor.* Albany: State University of New York Press.

Thorne, B. (1993). *Gender play.* New Brunswick, NJ: Rutgers University Press.

Thorne, B., & Henley, N. (Eds.). (1985). *Language, gender and society.* New York: Newbury House.

Tomlinson, A., & Yorganci, I. (1997). Male coach/female athlete relations: Gender and power relations in competitive sport. *Journal of Sport and Social Issues, 21,* 134-155.

Toscana, G., & Windau, J. (1994, October). The changing character of fatal work injuries. *Monthly Labor Review, 17.*

Treichler, P. (1987). AIDS, homophobia and biomedical discourse: An epidemic of signification. *Cultural Studies, 1,* 263-305.

Treichler, P. (1988). AIDS, gender and biomedical discourse: Current contests for meaning. In E. Fee & D. Fox (Eds.), *AIDS: the burden of history* (pp. 190-266). Berkeley: University of California Press.

Treichler, P. (1991). AIDS and HIV infection in the Third World: First World chronicles. In E. Fee & D. Fox (Eds.), *The contemporary historiography of AIDS* (pp. 187-210). Berkeley: University of California Press.

Trujillo, N. (1991). Hegemonic masculinity on the mound: Media representations of Nolan Ryan and American sports culture. *Critical Studies in Mass Communication, 8,* 290-308.

Trujillo, N. (1995). Machines, missiles, and men: Images of the male body on ABC's Monday Night Football. *Sociology of Sport Journal, 12,* 403-423.

Turner, B. (1984). *The body and society: Explorations in social theory.* Oxford, UK: Basil Blackwell.

Turner, B. (1991). Recent developments in the theory of the body. In M. Featherstone, M. Hepworth, & B. Turner (Eds.), *The body: Social processes and social theory* (pp. 1-35). Newbury Park, CA: Sage.

Tyler, S. (1996). Post-modern ethnography: From document of the occult to occult document. In J. Clifford & G. Marcus (Eds.), *Writing culture.* Berkeley: University of California Press.

U.S. Bureau of Labor Statistics. (1991, October 28). *Multiple jobholding unchanged in May 1991.* Washington, DC: Department of Labor.

U.S. Bureau of Labor Statistics. (1992, August 19). *Worker displacement increased sharply in recent recession.* Washington, DC: Department of Labor.

Vaid, U. (1995). *Virtual equality: The mainstreaming of gay and lesbian liberation.* New York: Anchor.

Vertinsky, P. (1995). The "racial" body and the anatomy of difference: Anti-Semitism, physical culture, and the Jew's foot. *Sport Science Review, 4*(1), 38-59.

Volkwein, K., Frauke, I., Schnell, F., Sherwood, D., & Livezey, A. (1997). Sexual harassment in sport: Perceptions and experiences of American female student-athletes. *International Review for the Sociology of Sport, 32,* 283-295.

Wachs, F. L., & Dworkin, S. L. (1997). There's no such thing as a gay hero: Magic = hero, Louganis = carrier: Sexual identity and media framing of HIV positive athletes. *Journal of Sport and Social Issues, 21,* 335-355.

Wacquant, L. (1992). The social logic of boxing in Black Chicago: Toward a sociology of pugilism. *Sociology of Sport Journal, 9,* 221-254.

Walk, S. (1994). *Information and injury: The experiences of student athletic trainers.* Unpublished doctoral dissertation, Michigan State University.

Walk, S. (1997). Peers in pain: The experiences of student athletic trainers. *Sociology of Sport Journal, 14,* 22-56.

Wallace, M. (1991). *Black macho and the myth of the superwoman.* London: Verso.

Wallenfeldt, E. C. (1994). *The six-minute fraternity: The rise and fall of NCAA tournament boxing, 1932-60.* New York: Praeger.

Wann, D. L. (1993). Aggression among highly identified spectators as a function of their need to maintain positive social identity. *Journal of Sport and Social Issues, 17,* 134-143.

Wann, D. L., Schrader, M. P., & Adamson, D. R. (1996, November). *The cognitive and somatic anxiety of sport spectators.* Paper presented at the annual meeting of the North American Society for the Sociology of Sport, Birmingham, AL.

Ward, S. K., Chapman, K., Cohn, E., White, S., & Williams, K. (1991). Acquaintance rape and the college coed social scene. *Family Relations, 40,* 65-71.

Warner, M. (Ed.). (1993). *Fear of a queer planet: Queer politics and social theory.* Minneapolis: University of Minnesota Press.

Warshaw, R. (1988). *I never called it rape.* New York: Harper & Row.

Watney, S. (1989). *Policing desire: Pornography, AIDS, and the media.* Minneapolis: University of Minnesota Press.

Weeks, J. (1985). *Sexuality and its discontents: Meanings, myths, and modern sexualities.* Boston: Routledge & Kegan Paul.

Weinberg, S., & Arond, H. (1969). The occupational culture of the boxer. In J. Loy & S. Kenyon (Eds.), *Sport, culture, and society.* New York: Macmillan.

Weinstein, M. (1995). *Culture/flesh: Explorations of post-civilized modernity.* Lanham, MD: Rowman & Littlefield.

Weinstein, M., Smith, M. D., & Wiesenthal, D. (1995). Masculinity and hockey violence. *Sex Roles, 33,* 831-847.

Welch, M. (1997). Violence against women by professional football players. *Journal of Sport and Social Issues, 21,* 393-411.

Wells, J. (1991, November 16-17). Fire them up Fred, before they go to pot. *The Weekend Australian,* p. 70.

Wenner, L. A. (1989). Media, sports, and society: The research agenda. In L. A. Wenner (Ed.), *Media, sports, and society* (pp. 13-48). Newbury Park, CA: Sage.

Wenner, L. A. (1996). The sports bar: Masculinity, alcohol, sports, and the mediation of public space. In S. J. Drucker & G. Gumpert (Eds.), *Voices in the street: Explorations in gender, media, and public space* (pp. 71-100). Creskill, NJ: Hampton.

Wenner, L. (Ed.). (1998a). *MediaSport: Cultural sensibilities and sport in the media age.* Boston: Routledge & Kegan Paul.

Wenner, L. A. (1998b). The sports bar: Masculinity, alcohol, sports, and the mediation of public space. In G. Rail & J. Harvey (Eds.), *Sport and postmodern times: Gender, sexuality, the body and sport* (pp. 301-332). Albany: State University of New York Press.

Wernick, A. (1991). *Promotional culture.* Newbury Park, CA: Sage.

West, C., & Zimmerman, D. (1987). Doing gender. *Gender and Society, 1,* 125-151.

West, C., & Zimmerman, D. H. (1991). Doing gender. In J. Lorber & S. Farrell (Eds.), *The social construction of gender* (pp. 13-37). Newbury Park, CA: Sage.

Wheaton, B., & Tomlinson, A. (1998). The changing gender order in sport? The case of windsurfing subcultures. *Journal of Sport and Social Issues, 22,* 252-274.

White, G. F., Katz, J., & Scarborough, K. E. (1992). The impact of professional football games upon violent assaults on women. *Violence and Victims, 7*(2), 157-171.

White, P., & Gillett, J. (1994). Reading the muscular body: A critical decoding of advertisements in *Flex* magazine. *Sociology of Sport Journal, 11,* 18-39.

White, P. G., & Vagi, A. B. (1990). Rugby in the 19th century British boarding-school system: A feminist psychoanalytic perspective. In M. Messner & D. Sabo (Eds.), *Sport, men and the gender order: Critical feminist perspectives* (pp. 67-78). Champaign, IL: Human Kinetics.

White, P., Young, K., & Gillett, J. (1995). Bodywork as a moral imperative: Some critical notes on health and fitness. *Loisir et Société, 18,* 159-182.

Whitson, D. (1984). Sport and hegemony: On the construction of the dominant culture. *Sociology of Sport Journal, 1,* 64-78.

Whitson, D. (1990). Sport in the social construction of masculinity. In M. Messner & D. Sabo (Eds.), *Sport, men and the gender order: Critical feminist perspectives* (pp. 19-29). Champaign, IL: Human Kinetics.

Williamson, J. (1988). AIDS and perceptions of the grim reaper. *Metro, 80,* 2-6 .

Wilson, B. (1997). "Good Blacks" and "bad Blacks": Media constructions of African-American athletes in Canadian basketball. *International Review for the Sociology of Sport, 32,* 177-189.

Wright, J. (1991). Gracefulness and strength: Sexuality in the Seoul Olympics. *Social Semiotics, 1,* 49-66.

Yates, P. D. (1987). A case of mistaken identity: Interethnic images in multicultural England. In G. Spindler & L. Spindler (Eds.), *Interpretive ethnography of education* (pp. 195-220). Hillsdale, NJ: Lawrence Erlbaum.

Young, K. (1990, August). *Treatment of sports violence in the Canadian mass media* (Report to Sport Canada's Applied Sport Research Programme). Ottawa: Government of Canada.

Young, K. (1993). Violence, risk, and liability in male sports culture. *Sociology of Sport Journal, 10,* 373-396.

Young, K. (1997). Women, sport, and physicality: Preliminary findings from a Canadian study. *International Review for the Sociology of Sport, 32,* 297-305.

Young, K., & Smith, M. (1988-1989). Mass media treatment of violence in sport and its effects. *Current Psychology: Research and Reviews, 7,* 298-312.

Young, K., & White, P. (1995). Sport, physical danger and injury: The experiences of elite women athletes. *Journal of Sport and Social Issues, 19,* 45-61.

Young, K., & White, P. (1998). Threats to sport careers: Elite athletes talk about injury and pain. In J. Coakley & P. Donnelly (Eds.), *Inside sports* (pp. 203-213). Boston: Routledge & Kegan Paul.

Young, K., White, P., & McTeer, W. (1994). Body talk: Male athletes reflect on sport, injury, and pain. *Sociology of Sport Journal, 11,* 175-194.

Yount, K. R. (1991). Ladies, flirts, and tomboys: Strategies for managing sexual harassment in an underground coal mine. *Journal of Contemporary Ethnography, 19,* 396-422.

Zaricznyj, B., Shattuck, L., Mast, T., Robertson, R., & D'elia, G. (1980). Sports-related injury in school-aged children. *American Journal of Sports Medicine, 8,* 318-324.

Zillmann, D., & Bryant, J. (1982). Pornography, sexual callousness, and the trivialization of rape. *Journal of Communication, 32,* 10-21.

Zillmann, D., & Bryant, J. (1984). Effects of massive exposure to pornography. In N. Malamuth & E. Donnerstein (Eds.), *Pornography and sexual aggression.* San Diego, CA: Academic Press.

Index

About the
Editors and Contributors

Jim McKay teaches courses on gender and popular culture in the Department of Anthropology and Sociology at the University of Queensland. He is the Editor of the *International Review for the Sociology of Sport*. His most recent book is *Managing Gender: Affirmative Action and Organizational Power in Australian, Canadian, and New Zealand Sport* (1997).

Michael A. Messner is Associate Professor of Sociology and Gender Studies at the University of Southern California. His books include *Power at Play: Sports and the Problem of Masculinity* (1992), *Sex, Violence, and Power in Sports: Rethinking Masculinity* (1994), and *Politics of Masculinities: Men in Movements* (1997). He has conducted several studies on gender in televised sports, and is a Past President of the North American Society for the Sociology of Sport.

Don Sabo, PhD, is Professor of Sociology at D'Youville College in Buffalo, New York, and an Adjunct Associate Professor of Sociology at the State University of New York at Buffalo. He has authored numerous articles and five books, most recently with David Gordon, *Men's Health and Illness: Gender, Power and the Body* (winner of the *Choice* magazine

325

Most Outstanding Academic Book Award for 1996). He lectures about issues ranging from gender equity in athletics, sport and masculinity, men's violence, and physical activity and health. His next book, *Confronting Prison Masculinities,* is being published by Temple University Press. Professor Sabo coauthored the President's Council on Physical Fitness and Sports report *Physical Activity and Sport in the Lives of Girls* (1997). He has directed several nationwide studies including the *Women's Sports Foundation Gender Equity Report Card: A Survey of Athletic Opportunity in American Higher Education* (1997) and the *Women's Sports Foundation Report: Sport and Teen Pregnancy* (1998).

Mathieu Albert, PhD, has worked for 10 years as a performance arts critic for *Le Devoir.* He has completed research and publications on the epistemology of historical knowledge associated with performance arts and, more recently, on extreme sports. Having completed a dissertation at the Université de Montréal on the impact of neoliberalism on social science research, he is currently a postdoctoral fellow at the Interuniversity Center for Research on Science and Technology in Montréal. His recent research focuses on the transformation of Canadian universities in the context of global economic restructuring.

Alan Bairner teaches politics at the University of Ulster in Jordanstown, Northern Ireland. He is coauthor of *Sport, Sectarianism and Society in a Divided Ireland* (1993) and joint editor of *Sport in Divided Societies* (1998). He has written numerous articles on sport in Ireland, Scotland, and Sweden and on the relation between sport and identity. His particular interests are masculinity and the role of sport in the construction and reproduction of national identities, on which theme he is completing a monograph for the State University of New York Press.

Todd Crosset, PhD, is Assistant Professor of Sport Studies in the Sport Management Program at the University of Massachusetts, Amherst. He did his doctoral work in sociology at Brandeis University. His academic interests in sport management include gender issues, elite athletes, ethics, and coach-athlete relations. His book *Outsiders in the Clubhouse,* about life on the LPGA golf tour, won the North American Society for the Sociology of Sport book of the year award in 1995. Prior to arriving at the University of Massachusetts, he held positions as a head coach of swimming at Northeastern University and assistant athletic director at

Dartmouth College. While an undergraduate at the University of Texas, Austin, he was an All-American swimmer and a member of the National Championship Team.

Timothy Jon Curry, PhD, is Associate Professor of Sociology at the Ohio State University. He earned his doctorate from the University of Washington and is a Past President of the North American Society for the Sociology of Sport and a member of the American Sociological Association, among other association memberships. He teaches courses in the sociology of sport, American society, and deviancy. He has published articles on various aspects of mass communication, sport, leisure, gender, and society. He has written three books, *Sports: A Social Perspective, Introducing Visual Sociology,* and *Sociology for the Twenty-First Century.* He currently is researching stadium controversies and urban renewal.

Laurence de Garis, PhD, at the time he wrote his chapter, was a Research Consultant at the University of Connecticut's Laboratory for Sport, Leisure and Tourism. When not writing about boxing, he prefers to be in the ring himself, where he is an active professional wrestler. Drawing on his experiences in the ring, he also frequently writes about professional wrestling and ethnographic research.

Michelle D. Dunbar is a graduate student at the University of Southern California. Her main research interest is in exploring how popular culture and the media influence individuals' ideas about race, gender, and class and how those ideas gets translated into social action. Her dissertation builds on the chapter presented here, extending the analysis of race, class, and masculinity in the image of Dennis Rodman to include audience research that seeks to find the meanings that viewers make of mediated sports figures.

Shari Lee Dworkin is a PhD candidate in the Department of Sociology at the University of Southern California (USC). Her substantive areas of research include gender, sexuality, and sport/fitness/bodies. Some of her published works include "Disciplining the Body: HIV Positive Male Athletes, Media Surveillance and the Policing of Sexuality," *Sociology of Sport Journal, 15* (1998), coauthored with Faye Linda Wachs; and (coauthored with Michael Messner) "Just Do . . . What? Sport, Bodies, Gender," in Judith Lorber, Myra Marx Ferree, and Beth Hess (Eds.),

Revisioning Gender (1999). She currently teaches courses in social theory and gender in the California State University system.

Philip M. Gray (PhD, State University of New York at Buffalo) is Associate Professor of Sociology at D'Youville College. As a Vietnam combat veteran, his past research interests have included posttraumatic stress disorder. His current research focuses on domestic violence issues. He is active in the AAUP-D'Youville College Chapter.

Othello Harris is Associate Professor and Chair of the Department of Physical Education, Health, and Sport Studies at Miami University, Ohio. He is a sport sociologist and book review editor for the *Sociology of Sport Journal*. His research interests focus on race and sport.

Cynthia A. Hasbrook, PhD, is Professor and Chair of the Department of Human Kinetics at the University of Wisconsin-Milwaukee. She is a sport sociologist, editor of *Sociology of Sport Journal,* and a member of the Board of Directors of the North American Society for the Sociology of Sport. Her primary research has focused on social factors affecting children's physicality, and she recently concluded a 3-year ethnographic study of a culturally diverse and working-class group of elementary school children in which the children's constructions of gender, physicality, and sexuality were examined.

Alan M. Klein, PhD, is Professor of Sociology-Anthropology at Northeastern University in Boston. He is author of *Sugarball: The American Game, The Dominican Dream* (1991), *Little Big Men: Bodybuilding Subculture and Gender Construction* (1993), and *Baseball on the Border: A Tale of Two Laredos* (1997). He is currently working on a book on globalization and baseball.

Suzanne Laberge, PhD, is a full professor in the Department of Kinesiology at the Université de Montréal. She teaches in sociology of sport and is mainly known for her neo-Bourdieusian and feminist analyses of gender, class, and health practices. She has published in a variety of journals, notably *Sociology of Sport Journal, Society and Leisure,* and *Sociologie et Sociétés,* on issues associated with extreme sports, doping in sport, and nationalism and elite sport. Her most recent research focuses on gender, cultural styles, and health practices.

Toby Miller is Associate Professor of Cinema Studies at New York University. He is the author of *The Well-Tempered Self* (1993), *Contemporary Australian Television* (with S. Cunningham, 1994), *The Avengers* (1997), *Technologies of Truth* (1998), and *Popular Culture and Everyday Life* (with A. McHoul, 1998) and the coeditor of *SportCult* (with R. Martin, 1999), *Film and Theory: An Anthology* (with R. Stam, 1999), and *A Companion to Film Theory* (with R. Stam, 1999). He currently edits the journals *Social Text* and *Television & New Media* and is a former editor of the *Journal of Sport and Social Issues.*

Linda A. Moore (M.Ed., State University of New York at Buffalo) has taught elementary school around the country and currently works in the field of curricular materials for teachers.

Brian Pronger, PhD, is the author of *The Arena of Masculinity: Sports, Homosexuality and the Meaning of Sex.* He has published articles on gender, sexuality, and sport as well as postmodern studies of the body, science, and physical fitness. He teaches philosophy in the faculty of Physical Education and Health at the University of Toronto.

David Rowe, PhD, teaches Media and Cultural Studies in the Department of Leisure and Tourism Studies at the University of Newcastle, Australia. His books include *Popular Cultures: Rock Music, Sport, and the Politics of Pleasure* (1995), *Tourism, Leisure, Sport: Critical Perspectives* (edited with Geoffrey Lawrence, 1998), and *Sport, Culture and the Media: The Unruly Trinity* (1999).

Faye Linda Wachs is Visiting Assistant Professor at Loyola Marymount University in Los Angeles. Some of her published works include "There's No Such Thing as a Gay Hero: Sexual Identity and Media Framing of HIV Positive Athletes" (1997) in *Journal of Sport and Social Issues, 21*(4): 335-355 (coauthored with Shari Lee Dworkin) and "I Was There: Gender, Power, and Discourse in the World of Co-ed Softball," in A. Bolin and J. Granskog (Eds.), *Bodies in Motion: Women, Culture, and Exercise/Sport* (in press). She teaches courses in methods, sport, and gender. She and Shari Lee Dworkin are working on an ongoing research project that analyzes men's and women's fitness magazines.

Stephan R. Walk earned PhDs in both sociology and physical education and exercise science from Michigan State University. He currently is

Assistant Professor in the Division of Kinesiology and Health Promotion at California State University-Fullerton. Specializing in the sociology of sport, his research centers on the normalization of risk, pain, and injury in sport and the social dynamics at work in systems of athlete health care. His work has appeared in the *Sociology of Sport Journal* as well as in books on the epidemiology of sports injuries and sports medicine.

Philip White is Professor of Kinesiology at McMaster University in Canada. He is coeditor (with Kevin Young) of *Sport and Gender in Canada* (forthcoming) and conducts research in various areas of the sociology of sport. He coaches the varsity men's rugby program at McMaster and the Ontario women's rugby program.

Kevin Young is Senior Research Fellow in the Department of Physical Education, Sports Science, and Recreation Management at Loughborough University, UK. He has published on a variety of sports-related topics and is coeditor, with Philip White, of *Sport and Gender in Canada* (1999). He has served on the editorial boards of *Sociology of Sport Journal* and *Avante,* and on the executive board of the North American Society for the Sociology of Sport. He is currently Vice President of the International Sociology of Sport Association.